D1236302

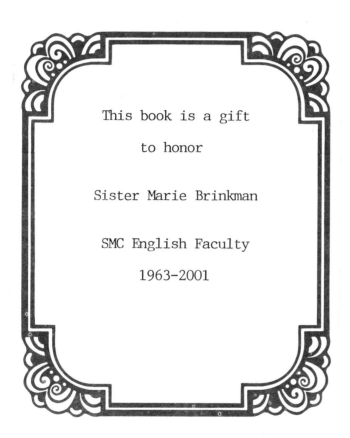

This book is a gift

to honor

Sister Marie Brinkman

SMC English Faculty

1963-2001

BY WHOSE AUTHORITY?

Henry Edward Manning
1808 - 1892

BY WHOSE AUTHORITY?

Newman, Manning and the *Magisterium*

edited by

V. ALAN McCLELLAND

DOWNSIDE ABBEY
BATH

152874

It is acknowledged with gratitude that the publication of this book would not have been possible without the generous waiver of copyrights by the contributors and the financial support of the following institutions:

The University of Hull, England

The Albert-Ludwigs-Universität, Freiburg, Germany

The Newman Fellowships Trust

Downside Abbey
Stratton on the Fosse
Bath, England, BA3 4RH

© 1996 V. Alan McClelland
All rights reserved. No part of this book may be reproduced, stored in a retrieval system or transmitted in any form or by any means without the permission of the editor.

British Library Cataloguing in Publication Data:
A catalogue record of this book is available from
The British Library.

ISBN 1-898663-06-8

All illustrations in this volume are from the collection at Downside Abbey.

Typeset at Downside Abbey, Bath.
Printed by Hobbs the Printers, Totton, Hampshire

John Henry Newman
1801 - 1890

CONTENTS

PREFACE

In contemplating the legitimacy of his pastoral ministry in Lavington, Manning asked himself two fundamental questions: 'What right have you to be teaching, admonishing, reforming, rebuking others? And by what authority do you lift the latch of a poor man's door and enter and sit down and begin to instruct or to correct him?' (*Autobiographical Notes*, IV, p. 26). This self-analysis enforces the recent view of David Nicholls that essentially 'the Catholic position is distinguished from the Protestant in being concerned not with a judgment about the content of Revelation but about who is the accredited teacher: whose voice is to be followed?' (David Nicholls and Fergus Kerr: *John Henry Newman: Reason, Rhetoric and Romanticism*, Bristol Press, 1991, p. 202). Both Newman and Manning identified that teacher as the Holy Spirit, with his regenerative and directive action ever at work within the *ecclesia docens* and the individual Christian soul. It was but a logical development of that subscription that led to the definition of the nature of the Petrine authority at the First Vatican Council at a time when authority itself in the political, social and ecclesiastical domains was being challenged and vitiated. The Church was not a democracy in which truth could be decided by majority or consensus opinion. In the event, the definition of 1870 could be accepted by Newman because his view as expressed in the pamphlet of 1859, 'On Consulting the Faithful in Matters of Doctrine', as Nicholls has argued, 'while emphasising the importance of the *consensus fidelium* depicted the rôle of the laity as essentially passive' (*ibidem,* p. 202).

The question of authority, however, could not rest solely upon the definition of 1870. As Manning prophetically wrote in 1883: 'it is easy to deceive ourselves but may we not reasonably believe that the next time the Church meets in Council, whether by the reassembling of the Council of the Vatican, or in any other way, the first duty will be to take up the work prepared and to define the Divine powers of the Episcopate and its relation to its Head' (*The Pastoral Office*, printed privately, 1883. p. 218).

The collection of essays in this volume explores further the nature of the authority resting in the Church as conceptualized in the teachings of Newman and Manning. With the exception of that by Michael Peterburs, the essays were contributed to symposia in 1993 and 1994 at the International Institute for the Advancement of Newman Research at Freiburg University in Germany. They formed part of a continuing research project on Newman/Manning studies subsidized by the British/German Academic Research Collaboration (ARC) Programme.

V.Alan McClelland

NOTES ON CONTRIBUTORS

Günter Biemer — is Emeritus Professor of Education and Catechesis in Albert-Ludwigs-Universität, Freiburg, and a leading European scholar in Newman studies. He is the author of *Newman on Tradition* (New York, 1967) and *John Henry Newman, Leben und Werk* (Mainz, 1989). He has also written on religious education and on the Jewish-Christian dialogue.

Vincent F. Blehl — is an American Jesuit and Postulator of the Cause for canonization of John Henry Newman. He is the author of a number of books and articles on Newman including *The White Stone: The Spiritual Theology of John Henry Newman* (Massachusetts, 1993). He has recently edited the second volume of *John Henry Newman's Sermons 1824-1843* (Oxford, 1993).

Sheridan Gilley — is Reader in Theology at Durham University. He has published *Newman and his Age* (London, 1990) and a large number of articles on modern Church history. Co-editor with Roger Swift of *The Irish in the Victorian City* (London, 1985) and *The Irish in Britain, 1812-1939,* he has recently co-edited with W.J. Sheils *A History of Religion in Britain* (Oxford, 1994).

Lothar Kuld — lives and lectures in Weingarten. He has worked on Newman's phenomenology of the act of faith and published in volume 13 of *International Cardinal Newman Studies* (Sigmaringendorf, 1989).

V. Alan McClelland — is Professor of Educational Studies at Hull University and the author of *Cardinal Manning: His Public Life & Influence, 1865-92* (O.U.P. London, 1962) and *English Roman Catholics & Higher Education 1830-1903* (Oxford, 1973). He has written a large number of articles on modern Church history and contributed to several books. He edited and contributed to *Christian Education in a Pluralist Society* (New York & London, 1988) and, with V.P. Varma, to *Advances in Teacher Education* (London, 1989).

Peter B Nockles — has responsibility for Methodist archives at the John Rylands University Library at Manchester. He wrote *The Oxford Movement in Context* (Cambridge, 1994) and has contributed several articles on eighteenth- and nineteenth-century ecclesiastical history. He has a chapter in the nineteenth-century volume of *The History of the University of Oxford*.

James Pereiro — is a priest of the Prelature of the Holy Cross and currently director of Grandpont House in Oxford. He has published on historical and theological themes and has written two important doctoral theses, one in 1980 on the theology of Melchior Cano and the other in 1995 on the theology of Henry Edward Manning.

Michael Peterburs — teaches religious studies and history at Ampleforth College. He read his first degree in theology at Durham University where he subsequently gained a doctorate in 1994 for a thesis on 'Divine Revelation and the Infallible Church: Newman, Vatican II and ARCIC'.

Geoffrey Rowell — is Anglican bishop of Basingstoke and formerly Chaplain, Fellow and Tutor at Keble College, Oxford. He has written extensively on nineteenth-century ecclesiastical history and is the author of *Hell and the Victorians* (Oxford, 1974) and *The Vision Glorious* (Oxford, 1983).

Bernhard Trocholepczy — lectures in Education and Catechesis at Albert-Ludwigs-Universität, Freiburg. He has written on religious philosophy and religious education, including *Rechtfertigung und Seinsfrage* (Freiburg, 1991).

I

SOURCES OF ENGLISH CONVERSIONS TO ROMAN CATHOLICISM IN THE ERA OF THE OXFORD MOVEMENT

Peter B. Nockles

A besetting sin of the historian of religious ideas is to over-context-ualise or over-particularise on the basis of individual and sometimes unrepresentative examples. The history of English conversions to Roman Catholicism in the era of the Oxford or Tractarian Movement provides ample room for historical pitfalls. As Sheridan Gilley has recently suggested in the case of the most celebrated of the Tractarian converts, John Henry Newman, there is an element of intrusive presumption in attempting to understand or explain the conversion of an individual to Roman Catholicism. To ascribe motives and reasons can lead to misrepresentation or distortion of the often unfathomable and mysterious inner workings of mind and soul. Even where the historian treads delicately, avoiding sociological or psychological reductionism in explaining motivation and viewing subjects through the eyes of Faith, there is always the danger of appearing to know those subjects better than they knew themselves. Converts were suspect.[1] It was precisely the danger of exposure to the prejudiced criticisms of opponents, that made Newman, in the immediate wake of his conver-sion, unwilling to record his reasons for becoming a Catholic. As Newman wrote in 1846:

> People shall not say, 'We have now got his reasons, and know their worth'. No, you have not got them, you cannot get them, except at the cost of some portion of the trouble I have been at myself. You cannot buy them for a crown piece — You cannot take them in your hand at your will, and toss them about, You must consent to think - and you must exercise such resignation to the Divine Hand which leads you, as to follow it ... Moral proofs are grown into, not learnt by heart.[2]

There exists a whole genre of literary and biographical evidence left by individual nineteenth-century English converts to Rome, of which, for all his initial reluctance to give reasons, Newman's *Loss and Gain* (1848), *Lectures on Anglican Difficulties* (1850) and *Apologia* (1864) are notable examples. Moreover, Newman's voluminous correspondence on the subject has ensured that he has become pre-eminently the convert's convert. Nevertheless in most conversion accounts the interior evidence, which might be more indicative of positive than negative factors in the conversion process, is often hidden from view and fails to find any written expression. Moreover, it was only the educated few who recorded their reasons for conversion. Yet, these provisos notwithstanding, an historical and part-biographical survey of an individual convert or groups of converts in a particularly fascinating epoch in modern English church history remains a rewarding subject of analysis for the religious historian. In recent years, there have been several valuable studies of English converts to Roman Catholicism in the nineteenth century, most notably by the late Louis Allen, V.A. McClelland, Sheridan Gilley, Pauline Adams, H.L. Morris, Elizabeth Stuart and Madeleine Beard. This study will concentrate on some of the processes by which certain individuals in the era of the Oxford Movement became Catholics rather than on the details of their later life as Catholics. It is unashamedly an historical survey not of conversions in general but of conversions primarily in the light of Tractarianism.

Conversion to Rome was and remains a very individualistic and personal matter. The process and pattern of conversion has tended to be viewed through the example of Newman. As one-time leader of the Oxford Movement and inspirer of a host of disciples, many of whom followed him to Rome just as some had preceded him along that path, the focus on Newman is hardly surprising. Nonetheless, Newman's way of conversion was manifestly not always the way of others. There was no premeditated union, inspired by Newman, among those who ended by becoming Catholics. Converts have always come in all shapes and sizes, mental and spiritual as well as physical. As one of the converts, Frederick Oakeley put it: 'we had, one and all, our individual peculiarities, which, like so many sharp edges, stood in the way of anything like effectual combination'.[3] The contrasts, even between disciple and leader, were often as instructive as the similarities. The impetuous and ebullient W.G. Ward presents an obvious contrast to the fastidious and cautious Newman of his later Anglican years. Moreover, differences in theological approach could be as significant as mere differences in temperament or even *ethos*. Polarisation occurred not merely between hereditary Catholics and converts. While a large number of converts such as F.W. Faber identified with the rising Ultramontane camp, there were others such as Peter Le Page Renouf and John Moore Capes who were more liberal or Gallican in their leaning. In selecting examples of English converts from the era of the Oxford Movement, I shall focus upon some of the many influences at work in the conversion process, the different theological routes taken, and the elements of contrast as well as affinity with Newman's path to Rome.

To disentangle the varied factors fostering English conversions to Roman Catholicism in the 1830s and 1840s might seem an invidious task. However, the following influences can be enumerated. For some, the attraction of Rome lay in realising intellectual certainty; for some it lay in a fulfilment of the claims of doctrinal authority or a manifestation of the visible unity of the Church; some were drawn by study of the Fathers into accepting Roman claims; some by visions of medieval Christianity and the age of chivalry; some by the evidence of supernatural life provided by the Catholic liturgical, devotional and penitential system, including devotion to the Blessed Virgin and the Saints; while many, Newman included, were partly inspired by the examples of self-denying holiness of Italian missioners such as the Rosminian Luigi Gentili and the Passionist Dominic Barberi. Many converts were particularly influenced by a new-found recognition of the special place assigned to Our Lady in the economy of salvation. They were struck by the inseparable link between the privileges of Our Lady and the doctrine of the Holy Trinity and Incarnation;[4] a link then denied by pre-Tractarian Anglican High Churchmen and Low Churchmen alike.

It would be possible to give innumerable examples of the positive impact of foreign travel on English men and women on a Continent which had opened up again after the Napoleonic Wars and which witnessed abundant evidence of a Catholic revival especially in France.[5] F.W. Faber's *Sights and Sounds in Foreign Churches* (1843) and T.W. Allies's *Diary in France* (1845) are just two examples of a whole genre of literature on this subject. Moreover, the rising Catholic spirit in Europe became harnessed rather than opposed to the cultural spirit of Romanticism. A Christianised Romanticism represented a search for eternal truths and found expression in renewed attachment to the ecclesiastical 'Gothic' past as well as the 'Roman' present. In Britain, the influence on the middle and upper classes of the writings of Sir Walter Scott served as an indication of a new Catholic spirit which spoke to the rising generation of the 1820s and 1830s reared in godly Protestant households. According to the Roman Catholic convert and disciple of Newman, William Lockhart writing in 1886,

> perhaps most of those who have become Catholic during the last fifty years can trace the attractions of Divine Grace, through the Providence of God, in the pure literature which came into their hands in early youth, as much as to the teaching and high example of religious men, whether of the Puritan or Catholic school, and also to their

reading of the English Bible, with which all were taught to be
familiar from their childhood.[6]

Further down the social scale, a key influence appears to have been
William Cobbett's *History of the Reformation* (1822) which portrayed
an England robbed of the old Faith by a profligate Henry VIII and the
new religion as being established by persecution.

Converts were drawn to Rome by one or a combination of several
of the above forces. Contemporaries recognised the variety of
influences at work. A list of the attractions of Rome for the potential
convert was provided by the Anglo-Catholic loyalist Pusey:

> Rome has many sympathies whereby to draw persons to herself. To
> those who would lean, she offers undoubting guidance; for those who
> would have certainty, she offers infallibility; for the devout, she has
> her churches ever open and her frequent public services, her retreats
> for devotion and contemplation; for the affectionate, she has the
> memory of the saints of old; for the imaginative, she has a nominal
> reverence for Antiquity and a visible unity of communion, spread
> over the whole world, and everywhere professing to teach the same
> truth. Her theory of Unity (to speak of the first) at once fills the
> imagination and contents the intellect.[7]

Given the profound influence of the Movement in reshaping the
Church of England in a more Catholic image, the compelling nature
of Newman's own religious odyssey and the literary power of his
account of it in the *Apologia*, it is not surprising that conversions from
the 1840s onwards should be directly linked to Tractarian Oxford. Of
course, for Protestant enemies of the Oxford Movement, the link was
causal; the converts of the 1840s onwards were the product of a
Romanising fifth-column and conspiracy within the Church of England
masterminded by Newman prior to 1845 and further fostered by Pusey
thereafter. High Churchmen were more than half papist and in secret
communication with Roman Catholics at home and abroad. The reality,
however, was more complex than this. Contact with individual Roman
Catholics on the part of English converts was rare and limited. There
were exceptions. The influence of French émigré clergy helped foster
some conversions, such as the Abbé Beaumont in the case of Henry
Digby Best (1768-1836), Fellow of Magdalen College, Oxford,[8] while
Kenelm Digby's path to Rome was encouraged by the hereditary
Catholic barrister, Charles Butler.[9] In contrast to a certain personal
knowledge of continental Catholicism, Newman and most of his
followers, however, had virtually no English Catholic contacts.
Frederick Oakeley later claimed that he had never set foot in an
English Catholic chapel prior to his conversion.[10] As William Lockhart

later recalled: 'it was a rare thing when any Anglican clergy or laity of the educated classes happened to make the acquaintance of a Catholic priest, until they came to ask to make in his hands their act of submission to the Catholic Church'.[11] The pull of Rome for English converts was always as much a response to spiritual and intellectual prompting from within as of external attraction from without.

The perception that Anglican High Churchmanship was a staging-post for conversion to Roman Catholicism was not confined to Low Churchmen or Protestant Dissenters, but shared by some Catholics themselves. In the 1790s and 1800s, the Catholic controversialist, Bishop John Milner had directed most of his anti-Anglican polemic at the Low Church or Latitudinarian tenets represented by Bishop Hoadly. The ultramontane Milner was notably more lenient on Anglican High Churchmen and respectful towards the Laudian tradition in Anglicanism represented by his friend, Bishop Samuel Horsley.[12] The conversion of a few pre-Tractarian High Churchmen such as Henry Best, and the influence of French émigré clergy in moderating anti-Catholic prejudice among some in this quarter, appeared good omens for the revival of Catholic fortunes. The rise of the Oxford Movement after 1833 further raised Roman Catholic hopes.

Nicholas Wiseman and Ambrose Phillipps de Lisle[13] were at the forefront of Catholic efforts to court the Tractarians as part of a stategy of encouraging conversions. For Phillipps de Lisle, the apparent similarities between the Catholicism of Oxford and Rome were proclaimed as a basis of future reunion. De Lisle cultivated ecumenical contacts with Tractarian Oxford, corresponding for some time on ecclesiastical matters with the liturgical scholar, J.R. Bloxam, Fellow of Magdalen.[14] By contrast, Wiseman's encouragement of the Oxford divines, which dated from his meeting with Newman and Hurrell Froude in Rome in 1833, did not entail any compromise on the Roman side. Wiseman recognised the gulf separating High Church Anglicanism and Rome, but he had reasons for entertaining higher hopes for conversions from the Oxford Movement compared to earlier High Church overtures in the days of Laud and Wake. Not only was he more sanguine because of the 'singular unworldliness of the leaders of the Movement', but because of the fact that 'in former times, men's minds were on the road from than to Catholic truth ... The tide of the Reformation was rolling in, not ebbing quietly back and restoring to the Church its usurped territories'.[15] This perception led Wiseman to challenge the High Church claims in favour of the Church of England being propagated in the *Tracts for the Times*, and provoked a lively controversy with the conservative High Churchman, William Palmer of Worcester College.[16] Some of Wiseman's controversial weapons hit home. As is well known, it was Wiseman's article in the *Dublin*

Review in 1839 which first inspired Newman's doubts about Anglicanism.

The gulf, however, between even Tractarian Oxford and Rome was
greater than the eirenic Phillipps de Lisle allowed. Many Roman
Catholics, of widely varying outlook, did not share his or Wiseman's
enthusiasm for the Movement. When Wiseman visited England in
1835, he was surprised to find how little attention the *Tracts for the
Times* had excited among Catholics.[17] When notice came to be taken,
it was not always favourable. *The Tablet*, under the editorship of
Frederick Lucas, a Quaker convert to Ultramontane Catholicism, was
particularly hostile to the Movement.[18] From an opposite perspective,
Old Catholics such as John Lingard and Bishop Baines and their
mouthpiece the *Catholic Magazine* dampened down schemes for the
conversion of England, which Baines regarded as 'a moral impos-
sibility'[19] likely to take many thousands of years at the then rate of
progress. Old Catholics were suspicious of the Tractarians whom they
regarded as dreamers, enthusiasts and disturbers of the peace. While
respecting their integrity and unworldliness, the *Catholic Magazine*
regarded the Oxford divines as 'the most obstinate and tenacious of all
our opponents',[20] whose teaching appeared liable to entrench rather
than remove Anglican self-delusion. The author of *Tract 83*, who
happened to be Newman, was commended in 1840 as sincere, but was
described as being impelled 'more by the spirit of Toryism and High
Churchism, than by the spirit of religion'.[21] Lingard remained anxious
that those who did convert should be usefully employed, but felt that
the Oxford Movement would yield few converts and foretold that
Pusey would not enter the Church.[22] In the immediate wake of Newman's conversion in 1845, he observed: 'I think the Anglican Church
will become more powerful after it has been left by the more catholicly
inclined'.[23] For Lingard, the Tractarian converts represented 'nothing
more than the travail of their own minds and that of a portion of their
congregations' who 'were in no real touch with the great mass of
English Protestantism'.[24] Even de Lisle's patron and opponent of
Bishop Baines, Lord Shrewsbury, in an almost eighteenth-century tone
of cool rationality, was constantly urging him to check his ardour for
his Tractarian friends and abandon utopian schemes of reunion
involving the Oxford divines. It was the experience of Isabella Young,
one of Pusey's female protégés, which convinced Lord Shrewsbury
that Pusey was wrong-headed and untrustworthy, while the extreme
asceticism of Newman's 'Littlemore party' also earned his mistrust. As
the Earl told de Lisle in 1842:

> There never was a more deluded mind than Pusey's, and I am now
> more convinced of it. I hear from various quarters, and I have very

good proof of it, that the reigning fanaticism of the day with them...
is the seeking after supernatural Evidences or Inspirations in favour
of Anglicanism. It is the most common and most fatal resource of all
Heresiarchs — only for the moment to instance Luther, Calvin,
Wesley, etc — and joined, as it commonly is, with great fasting and
austerities, is sure to make the Imagination an overmatch for the
Reason.[25]

Given Lord Shrewsbury's own preoccupation at this time with the
evidence of supernatural revelations and miraculous signs in favour of
the Catholic Church associated with the so-called 'Miraculous Virgins
of the Tyroll', a preoccupation which he shared with de Lisle,[26] his
criticism of Tractarian enthusiasm was all the more pointed.

The path to Rome of English converts was by no means always a
by-product of High Church values taken to a logical conclusion. It is
easy to overlook the large numbers of converts who predated, or had
no connection with Newman or the Oxford Movement. As Pauline
Adams has shown, the records of Catholic Missions reveal that the rise
in conversions to Rome not only anteceded the Movement but were
only slightly affected by it. The peak periods of Tractarian conversion
in 1845/6 and 1850/1 were not reflected in the figures for conversions
in general.[27] Oxford converts represented an intellectual and social élite
but were far from typical even in the Tractarian era. Of the four
hundred Anglican clerical converts in the nineteenth century, one
hundred dated from the period 1845-55.[28] Roman Catholic converts,
however, were not recruited solely from the Anglican establishment;
many were former Nonconformists, reclaimed pagans or lapsed
Catholics. The lapsed Irish immigrant was more statistically significant
in conversion figures than the Oxonian academic. One needs to be
aware of the danger of which a writer in *The Tablet* complained in
1855, when he criticised 'the continual harping on the conversion of
great people' as 'a sort of spiritual flunkeyism'.[29] Nonetheless, while
Oxford Tractarian converts may not have been representative of
converts in general, their importance was necessarily out of all
proportion to their numbers on account of their educational, intellectual
and cultural status. The Tractarian converts would prove an indispensable revitalising force for the Catholic Church in England in the
second half of the century.

If Tractarian Oxford, however, was to gain a reputation as a nursery
for converts to Rome, at a somewhat earlier date it was the sister
university of Cambridge which had attracted and nurtured several
notable Roman Catholics such as Ambrose Phillipps de Lisle and
Kenelm Digby, and spawned many converts in the 1840s. George
Spencer, the future Passionist,[30] and William Dodsworth, a Tractarian
leader in London, are just two examples of numerous Cambridge-

educated converts to Rome. Cambridge itself had no direct equivalent of the Oxford Movement; its apostolical enthusiasms being channelled into the ecclesiological preoccupations of the Cambridge Camden Society and the Romantic social paternalism of the 'Young England' movement. Yet the number of Cambridge converts, many educated at Trinity and St John's College and some such as Frederick Apthorp Paley (1815-88), John Hanmer (1817-1907), Edward Healy Thompson (1813-88) and Henry Austin Mills (1823-1903) influenced by Newman, is striking. This Cambridge dimension has been overshadowed by the more familiar conversion path from Oxford to Rome. Some explanation for the apparent anomaly is called for.

In comparison to Royalist, Tory, Jacobite and High Church Oxford, Cambridge has been viewed historically as Roundhead, Whig, Hanoverian and Latitudinarian. Cambridge was not without its High Church Anglican representatives such as Christopher Wordsworth, Master of Trinity, Hugh James Rose, a forerunner and early patron of the Oxford Tractarians, William Hodge Mill and S.R. Maitland, both detached supporters of the Movement. Tractarianism also inspired Cambridge Camdenites such as John Mason Neale, Thomas Thorp and Benjamin Webb. Nor were Cambridge graduates absent from the ranks of notable Tractarian sympathisers in the public life of the 1840s, Lord John Manners, Alexander Beresford Hope and Richard Monckton-Milnes, a contemporary of Phillipps de Lisle, being among the more noteworthy examples. Yet it is a moot point of conjecture whether if Newman had gone to Cambridge, he would ever have emerged as a leader of a religious movement of the character of that which he inspired at Oxford. Rose felt his isolation at Cambridge and had to look to Oxford for support in 1833.[31]

In the condescending eyes of Tractarian Oxford, the *ethos* of the University of Cambridge was cold, utilitarian and uncatholic. In the Oxford of the 1830s, the High Church campaign in defence of the university's Anglican monopoly against proposals to admit Dissenters without subscribing to the Thirty-Nine Articles and Oath of Supremacy at matriculation proved a formative experience for the Tractarians. For all their later popular association with crypto-Romanism, the Tractarians were battling at this date to defend an essentially High Church Protestant hegemony to the utter exclusion of Catholics as well as Protestant Dissenters. On the other hand, from the perspective of Tractarian Oxford, Cambridge had already fatally compromised with the forces of liberalism and secularity by having admitted to residence Roman Catholics and Dissenters and only excluding them from actually taking degrees.[32] Oxford High Churchmen poured scorn on such liberality and presented it as indifferentism. Writing of Cambridge in 1834, George Moberly, a Fellow of Balliol, maintained:

how different is their religious system from ours. In our colleges a Roman Catholic, or Socinian, would feel their doctrines denied more or less directly every day of their lives. In the regular course of our religious reading, every form of Dissent would in turn be exposed and refuted. We have instituted, and we wish to perfect, a higher system of religious education than is there possible.[33]

From a narrowly High Anglican perspective, this argument had validity, but it meant that, prior to the Oxford Movement and even beyond, Roman Catholics would feel an affinity with Cambridge which they could not bestow upon her more exclusive sister university. Phillipps de Lisle and Digby might appear to have been more in tune with Oxford's medieval spirit than with Cambridge's prosaic, rational tone, but their Catholicism excluded them from Oxford while it did not from Cambridge.

To be High Church in the early decades of the nineteenth century was to be both politically and theologically Protestant and anti-Roman. The Oxford Movement originated from a cause directly hostile to Roman Catholicism — indignation at the concession to Irish Catholics of the annihilation of the Protestant sees.[34] In contrast, it was often Whigs and liberals, much better represented at Cambridge than Oxford, who were the more natural patrons and allies of Roman Catholicism. The very eclecticism of Cambridge liberals could encompass remarkably tolerant attitudes towards Catholicism. For example, Julius Hare, a not untypical Cambridge-educated Whig Latitudinarian, combined veneration of Martin Luther with devoted study of and admiration for continental Ultramontane authors such as Bonald and De Maistre. Connop Thirlwall of Trinity was another Cambridge liberal who was eirenic towards Catholicism. As Bishop of St.David's, Thirlwall was one of the very few Anglican bishops who engaged with the Tractarians with intellectual sympathy and understanding.[35] In this context, the Roman Catholic alliance with Whigs in the age of Reform, an alliance supported by Wiseman but deplored by Catholic Romantics such as Phillipps de Lisle, the 'Young-Englander' Lord John Manners and the Tractarian Newman alike, appears less than surprising.

The seeds of a later opening-up to Rome among the Tractarians may well have been sown by the lectures on the Roman Breviary given by the unusually eirenic High Churchman, Charles Lloyd, Regius Professor of Divinity at Oxford, in 1826.[36] However, the early phase of the Oxford Movement as exemplified in the earlier numbers of the *Tracts for the Times* and Newman's *Lectures on the Prophetical Office of the Church* was no less anti-Roman than it was anti-Protestant Dissent. In High Church rhetoric, Rome may have been a true church but she was deemed to have abandoned Antiquity by adding to as well as corrupting the Faith with tenets such as Transubstantiation,

Purgatory, the Invocation of Saints, devotion to the Blessed Virgin
Mary, Indulgences, and obligatory private confession. The necessity
of the Reformation, defined as conservative restoration rather than
radical departure, was deemed self-evident. It was a High Church
shibboleth that the Roman communion was schismatical in Britain,
because her bishops apparently could trace 'no descent nor do they
pretend to be descended from the ancient church in this island'.[37]

Although many Tractarians gradually softened their line on Rome's
supposedly idolatrous practices, Rome's 'schism' and especially her
political alliance in England and Ireland with Whigs and liberals
continued to offend the High Church and Tory sensitivities of the
Tractarians. The hopes of Tory Romantics like Phillipps de Lisle and
Lord John Manners that High Church principles would mitigate Irish
Protestantism and render Ireland 'the La Vendée of the British
Monarchy'[38] were fanciful given the enduring link between Tory High
Churchmanship and Protestantism; a link which underpinned the
original Tractarian protest against the suppression of Irish bishoprics.[39]

Many moderate Tractarians and their sympathisers continued to
regard High Church principles as the only sure bulwark of the Church
of England against Rome. Secessions to Rome were blamed on the
excesses of either Anglican Evangelicals or Liberals. One High
Churchman in 1850 went so far as to assert that 'amongst all those
who have seceded there is not to be found a single individual who had
been brought up from early youth in High Church principles. Men
who were so taught and trained are with us still'.[40] A correlation
between Low Church ascendancy and Roman Catholic conversions was
demonstrated from the example of the city of Birmingham:

> the Low Church party ... had everything their own way. The only
> High Church clergyman ... was opposed in every possible way ...
> Mark the consequence. That town is now one of the greatest
> strongholds of Romanism in England.[41]

Protestant critics of the Oxford Movement might blame contemporary
secessions to Rome on the Tractarians, but the first converts of the
1840s roundly denied any Tractarian influence on their life's decision.
One of the earliest converts of the Tractarian era, Richard Waldo
Sibthorp, one-time Fellow of Magdalen College, Oxford, justified his
conversion to Rome on what were construed as essentially Protestant
grounds. For Sibthorp, the key to conversion was a realisation that the
modern Church of Rome corresponded to the Scriptural type or figure
of the True Church as represented by ancient Israel under the Mosaic
dispensation. It was precisely Sibthorp's Evangelical Protestant
preoccupation with the biblical Mosaic dispensation which prompted

him 'to look for a church characterised by visible oneness ... by the strictest required holiness, — by Catholicity, as to the land of its inheritance ... by a supreme Spiritual Rule ... by continual daily sacrifice'.[42] Tractarianism checked rather than fostered Sibthorp's spiritual quest. Although his former Low Church friends denied his claim,[43] Sibthorp maintained that as a Protestant he had known no 'Protestant controversial writer (the authors of the Oxford *Tracts* alone excepted) whose words did not leave me more a Catholic than before'.[44] Having nearly become a Catholic when under age, Sibthorp had fallen back into Evangelical Protestantism. Tractarian Oxford disowned him as having been 'for many years an extempore preacher and all but a Dissenter'.[45] According to one Tractarian sympathiser, if Mr Sibthorp had turned Mahometan no one would have been astonished, as his life was a series of changes from beginning to end'. He was dismissed as being quite unknown till the other day'.[46] As late as 1839 Sibthorp was deemed to have preached a highly Protestant sermon at Oxford, before progressing almost directly to Rome without an intermediary High Church phase. Sibthorp was positively scornful of the *Tracts for the Times*, and like most Protestant critics regarded Newman's *Tract 90*, which sought to reconcile the Thirty-Nine Articles with the Tridentine decrees, as sophistical and erroneous.[47]

The example of Sibthorp's path of conversion initially seemed to give credence to the High Church and Tractarian assertion 'that the way to Rome is through Geneva'.[48] William Dodsworth, a Tractarian and later convert to Rome, poured scorn on Sibthorp's published reasons for converting, as betraying 'your extreme unacquaintance with the writings of our best English divines, and the baneful influence of that school of Ultra-Protestantism in which you have been trained'. Dodsworth patronisingly informed Sibthorp that a better knowledge of Anglican divines 'might, by God's blessing, have saved you from your present unhappy course'.[49] In the early-1840s, Pusey was no less dismissive of any link between Tractarian teaching and conversions to Rome such as that of the Cambridge graduate F.D. Wackerbath as well as of Sibthorp, though this would be harder to prove in the case of another convert of 1842, the former Magdalen Fellow, Bernard Smith. The authors of the *Tracts for the Times*, Pusey insisted, had not been responsible for 'the extent of the tendency to Romanism'.[50]

There had been numerous secessions before the *Tracts* began — 'in Edinburgh alone, the annual converts to Romanism were calculated at one hundred; but from the Kirk, not from our Church'. Thus far Pusey's view accords with current historical evidence. On more debatable ground, he also maintained that the converts and potential converts were not, for the most part, persons formed by any one of us or by our writings. Those who have gone over, have been mostly persons, not at all instructed in the character of our church, who sought in Rome what they might have found in our own church, had they allowed themselves time to be instructed in her teaching.[51]

There were other academic converts, besides Sibthorp, for whom the Oxford Movement had little to say. The conversion of John Moore Capes, who entered the Catholic Church in 1845, came about in spite of, rather than because of the Oxford Movement. Capes had actually written against the Movement. Like Sibthorp, he started from a point far removed from the High Church position and scarcely even passed through that phase on his religious journey. Although Capes's conversion came about in the same year as that of Newman and many of his followers, it followed a different pattern. Capes never felt himself to have been a disciple of Newman, and later stated: 'I had none of that... feeling of utter intellectual helplessness, or that dependence upon the example and opinion of others, which in some cases, predispose the mind to seek for rest in the bosom of Catholicism'.[52]

The submission to Rome of the twenty-year old Pembroke College, Oxford undergraduate, Peter Le Page Renouf in 1842, while more subject to Tractarian influence, was no less independent of Newman's guidance. Whereas Newman was to remain four years on his Anglican 'deathbed', for Renouf there was no time-lag between initial doubts over Anglicanism and conversion. Renouf's fascinating undergraduate correspondence with his parents, preserved in the archives of Pembroke College, reveals at most a detached supporter of the Movement who followed his own original and creative line of religious enquiry. At the time of his conversion, Renouf insisted to his parents that he had only read the first volume of the *Tracts for the Times*.[53] He was enthusiastic about some of Newman's university sermons on the connection between philosophy and religion but was unmoved by his *Parochial Sermons* 'where he never says anything which the most illiterate person cannot understand'.[54]

The reasoning employed in Renouf's learned apologetic on the doctrine of the Eucharist, published in 1841 on the eve of his conversion, bore some affinity to that of Newman's *Tract 90*.[55] The work, which was fulsomely praised by Wiseman,[56] was widely ascribed to Newman himself.[57] The Anglican Newman, however, was not flattered by the misconception, while Pusey was uneasy about Renouf's precocity. As a Catholic, after some intial controversial forays against Anglicanism, Renouf increasingly revealed his mental distance from the enthusiasms of Tractarian Oxford. By the late-1840s, the liberal Catholic Renouf was privately deriding Tractarian Oxford as a sink of religious bigotry, exclusiveness and fanaticism, and unflatteringly contrasting it with the tolerant religious atmosphere in Besançon, France, where he then resided as a language tutor. Renouf had never understood the Tractarian outcry over Dr Hampden which the Anglican Newman had helped orchestrate. In stark contrast to the Anglican Newman's harsh verdict on Hampden, the Catholic Renouf later confided that he had always regarded the apparently heterodox Regius Professor as 'entirely innocent in intention of the charges brought against him'.[58]

By way of contrast to the above experiences, the conversion of John Gordon, the later Oratorian, was strongly determined by the character, ability and learning of converts who had preceded him on the path to Rome and whose previous adherence to the Church of England had been constantly held up to him as a positive 'note of the church to which they belonged'. It was clear, Gordon concluded, 'that whatever was gained to the English Church by the personal character and abilities of the persons alluded to, was not only lost to it by their secession, but became thus far a note against it'.[59] It would be wrong, however, to infer that Newman's influence as leader of the Movement was always paramount. For example, James Hope was 'put off' by Newman's theory of development of doctrine, complaining that Newman's work gave up the Fathers 'which had been the foundation of the Oxford Movement'.[60] Hope's conversion was delayed until 1851 and the impact of the Gorham Judgment. Far from encouraging followers like Ward and Oakeley or his Littlemore disciples such as Lockhart and Dalgairns to convert, for a long period Newman tried to hold them back. One Anglican critic of the converts in 1846 conceded that Newman had not been very 'instrumental in detaching others from that church which he has not, till very lately, himself abandoned'. Several young men of wavering opinions had been committed to Newman's charge. Their secession to Rome, however, it was admitted, had been 'to his great annoyance ... and left him grieving and offended'.[61]

While individual converts undoubtedly made up their own minds in the face of their own personal dilemmas and circumstances, it would be idle to deny that the theological and spiritual power of the Movement which Newman helped shape and direct was not a key element in determining the conversions of many. When Newman later maintained that it was 'Oxford which made us Catholics',[62] he was asserting an important truth. As a Catholic, Newman insisted that the whole direction, albeit unconsciously, of the Oxford Movement had been providentially towards Rome and had ever been alien to the national establishment.[63] Even leading Tractarian figures who remained Anglican, such as William Copeland, Frederic Rogers and Richard

Church, would have had to admit at least that the Movement was more than a mere defensive response to a 'church in danger' scenario of the type which had frequently agitated Anglican High Churchmen over the preceding century and a half. Newman went further, concluding that the Movement had from the first been engaged in propagating an unreality or dream — the congeniality of sentiments, ways and moral life of the national religion with the principles, doctrines and traditions of Apostolical Christianity.[64]

Gladstone, like other High Church Anglican supporters of the Movement, was astonished that Newman and his disciples should begin to abandon the Church of England just when Catholic principles had appeared to gain ground within her. Was this not a paradox? Gladstone wondered how Newman could fail to see that the Anglican Church in her members was growing more Catholic by the year.[65] For the converts, such a view was blinkered. It was not enough for individuals to have become more 'Catholic', if the Church of England as a church could not be proved Catholic. Puseyites maintained that it was possible to catholicise, the national church from within and that the converts had betrayed the Tractarian cause. Newman himself had once held as much, but after 1845 this view seemed less sustainable or in accord with reality. For the converts, it represented a second-best settling for a mere permission to hold certain doctrines or adopt certain practices.[66]

The view that Newman and his convert disciples misunderstood or were not deeply acquainted with the teaching or spirit of Anglicanism cannot be sustained. As the convert Newman later recalled, he and his followers had always sought 'to make the Anglican divines real vouchers and sanctions of their own teaching, and they used their words rather than their own'.[67] It was precisely because so many of the English converts of the Tractarian era had been ardently believing Anglicans, albeit often with Evangelical roots, rather than liberals or men of no faith, that they spent so much time thereafter trying to counteract the force of a religious viewpoint which had once beguiled them. Newman himself in the wake of his conversion in 1845 paid a back-handed compliment to the strength of the High Church case in Anglican apologetic when he conceded that High Church Anglican principles of unity, authority and apostolicity were 'still the firmest, strongest bulwark against Rome — that is if they could be held. They have been held by many, and are far more difficult to refute than those of any other religious body'.[68]

Other converts were more dismissive of their abandoned High Anglican principles, while remaining conscious of their continued plausibility for those they had left behind. According to Frederick Paley in 1848: 'Of all the theories in defence of the Anglican position, the "Catholic" claim is the most unreasonable and the most inconsistent in its conclusions'.[69] The inconsistencies of High Churchmen in their respective rebuttals of Protestant Dissent and Romanism were frequently insisted upon. In effect, High Church Anglicans maintained 'a visible church against dissenters and an invisible one against the Holy See. You must have a visible succession they say to one, to be a church; you need not have a visible communion with the rest of Christendom, they say to the other'.[70] The High Church position was unreal in its selectivity. Bishop Phillpotts, for example, was criticised for using 'weapons pilfered from the armoury of the Church' against Evangelicals, Methodists and Latitudinarians, but which could just as consistently be turned against his own position.[71] Old Catholics could be no less scathing about High Church Anglican pretensions; with Lingard in 1839 urging his friend John Walker of Scarborough in a sermon, to 'speak with sovereign contempt of the miserable sophistry by which it is sought to humbug the people and preach that the present is the old Church of England'.[72]

Pusey deluded himself in blaming what he called 'Ultra-Protestant-ism' rather than Tractarian teaching for secessions to Rome. If prior to 1842 Pusey had a point, subsequent conversions and lapses rendered his argument mere special pleading. Although many of the converts had emerged from Evangelical Protestant backgrounds, most had for a time become enthusiastic proponents of the High Church Anglican notions of the '*via media*' and 'branch theory'. It was these who never wavered once they had become Catholics. Those converts such as Sibthorp and Capes, however, who stood aside from Tractarian involvement were precisely those who proved to be the least stable and returned to the Church of England; in the case of Sibthorp making the journey back again to Rome and finally dying on the apparent brink of another lapse. Of course, Sibthorp was not typical of the Tractarian converts, but it was his unfortunate example which confirmed those Old Catholics such as Lingard who had profound misgivings about the Oxford Movement. As Lingard correctly foretold at the time of Sibthorp's lapse in 1845:

> I consider him as one of those weak men who consult others, and always feel disposed to agree with their last adviser. I suspect that he will continue to oscillate between the two churches till the end: and that end will be made in the church to which the person into whose hands he may chance to fall may belong.[73]

Tractarianism made a unique contribution to the process of conversion in the following ways. The Tractarian converts recognised that it had been the very signs of life exhibited by a renewed Anglicanism after 1833 which had first drawn them to the Movement, giving High Churchmanship an appeal which it had hitherto lacked. Yet this

Anglican revival had raised a desire for unity and authority which the Church of England could not hope to supply or sustain. The Oxford Movement had the double-edged effect of raising the Church of England to its highest pitch of Catholic doctrine and spirituality on the one hand, while ultimately exposing the limitations and defects of the Anglican system on the other. The leaders of the Movement encouraged followers to look to the roots of their theological and liturgical tradition as well as of their own spiritual life. For the converts, that tradition was tested to destruction and found wanting.

Newman and his convert disciples had been genuinely convinced that the Anglican system as enshrined in the Church's formularies and expounded by the seventeenth-century divines represented the authentic teaching of Antiquity. This was the underlying assumption on which the whole Tractarian edifice rested, even if the Church's abandonment of various primitive practices was deemed a matter of profound regret. However, whereas for conservative High Churchmen, the appeal to Antiquity had already been made by the Church and could not be superseded, for the Tractarians, Antiquity was an absolute standard to which the Church remained subject.[74] Compared to the old High Churchmen, there was always a provisional quality to the Anglican allegiance of Newman and his younger followers, which would prove vulnerable to the more searching study of the Fathers which they undertook after the late-1830s.

Far from giving up the vantage-point of Antiquity in their submission to Rome, according to William Lockhart, the Tractarian conversions to Rome 'were for the most part the pure logical outcome of the study of the Holy Fathers and of the History of the Ancient Church, aided by the Divine Spirit'.[75] The process was gradual. At first it was enough that the Fathers were utterly anti-Protestant without enquiring too closely if they told in favour of the Church of Rome or not. The 'Library of the Fathers' set up in 1836 was a Tractarian-inspired project which enjoyed wide support among conservative High Churchmen. It was at this date taken for granted by Tractarians that Anglicanism could be vindicated and Romanism condemned by the verdict of Antiquity. For William Lockhart and his collaborators on the project, however, the patristic study involved first led them to consider seriously the Roman claims for authority and unity. As Lockhart later recalled, he and his friends 'observed that the supreme characteristic of Primitive Christianity was an intense conviction that the Church was a divine power in the world'.[76] Moreover, Lockhart and others found in early writings such as those of St Ireneaus, 'set forth in the most luminous manner, that Primitive Christianity adhered to the teaching of a living body, already called the catholic or universal church, spread everywhere'. Lockhart found implied in the *Catechetical Instructions of St Cyril of Jerusalem*, the basis of the later doctrine of Transubstantiation. In St Ireneaus and other writers, he found evidence for the Petrine Headship of the Church and the honour due to the Blessed Virgin and the Saints.[77] The Oxford convert, R.K. Sconce, devoted a major treatise to 'the testimony of Antiquity to the Supremacy of the Holy See'.[78] In this way, a key source of apparent support for the Anglican position had been turned into a potent agent of its destruction. For as the convert Newman memorably put it, many of the Movement's followers came at length to find in the Fathers:

> at least the rudiments, the anticipation, the justification of what they had been accustomed to consider the corruptions of Rome.... They had raised a goodly house, but their foundations were falling in. The soil and the masonry were both bad. The Fathers would protect Romanists as well as extinguish Dissenters.[79]

The Anglican 'branch theory' was another casualty of the deeper patristic researches of the future converts. 'For the first time', Lockhart concluded, 'the vision of the world-wide Church, in its majestic unity, had come before us. We saw it for the first time, not as we had supposed it to be, an aggregate of congregations — a voluntary union of spiritual families, but as a world-wide essentially united kingdom'.[80] Newman and his convert disciples had embraced the Anglican theory and teaching of the Caroline Divines essentially on trust. They felt betrayed by the Caroline Divines once their own deeper study of the Fathers destroyed their faith in Anglicanism.[81] Peter Le Page Renouf in 1843 indignantly turned on that most learned High Churchman, William Palmer of Worcester College, for what Renouf regarded as Palmer's unfair and selective use of the Fathers in controversy with Wiseman. According to Renouf, Palmer — like other Anglican controversialists — had appealed to Antiquity in an entirely subjective way. As Renouf put it:

> Having made up his mind that the Ancient Church believed just as little as his own Church does, and that his own Church believes just as much as the Primitive Church, he refuses, upon examination, to see more in one than in the other. So by Anglicanizing in his mind the Primitive Church, and Catholizing Anglicanism, he has at last finished by establishing some sort of identity between the two.[82]

High Church Anglicans might decry the religion of extreme Protestantism based on the Bible only as one of private judgment, but Catholic converts, echoing Protestant complaints in the same vein, maintained that it was much 'more an act of private judgment to form a creed out of the folios of Antiquity'. High Churchmen would retort that the

Anglican divines and formularies along with Holy Scripture, councils and episcopal authority were all indispensable guides in perusing the Fathers. But granting the verdict of early Councils, 'why', came the Catholic rejoinder, should Anglican divines 'be able to inform us more about the early church than their contemporaries of the Roman communion?'.[83]

Knowledge of the Fathers in itself was not enough, since one could spend years in patristic study without reaching a conclusive decision as to which church embodied the fullness of religious truth.[84] A one-sided study of the Fathers might only lead down blind alleys. The telling example of the later Nonjurors was cited. Thomas Brett, Thomas Deacon and others had devoted enormous zeal to the study of primitive liturgies in order to 'prove the necessity of particular observances to which they had taken a fancy'. Yet at the same time, they revealed 'their utter blindness to matters a hundred times more momentous, such as the real nature of the eucharistic sacrifice, and the intercession of the saints'. On these points, from a Roman Catholic perspective, even the Nonjurors were incurably Protestant. It was conceded that 'the Puseyite school is a real advance on the non-juring',[85] but they remained blinded by a similar patristic fundamental-ism. What was necessary was to form a correct principle to the knowledge which one acquired in patristic scholarship. Without this, moral certainty was impossible. The lesson was that one could only appeal to the Church of the Fathers, if one had a final living judge as well as the means of determining what the belief of that church was.[86]

It was not denied that individual Anglican divines had held such and such doctrines in conformity with Antiquity, but as Wiseman's *Dublin Review* article had demonstrated, the Roman and not Anglican theory of the Church had been the one foreshadowed in Antiquity. On the primitive model of the Church, the Anglican theory would have to be proved to be the authoritative teaching of the Church of England in order to show that the latter was a living body. The converts concluded that this was impossible. It was because, as John Gordon put it, Anglicans could not insist on their doctrines on authority, on the authority of their church as their church' that 'their whole theory falls to pieces; their doctrines are mere opinions, matters of private judgment'.[87] The 'branch theory' was flawed primarily because it substituted a purely local and subjective idea of Catholicity in place of a supra-national one guided by a central teaching authority, as foreshadowed in Antiquity. The 'trunk' or parent tree from which the so-called 'branches' in the Anglican theory stemmed, was, maintained by Frederick Paley, but a mere abstraction or paper fiction, never adequately defined and not endowed with any concept of the household of faith.[88] By conceding, however, that the churches of France, Italy etc. were the Catholic churches of their respective countries, modern Tractarian Anglicans had cut the vital theological ground from under the feet of the branch theory as expounded by their seventeenth-century forebears such as Bramhall.[89] Unlike the Caroline Divines, the modern High Churchman in practice had reduced Catholicity to a matter of mere geographical location. Ironically, therefore, the more moderate and candid modern High Church divines were in their dealings with Rome, the less consistent and more vulnerable their position became. In short, Tractarians who clung to the Church of England were able to give far less solid grounds for the Anglican schism than those Caroline apologists such as Bramhall who had thrown the charge of schism back upon Rome itself.[90] Catholic controversialists could plausibly claim that whereas at least the early *Tracts* had advanced definite and tangible arguments against Rome, by the mid-1840s, Pusey and Keble had abandoned 'the domain of facts' and taken refuge in misty notions of individual contentment and intellectual modesty. Wiseman was congratulated for showing how such vague and defensive reasons 'would just as much operate in keeping any sectaries whatever, nay even Turks and savages, where they are, as well as Anglicans'.[91]

Anglican High Churchmen might regard the notion of a 'branch church' as an antidote to subservience to the state and guarantor of ecclesiastical independence. The convert Newman, however, argued that a branch church was necessarily Erastian, 'for as a branch cannot live of itself, therefore as soon as it is lopped off from the Body of Christ, it is straightway grafted of sheer necessity upon the civil constitution, if it is to preserve life of any kind'.[92] Doctrinal conformity with the other 'branches' of both East and West had been severed, while the prospective appeal to a future Ecumenical Council was a theoretical option, never likely to be realised. According to Renouf, the 'branch theory' itself, as a viable ecclesial concept, was only a latter-day rationalisation of the Church of England's isolation, having been 'first broached by the Court divines of James I', then 'scouted' by the infinite majority of Anglicans in its day,' and only revived within living memory.[93] Only a very selective reading of Anglican history could have prompted High Churchmen such as William Palmer of Worcester to argue that the Church of England had always believed in the necessity of apostolical succession or that their own deference to Antiquity was normative. The Laudian divines could not be taken as a proof of what the Anglican Church believed, since 'they were clearly in a minority, even in their day'.[94]

The Thirty-Nine Articles had vindicated the rights of a national church but had contemplated no branch theory on the High Church model. The teaching of the Reformers and the Book of Homilies had been emphatic in proclaiming the Western Church as Antichrist and intercourse with it as pollution. Far from sorrowing at the Church of England's visible separation from the Catholic world, as did the Tractarians, generations of her worthiest divines had gloried in it.[95] Nor was this altogether surprising. The Caroline Divines had felt the Anglican church to be less isolated than did their modern Tractarian successors. In the seventeenth century, the Church of England had not yet been disowned by the churches of the East. Moreover, the Caroline Divines still retained hopes of foreign Protestantism while they confidently looked forward to a dissolution of the power of Rome.[96] By the mid-nineteenth century there were fewer grounds for harbouring such illusions.

The Church of England, according to the convert Thomas Allies, claimed 'in the letter of its documents, powers which as a system, it does not exercise, and which it will not warrant individual members in claiming or exercising'.[97] Such episodes as that of the Jerusalem bishopric in 1841-2 and of the Gorham Judgment over baptismal regeneration in 1850-1 were sources of Anglican converts to Rome because they exposed this apparent want of doctrinal authority in the Church of England and hence her separation from the primitive Church. For hitherto stalwart Anglican High Churchmen such as William Maskell, James Hope, Thomas Allies, William Dodsworth, Henry Wilberforce and Manning, the Gorham Judgment was a revelation both of the intrinsic doctrinal ambiguity of Anglicanism and of the Church of England's essential Erastianism. By revealing that the Royal Supremacy extended to spiritual matters, the Gorham Judgment, as Wiseman remarked, made Queen Victoria into a sort of female Pope.[98]

The unfolding of Manning's position has been excellently delineated by Professor McClelland, Father Pereiro[99] and others. The position of Allies underwent a no less significant change. As late as 1846-8 Allies sought to defend the Anglican Church from schism in a major work of apologetic based not on Reformation formularies but on patristic and conciliar evidence, in which he claimed that the primitive system of church authority was patriarchal rather than papal.[100] Further patristic study led Allies to revise his earlier opinions, convincing him that the Anglican High Church assumption that the Papal Supremacy only originated in the false decretals of Isidore Mercator was groundless.[101] The Gorham Judgment now revealed the Royal Supremacy to be no mere abuse of those currently in political power as High Churchmen contended, but in Allies's words, 'the *Cathedra Petri* of Anglicanism', with the Church of England's public authority derived from the state from the Reformation onwards.[102] The Royal Supremacy had not only separated the Anglican Church from the rest of Christendom but the very act of denial of St Peter's Primacy on which Anglicanism had been founded had enshrined a principle of isolation and severence. In contrast with the separation of the Eastern churches, the Anglican Royal Supremacy had consecrated the schismatical principle.[103] The Church of England could not, therefore, even if she wished, act as a living, teaching or prophetical body in conformity with the Church of Antiquity. In short, as Frederick Paley argued, conversion from Protestantism to the Catholic faith lay not in any 'mere capricious preference for the working of one system over another (to express a popular notion of the subject), but simply in realising the true idea of the Church'.[104]

Newman's theological rationale for converting remained distinctive, not only in terms of his theory of development of doctrine but in his Evangelical Protestant emphasis on the prophetical interpretation of Scripture.[105] Newman's role in fostering conversion to Rome among his disciples, however, lay not so much through his Tractarian doctrinal teaching as by his spiritual influence. His guiding vision of the Church of the Fathers comprised not only dogmatic orthodoxy but the quest for holiness. Newman complained that Anglican critics of his conversion such as James Mozley missed the point by assuming that he 'went to books in the first instance not to life'. Mozley's criticism 'fidgetted' Newman. Contrary to Mozley's claim, Newman felt that he 'was the first writer who made *life* the mark of a true Church'. He regarded his own *Sermons* as 'a wholesale refutation' of Mozley's theory about his conversion.[106] Newman's convert disciples bore out this point. According to Lockhart, the effect of Newman's preaching 'was to turn our souls inside out'.[107] Newman taught his followers to look for sanctity, not only catholicity, apostolicity and authority, as notes of the true Church. Examples of sanctity and evidence of the miraculous were to be sought in the Catholic Church of the current as well as primitive era; these were crucial tests of the Church's continuing divine life. According to the convert Henry Wilberforce in 1851, a key sign that the Catholic Church was the one and only true Church was the importance which it assigned to the scriptural concept of 'counsels of perfection' such as obedience, virginity, self-denial and poverty as essential aids to spiritual growth.[108] Other future converts, such as Faber, George Ryder and Allies on their respective Italian and French travels in the 1840s, were particularly impressed by the sheer spiritual power of the Catholic Church on the Continent, as evidenced by the practical impact of the dogma of the Real Presence and doctrines of the Intercession of Saints and of the Blessed Virgin in inspiring popular devotion.[109]

A recurring theme in conversion accounts from Newman downwards, was the claim that the Catholic Church alone embraced the union of external with internal notes of God's favour. W.R. Brownlow, a Cambridge convert, explained that as a High Church Anglican who had sought to combine Evangelical doctrines of grace with Catholic doctrines of order and the sacraments he had alienated both the Evangelical and High Church parties in the Church of England. It was only in the Catholic Church that he found the two elements to be happily combined without tension. Brownlow was primarily drawn to Rome by finding 'in Roman Catholic writers, as well as in the works of St Cyprian and St Augustine and other Fathers, the fullest recognition of the interior workings of grace in the soul'.[110]

While Newman's preaching was not doctrinally focused in a technical High Church sense, the broader quest for holiness which he inspired took an increasingly Catholic form which could only be fully realised in the sacramental, liturgical and penitential system of Rome. One of the distinctive ways in which Tractarian practical teaching diverged from that of contemporary conservative High Churchmen was in its emphasis on the need to combat post-baptismal sin by recourse to a regular regimen of auricular confession and absolution. By the late-1830s, perceiving this to be a want in current Anglican discipline, individual Tractarians begin to recover it for themselves and to practise confession. Far from regarding this as a 'Romish' innovation, they justified their conduct by reference both to the practice of the primitive Church and also of that of seventeenth-century Anglican divines.[111]

William Lockhart revealed that it was only by reading the Roman Catholic John Milner's, *End of Religious Controversy* (1818) that he first heard that there was a sacrament of confession. As he recalled: 'it was Milner who sent me to the Anglican Prayer Book for the same doctrine of Confession and Absolution'. Lockhart duly found the doctrine enshrined in the Prayer Book Office for the Visitation of the Sick and in the writings of Jeremy Taylor and others.[112] However, though private confession had only ever been the exception rather than the rule in Anglican practice, Lockhart interpreted the Church of England's neglect of its own professed doctrine as a serious 'note' against the validity of her spiritual claims. For Pusey, it was enough to restore what had been lost and even to model Anglican penitential practice more closely on that of Rome. For the converts, however, this only disguised the root of the problem of loss of discipline, which was loss of teaching authority. As Lockhart concluded:

> What then was to be thought of a church which had neglected for 300 years an essential sacrament in which it professed in words to believe — what confidence could we have that in other weighty matters it had not neglected its trust?[113]

One of the crucial factors in prompting Lockhart's own conversion in 1843 was Newman's reluctance in granting him absolution at Littlemore on the ground that he no longer felt he had the power or authority to do so.[114]

For the later converts, Allies and Dodsworth, Pusey's importation of Roman Catholic penitential practice, along with Roman devotional manuals, into the Church of England was both morally disingenuous and uncatholic in terms of valid order and jurisdiction.[115] As Newman told Pusey in 1843 it was 'like sewing a new piece of cloth on an old garment'.[116] The rationale for what Newman called 'Patristico-Protestantism' or what William Maskell would come to term 'Protestant Ritualism' was essentially eclectic; Catholic doctrine or practice tolerated by the laxity of a liberal establishment rather than owned as the authoritative teaching of a living Church speaking with one voice as the movement of 1833 had originally envisaged.[117] In short, Anglo-Catholicism had become sectarian.

Among the converts, differences in perceptions of the Church of England were evident. In explaining their conversion, some disowned their Anglican past, and even applied to the conversion proceess the image of death or renunciation of the visible world.[118] According to Frederick Paley: 'we act irrespectively of what we have been; we give up nothing out of the church. our spiritual existence is not recognised; we begin to be Christians only when we are in the church of Christ'.[119] In similar vein, William Lockhart maintained: 'we utterly deny that Anglicans form any part of the Visible Church. It was only by slow and sad steps we became convinced of this, that we, who are converts, were forced to make our submission'.[120] Even J.M. Capes who was to return to the Church of England, maintained in 1849 after four years of convert life:

> The moment I entered the Church, the Anglican Establishment became to me as nothing more than what a dream is to a waking man. A gulf — wide, deep, and impenetrable — separated my present from my past interests ... I ceased to feel the slightest interest in their opinions, their system, their conduct, — except so far as it indicated a tendency to Catholicism, and created hopes, that they might do, as I had done.[121]

Renouf, on the other hand, matched his complaints at the misrepresentations of the Catholic religion by Protestant controversialists with a plea for greater understanding by Catholics towards Protestants. In contrast to many contemporaries, Renouf's own conversion led to no family breach or 'parting of friends'. On the contrary, when Renouf returned to Oxford to collect his possessions in the wake of his conversion at Easter 1842, university friends and even some in authority rallied round. The Rector of Exeter College, Dr Richards, commended Renouf for not running away. According to Renouf, the

Rector maintained that 'my having acted conscientiously was no reason for any of my friends giving me up'.[122] Renouf's prospective engagement to a Protestant lady in 1845 led him, while still at Oscott, to expound some unusually eirenic sentiments in correspondence with his parents. Renouf clearly had his own experience of conversion in mind, when he argued:

> God's religion is not of a nature to need controversy. It is of such a kind as compels assent, immediately when understood. And so we find that hardly one person in a thousand becomes a Catholic by controversy, they all become so immediately when they hear what the Catholic faith really is.[123]

Having been brought up a pious Protestant with many pious Protestant friends, Renouf considered 'that Protestants are very different from what Catholics generally believe them to be'. He assured his parents that 'in embracing Catholicism I have not renounced a single Protestant doctrine that you taught me'. Renouf conceded that his was an unusual position among the run of converts:

> Converts are proverbially the most fiery & hot headed partisans of the side they have embraced. I have myself already considerably cooled, not indeed (God forbid!) in my acceptance of any Catholic doctrine, but in my low estimate of people differing from myself.

As a Catholic, Renouf regarded his earlier Anglican 'aversion to Low Church people and Dissenters' as unreasonable and grossly unchristian'. He stressed that his religious tolerance had grown since his conversion and while residing at Oscott, 'living in an ecclesiastical college, under the immediate guidance of Catholics, in constant intercourse with Catholics only... in short in a red-hot Catholic atmosphere'.[124]

Personal factors shaped Renouf's attitude. He was strongly committed to the principle of toleration but never regretted leaving the Church of England. A few converts, however, did publicly avow a sense of disillusionment with current Roman Catholic attitudes towards Anglicanism. The convert Henry Collins, one-time curate of St Mary Magdalen, Oxford, complained in 1857 that owing to the bitterness of the Catholic controversial tone against Protestants, 'the number of conversions that have been either impeded, or altogether hindered, cannot be fully known'.[125] In contrast to other converts such as Faber whose main reason for becoming a Catholic was a conviction of the invalidity of his Anglican orders,[126] Collins defended the validity of Anglican orders. For Collins, as for the equally eirenic Phillipps de Lisle, differences between the Catholic and Anglican churches were narrow and insignificant.[127] It was only on this understanding that Collins had converted at all:

> I had been told by various converts that, if I were received into the Catholic Church, I should find it to be an entirely different faith — nay, a new God. Here was another difficulty I had to undergo: to receive a new faith was utterly abhorrent to me, and yet I was assured of it again and again. Thank God, I can now tell Anglicans that it is no new faith at all, but the same which the old Creeds contain, the same which is to be found in all the works of the Catholic Fathers; the same substantially on which we fixed our love and years, if we did not from childhood learn to lisp its accents; the same faith, but not the same atmosphere.[128]

Edmund Ffoulkes, one-time tutor of Jesus College, Oxford, was another convert clergyman, who was similarly inclined to minimise the distance from his Anglican past. In later controversy with Manning, Ffoulkes conceded that he would never have joined the Catholic Church had he been then pressed to hold that Rome could never be mistaken:

> For I considered that after the extreme rigour with which the claims of the Church of England had been examined by us all, it would be the height of disingenuosness in us to shut our eyes to any weak points of the system that we were embracing in preference, should any such exist.

In an unusual reversal of the more submissive spirit embraced by a convert, Ffoulkes felt freer to criticise Rome from within than he had been from without. He had been told that he had been in no position to judge Rome fairly while he was an Anglican, 'and this was one of my chief reasons for embracing it when I did'.[129]

Among the converts, Ffoulkes's position represented an opposite polarity to that of Manning, but there was plenty of middle ground. Thus, whereas for the Catholic Manning, Anglicanism was identical in principle with all other forms of the Protestant Reformation,[130] Frederick Oakeley remained convinced that the Anglican Church, for all its grave faults and errors, was superior to that of Dissenting bodies. Oakeley's attitude was shaped by his Tractarian background. He was convinced that 'no dissenting body could have operated the Tract movement'. Significantly, Manning's view was explained by Oakeley on his seeing 'things far more through an Italian medium than I can do' and because he was 'never absorbed by the Oxford Movement like some of us'.[131]

In conclusion, the Oxford Movement played a crucial role in fostering conversions to Rome, even if they represented a minority of

conversions overall. Of the one hundred Anglican clerical converts of
the period 1845-55, most were the product of Tractarian influence.
These Tractarian converts, however, were not the result of mere
negative dissatisfaction with the Church of England, still less of
episcopal or academical persecution, as Anglican apologists of the
Movement implied. The Movement's celebrated historian, Dean
Church, made the Anglican authorities who condemned Newman a
convenient scapegoat for his secession. For Anglo-Catholics, Newman
was the 'great lost leader' whose defection had to be explained away.
Newman had departed because the Church of England had not known
'how to employ him'[132] or because he had never realised a state of
pastoral contentment.

Some Anglo-Catholics turned against their former leader with
bitterness. Whereas Pusey regarded Newman's departure as a mere
transfer to another 'vineyard',[133] there were others who viewed the
converts in the light of the old High Church theory that English
Romanists were schismatics. Thus for William Bennett, there was 'no
church to which we can go over in this country; we may go over to a
schismatic place of worship, but we cannot go over to a church'.[134] It
might be excusable for foreigners to be Roman Catholics as they often
had no choice, but for those baptised in the Church of England to
abandon her was deemed schismatic and sinful.[135] Newman, on this
reckoning, was guilty of a great fall from grace. He was likened to 'a
noble vessel, that has slipped his anchor'; even his sanity was
questioned.[136] The very *esprit de corps* and party spirit of the Puseyites
made it hard for some to refrain from regarding secessions to Rome as
other than treachery to the Tractarian cause. Some even suggested that
Newman was motivated by mere pique and wounded pride, and later
argued that many of the converts subsequently deteriorated in
character.[137] They were reluctant to accept that Newman and his
convert followers went because they chose. They were inclined to
overlook the extent to which converts lost friends, family and
sometimes worldly prospects. Newman and other converts, however,
became Catholics because of positive belief in and attraction towards
the Church of Rome and a conviction that for them personal salvation
lay only within its fold.[138] For the converts, the harder-line High
Church attitude was more consistent and intelligible than that of latter-
day Puseyites inclined to blur the lines of communion. Conversion to
Rome was not a question of merely passing from one branch of the
Catholic Church to another. Although Newman once maintained that
he had 'never acted in direct hostility to the Church of England',[139] he
also asserted, albeit in a qualified sense, that 'a convert, if justifiable
in the grounds of his conversion, must be an enemy of the communion
he has left'.[140] Dismayed by what he regarded as James Mozley's

breach of confidentiality in presuming to pass judgment on his reasons for conversion, Newman privately repaid Mozley for his public strictures. For Newman, Mozley and his Puseyite friends were guilty of making 'esprit de corps everything', and 'of going by party, not by truth'.[141] The Tractarian 'parting of friends' could be real and painful.

Some mid-century Catholic predictions of a mass conversion of the English nation to Rome within a generation would prove ludicrously over-optimistic.[142] The Oxford Movement retained far more adherents for Anglicanism than it yielded to Rome. Pusey and Keble argued that the transformation wrought by the Movement was a clear indication of the presence of Christ in the Church of England; in later years, they both became less, rather than more, sympathetic towards Rome.[143] Newman's contention that the providential direction of the Movement of 1833 was directed towards Rome, was repudiated.[144] Lingard's scepticism was not without foundation. England was never going to be converted through Oxford. Catholic conversion expectations over-looked the fact that England as a whole was not Puseyite. As one Catholic commentator conceded, with reference to the best means of promoting the conversion of England:

> until we can thoroughly disabuse ourselves of the theory that what converts the Puseyite will convert the nation, we shall not make one single step towards this glorious end.[145]

Oxford convert testimonies had their intrinsic value, but in surveying some of this literature, one contemporary Catholic reviewer felt the need to issue the reminder that conversion was more than a mere intellectual process. Hearts as well as minds needed to be moved. The way to win over Protestants was best served by persuasion rather than confutation; by treating an ordinary Protestant opponent not so much as an ecclesiastic in an inconsistent position, but 'as a soul in peril of damnation'.[146]

Even the Gorham Judgment, whose implications in Catholic eyes should have removed any residual basis for self-deception among High Church Anglicans,[147] did not yield the harvest of converts which at one time was confidently foretold. In fact, by reluctantly tolerating an increasingly extreme Anglo-Catholicism in the wake of the Gorham Judgment, the Anglican establishment removed the incentive of many to secede to Rome.[148] From a Catholic perspective, the emergence of Ritualism within the Church of England represented a 'countefeit Catholicism', or 'Protestantism on stilts' and a real set-back to potential conversions, though Ritualism did act for some as a staging-post to Rome.[149] Another check to conversion was the promotion of corporate reunion as a substitute for individual submission to the Catholic Church[150] The fanciful hope was even expressed that disestablishment of the Church of England might permit the Anglo-Catholic party to unite with Rome on its own terms leaving the 'Calvinist element' to join the Dissenters.[151] Nor should one forget the spiritual and psychological casualties of the Oxford Movement; those one-time Tractarians such as Arthur Hugh Clough, James Anthony Froude, Mark Pattison and J.A. Foxton, who became rationalist or men of no faith in recoil from the Movement. Moreover, while Catholics could fairly insist that there was no comparison in terms of character or moral worth between the two classes of convert,[152] there were a number of Catholic desertions to Protestantism which somewhat offset the spiritual traffic in the other direction.

Tractarianism, however, acted for many as an essential spiritual and theological conduit for Rome. The recovery of Catholic elements within the Anglican tradition, such as stricter adherence to the Prayer Book, created a longing for others, such as the fuller liturgical richness of the Roman Breviary, which went beyond Anglican confines. Thus, for example, the original Tractarian attempt to prove the continuity between the primitive and Anglican liturgies, came to be abandoned by some in favour of a growing perception of the discontinuities. This in itself sharpened a sense of Anglican deficiencies among the movement's followers. For many Tractarians, Newman included, familiarity with the Roman liturgy, first gleaned through Anglican sources, proved a decisive factor on the path to Rome.[153] Typical of the Tractarian convert was John Gordon's avowal: 'it was Anglicanism that led me to the Church of Rome... It first gave birth in my mind to the glorious vision of the Visible Church'. Certain wants and even seeds of certain doctrines were sown, but ultimately it 'failed in every respect to satisfy the needs it had created'.[154]

But the approach to Rome had been entirely over Anglican domain. The submission of the Tractarian convert was the direct outcome of principles learned in the Church of England. As the convert W.R. Brownlow put it in 1864:

> the tide of the Oxford Movement, starting from the simplest Christian principles, carried men forward even against their will far beyond the artificial limits of Anglicanism into the wide ocean of Catholic faith.... And yet the Prayer Book has been all along the ladder up which men have climbed to the Church from which our fathers fell 300 years ago. There seemed to me a beautiful retributive justice in this. That, as England, once Catholic, had descended to Protestantism by the means of the Prayer Book, so in almost every case it is by the Prayer-Book that we have been led, and we trust our countrymen will be led, up to Catholicism again.[155]

Catholic controversialists conceded that by leading many of their recipients towards Rome, Anglican sacramental rites revivified by the Tractarians had done spiritual good, in spite of their formal invalidity. The confessions made to Pusey and other Anglo-Catholics had sometimes 'distinctly led to conversion to the Catholic faith, and to absolution from one who really possesses the power of the keys'.[156]

In the last resort, perhaps the greatest impact of the Oxford Movement in relation to English Catholicism lay not in the number of converts it inspired, but in familiarising especially the English upper and middle classes with Catholic doctrine and in the long-term diminution of anti-Catholic prejudice.[157] One Catholic observer noted in 1851:

> from the moment that the Oxford Tracts commenced, the Catholic Church assumed a position in this country which she had never before attained since the schism of the sixteenth century.[158]

The bulk of the English people remained staunchly Protestant but the outcry over the 'papal aggression' in 1850-51 proved short-lived and came to be directed more against Puseyism within the Church of England than Roman Catholicism without. Although the Tractarian conversions produced no appreciable impression on the great mass of English society, the converts themselves gave a new respectability to Roman claims among educated Protestants. Within a very few years the accepted image of English Catholicism early in the century as 'an effete, decrepit, worn-out, exploded, crumbling superstition', was transformed[159] and the Catholic religion at length came to be regarded as a power which it was 'neither possible to ignore nor prudent to despise'.[160] Earlier Whig toleration of Catholic claims had been partly predicated on an inaccurate image of English Catholic weakness and decay. Likewise, the temporary revival of Protestant intolerance from the 1830s and into the 1850s was in itself an index of the reinvigoration and growing self-confidence of English Catholicism in the wake of Tractarian conversions.[161]

Tractarian converts to Rome were the first to appreciate that Anglicanism was

> the growth not merely of a one-sided study of the Fathers, but of all those influences which make up the English gentleman as he is fashioned by Oxford University. The indistinctness and eclecticism of the English mind was one element; the dislike of anything foreign another'.[162]

For all their reputation for Ultramontanism, the Tractarian converts by the very nature of their Anglican and Oxford background helped prove the compatibility of being 'Catholic' and 'English' at the same time.

The mid-nineteenth century revival of English Catholicism was only very partially the result of proselytising efforts of Catholics themselves. The external agency of the Tractarian movement leavening the Church of England played a crucial role. Anglican Oxford was by no means the only path to Rome in the mid-nineteenth century, but it was a vitally important one. For as Newman rightly concluded: 'Catholics did not make us Catholics; Oxford made us Catholics'.

NOTES

1.   S. Gilley, 'Loss and Gain: Conversions to Roman Catholicism in Britain, 1800-1994' Annual Lecture of the Friends of Cardinal Newman, 1994, *Friends of Cardinal Newman Newsletter* (Christmas, 1994), pp. 4-8.

2.   J.H. Newman to J. Spencer Northcote, 8 February 1846, *Letters and Diaries of John Henry Newman*, ed. C.S. Dessain, vol. 11, (London, 1961), p. 110. Newman's point was that the grounds which 'a person gives for his conversion cannot be expressed in a formula'. 'Catholicism', Newman stated memorably, 'is a deep matter — you cannot take it in a teacup'.

3.   F. Oakeley, *Personal Reminiscences of the Oxford Movement, with Illustrations from Dr Newman's 'Loss and Gain'* (London, 1855), pp. 6-7. On Frederick Oakeley (1811-80), see *DNB*; J. Gillow, *A Literary and Biographical History, or Bibliographical Dictionary of the English Catholics*, 5 vols, (London, [1885-1902]), vol. 5, pp. 204-10.

4.   For example, see J.B. Morris, *Jesus the Son of Mary or the Doctrine of the Catholic Church upon the Incarnation of the Son, Considered in its Bearing upon the Honour shown by Catholics to His Blessed Mother*, 2 vols, (London, 1851).

5.   On this, see M. Beard, 'Faith and Fortune: English Aristocratic Converts to Roman Catholicism in the Nineteenth Century' (forthcoming).

6   W. Lockhart (ed), *The Life of Antonio Rosmini Serbati. Founder of the Institute of Charity*, 2 vols, (London, 1886), vol. 2, p. 97. On William Lockhart (1819-92), see *DNB*; Gillow, *Biographical Dictionary of the English Catholics*, vol. 4, pp. 301-8.

7.   E.B. Pusey, *The Articles Treated in Tract 90 Reconsidered and their Interpretation Vindicated in a Letter to the Rev. R.W. Jelf* (Oxford, 1841), pp. 154-5.

8.   H.D. Best, *A Sermon on Priestly Absolution Preached before the University of Oxford at St. Mary's on Sunday, November 24, 1793. Third edition with Notes and other Autobiographical Writings*, (London, 1874), pp. 173-6. On the impact and influence of the French émigré clergy in England, see B. Ward, *The Dawn of the Catholic Revival in England, 1781-1803*, 2 vols, (London, 1909), vol. 1, pp. 163-175 and D.A. Bellenger, *The French Exiled Clergy in the British Isles after 1789* (Bath, 1986).

9.   B. Holland, *Memoir of Kenelm Digby* [Reprint of 1st edn, 1919] (Sevenoaks, 1992), p. 38. See also, Gillow, Op. Cit., vol. 2, pp. 81-3.

10.   F. Oakeley, 'English Views of Catholicism Fifty Years Ago and Now',*Contemporary Review* 35 (1879), p. 670.

11.   Lockhart (ed), *Life of Antonio Rosmini*, vol. 1, p. 96.

12.   F.C. Mather, *High Church Prophet: Bishop Samuel Horsley (1733-1806) and the Caroline Tradition in the Later Georgian Church*, (Oxford, 1992), p. 307.

13.   On de Lisle (1809-78), see *DNB*; Gillow, Op. Cit., vol. 2, pp. 38-47; M. Pawley, *The Life and Circle of Ambrose Phillipps de Lisle* (Norwich, 1993).

14.   A.L. Phillipps, *Some Remarks on a Letter Addressed to the Rev. R.W. Jelf D.D. Canon of Christ Church, in Explanation of No. 90 in the Series called the 'Tracts for the Times'* (London, 1841). See also, Pawley, *Life of Phillipps de Lisle*, ch. 4.

15.   Quoted in W. Ward, *The Life and Times of Cardinal Wiseman*, 2 vols, (London, 1897). vol. 1, p. 402.

16.   See N. Wiseman, *High Church Claims: or, a Series of Papers on the Oxford Controversy, the High Church Theory of Dogmatical Authority, Anglican Claim to Apostolical Succession etc. No. 5. Occasioned by the Publication of the Tracts for the Times* [1836] (London, [1838?]), pp. 87-117.

17.   *Rambler*, 12, 'Cardinal Wiseman and the Tractarians', (September, 1853), p. 224.

18.   S. Gilley, 'Frederick Lucas' in S. Mews (ed), *Modern Religious Rebels. Presented to John Kent* (London, 1993), pp. 65-6.

19.   P. Adams, 'English Catholic Converts in the Nineteenth Century', Oxford M. Litt thesis, 1977, p. 13.

20.   *Catholic Magazine*, 4, 'Tracts for the Times', (Nov. 1840) p. 669.

21.   *Ibidem*, p. 677.

22.   M. Haile & E. Bonney, *The Life and Letters of John Lingard* (London [1911]), p. 305. On Lingard (1771-1850), see *DNB*; Gillow, Op. Cit., vol. 4, pp. 254-78.

23.   J. Lingard to F.C. Husenbeth, 5 November 1845, *Life and Letters of Lingard*, p. 323.

24.   *Ibidem*, p. 361. Lingard deplored what he regarded as 'a superabundance of wordiness and dreaminess in all the writings of the Oxford Tractarians, whether they come over to us or not'. J. Lingard to J. Walker, 27 April 1848, *ibidem*, p. 324.

25.   Quoted in D. Gwynn, *Lord Shrewsbury, Pugin and the Catholic Revival* (London, 1946), p. 96.

26.   *Letters from the Earl of Shrewsbury to Ambrose Phillipps de Lisle, Esq. descriptive of the Estatica of Caldaro and the Addolorata of Capriana.*

To which is added the Relation of three Visits to the Estatica of Monte Sansavino in May 1842 (London, 1842).

27.   Adams, 'English Catholic Converts', p. 1.

28.   See E.G.K. Browne, *Annals of the Tractarian Movement from 1842 to 1860*, 3rd edn, (London, 1861); W. Gordon Gorman (ed), *Converts to Rome: a Biographical List of the more Notable Converts to the Catholic Church in the United Kingdom during the last Sixty Years* (London, 1910).

29.   *Tablet*, (1855), vol. 16, p. 266.

30.   On George Spencer, Ignatius of St.Paul (1799-1864), see *DNB*; Gillow, Op. Cit., vol. 5, pp. 519-20; *Life of Father Ignatius of St.Paul, Passionist (the Hon. and Rev. George Spencer). Compiled by the Rev. Father Pius a Sp. Sancto [Devine], Passionist* (Dublin, 1866); U. Young, *Life of Father Ignatius Spencer* (London, 1933).

31.   See W.J. Sparrow Simpson, *The Contribution of Cambridge to the Anglo-Catholic Revival* (London, 1933) especially pp. 15-33.

32.   See Newman's comment: 'these [Cambridge] fellows take up everything as a matter of literature — and their opinions come and go like Spring fashions'. J.H. Newman to C. Cornish, 28 December 1838, *Letters and Diaries*, ed. G. Tracey, vol.6, p. 363. For further discussion of comparisons between the religious ethos of Oxford and Cambridge see P. Nockles, 'An Academic Counter-Revolution: Newman & Tractarian Oxford's Idea of a University', *History of Universities*, 10 (1991), pp. 143-47; P. Nockles, 'Lost Causes and Impossible Loyalties: the Oxford Movement and the University, 1829-54', *History of the University of Oxford*, vol. 6, (forthcoming).

33.   G. Moberly, *A Few Thoughts on the Proposed Admission of Dissenters into the University of Oxford* (Oxford, 1834), p. 14. The one-time Balliol College tutor and Catholic convert, Frederick Oakeley, argued that Oxford's Aristotelian curriculum bias made it more responsive than Cambridge towards Tractarianism. F. Oakeley, *Historical Notes on the Tractarian Movement* (London, 1865), p. 180; F. Oakeley, *Remarks on the Study of Aristotelian and Platonic Ethics as a Branch of the Oxford System of Education* (Oxford, 1837), pp. 26-28.

34.   The Whig ministry's abolition of ten Irish bishoprics in 1833 (which helped provoke Keble's sermon on 'National Apostasy') marked the dawn of the Movement. The Tractarians objected to 'state interference in matters spiritual'.

35.   J.J.S. Perowne & C. Stokes, *Letters Literary and Theological of Connop Thirlwall* (London, 1881), p. 349.

36.   On Lloyd's influence on the Tractarians, see Oakeley, *Historical Notes on the Tractarian Movement*, pp. 12-14; Oakeley, *Personal Reminiscences of the 'Oxford Movement'*, pp. 4-6; J.H. Philpot, *The Seceders* (1829-1869) (London, 1930), pp. 15-16. See also, W.J. Baker, *Beyond Port and Prejudice: Charles Lloyd of Oxford* (Maine, 1981), pp. 214-15.

37.   A.P. Perceval, *The Roman Schism Illustrated from the Records of the Catholic Church* (London, 1836), p. xxxi; W. Palmer, *The Apostolical Jurisdiction and Succession of Episcopacy in the British Churches Vindicated against the Objections of Dr. Wiseman in the 'Dublin Review'* (London, 1840), p. 197; W. Palmer, *A Treatise on the Church of Christ*, 2 vols (London, 1838), vol. 1, p. 454. Wiseman's episcopal rank was even denied by Palmer. W. Palmer, *Letters to N. Wiseman, D.D. on the Errors of Romanism* (Oxford, 1842), pp. 3-4.

38   A. Phillipps de Lisle to Lord John Manners, 13 April 1857, E.S. Purcell, *The Life and Letters of Ambrose Phillipps de Lisle ... Edited and finished by Edwin de Lisle*, 2 vols (London, 1900), voi. 2, p. 311; A. Phillipps to Count de Montalembert, 6 October 1841, L. Allen, 'Letters of Phillipps de Lisle to Count de Montalembert', in *Dublin Review*, no.463 (1954), p. 63.

39.   P.B. Nockles, *The Oxford Movement in Context: Anglican High Churchmanship, 1760-1857* (Cambridge, 1994), pp. 67-72.

40.   J. Ingle, *Puseyites (so called) no friends of Popery. A Letter to Sir J. Trayton Fuller Elliott Drake, Bart, containing some Remarks on the Letter of Lord John Russell to the Bishop of Durham* (Exeter, 1850), p. 18.

41.   *Ibidem*, p. 19.

42.   R.W. Sibthorp, *Some Answer to the Enquiry: 'Why are you become a Romanist?* (London, 1842), p. 10.

43.   *A Serious Remonstrance Addressed to the Rev. R.W. Sibthorp, B.D. occasioned by his recent Publication entitled 'Some Answer to the Enquiry: Why are you become a Romanist?' By some of the Hull clergy who were Personally known to him* (London, 1842), p. 70.

44.   Sibthorp, *Some Answer to the Enquiry*, p. 36.

45.   PH, Hamilton Papers, HAM 6/115.1, W. Palmer of Magdalen to W.K. Hamilton, 18 November 1841.

46.   PCA, Renouf Papers, 13/9/1/119, P. Le Page Renouf to Mr Renouf, n.d. [March, 1841].

47.   Sibthorp, *Some Answer to the Enquiry*, p. 42; R. W. Sibthorp, *A Further Answer to the Enquiry: Why are you become a Catholic? in a Second Letter to a Friend, containing a notice of the Strictures of the Rev. Messrs. Palmer and Dodsworth, upon a former Letter* (London, 1842), p. 61.

48.   W. Dodsworth, *Why have you become a Romanist? A Letter to the Rev. Richard Waldo Sibthorp, B.D. occasioned by his Letter entitled 'Some Answer to the Enquiry: Why are you become a Romanist?'* (London, 1842); W. Palmer, *An Examination of the Rev. W. Sibthorp's Reasons for his Secession from the Church* (Oxford, 1842); E.B. Pusey, *A Letter to his Grace the Archbishop of Canterbury, on some Circumstances connected with the Present Crisis in the English Church* (Oxford, 1842), p. 35.

49.   Dodsworth, *Why have you become a Romanist?*, pp. 25-8.

50.   E.B. Pusey, *The Articles Treated in Tract 90 Reconsidered* (Oxford, 1841), p. 154.

51.   Pusey, *Letter to the Archbishop of Canterbury*, p. 35.

52.   J.M. Capes [1812-1889], *Four Years' Experience of the Catholic Religion with Observations on its Effects upon the Character, Intellectual, Moral and Spiritual* (Philadelphia, 1849), p. 3.

53.   PCA, Renouf Papers, 69/9/1/37, P. Le Page Renouf to Mr Renouf, 8 March 1842. Born in Guernsey, Renouf (1822-97), was a Bible-clerk at Pembroke College, Oxford, 1840-42. On his conversion to Roman Catholicism in 1842, he migrated to St.Mary's College, Oscott, where he taught. From 1846-55, he resided in Besançon, France, where he acted as tutor to the Comte de Vaulchier. He taught at Newman's Catholic University, Dublin, and in 1865 became Inspector of Catholic Schools in England. In 1885, he was appointed Keeper of Egyptian Antiquities, British Museum. See *DNB*; E. Le Page Renouf (ed), *The Life Work of Sir Peter Le Page Renouf* (London, 1910); Gillow, Op. Cit., vol. 5, pp. 405-6; J. Bowes Gwatkin, *Memor et Fidelis: A Study of the Life and Role of Peter Le Page Renouf* (unpublished MSS.).

54.   PCA, Renouf Papers, 69/9/1/25, P. Le Page Renouf to Mr Renouf, 7 May 1841.

55.   [P. Le Page Renouf], *The Doctrine of the Catholic Church in England on the Holy Eucharist, Illustrated by Extracts from her Great Divines. With an Appendix on various other Points of Faith and Practice* (Oxford, 1841), especially p. 11.

56.   PCA, Renouf Papers, 63/9/36/2, J.P. Tweed to P. Le Page Renouf, n.d. [December 1841].

57.   PCA, Renouf Papers, 63/9/36/3, J.H. Parker to P. Le Page Renouf, 22 December 1841.

58.   PCA, Renouf Papers, 6319/1/123, P. Le Page Renouf to Mr & Mrs Renouf, 13 January 1848.

59.   J. Gordon, *Reasons of my Conversion to the Catholic Church. Letters to a Friend* (London, 1849), p. 14.

60.   *Letters and Diaries*, vol. 11, p. 76; R. Ornsby, *Memoirs of James Robert Hope-Scott of Abbotsford. With Selections from his Correspondence*, 2 vols, (London, 1884), vol. 2, p. 64.

61.   J. Irvine, *Romanism, as Represented by the Rev. John Henry Newman, briefly Considered, with some Illustrations of its Necessary Tendency, from Personal Observations made at Rome* (London, 1846), p. 30.

62.   J.H. Newman to E.E. Estcourt, 2 June 1864, *Letters and Diaries*, ed. C.S. Dessain, vol. 19, (London, 1969), p. 352.

63.   J.H. Newman, *Lectures on Certain Difficulties Felt by Anglicans in Submitting to the Catholic Church* (London, 1850), especially Lecture 2.

64.   *Ibidem*, pp. 30-31.

65.   BL, Gladstone Papers, Ms Add 44247, fols. 173-4, W.E. Gladstone to H.E. Manning, 24 October 1843.

66.   W. Maskell, *Protestant Ritualists* (London, 1872), p. 12.

67.   Newman, *Anglican Difficulties*, p. 123; J.H. Newman, *Apologia Pro Vita Sua* (London, 1864), p. 328. See also Nockles, *Oxford Movement in Context*, pp. 129-33.

68.   J.H. Newman to S. Wilks, 8 November 1845, *Letters and Diaries*, vol. 11, p. 28.

69.   F.A. Paley, *A Brief Review of the Arguments Alleged in Defence of the Protestant Position. Addressed to those who call themselves 'Anglo-Catholics' in the Church of England* (London, 1848), p. 25. On Frederick Apthorp Paley (1815-88), see *DNB*; Gillow, Op. Cit., vol. 5, pp. 234-7.

70.   KCA, Keble Papers, 'Miscellaneous Letters', no. 164, J.B. Morris to J.M. Gresley, 1 February 1846.

71.   *Rambler*, 9, 'Dr Phillpotts and the *Edinburgh Review*', (May, 1852), pp. 394-6.

72.   *Life and Letters of Lingard*, p. 281.

73.   J. Lingard to J. Walker, 14 November 1845, *Ibidem*, pp. 324-5.

74.   Nockles, *Oxford Movement in Context*, pp. 113-27.

75.   Lockhart, *Life of Antonio Rosmini*, vol. 2, p. 96.

76.   W. Lockhart, *Cardinal Newman: Reminiscences of Fifty Years Since. By one of his Leading Disciples* (London, 1891). p. 37.

77.   *Ibidem*, pp. 47-8.

78.   W.K. Sconce, *The Testimony of Antiquity to the Holy See, to which are Appended, a View of the Scripture Proof of St Peter's Pre-Eminence, and a List of Anglican Misrepresentations* (Sydney, 1848).

79.   Newman, *Lectures on Anglican Difficulties*, pp. 124-5.

80.   Lockhart, *Reminiscences*, p. 49.

81.   PH, Pusey Papers, LBV [Transcripts], J.H. Newman to E.B. Pusey, 19 February 1844.

82.   P. Le Page Renouf, *The Character of the Rev. William Palmer, MA of Worcester College, as a Controversialist ... Considered in a Letter to a Friend at Oxford* (London, 1843), p. 7.

83.   [G.J.L. Crawley], *England, Greece or Rome? A Letter to a Friend. By a Convert from Anglicanism* (York, [1853]), pp. 4-5; A.J. Hanmer, *Submission to the Catholic Church. Addressed to the Inhabitants of the Parish of Tiverton* (London, 1850), pp. 15-20.

84.   E.H. Thompson, *The Unity of the Episcopate Considered, in Reply to the Work of the Rev. T.W. Allies, M.A. Entitled 'The Church of England Cleared from Schism upon Testimonies and Councils of the Fathers of the First Six Centuries'* (London, 1847), p. xi.

85.   *Rambler*, 11, 'Protestant Rosaries' (May, 1853), p. 432.

86.   [Crawley], *England, Greece or Rome?*, p. 6.

87.   Gordon, *Reasons of my Conversion*, p. 19; W.H. Anderdon, *A Letter to the Parishioners of St. Margaret's, Leicester* (London, 1851), p. 8; F. Oakeley, *A Letter on Submitting to the Catholic Church, Addressed to a Friend* (London, 1845), p. 11-12.

88.   Paley, *Arguments alleged in Defence of the Protestant Position*, pp. 20-29; E.H. Thompson, *Remarks on Certain Anglican Theories of Unity* (London, 1846), p. 29; Hanmer, *Submission to the Catholic Church*, pp. 50-52.

89.   Thompson, *Anglican Theories of Unity*, p. 30.   Edward Healy Thompson (1813?-91), Emmanuel College, Cambridge, 1832-6; several curacies; influenced by Newman and converted to Catholicism, 1846. See *DNB*; Gillow, Op. Cit., vol. 5, pp. 540-41.

90.   Thompson, *Unity of the Episcopate*, p. 15; *Anglican Theories of Unity*, p. 43.

91.   *Rambler*, 12, 'Cardinal Wiseman and the Tractarians', 227; *Dublin Review*, p. 33, 'Present Position of the High-Church Theory', (December, 1847), p. 502.

92.   Newman, *Lectures on Anglican Difficulties*, p. 155.

93.   P. Le Page Renouf, *The Greek and Anglican Communions: a Letter respectfully Addressed to the Rev. T. Allies* (London, 1847), pp. 5-6.

94.   Renouf, *Character of the Rev. William Palmer*, p. 9; [G.D. Ryder], *Thoughts on Some Questions of the Day*, 'Notes preparatory to a History of the Church of England's claim to the Apostolical Succession, previous to 1832' (London, 1869), p. 33.

95.   Renouf, *The Greek and Anglican Communions*, pp. 5-7.

96.   Thompson, *Anglican Theories of Unity*, p. 50.

97.   T.W. Allies, *A Life's Decision* (London, 1880), p. 272.

98.   On the High Church Anglican response to the Gorham Judgment, see Nockles, *Oxford Movement in Context*, pp. 93-103.

99.   V.A. McClelland, 'Gladstone and Manning: a question of authority'; P.J. Jagger (ed), *Gladstone, Politics and Religion* (London, 1985). pp. 148-70; J. Pereiro, 'Truth before Peace: Manning and Infallibility', *Recusant History*, 22 (October, 1992), pp. 218-53.

100.   T.W. Allies, *The Church of England cleared from the Charge of Schism, by the Decrees of the Seven Ecumenical Councils and the Traditions of the Fathers*, 2nd edn, (Oxford, 1848).

101.   T.W. Allies, *The See of St Peter, the Rock of the Church, the Source of Jurisdiction and the Centre of Unity* (London, 1850). p. xii.

102.   *Ibidem*, p. xi; M. Allies, *Thomas William Allies* (London, 1924). p. 76.

103.   *Ibidem*, p. 155.

104.   Paley, *Arguments Alleged in Defence of the Protestant Position*, p. 27.

105.   S. Gilley, 'Newman and Prophecy, Evangelical and Catholic', *Journal of the United Reformed Church History Society*, 3 (March, 1985), 160-83; P. Misner, *Papacy and Development: Newman and the Primacy of the Pope* (Leiden, 1976), pp. 50-57.

106.   J.H. Newman to H.W. Wilberforce, 28 January 1846, *Letters and Diaries*, vol. 11, p. 101; J.H. Newman to Ambrose St John, 8 January 1846, *Ibidem*, p. 87.

107.   Lockhart, *Reminiscences*, p. 5.

108.   [H.W. Wilberforce], *Reasons for Submitting to the Catholic Church. A Farewell Letter to his Parishioners from a Clergyman of the Established Church* (London, 1851), pp. 27-34; Oakeley, *Letter on Submitting to the Catholic Church*, p. 12.

109.   T.W. Allies, *Journal in France in 1845 and 1848. with Letters from Italy in 1847. of Things and Persons concerning the Church and Education* (London, 1849), especially pp. 331-5, 339, 346; J.E. Bowden, *The Life and Letters of Frederick William Faber, D.D.* (London, 1869), chs. 4-5.

110.   W.R. Brownlow, *How and Why I became a Catholic. A Letter to a Friend in the Church of England* (London, 1864), pp. 13-14.

111.   Nockles, *Oxford Movement in Context*, pp. 148-56.

112.   Lockhart, *Reminiscences*, p. 7.

113.   *Ibidem*, p. 8.

114.   *Ibidem*, p. 13.

115.   W. Dodsworth, *A Few Comments on Dr Pusey's Letter to the Bishop of London* (London, 1851), p. 6; T.W. Allies, *The Royal Supremacy Viewed in Reference to the Two Spiritual Powers of Order and Jurisdiction* (London, 1850). pp. 56-8; *Dublin Review*, 30, 'Dr Pusey's Teaching and Practice', (March, 1851). pp. 153-76.

116.   PH, Pusey Papers, LBV [Transcripts], J.H. Newman to E.B. Pusey, 2 December 1843. The convert Dodsworth criticised Pusey for seeking 'to satisfy persons out of the pale of the [Roman Catholic] church with devotions designed for her own children', and for quoting an author 'partially either in defect or excess, in order to accommodate his writings to a purpose which he himself never contemplated'. W. Dodsworth, *Further Comments on Dr Pusey's Renewed Explanation* (London, 1851), p. 7.

117.   Maskell, *Protestant Ritualists*, pp. 12-13; H.E. Manning, *The Crown in Council on the 'Essays and Reviews': a Letter to an Anglican Friend* (London, 1864), p. 16.

118.   'Ordinarily speaking, men must enter the Church as though they were approaching death. They must enter it one by one; singly, awfully, coming forward in the presence of men and angels, to say their own Confiteor: - leaving others behind, as though they were, indeed, and altogether, quitting

the visible world'. Hanmer, *Submission to the Catholic Church*, p. 178.

119. Paley, *Arguments Alleged in Defence of the Protestant Position* pp. 27-8.

120. W. Lockhart, *Secession or Schism: a Review of the late Dr Neale's Sermon on Secession* (London, [1869]), p. 5.

121. Capes, *Four Years' Experience of the Catholic Religion*, p. 68.

122. PCA, Renouf Papers, 69/9/1/41, P. Le Page Renouf to Mr & Mrs Renouf, 10 April 1842.

123. PCA, Renouf Papers, 69/9/1/40, P. Le Page Renouf to Mr & Mrs Renouf, 24 March 1842.

124. PCA, Renouf Papers, 69/9/1/75, P. Le Page Renouf to Mrs Renouf, 6 May 1845.

125. H. Collins, *Difficulties of a Convert from the Anglican to the Catholic Church* (London, 1857), p. 6.

126. *Ibidem*, p. 10.

127. For a statement of de Lisle's eirenicism towards Anglicanism, see A. Phillipps de Lisle, *On the Future Unity of Christendom* (London, 1857).

128. Collins, *Difficulties of a Convert*, p. 13.

129. E.S. Ffoulkes, *The Church's Creed or the Crown's Creed? A Letter to the Most Rev. Archbishop Manning* (London, 1868), pp. 2-3.

130. H.E. Manning, *The Convocation and the Crown in Council: a Second Letter to an Anglican Friend* (London, 1864), pp. 13-14.

131. PH, Pusey Papers, LBV 58 (Originals), F. Oakeley to E.B. Pusey, 22 January 1860.

132. R.W. Church, *The Oxford Movement. Twelve Years* (London, 1891), ch. 13.

133. H.P. Liddon, *Life of Edward Bouverie Pusey*, 4 vols, (London, 1894), vol. 2, p. 461.

134. W.J.E. Bennett, *A Schism of certain Priests and others lately in Communion with the Church. A Sermon* (London, 1845), p. 16.

135. C. Wordsworth, *Sequel to Letters to M. Gondon, on the Destructive Character of the Church of Rome both in Religion and Polity* (London, 1848), pp. 240-43.

136. PH, Churton Papers, Chur 3/7/46, E. Churton to W. Gresley, 22 November 1843.

137. *Recent Secessions and Corporate Re-Union. A Letter to an Anglican Friend* (London, 1868), pp. 5-7.

138. 'For myself, I came into the Church to save my soul, which I considered I could not save by remaining in the Establishment'. J.H. Newman to E. Walford, 10 May 1860, *Letters and Diaries*, vol. 19, p. 336.

139.   J.H. Newman to E.E. Estcourt, 4 June 1860, *ibidem*, p. 353.

140.   J.H. Newman to T.W. Allies, 20 February 1849, Allies, *A Life's Decision*, p. 176.

141.   J.H. Newman to Ambrose St John, 8 January 1846, *Letters and Diaries*, vol. 11, p. 87. According to Frederick Oakeley, Anglicans who deplored secessions to Rome, 'speak more like members of a club, than of one section of the church catholic'.   Oakeley, *Letter on Submitting to the Catholic Church*, pp. 22-3.

142.   *Rambler*, 3, 'Will England ever be a Catholic country?', (September, 1849), pp. 81-2; *Rambler*, 7, 'Catholic Prospects', (January, 1851), pp. 1-6.

143.   PH, Pusey Papers, LBV, E.B. Pusey to R.F. Wilson, 23 February 1875. However, see Newman's mature estimate of Pusey's position: 'People are apt to say that he was once nearer to the Catholic Church than he is now; I pray God that he may be one day far nearer than he was then; for I believe that, in his reason and judgment, all the time that I knew him, he never was near to it at all'.   Newman, *Apologia*, p. 138.

144.   J.M. Neale, 'The Providential Direction of the Movement of 1833 not towards Rome', *Lectures on Church Difficulties*, (London, 1852), Lecture 3.

145.   *Rambler*, New Series, 1, 'How to convert a Protestant', (January, 1854), p. 4.

146.   *Dublin Review*, 21, 'The reasonableness of forebearance to some not yet converted', (January, 1847), pp. 316-27.

147.   *Rambler*, 5, 'Gorham Judgment', (May, 1850), pp. 396-7; *Rambler*, 12, 'Cardinal Wiseman and the Tractarians', p. 228; *Dublin Review*, 28, 'Gorham Judgment, (March, 1850), p. 249.

148.   [Ryder], *Thoughts on some Questions of the Day*, 'Ritualism' (London, 1869), pp. 5-6.

149.   H.I.D. Ryder, 'Ritualism, Roman Catholics and Converts: some strictures on Dr Littledale's article "Why ritualists do not become Roman Catholics".', *Contemporary Review*, 34 (1879), pp. 458-9.

150.   V.A. McClelland, 'Corporate Reunion: a Nineteenth-Century Dilemma', *Theological Studies*, 43 (1982), pp. 3-29.

151.   R. Strong, *Alexander Forbes. The First Tractarian Bishop* (Oxford, 1995), p. 222.

152.   According to Father Dominic Barberi, who received Newman into the Catholic Church: 'They [Protestants] take the worst of ours, and we take the best of theirs!'. U. Young, *Life and Letters of the Venerable Father Dominic (Barberi), C.P. Founder of the Passionists in Belgium and England* (London, 1926), p. 264.

153.   D. Withey, *John Henry Newman. The Liturgy and the Breviary* (London, 1992), pp. 110-11; Nockles, *Oxford Movement in Context*, pp. 223-7.

154. Gordon, *Reasons of my Conversion to the Catholic Church*, p. 34.

155. Brownlow, *How and Why I became a Catholic*, p. 63.

156. *Rambler*, New Series, 2, 'Suggestions to "Contented" Anglicans', (November, 1854). pp. 429-32.

157. *Rambler*, 3. 'Will England ever be a Catholic country?' (September, 1849). p. 87.

158. *Rambler*, 7, [J.M. Capes]. 'Rise, Progress and Results of Puseyism', (March, 1851), p. 246.

159. J.C. Hare, *The Contest with Rome: a Charge to the Clergy of the Archdeaconry of Lewes, Delivered at the Ordinary Visitation in 1851. With Notes, especially in Answer to Dr Newman's recent Lectures* (London, 1852), p. 11.

160. Oakeley, 'English Views of Catholicism', *Contemporary Review*, 35. (1879), p. 458.

161. On the revival of Protestant intolerance in the early and mid-Victorian era, see J. Wolffe, *The Protestant Crusade in Great Britain, 1829-1860* (Oxford, 1991); W.L. Arnstein, *Protestant versus Catholic in Mid-Victorian England: Mr Newdegate and the Nuns* (London 1982), pp. 212-14; E.R. Norman, *Anti-Catholicism in Victorian England* (London, 1968), F.M. Wallis, *Popular Anti-Catholicism in Mid-Victorian Britain* (New York, 1993).

162. *Rambler*, 12, 'Cardinal Wiseman and the Tractarians', p. 228.

II

NEWMAN AND THE CHURCH OF ENGLAND

Vincent Ferrer Blehl

In October 1845 Newman's sister Jemima received a letter from her brother stating his intention of becoming a Roman Catholic. Apparently apprehensive of his influence on persons remaining in the Church of England, she wrote that she was not alone in thinking he should not remain at Littlemore. Newman replied on the morning of his reception into the Roman Catholic Church, 'It is very natural that persons should have the feeling you express about my leaving Littlemore, but in having it, they do not put themselves in *my* position, but view me from their own. Few people can put themselves in another's position'. Newman, I believe, belonged to that select few who are gifted with a special empathy and projective imagination which enable them to enter into the ideas and feelings of others, and I hope some instances of it will emerge from the contents of this paper.

Perhaps with the enthusiastic zeal of the newly converted Newman continued, 'the Apostles were told to begin with Jerusalem, not to quit it'. He then affirmed his belief in the Catholic Church: 'If I thought any other body but that which I recognize to be the Catholic to be recognised by the Saviour of the world, I would not have left that body'. At the same time he affirmed that this was consistent with his firm belief that there are 'individuals in the English Church ... invisibly knit into that true body of which they are not outwardly members — and consistent too with thinking it highly injudicious, indiscreet, wanton, to interfere with them in particular cases — only it is a matter of judgment *in* the particular case'.[1]

The fundamental principle of discretion in urging persons to become Catholics remained throughout Newman's life as a Catholic, and he held it against those who wanted him to make many conversions, especially prominent ones, and criticized him for not so doing. He was afraid of such conversions because the hasty convert, not having counted the cost, might encounter difficulties in the Catholic Church and return to the Church of England, or more probably fall into scepticism and unbelief.[2] On the other hand, he would never deny or conceal his belief that salvation was in the Roman Catholic Church *as such*. Thus Newman distinguished between the Anglican Church as a *body* and individuals in it.

Frederick Faber shortly after his own conversion wrote an apology in the form of a letter to a High Church friend entitled *Grounds for Remaining in the Anglican Communion*. Faber's biographer, Ronald Chapman, calls it 'a violent amorphous piece of writing ill calculated to help Anglicans in doubt'. He describes it as 'written in a harsh tone of polemical triumph', and that 'it infuriated the Anglicans and upset his friends'. Newman wrote to Ambrose St. John, 'If anything could stop the movement, it would be such writings'.[3]

But it was not merely that such attacks would turn away prospective converts. Newman believed that in the concrete situation in England, the Anglican Church represented a breakwater against Unitarianism, fanaticism and infidelity, and therefore he did not want to see it weakened or destroyed. On this basis he declined, in June 1860, to take part in a plan to build a Roman Catholic church in Oxford, which could in the circumstances be construed as an attack on the Church of England there. In the same letter he affirmed, 'I have never acted in direct hostility to the Church of England'.[4]

Do the *Lectures on Difficulties of Anglicans* contradict his assertion? In Newman's eyes they were not delivered in hostility. His purpose in the *Lectures*, he said, was to lead Puseyites to pursue the consequences of their Catholic principles and hence, he argued, that the true direction and fulfilment of the Tractarian Movement was the Church of Rome. He admitted, however, that he did disparage the Anglican Church in the eyes of Puseyites, 'who ought to leave it'.[5]

These lectures delivered in 1850 contributed to the conversion of a number of persons and increased the number of those who wrote to him about their doubts and difficulties. Newman found personal contact by letter more satisfactory than such lectures. As Ward remarks:

> He felt that words used publicly and afterwards printed would be read by persons representing the most various standpoints. What was most cogent to those who were already far advanced towards Rome would seem trivial and inconclusive to others ... All this made the lectures unsatisfactory to him. In his correspondence, on the other hand, he could take account of such differences, and play on each mind as the special instrument demanded.[6]

The evidence of the letters shows a marvellous ability to enter into diverse psychologies and to handle the individual's difficulties with clarity and persuasiveness. Mrs William Froude, for example, wrote to Newman, 'Other Catholics always seemed making a case when they said things to me, — you always contrived to say exactly what suited my mind'.[7] As regards the *Lectures on the Present Position of Catholics* Newman viewed them as opposing 'not the Anglican Church, but national Protestantism, and Anglicans only so far as they belong to it'.[8]

With regard to individuals in the Church of England Newman took a broad view of what was called 'invincible ignorance'. He interpreted it to mean 'being in good faith':

> I cannot get myself to believe that the many dear friends and relatives I have lost are without the hope of salvation; I do not know what obliges me to think so; I do not see why I should adopt the contrary views of this Catholic or that who is narrowminded in his view of doctrine, and has not the experience of fact, of the lives of Protestants, as I have. Till then I am called by the voice of the Church to think otherwise, I shall think hopefully where others who have no means of judging, rashly despair.[9]

Who was and who was not in good faith he did not think any one except God could determine. In this respect he differed from Manning 'who attempted to define the classes, who are, and who are not'.[10]

In the *Apologia* Newman went out of his way to show a kindly spirit towards the Anglican Church and his former friends and enemies in it. Though he makes it clear that he believes the Anglican Church is not the Church of Christ's promises but only a national institution, he nevertheless affirmed:

> I recognized in the Anglican Church a time-honoured institution, of noble historical memories, a monument of ancient wisdom, a momentous arm of political strength, a great national organ, a source of vast popular advantage, and, to a certain point, a witness and teacher of religious truth.

He continued his appreciation of the Anglican Church by expressing his gratitude for the benefits he had received in being baptised and having lived in it. Newman concluded this eulogy with an affirmation to which Manning and the Ultramontanes objected:

> Doubtless the National Church has hitherto been a serviceable breakwater against doctrinal errors, more fundamental than its own ... and my own idea of a Catholic's fitting attitude towards the National Church in this its supreme hour, is that of assisting and sustaining it, if it be in our power, in the interest of dogmatic truth. I should wish to avoid every thing (except indeed under the direct call of duty, and this is a material exception,) which went to weaken its hold upon the public mind, or to unsettle its establishment, or to embarrass and lessen its maintenance of those great Christian and Catholic prin-

ciples and doctrines which it has up to this time successfully preached.[11]

At least two periodicals thanked Newman and contrasted his friendly
attitude with that of others particularly Manning. Manning was disturbed by this contrast. It was not the last time it was made, and he
remained sensitive to it even into his old age. There was in his eyes,
however, a more important reason for his opposition to the *Apologia*.
As he wrote to Talbot, the representative of the English hierarchy at
the Vatican: 'I know that the Anglicans look on the *Apologia* as a plea
for remaining as they are'. There is no way of determining how many
did so, but certainly the *Union Review* and the *Quarterly Review* interpreted Newman's remarks in this way. Rumours in Rome that Manning tried to have the *Apologia* put on the Index of Forbidden Books
reached Newman from several sources.

At this time the controversy over the publication of *Essays and
Reviews* had reached a new stage. The Crown in Council reversed the
decision to censure those writers of the *Essays and Reviews* who had
denied the inspiration of Scripture and eternal punishment. Manning
published the first of three pamphlets in which he pointed out rather
harshly that this was an indication that the Church of England was
ultimately subject not to a divinely guided Church but to a national
institution.

> My belief is that when the Church of England lost its inherence in
> the universal Church, the principle of all spiritual and intellectual
> disease was developed in its blood, and ate into its bone. I do not
> believe that it is a poisoned vestment which is put upon it from with-
> out, but a morbid and manifold disease which is ever reproducing
> itself from within.[12]

In a second pamphlet, *The Convocation and the Crown in Council*,
Manning referred to the final part of the *Apologia* and refused to grant
to Anglicanism in the Church of England the special place Newman
had accorded it. 'What I wish to show is, that Anglicanism is identical
in principle with all other forms of the Protestant Reformation'. He
denied that there was for the present generation an alternative between
Anglo-Catholicism and Roman Catholicism, presumably blocking off
any interpretation that Newman meant one could or should remain in
the Church of England.

Pusey published an answer to this pamphlet, *Legal Force of Judgement of the Privy Council*. At one point he wrote,

> And while I know that a very earnest body of Roman Catholics
> rejoice in all the workings of God the Holy Ghost in the Church of

> England (whatever they think of her), and are saddened in what
> weakens her who is, in God's hands, the great bulwark against
> infidelity in this land, others seemed to be in an ecstasy of triumph
> at this victory of Satan.

What Newman had written, however, was not 'a great bulwark against
infidelity in this land', but 'a serviceable breakwater against doctrinal
errors, more fundamental than its own'.

In his third pamphlet, *The Workings of the Holy Spirit in the
Church of England*, published in November 1864, Manning answered
Pusey directly but Newman indirectly. Rather than being a bulwark
against infidelity, the Church of England, he affirmed, was 'the mother of all the intellectual and spiritual aberrations which now cover
the face of England'.[13]

The *Apologia* gave a new impetus to the movement for corporate
reunion between the Churches. In 1857 Ambrose Lisle Phillipps had
published a pamphlet *On the Future Unity of Christendom* and shortly
afterwards became one of the founders of the Association for the
Promotion of the Unity of Christendom. Newman was encouraging,
but cautious. One obstacle, he thought, was the difficulty of proving
the validity of Anglican orders, a problem Phillipps thought could be
met.[14] At first the Vatican gave a favourable response, but the atmosphere changed.

When Phillipps de Lisle, who had changed his name from Lisle
Phillipps on the death of his father, praised the *Apologia* for the stim-
ulus it gave toward reunion, Newman remarked:

> The mixture of good and bad, which makes up the Protestantism of
> England, is a great mystery; He alone, whose infinite Intelligence
> can understand the union of the two, can also dissolve it, and set the
> truth and the right free; but, if an human agency is to be much His
> instrument in any part of this work, surely it must begin by ack-
> nowledging, not denying, what Protestants have that is good and
> true, and honouring it in them as coming from the one source of all
> light and holiness. Certainly, to my own mind one of the most
> affecting and discouraging elements in the action of Catholicism just
> now on English Society, is the scorn with which some of us treat
> proceedings and works among Protestants which it is but Christian
> charity to ascribe to the influence of divine grace.[15]

Newman here seems to be responding to de Lisle's complaint that
attitudes toward reunion had changed in the English Catholic Church.
Indeed shortly afterwards in September 1864 Catholics were forbidden
to be members of the Association. It was a crushing blow to de Lisle,
but he did not give up.

Pusey for his part prepared an answer to Manning's third pamphlet, calling it *An Eirenicon*, in which he expressed a wish for reunion with Rome but cited as obstacles Marian devotions and infallibility. Catholics took it as an attack on Catholicism. Newman remonstrated indirectly through Keble, to whom the *Eirenicon* had been addressed, and directly to Pusey himself. To Keble he wrote the memorable sentence, 'The first duty of charity is to try and enter into the minds and feelings of others', and to Pusey, 'An Irenicon smooths difficulties; I am sure people will think you increase them'. When Pusey replied that he had no 'idea of attacking anything', Newman assured Pusey he would 'treat the book simply as an Irenicon, as you wish', and this he did in his *Letter*, but he gently chided him, 'You discharge your olive branch as if from a catapult'.[16]

Adopting common ground between High Anglicanism and Catholicism, i.e. 'Antiquity', Newman cited the Fathers of the Church who refer to Mary as the second Eve, from which he deduced the privileges and prerogatives of Mary both as regards dogma and devotion, a distinction he felt Pusey had blurred. 'The faith is everywhere one and the same, but a large liberty is accorded to private judgment and inclination as regards matters of devotion'.[17] He declared his preference for English habits of devotion and repudiated the exaggerations of Ward and Faber, whom Pusey had quoted, and would not allow that they were spokemen for English Catholics.

There was general satisfaction with the *Letter* with certain reservations on the part of Manning and Ward, who tried to have Newman's bishop Ullathorne censure it. Pusey was pleased and so was Phillipps de Lisle who wrote that the *Letter* would give an 'immense impulse to the Reunion Movement'. Newman in reply described how careful he had been to avoid hurting or offending. 'I have an especial desire to act considerately towards the Catholic movement in the Anglican Church because they have been severely handled, and because kindness seems a better way of dealing with them'. According to Malcolm MacColl Newman was successful in so doing.[18]

At this time Manning, now Archbishop of Westminster, issued a pastoral, *On the Reunion of Christendom*. In February 1866 de Lisle complained to Newman of its 'harsh and repulsive line'. Newman, however, defended Manning and wrote to de Lisle, 'I do not think it right to judge of such publications as the Archbishop's *Pastoral*, as if they were merely private and personal compositions. An Archbishop has great duties to perform — he has to defend the faith — he must beware of betraying it — and he must emphatically put truth in the first place, and charity in the second. He cannot, by virtue of his office, indulge his feelings, and he seems to be stern, when really he is but faithful to his trust'.[19] At the same time Newman expressed gratification with de Lisle's recent article, 'Mr de Lisle on Reunion', in the *Union Review* of January 1866, which was written 'with the express purpose of diminishing difficulties in the way of corporate reunion'.

Pressed by de Lisle to reveal his mind on corporate reunion Newman replied at length, the gist of which was that in the concrete situation he did not see it coming about, because the three main parties in the Church of England were unlikely to coalesce, which would be necessary for reunion. He concluded 'I can no more see the Establishment running into Catholicism any more than I can conceive the Thames running into the Wash'.[20]

The success of the republication of Newman's *Anglican Sermons* in 1868 prompted Newman to republish his other Anglican works, and he collaborated with Copeland in publishing a selection of the sermons that would appeal equally to Anglicans and Catholics with the irenic purpose of cultivating 'a unity of *ethos* among those who otherwise differ'. In his correspondence he tried to maintain charitable relations with all those, whether within or without the Establishment, who showed any interest in promoting religion and opposing scepticism and unbelief. He tried to emphasize what was common and to build on this in a cooperative effort to halt the spread of 'infidelity'. For example, in thanking David Brown for his lecture, "Helplessness of Modern Unbelief", Newman wrote, 'I rejoice in it as one compensation of the cruel overthrow of faith which we see on all sides of us, that, as the setting of the sun brings out the stars, so great principles are found to shine out, which are hailed by men of various religions as their own in common, when infidelity prevails'.[21]

A few years before he had responded to a letter of the same theologian:

> What a mystery it is in this day that there should be so much which draws religious minds together, and so much which separates them from each other. Never did members of the various Christian communions feel such tenderness for each other, yet never were the obstacles greater or stronger which divide them. What a melancholy thought is this — and when will a better day come?[22]

NOTES

1. C.Dessain (Ed.) *et al.*, *Letters and Diaries of John Henry Newman, [LD]* (Edinburgh, 1961), XI, pp. 13-14.
2. *Autobiographical Writings, [AW]* (London, 1956), pp. 257-258.
3. *LD* XI, p. 118.
4. *LD* XIX, p. 353.

5. *LD* XIV, p. 173.
6. W. Ward, *The Life of John Henry Cardinal Newman* (London, 1912), I, p. 235.
7. *LD* XVII, p. 544, n. 2.
8. *LD* XIX, p. 353.
9. *LD* XX, p. 269 and *LD* XVIII, pp. 467-68.
10. *LD* XXI, p. 315; 'Workings of the Holy Spirit in the Church of England', pp. 10-21, reprinted in *England and Christendom* (London, 1867), pp. 91-104.
11. *Apologia pro Vita Sua* (London, 1873), p. 342.
12. 'The Crown in Council on the *Essays and Reviews*', in *England and Christendom* (London 1867), p. 24.
13. *E & C*, p. 115.
14. *LD* XVIII, pp. 104-05 and n. 2 (p. 105).
15. *LD* XXI, p. 228.
16. *LD* XXII, pp. 69, 90, 93, and n. 2 (p. 93); *Certain Difficulties felt by Anglicans in Catholic Teaching* (London, 1879), II, p. 4.
17. *Ibidem,* II, pp. 26-31.
18. *LD* XXII, pp. 146-47, and n. 1 (p. 146).
19. *LD* XXII, p. 165.
20. *LD* XXII, pp. 170-72.
21. *LD* XXVII, p. 188.
22. *LD* XXVI, p. 187.

III

NEWMAN AND THE DEVELOPMENT OF DOCTRINE

Michael Peterburs

Firmly I believe and truly
God is Three and God is One
And I next acknowledge duly
Manhood taken by the Son.[1]

Although the subject of papal infallibility was to exercise Newman's mind greatly in the 1860s and '70s, it was not in itself a major theme of the *Essay on the Development of Christian Doctrine* of 1845 and it was not his acceptance of it that led to his conversion to Catholicism. Rather it was the 'hypothesis' of development which enabled him to regard the Catholic Church of the nineteenth century as being one with the Church of the Fathers. The generally accepted opinion of the genesis of the *Essay of Development* is that the theory 'was something almost entirely new, although Newman first adumbrated it in his *Arians of the Fourth Century*'.[2] It is in the last of the *University Sermons* on 'The Theory of Developments in Religious Doctrine' that the theory is first reckoned to have seen the light of day, reaching its culmination in the *Essay*. In other words, the chronology of his conversion is thought to be *Tract XC,* Development (*University Sermon XV* as prologue to the *Essay*) and then Rome. Such an impression, however, is misleading. His first attempt to work out a coherent theory of development appears in two, as yet unpublished and unconsidered, letters to his brother, Francis William, in October and November 1840, and these, along with the last of the *University Sermons*, form the groundwork to the *Essay*. Furthermore, the controversy with the Abbé Jager, and discussions with Samuel Francis Wood on the development of doctrine, seem to have affected the development of his thought. Notes made in the appendices to his private diaries between 1843 and 1846 show how his mind dwelt on this subject during those years, and a plan for the *Essay* is to be found in the 'Copybook on Development', dated 7 March 1844.

THE ARIANS OF THE FOURTH CENTURY

In *The Arians of the Fourth Century,* Newman seems to have recognised that, in the doctrines of the *Homoousion* and the Trinity, some sort of development had taken place.[3] Following Hawkins,[4] he rejected the idea of *sola scriptura* arguing that:

> Surely the Sacred Volume was never intended, and is not adapted, to teach us our creed: however certain it is that we can prove our creed from it, when it has once been taught us.[5]

He does, however, take a distinctly negative approach towards developed dogma, almost regarding it as a necessary evil:

> On the other hand, while the line of tradition, drawn out as it was to the distance of two centuries from the Apostles, had at length become too frail a texture, to resist the touch of subtle and ill-directed reason, the Church was naturally unwilling to have recourse to the novel, though necessary measure, in imposing an authoritative creed upon those whom it invested with the office of teaching. If I avow my belief, that freedom from symbols and articles is absolutely the highest state of Christian communion, and the peculiar privilege of the primitive Church, it is not from any tenderness towards that proud impatience of control in which many exult, as in a virtue: but first, because technicality and formalism are, in their degree, inevitable results of public confessions of faith; — and next, because when confessions do not exist, the mysteries of divine truth, instead of being exposed to the gaze of the profane and uninstructed, are kept hidden in the bosom of the Church, far more faithfully than is otherwise possible: and reserved by a private teaching, through the channel of her ministers, as rewards in due measure and season, for those who are prepared to profit by them: for those, that is, who are diligently passing through the successive stages of faith and obedience.[6]

This reservation about formal dogma partly resulted from Newman's understanding of the inadequacy of human language for expressing the divine mysteries. This in turn was based upon the principle of 'economy' practised by the Early Church, and which he learnt from his study of the Alexandrian Fathers.[7] This belief is also expressed in *Tract LXXIII* (1835),[8] which was later published under the title 'On the Introduction of Rationalistic Principles into Revealed Religion'.[9]

> Thus the systematic doctrine of the Trinity may be considered as the shadow, projected for the contemplation of the intellect, of the Object of scripturally-informed piety: a representation, economical, necessarily imperfect, as being exhibited in a foreign medium, and

therefore involving apparent inconsistencies or mysteries; given to the Church by tradition contemporaneously with those apostolic writings, which are addressed more directly to the heart; kept in the background in the infancy of Christianity, when faith and obedience were vigorous, and brought forward at the time when, reason being disproportionately developed, and aiming at sovereignty in the province of religion, its presence became necessary to expel a usurping idol from the house of God.[10]

Having outlined, however, how undesirable formalised religious doctrines are, Newman then goes on to show how necessary they are to

restrain the rovings of the intellect, or silence its clamorous demand for a formal statement concerning the Object of our worship. If, for instance, Scripture bids us adore God, and adore His Son, our reason at once asks, whether it does not follow that there are two Gods; and a system of doctrine becomes unavoidable; being framed, let it be observed, not with a view of explaining, but of arranging the inspired notices concerning the Supreme Being, of providing not a consistent, but a connected statement.[11]

Newman did not regard formal statements of doctrine as merely human constructs. They were part of Revealed Truth.[12] This can be seen from his discussion of ecumenical councils, in which he makes further use of the theory of the *Disciplina Arcani*:

Lastly, the secret tradition soon ceased to exist even in theory. It was authoritatively divulged, and perpetuated in the form of symbols according as the successive innovations of heretics called for its publication. In the creeds of the early Councils, it may be considered as having come to light, and so ended; so that whatever has not been thus authenticated, whether it was prophetical information, or comment on the past dispensations, is, from the circumstances of the case, lost to the Church. What, however, was then (by God's good providence) seasonably preserved, is of some sense of apostolic authority still; and at least serves the chief office of the early traditions, viz. that of interpreting and harmonising the statements of scripture.[13]

As such, not only do such theological expressions 'assist acts of religious worship and obedience', they also 'exclude heresy'.[14] It is the task of the Church, 'the pillar and the ground of truth',[15] to preserve these divinely revealed truths. Two of the main themes of the *Essay on Development* are already present in Newman's thought: first, the creative role of heresy; and secondly, that which underpins the whole process of development — Divine Providence.

So, in *Arians,* Newman regarded dogma as the necessary, if unfortunate, consequence of an increasing disdain for the apostolic witness, incapable of fully expressing the divine mysteries it represents. It is, however, also part of Revealed Truth, being the formal statement of the secret, unwritten tradition of which the apostles were in possession. That being said, he still felt it to be regrettable that dogma was at all necessary, but it is regarded as excluding heresy from the Church, whose task it is to protect Christian truth. In connection with this, he thought of the creeds as a test of authority, not of communion:

> the test has been used, not as a condition of communion, but of authority. As learning is not necessary for a private Christian, so neither is the full knowledge of the theological system. The clergy, and others in station, must be questioned as to their doctrinal views: but for the mass of the laity, it is enough if they do not set up such counter-statements of their own.[16]

Some other elements of the *Essay* of 1845 can also be detected in 1833. This includes the idea of the interdependence of Scripture and Tradition, although the latter was regarded as 'unauthoritative' and static, rather than as a dynamic, organic reality as it was in the *Essay*. There is not at this stage a formal attempt to outline a theory of the development of doctrine.

The question of the relationship between faith and the Church, however, was to occupy his mind considerably during the following years: 'There was a contrariety of claims between the Roman and the Anglican religions, and the history of my conversion is simply the process of working it out to a solution'.[17]

CONTROVERSY WITH THE ABBÉ JAGER

In 1834 Newman entered into direct controversy with the Roman claims in a correspondence, which he took over from Benjamin Harrison,[18] with the Abbé Jager.[19] In his discussions with the Abbé, Newman argued that Anglicanism represented a middle way between 'Romanism' on the one side and popular Protestantism on the other. Both, as he saw it, were corruptions of the primitive faith of the undivided Church, which found its fullest expression in Antiquity. His argument with Jager, which centred around St Vincent's *Commonitorium*, was that the Church of Rome had committed 'the intolerable offence of having added to the Faith'.[20] This 'offence' was based on the fallacious belief that 'Tradition *per se* (is) ... sufficient authority for the Church considering a doctrine fundamental'. [21] This was not an error into which Anglicans would fall because 'we consider tradition subordinate, not co-ordinate to Scripture'.[22]

For Newman there were two types of Tradition. First, Episcopal Tradition which was the Creed, 'a collection of definite articles committed and received from bishop to bishop and forced upon the attention of each individual Christian'.[23] The development of Episcopal Tradition was limited to Antiquity, by which Newman meant approximately the first 450 years after Christ.[24] Secondly, Prophetical Tradition, which he understood to be the interpretation of the Revelation, and which consisted in theological rather than doctrinal development. That which was brought to light through Prophetical Tradition was entitled to attention, although different statements were entitled to very different degrees of credit. The seeds of the idea of the development of doctrine can be found in Newman's discussion of Prophetical Tradition.[25]

Through her Prophetical Office, Newman believed that the Church had 'the power to develop its fundamental Creed into Articles of Religion, according to times and circumstances; (but) to develop is not to create. Articles of religion are not essentially fundamental articles as articles of faith are'.[26]

Jager agreed that 'to develop is not to create', but he asked Newman for proof that the 'Thirty-nine Articles are the development of the Creed',[27] for example 'that there are only two sacraments ... that the Pope has no jurisdiction over the Catholic Church [and] that Queen Elizabeth has the chief power in all kinds of causes, whether ecclesiastical or civil'.[28] More irenically:

> No doubt, there is a difference between apostolic tradition and prophetic exposition. The prophets or the doctors of the Church are obliged to define, to comment, to develop the mysteries of religion, and to put them within the people's reach. But as Vincent says, they must do it 'while preserving the same doctrine, the same sense, the same judgement'. When you develop a truth, you do not change it, on the contrary, you give it more force, more lustre, greater scope. That is what the Fathers and the Doctors of the Church did. The Church took care to warn those who had the misfortune to stray from the apostolic doctrine as in their explanations, she pointed out their errors, and condemned them when necessary. And so apostolic tradition has remained pure and intact until our own day, and will remain so until the end of time.[29]

This point evidently weighed heavily with Newman because in the *Essay on Development* it is embodied in the first note of a genuine development 'preservation of type'. In addition, he was not so keen to diminish the authority of prophetic Tradition in the *Lectures on the*

Prophetical Office (1837) as he was when he first described it to Froude in 1835. Compare these two quite contrasting attitudes. To Froude he wrote that Prophetical Tradition 'does not carry with it any witness of its reception being necessary for Church Communion. Its reception is the privilege of the Christian when admitted, not of his admission'.[30] Yet two years later, in the *Prophetical Office* he described it as:

> existing primarily in the bosom of the Church itself, and recorded in such measure as Providence has determined in the writings of eminent men. This is obviously of a very different kind from Episcopal Tradition, yet in its origin it is equally Apostolic, and equally claims our zealous maintenance ... This is that body of teaching which is offered to all Christians, partly being a comment, partly an addition upon the articles of the Creed.[31]

A second point which was to have its effect upon Newman's thought later was Jager's accusation that the Church of England was in the same position as the Donatists, who had separated themselves from the Church 'for articles which were not fundamental':[32]

> You hurl at me darts which you think are lethal, namely that the Donatists were considered by the Church as excluded from salvation, although their error was against Scripture. I answer, almost in your own words, that to maintain an opinion against the voice of the whole Church stubbornly and publicly is of itself without any doubt a mortal sin, and such was the flagrant sin of the Donatists, as St Augustine tells us.[33]

From the *Apologia*[34] it may perhaps be inferred that in 1839 Newman regarded himself as condemned by his own arguments of four years before.

In summary, then, it may be concluded that the controversy with the Abbé Jager left its mark upon Newman. Already present in his own mind were the seeds of a theory of the development of doctrine, and his correspondence with the Abbé pushed him further in that direction. This can be seen from the discussion on the difference between 'develop' and 'create' which is essential to the *Essay on Development*. Furthermore, 'the conjunction which so startled him in 1839, of Donatists, Anglicans and St Augustine, had been present to his mind in 1835, without producing the dramatic effect it had later'.[35] It would appear fair to conclude that the controversy had some effect in changing Newman's opinions, but that where the subject of development occurs in his early work, he is usually found to be attacking it. This is true of the *Letters on the Prophetical Office* as well as of the controversy with Jager.[36]

SAMUEL FRANCIS WOOD

In 1835, Newman was also confronted with the idea of development in doctrine by Samuel Francis Wood, a former Oriel pupil, and now a friend and disciple in the Oxford Movement.[37] Wood's theory, which he discussed with both Newman and Henry Edward Manning, then Rector of Lavington,[38] may be set out as follows:

> 1. Under the direction of the Holy Spirit, and pursuant to Christ's commands, the Apostles committed to the charge of the Church a formal system of doctrines, ordinances, disciplines etc. And this *orally*, their *writings imply* or presuppose, but do not contain it.
> 2. It is therefore only *incidentally* that the obligation to receive doctrines arises from their being found in Scripture; *primarily*, it results from them being *ascertained* Apostolical Tradition.
> 3. In common with other societies the Church has the inherent power of expanding or modifying her organisation, of bringing her ideas of Truth into more distinct consciousness, or of developing the Truth itself more fully.
> 4. It follows that the doctrines may be true, tho' not traceable [amended to 'apparent' following criticism from Manning] to the Apostles.
> 5. And further, that the Church retains the right of authoritatively exhibiting them, subject only to the condition — arising from the withdrawal of her inspiring guides and from her infallibility — of their being true.
> 6. But the only mode of providing this is by showing their accordance with Scripture. So that while the Church has ever been our sole *expositrix*, we have now two co-ordinate tests of doctrine: Apostolical Tradition and Scripture.[39]

Newman reacted against this theory employing the same arguments he had used against Jager. These are summarised by Wood in a letter to Manning, dated 29 January 1836, which he wrote following a visit from Newman during which the theory had been discussed.

> Well then! Newman holds that from the time the Church ceased to be One, the right of it to propound *Articles of Faith*, as such, is suspended, all that remains to them is to impose terms of communion, articles of peace etc. Further, he says that before the Reformation the Church never *deduced* any doctrine from Scripture, and by inference blames our Reformers for doing so. Moreover, he objects to their doctrine in itself as to Justification by Faith, and complains of their attempt to prove it from the Fathers, as a perversion of their meaning. Generally, his result is, not merely to *refer* us to antiquity but to *shut us up* in it, and to deprive, not only individuals but the Church, of all those doctrines of Scripture not fully commented on by the Fathers: and he seems to consider that

our Reformed Church has erred as much in one direction as the
Council of Trent in another, and the fact of our churches holding
different views e.g. on justification, requires the suspension of our
judgement, or at least prevents full acceptance of our doctrine
concerning it.[40]

The argument that doctrine is not to be deduced from Scripture shows
that Newman still held to the *Disciplina Arcani*, and that he rejected
the idea of doctrinal development. Theological development was,
however, permissible in his view, but its role was limited to drawing
up terms of communion; what he described to Jager as 'Articles of
Religion'. This, however, is a development of his view in *Arians* that
the creeds provide only a test of authority, not of communion, and, as
will be suggested below, his discussions with Wood, as well as the
controversy with Jager, left their imprint upon him. In fact, by 1840,
he had formulated an organic theory of the development of doctrine.[41]

LETTERS TO FRANCIS NEWMAN

In 1840, Newman resumed an as yet unpublished and unconsidered
correspondence with his brother, Francis, with whom he had long been
out of contact. In his letters, Francis (who had definite Unitarian
sympathies) challenged John Henry to state why he could call himself
an Apostolical Christian, when it seemed to Francis that Wiseman's
claim was just as good, if not better, than John Henry's. John Henry
approached this issue from the direction of Revelation and development.

In a letter of 22 October 1840, John Henry argued that:

> ... if the fact of a revelation be granted, it is most extravagant and
> revolting to our reason to suppose that after all its message is not
> ascertainable and that the divine interposition reveals nothing.[42]

He then went on to draw out what he saw to be the difference between
a Unitarian and an orthodox Christian:

> 'I regard the Unitarian controversy as a singularly difficult one'; I
> grant it on the assumption that the books of the New Testament are
> the appointed or direct means by which truth is to be ascertained on
> the subject, or that nothing need be received as true, but what
> necessarily follows from the text by the mere force of words, or that
> nothing is important which though apparently taught in one portion,
> is not taught in all others also; positions which I deny.[43]

Newman's argument is that the Unitarian picks and chooses the parts
of Scripture which suit his argument best, but that the Trinitarian takes
Scripture as a whole, interpreted by the creeds. Thus, Trinitarian

thought is based on Scripture and Tradition, but the Unitarian approach is distorted by the

> assumption that 'He who is literally and wholly man, cannot be literally and wholly God'.[44]

He then continues with the argument that Scripture must be taken and interpreted as a whole:

> 'If I had not Scripture but Paul's epistles, I should believe him an Arian; if I had none but the opening of the 4th Gospel, I might think the writer a Sabellian; if I had the first 3 gospels and the Acts alone, I should most unhesitatingly be a follower of Dr. Priestley'. Granting this for argument-sake, the question is what ought I to believe, when I have *ALL* these informants [?]. Now the Catholic creed is pretty much the *union* of *all* these antagonistic opinions which separately become heresies; and heresy in each case is not so much a positive doctrine, as the holding of a particular doctrine to the exclusion of other doctrines. The question then resolves itself into this. Is such union of antagonistic doctrines an absurdity? Is it more likely that the various writers of the New Testament should agree by holding a mystery, or should differ, by holding each of them only what is on the surface of their respective writings? Is it not a more probable assumption than not, that in your words 'every writer of the New Testament held the very same?' You think not, I think it is.[45]

Newman's thought leads to the conclusion that an authoritative interpreter of Scripture is required, something he had already established to his own satisfaction in *Arians*. Since he believed that one can understand God's Revelation with certainty, it is not surprising that he saw the creeds, authoritatively laid down by the early ecumenical Councils, as the interpreter of the whole of Scripture, and as catechetical material. Revelation in Scripture is not a series of disunited arguments and opinions. It forms a coherent whole and is intended, by God, to be understood by man. The creeds are the key to understanding Scripture, because they are the explicit statement of unwritten Tradition which explains that Revelation given in Scripture. More will be said below about Newman's understanding of Tradition in 1840 as opposed to 1833, in the discussion of his second letter to Francis.

To John Henry, Francis had approached the issue from the wrong direction. Rather than starting at the position outlined in *Arians* that faith is taught by the creeds, which are in turn proved by Scripture, Francis started from Scripture, ignoring the existence of Tradition. It was, therefore, not surprising to John Henry that Francis should speak of the authority of the Church as 'the authority of an unseen abstraction'.[46] John Henry responded:

> If the Church is nothing more than this, and so far as it is nothing
> more, I do not maintain its authority. Supposing one said 'Philo-
> sophers are now agreed that the earth goes round the sun' or 'the
> House of Commons has ruled that it has a right to publish libels'; are
> 'Philosophers' ideal and the 'House of Commons' an abstraction? So
> far as the Church does not answer to these illustrations, I do not
> maintain its authority.[47]

So, in this letter, Newman has, in effect, reproduced the arguments of
Arians. Man can understand God's Revelation with certainty, but this
Revelation is not *taught* generally to Christians by the Bible. Rather,
it is taught authoritatively by the creeds, which can be proved from
Scripture. In consequence of this, the Church has authority to perform
her role as guardian of the Revealed Truth. There is, however, no
mention in this letter of the inadequacy of human language in this
context. Since this was a belief he retained in his later theology, it
would seem that he had avoided this point for the moment so as not to
over-complicate the issue and perhaps to avoid giving Francis further
ammunition. It is also to be noted that he does not comment on the
desirability, or otherwise, of formal doctrine, even by implication.
That which is implied is that doctrine is necessary for the interpretation
of Scripture. Whether this is regrettable or not he does not say.

   In the second letter, Newman goes on to set out his first formal
attempt at establishing a theory of development. He no longer held the
view that there was at one time an age of 'pristine' Christianity, but
was of the opinion that Christianity, as it is now known, had developed
by fits and starts, in a rather haphazard fashion. He was concerned to
show that these developments were legitimate, and that he, who held
the developed doctrines of Christianity, was right to call himself an
Apostolical Christian. Before setting out his theory, however, he
turned first to the 'question whether I go by private judgement though
I proscribe it'.[48] Newman wished to demonstrate that

> there would be no inconsistency in upholding the authority of the
> Church, and yet, when she did not speak or could not be heard,
> going by private judgement.[49]

To illustrate his point, Newman gives three examples of how following
one's private judgement need not necessarily conflict with giving way
to a higher authority.[50] The general point that is made in these
examples is that he did not regard it as illegitimate to rely on one's
own private judgement in a situation in which one did not receive, or
have access to, commands from a legitimate higher authority. That
being the case:

there is nothing impossible in Almighty God having granted the Church a power of speaking truth within certain limits, viz. on certain subjects or for a certain time, or under certain conditions; and that external to those limits private judgement should have its range. There may be moral uses in the freedom of judgement in some things as well as its restraint in others. As to the fact, whether Providence has thus appointed, and its antecedent probability, these are distinct and essential points of course; but I am describing a case in which a use of private judgement is not inconsistent with implicit submission to an external decisive.[51]

Regarding the theory of development, the important point to note is that Newman is repeating the argument that the Church has authority to protect the faith, authoritatively defined by the early ecumenical councils. On the issues thus decided there is no scope for the use of private judgement, but in those matters where no such decision had been made, private judgement is the correct means by which to proceed. This argument is also to be found in the fifth, sixth and seventh lectures on the *Prophetical Office*.[52]

Having said a few words about the use of private judgement, Newman then addresses the issue on which Francis has accused him of inconsistency:

You observe then that, if a generally received opinion be of authority, this must be because what is generally received in any age is *therefore* true, or because its general reception is an *index* of a reception from the first age; whereas I virtually abandon the former ground by giving up a later age when it contradicts an earlier, and the latter by never attempting to prove the opinions of the Christian body higher than century iv, nay by granting differences prior to the ivth. You call on me to make good the *first* link in the chain.[53]

It is at this point that Newman sets out his theory, which, given that it is yet to be published, will be quoted in full:

The link in the argument, which you think may be weak, may yet be felt by others. That argument I shall sketch as follows:

1. From the first, running into the obscurity of the Apostolic century, there has been a large body called the Church, claiming the exclusive dispensation of the gospel; and there has been but one such, — large, continuous and commanding.

2. This body in centuries iv and v, is known to have been of a certain temper, cast of principle, system of doctrine, and character of conduct; in a word of a certain *religion*.

3. On tracing backwards, the evidences of the existence of this religion are fainter, but still they exist in their degree.

4. Evidence of any other system of religion, (i.e. in temper, principle, doctrine, conduct) calling itself Christianity, is altogether unproducible. Either this is Christianity, or we do not know (historically) *what* Christianity is. Everything else is the history of mere sects with known authors. The Christian religion, when traced back from the fourth century, vanishes in this form from the pages of history. In proportion as it is known it is this.

5. There is no reason why this should not be Apostolic Christianity; as it does not differ from Scripture more than the parts of Scripture differ from each other, and does not resemble foreign systems, which came into contact with it between the first and fourth centuries, more than systems resemble each other which are acknowledged by all to be independent and distinct.

6. This temper, cast of principle, doctrine, conduct, are singularly consistent with each other, or one; so that the existence of e.g. the temper, makes the co-existence of the doctrine at least not impossible.

7. The *temper and principles* of the Church have been precisely the same from the first to last, from the Apostolic age to this; viz. what her enemies call dogmatic, mystical, credulous, superstitious, bigoted, legal. I consider no persons doubt this great fact.

8. Its doctrines and course of conduct have developed from external and internal causes, where by development I mean the more accurate statement and the varied application of ideas from the action of the reason upon them according to new circumstances.

9. All systems which have life, have a development, yet do not cease to have an identity though they develop. E.g. Locke and Luther have done far more than they themselves saw.

10. While there is no antecedent objection to developments, while they harmonise with its temper and principles, are consistent with the ideas from which they profess to spring, and are professed unanimously by its members. In proportion as these (or if so be, other) tests fail, they become doubtful.

11. Since the 4th century does not present greater developments upon the first, than the 7th upon the 4th, and no one (except *thesin diaphulatton*) would deny that the 7th professes the same religion as the 4th, it is unreasonable on account of its developments to deny that the 4th has the same religion as the first.

12. There are sufficient doctrines developed from a very early date both to remove the difficulty of the notion of a dogmatic system, and

actually to furnish portions and indices of the whole system afterwards confessedly existing. Ignatius has unfolded the episcopal and
sanctioned the magisterial principle; from Justin downwards we have
an uninterrupted testimony to the Homoousion, (as I consider it will
be felt that Bull has shown) and to baptismal regeneration; in
Irenaeus, not to say in Ignatius, we find the doctrine of the Incarnation fully developed. All bear witness to the doctrine of the
Trinity, and [?] to the rule of celibacy.

My analysis might be more exact; but it is the best I can make of
the line of proof, which will, I think, and justly, weigh with men
practically, whether they submit to the religion thus ascertained or
not, and which I think, even opponents grant by not assailing. All
they can do is dispute about *details*.[54]

So far, then, Newman has addressed the issue of the identity of the
nineteenth-century Church with the Church of the early centuries AD,
arguing that the Early Church has, quite legitimately, developed into
the current Church. As regards Francis's claim that Wiseman's
argument is just as good as his, he continued that

no one seems to deny that from the first the mass of Christianity
tended straight to what is afterwards known as Catholicism, and was
such, as far as it went; no one pretends to produce from the records
the history of an early religion professing to be Christian (e.g.
Gnostic or Platonic) with greater claims so to be considered, and
never to modern opinions than the Catholic; every one grants or
rather urges the sameness of Roman, Greek and Anglican here,
every one sees that, whatever superstition may have done for them,
and rationalism for us, we and they are on the whole the same,
Archbishop Whately[55] having written on the Popery in our Church,
and Mr Taylor[56] preferring [?] Popery to early Christianity. Here
then we have one religion in all ages; I profess it, I sacrifice my
private judgement to it whenever it speaks; I use my private
judgement only in accidental details, where it does not speak, or to
determine what it speaks.[57]

In other words, Newman is here relying on the branch theory, i.e. that
Roman Catholicism, Orthodoxy and Anglicanism are all branches of
the true Catholic Church, being in substance identical with the
undivided Early Church; the differences between them being merely
in changeable details.

Two points, however, illustrate the fluid nature of Newman's
thought during this period. First, among those doctrines 'developed
from a very early date (which) .... remove the difficulty of the notion
of a dogmatic system, and actually ... furnish portions and indices of
the whole system afterwards confessedly existing', he cites the

'uninterrupted testimony to the Homoousion' (point 12), giving Bull as his authority. This view he came to reject in the *Essay*, in effect arguing that if the ante-Nicene Fathers were to be judged by the standard of Nicaea they would be heretics.[58]

Secondly, in his letter to Francis, John Henry availed himself of the branch theory to justify his claim to be an Apostolic Christian. This was a theory which he rejected not only before his conversion to Catholicism, but which he attacked in a review[59] of William Palmer's *Treatise on the Church of Christ* (1838), i.e. before using it to defend his position to Francis.

It is suggested here, therefore, that there was a certain amount of inconsistency in Newman's thought during this period, but that it appears to have given rise to a creative tension, which resulted in the further development of his own opinions. Furthermore, it would seem that he himself was to realise this much later on, and made use of this insight in his description of the relationship among the offices of Prophet, Priest and King, as exercised by the Church.

In addition, there are certain similarities with Wood's theory of development. Newman had always accepted Wood's first two points, but by 1840 he had come to accept doctrinal, as well as theological, development. To use Wood's terminology, Newman now accepted that the Church has 'the power... of bringing her ideas of Truth into more distinct consciousness' (point 3) and that this implied that not all true doctrines were necessarily 'apparent to the Apostles' (point 4). Furthermore, Newman now held that Tradition and Scripture were 'two co-ordinate tests of doctrine' (point 6), but it was not until 1845 that he became finally convinced that it was the Roman Catholic Church alone that was the judge in such matters.

In summary, then, Newman set out here the basic structure of a theory of the development of doctrine. In points 1 to 7 he identified the nineteenth-century Christian Church with that of the early centuries. He argued that they are identical in 'temper and principles', noting as he did in the *Essay* that although doctrine may change, the principles that underlie it can be consistent. The obvious differences between the Churches of the different ages he attributed to development, point 8 anticipating his description of the development of an idea in the *Essay*. In fact the necessity of development is emphasised (point 9) in terms resembling the famous dictum of the *Essay* that 'to live is to change and to be perfect is to have changed often'. He also recognised that not all developments are true developments. In point 10 therefore, he outlined the necessity of tests. He acknowledged the same point in the *Essay*, but in the 1878 edition he called the tests 'notes', thus suggesting their tentative nature. Another theme covered in point 10 is that of antecedent probability. This takes one back to a point made earlier in the letter about the necessity of judging by antecedent probability[60]in matters of religion. This, of course, has links with the idea of Divine Providence discussed in his earlier letter to Francis.

> I have for some years been preaching University Sermons, as I have had opportunity, on this one subject, that men judge in religion, and are meant to judge by antecedent probability much more than by external evidences, and that their view of antecedent probability depends upon their particular state of mind. I consider with you that 'the alleged historical proof of miracles is unsatisfactory', separate from the moral character of the doctrine. Accordingly I think a Churchman is (abstractly speaking) a man of certain *ethos* — and a Dissenter of another. And in like manner, abstractedly, the Church has a tendency to produce in individuals a Church *ethos*, and Dissent a Dissenting *ethos*. At the same time of course I know that in matter of fact, considering the accidents of birth, influence, interest, politics etc. etc., men of a Church temper are found among Dissenters, and men of a Dissenting temper among Churchmen.[61]

This belief in antecedent probability allowed Newman to read back from later centuries into earlier as he did in point 11.[62] He provided evidence to support this method in point 12. As regards the branch theory, it can be noted that by the time of his conversion to Catholicism in 1845 he believed it to be untenable. In effect, Francis had made his point, although he would not have agreed with Wiseman either! John Henry's view, however, that private judgement was valid only in circumstances when the Church had not pronounced remained. This obviously links in with his argument that the creeds are the authoritative interpretation of Scripture.

Again, there is no mention of the inadequacy of human language for expressing the divine mysteries — presumably for the same reason suggested above. There is also no mention of dogmatic formulations being necessary, if unfortunate in some of their consequences. Nor, however, is there any mention of their benefits. As such, we cannot be sure whether his attitude to formal dogma, at this stage in the development of his thought, has changed since 1833.

His attitude towards Tradition, however, has undergone some change. Its working still appears limited to the years of the Patristic Church, but what he expounded in the above letter to Francis is an organic theory of development. He no longer thought of Tradition as something static, secretive and present from the beginning in explicit form, only made known by the ecumenical councils. Rather, Tradition was now regarded as having life in itself. Newman was therefore approaching the view of Tradition outlined in the *Essay on Development*, having rejected the notion that there was once an age of 'pristine' Christianity. He had jettisoned his belief in the *Disciplina Arcani*.

The issue of development was to occupy Newman still further during the coming years. During the period 1839-45 he was to move, as a result of his study of development and various blows received within the Church of England,[63] from a position of supreme confidence in himself and his Anglican theological opinions, to a position where he questioned them seriously enough to relinquish them, and to seek admittance into the Catholic Church. The events of this period are well known, and so will not be repeated here, except where necessary to illustrate a point.[64]

Newman's doctrinal difficulties, during this period, resulted from his study of the Fathers. The more he read, the more he became convinced that the Church of England was in schism from the Catholic Church, and that Wiseman's comparison, in 1839,[65] of the Church of England with the Donatists was accurate. That he was working on the idea of doctrinal development during this period is evident from the last of the *University Sermons* which he preached in 1843 on 'The Theory of Developments in Religious Doctrine'. Taken together with the letter to Francis, the ideas contained therein form the groundwork for the *Essay on Development*.

UNIVERSITY SERMON XV

The sermon was preached on the theme of 'But Mary kept all these things, and pondered them in her heart' (Lk. 2:19):

> Thus St Mary is our pattern of Faith, both in the reception and the study of Divine Truth. She does not think it enough to accept, she dwells upon it; not enough to possess, she uses it; not enough to assent, she develops it; not enough to submit the Reason, she reasons upon it; not indeed reasoning first, and believing afterwards... yet first believing without reasoning, next from love and reverence, reasoning after believing.... [Thus] at the marriage-feast in Cana, her faith anticipated His first miracle, and she said to the servants, 'Whatsoever He saith unto you, do it.'[66]

The point that is being made here is that, like Mary, the Church must reflect upon that faith which has been entrusted to her. If she does this development occurs. Dogma is therefore seen in a more positive light than it was in 1833 and 1840, if only because Newman now regarded doctrinal development as a sign of life in the Church:

> Here, too, is the badge of heresy; its dogmas are unfruitful; it has no theology; so far forth as it is a heresy, it has none. Deduct its remnant of Catholic theology, and what remains? Polemics, explanations, protests. It turns to Biblical Criticism, or to the Evidences of

Religion, for want of a province. Its formulae end in themselves, without development, because they are words; they are barren, because they are dead. If they had life, they would increase and multiply, or, if they do live and bear fruit, it is but as 'sin, when it is finished, bringeth forth death'. It develops into dissolution; but it creates nothing, it tends to no system, its resultant dogma is but the denial of all dogmas, any theology, under the Gospel. No wonder it denies what it cannot attain.[67]

But formal doctrinal statements are necessary

> only because the human mind cannot reflect upon that idea [that they are designed to express] except piecemeal.... And in matter of fact these expressions are never equivalent to it; ... thus the Catholic dogmas are, after all, but symbols of a Divine fact, which, far from being compassed by those very propositions, would not be exhausted, nor fathomed, by a thousand.[68]

So, as in 1833, Newman still regarded human language as inadequate to express the divine mysteries, but that being said, he did not see a contradiction between a personal faith in Christ and a dogmatic creed. The latter gives expression and substance to the former, and is therefore necessary for realising Revelation:

> Theological dogmas are propositions expressive of the judgements which the mind forms, or the impressions which it receives, of Revealed Truth. Revelation sets before it certain supernatural facts and actions, beings and principles; these make a certain impression or image upon it; and this impression spontaneously, or even necessarily, becomes the subject of reflection on the part of the mind itself, which proceeds to investigate it, and to draw it forth in successive and distinct sentences.[69]

This raises the question whether Newman regarded propositions as having any role in God's communication, to man, of Revealed Truth. It is not clear from the above passage whether 'principles' are something which are to be regarded as pre-linguistic, or whether they are propositions.[70] This ambiguity[71] is, however, resolved in the sermon, during a discussion of the 'idea' of Christianity; that idea being the sum total of God's self-Revelation:[72]

> Particular propositions, then, which are used to express portions of the great idea vouchsafed to us, can never really be confused with the idea itself, which all such propositions taken together can but reach, and cannot exceed ... That idea is not enlarged, if propositions are added, nor impaired if they are withdrawn: if they are added, this is with a view of conveying that one integral view, not

> of amplifying it. That view does not depend on such propositions: it
> does not consist in them; they are but specimens and indications of
> it. And they may be multiplied without limit. *They are necessary, but
> not needful to it,* [my italics], being but portions or aspects of that
> previous impression which has at length come under the cognisance
> of Reason and the terminology of science. One thing alone has to be
> impressed on us by Scripture, the Catholic idea, and in it they are all
> included. To object, then, to the number of propositions, upon which
> an anathema is placed, is altogether to mistake their use; for their
> multiplication is not intended to enforce many things, but to express
> one, — to form within us that one impression concerning Almighty
> God.[73]

It would, therefore, appear that for Newman Revelation is in the first
instance purely personal. It is God's self-communication to man,
person to person, through the senses,[74] without means of language.
That being said, it is then perfectly legitimate, indeed necessary, to
express this Revelation in propositional form.

Vital to the understanding of this process is the distinction between
implicit and explicit knowledge. This distinction enabled Newman to
regard explicit, formal doctrinal statements as being already present in
Revelation (which was not given in a credal form), because they were
implicit in it. Thus, when a doctrine was defined, it was not an
addition to the faith. Rather, it was the making explicit of what was
already implicit. This distinction was discussed in an earlier University
Sermon on 'Implicit and Explicit Reason'[75] and was also present
(though perhaps not in so highly developed a fashion) in *Arians*:[76]

> Yet it does not seem too much to affirm, that copious as (doctrine)
> may be in theological terms, yet hardly one can be pointed out which
> is not found or strictly implied in the New Testament itself.[77]

In the sermon Newman commented:

> Now, it is important to insist on this circumstance, because it
> suggests the reality and permanence of inward knowledge, as distinct
> from inward confession. The absence, or partial absence, or
> incompleteness of dogmatic statements is not proof of the absence of
> impressions or implicit judgements, in the mind of the Church. Even
> centuries might pass without the formal expression of a truth, which
> had been all along the secret life of millions of faithful souls.[78]

In summary, then, the Church, like Mary, is to reflect on the faith
entrusted to her. This faith did not come in the form of credal
statements, but was given at a deeper level than that at which it came
to be articulated. As time passed, the idea of Christianity developed,

and that which was implicit in it was made explicit. Formal statements of doctrine were necessary for this realisation to take place, but they are in themselves an inadequate means of expressing the divine mysteries. Obviously this process was to be guided by Divine Providence.

Taken together with the letters to Francis, it can be remarked that, for Newman, the ecumenical councils of the Early Church played a decisive role in the formation of doctrine, authoritatively defining the creeds. In addition, Tradition was now regarded as a dynamic, organic reality — the process by which that which was implicit in Revelation was made explicit. He had also softened his position with regard to doctrine. It was now thought of as something more than an unfortunate necessity, but nevertheless he did not regard it as indispensable for personal faith (as he did in the *Grammar of Assent*),[79] which was his mature view. One can still detect traces of the idea in *Arians*, that although the believer cannot worship Christ without knowing something of his divinity, it was unfortunate that the Church in the nineteenth century could not retain the 'peculiar privilege' of the Early Church, which rested in the simplest kind of proclamation of faith.[80]

Another important difference between this sermon and the *Essay on Development*, is that the operation of Tradition in the sermon appears to be limited to the Patristic Church. Notes in Newman's diaries from this period suggest that it was not until 1844-5 that he was fully convinced that the Catholic Church's so-called 'additions' to the faith were in fact true developments. This implies that in 1843 he still had some doubts as to whether legitimate developments could occur after the end of the Patristic Age. As such, he had not quite arrived at the conclusion of the *Essay* that 'to live is to change, and to be perfect is to have changed often'.[81]

The effect that this study was having on his state of mind is evident from the various, still unpublished and largely unconsidered,[82] dated entries in the appendices to his private diaries between 1843 and 1846. In these, he asked himself a series of questions as to which of the nineteenth-century Churches was to be considered one with the Early Church.

DIARY APPENDICES AND COPYBOOK ON DEVELOPMENT

On 17th March 1843 Newman wrote:

> Supposing the Catholic religion to be true, qu. whether some great judgement is and likely to have come upon the English for our dreadful suppression of it through three centuries by our national acts — If so, are not the misconceptions we form of it and the horror we have of it, only the expected conformably with the state of the case?[83]

His thought had progressed further along such lines by the following
month:

> Is not the RC system the nearest by far to the primitive? Looking at
> the saints in all ages as one company [,] is not the Roman Church
> decidedly on their side, not on the other, ours, as a Church, on the
> other, and on theirs? — Are we not *in loco haereticorum?* is there
> any doubt what the saints whom we admire would think of our
> Church? Is there much doubt that they would recommend us to
> do?[84]

From these questions, it can be seen that Newman has changed his
mind about the branch theory since he wrote to Francis in November
1840. To him, it appeared that it was only the Roman Catholic Church
that may be considered one with the Church of the Patristic Age, the
Anglican Church being in the position of the Donatists, Monophysites
and Semi-Arians. 'The theory of the *Via Media* was absolutely
pulverised'.[85]

Newman still clung on to the Church of England, however, since he
needed to satisfy himself that Catholic doctrines, such as the invocation
of saints, were true developments and not corruptions of the Gospels.
He broached this issue in his diary on 7th October 1843:

> If the developed doctrine of the Holy Trinity is universally received,
> must be true, else the whole Church has fallen into the most awful
> idolatry, for the same reason may not the doctrine of saint worship
> wh[ich] is universal, be considered religious, lest the same conclus-
> ion follow?[86]

It is apparent from the way in which this question was framed that
Newman was now in the process of trying to persuade himself
intellectually of the truth which he had, on one level, already received,
viz. that 'The Church of Rome will be found right after all'.[87] This
he approached from the direction of development. As for the Church
of England:

> It would be curious to trace the Via Media in antiquity ... what has
> been called the extreme view is the *right* one e.g. Dionysius against
> Eusebius and the Semi-Arians, Cyril against Theodore — Leo against
> the Monophysites.[88]

This statement echoes Newman's feelings of 1839 (as recounted in the
Apologia) when, having seen the Monophysite in the mirror,[89] he
came to the conclusion that

> The Church of the *Via Media* was in the position of the oriental communion, Rome was where she now is; and the Protestants were the Eutychians.[90]

In other words, the Church of England was in schism. It was not, in Newman's view, one with the Patristic Church. He did not regard her doctrines as a true development of primitive doctrines. Rather, he saw the Church of England as occupying the same ground in the nineteenth century that had been occupied by schismatical and heretical bodies in the patristic Age:

> The Fathers say 'If a body has certain irregularities in its first foundation, certain evils will follow ... heresy, schism etc. Now this is almost prophetic as regards us ...[91]

By 4th May Newman had arrived at the point where:

> 1. I am more sure that we are in schism than that the Creed of Pope Pius is not a development from primitive doctrine. 2. I am far more certain that we have taken from the faith, than that Rome has added to it. On the other side, 1. There is more responsibility in changing to a new communion than remaining where you are placed. 2. One ought to have some clear proof to outweigh the misery it would occasion to others. 3. One ought not to go by private judgement but with others.[92]

Here it is quite clear that Newman had now come to the conclusion that it was only the Catholic Church that was one with the Church of the Patristic Age, and that she alone had preserved the faith in its purity and entirety. He was, however, still held back from seeking reception into her fold by persistent doubts. Perhaps the state of his mind at this juncture can be judged from two comments he made in his diary after his conversion to Catholicism. In June 1846 he wrote:

> It is a want of *faith*, which makes men look at the adoration of the Host as idolatry — of course. To worship it is the natural obvious direct act of an actual faith.[93]

Then in July he added:

> The doctrine of honour to St Mary and the Saints brings out a class of feelings unknown to Protestants. Hence the difficulty of talking to them about it ... They say it is red or yellow, not knowing the existence of blue.[94]

It could be that he was held back from seeking admittance into the Catholic Church by difficulties with certain Catholic doctrines brought about by not sharing in what he termed "the Catholic *ethos*".[95] By 1841 he was of the opinion that the Anglican Church was in schism, but it nevertheless took another four years for him to seek reception into the Catholic Church. Why the delay? It is perhaps too simplistic to speak first of an emotional and then an intellectual conversion, but both elements certainly played a role in his thoughts. At the risk of constructing too crude an anthropology, it appears fair to say that Newman's conversion was in the first instance experimental: he says he felt as if he had seen a ghost.[96] He then embarked upon a prolonged period of study to establish the intellectual validity of this experience. This he had done by May 1844. It appears, however, that his conversion was delayed by doubts. Given his understanding of *ethos*, in his letter of November 1840 to Francis, it could well be that in 1846, he was explaining in his diary, that his conversion did not take place in 1844, because a certain 'class of feelings' was still foreign to him. As such, although he was practically convinced of the truth of the Catholic claim by May 1844, there was still a certain difficulty. It would also seem that where he spoke of 'some clear proof', he was almost rejecting the force of antecedent probabilities, which he had championed in his letter to Francis. He was resisting the intellectual force of these probabilities because of the experiential difficulties, concerning certain Catholic doctrines, suggested above.[97]

In summary, then, Newman's views on the subject of development underwent a certain amount of change following the writing of his letters to Francis in 1840. He still accepted that the external differences between the Early Church and the Church of the nineteenth century were due to organic development, but he had come to the opinion that it was only the Catholic Church, and not others, that was one in 'principle and temper' with the Early Church. His study of the Fathers revealed to him that the Anglican Church was in a state of schism. Before seeking admittance into the Catholic Church, however, he had to establish to his own satisfaction that various Catholic practices were not corruptions of the Gospel, but were true developments. A summary of his conclusions is provided in the unpublished 'Copybook on Development', dated 7th March 1844.[98]

Developments are likely or necessary

1. from the natural *growth* of any idea

2. from the terms as admitting of development in Scripture and Antiquity

3. from the heretical attempts: Montanists, Novatianists, Tertullian and Origen

4. from the strange mixture of true and false eruditio [?] and consistence [?] in Tertullian, Origen, Hippolytus, etc

5. from the remarkable fact that heretical writing are absorbed and purified by the Church writers — Origen by Basil and Ambrose, Eusebius (Luke) by Ambrose, Tertullian by Cyprian and S Leo etc — heretics or heterodox (e.g. *in Praxeam*) are raw material

6. from the inconsistencies in words and evident in extremity [?] of the greatest writers on certain subjects e.g. Athan, about our Lord's ignorance.[99]

This development, however, convinced Newman that the Church of England was

> *In loco haereticorum*: Put aside doctrine — since it is not clearly found in Scripture. Take what is *plain* in Scripture, the duties, acts, works, fruits of a Christian as given in the N.T. *When* are they fulfilled? Where *can* they be fulfilled? Are they, can they, be fulfilled among us?[100]

Newman no longer regarded Tradition as limited to the Patristic Age. Growth was seen to be the only evidence of life, and so his answer to the last question had to be 'No'. He had come to the conclusion that:

> St. Augustine's position towards the *ancient sects* of the Donatists[101] [was the same as] the Church of Rome's to us ... [He was] more certain that the E[nglish] Ch[urch] is in schism, than that the Roman doctrines are not developments ... [He believed that there was] enough evidence to convince those who believe in the probability of the R.C. being right [and that] the present RC system is by far the nearest of any existing system to the Primitive.[102]

He had now satisfied himself that certain 'Roman' doctrines were not a bar to his reception into the Catholic Church. Regarding Purgatory, for example:

> Is not this doctrine, also, the vivid representation of the feelings and ideas which primitive principles involve? does any other system contain and secure those ideas and feelings?[103]

CONCLUSION

In conclusion, the following points can be made: development was a subject that had occupied Newman for many years, although before 1840 he was often found to be arguing against it. This means that it is misleading to think only of the chronology of the events that led up to his conversion as *Tract XC,* Development and then Rome. This is not to deny the effect of the *Tract XC* Affair, his study of Arianism and the Jerusalem Bishopric, the combined force of which certainly helped to push him from the Church of England. Rather it is suggested that, along with these events, Newman also felt a pull towards the Catholic Church, which was brought about by his contact with theories of the development of doctrine between 1833 and 1840. After all, he wrote to Francis before the 'three blows'. It was intellectual honesty, as well as disillusionment with the Church of England, that led to his conversion. As such, the chronology of his conversion may perhaps be seen as Development, *Tract XC,* Further Development, Rome. Furthermore, it is clear that his own thought on the subject of development underwent considerable change between 1833 and 1845. It would appear that the development in his thought parallels his description of the development of an idea in the *Essay on Development*, and that, as a consequence of this development, he came to see the Catholic Church as being one with the Church of the Patristic Age, thus leading him to seek admittance into her fold. Looking back with Newman, one can see how he was able to conclude:

> I *seem* to have many things which I did not consciously hold at the time, but which my present opinions show to be a germ, 'astonishing I saw this *so early*'.[104]

NOTES

1. A.N. Wilson (ed), *John Henry Newman: Prayers, Poems, Meditations* (SPCK: London, 1989), p. 32.
2. C.S. Dessain, *John Henry Newman* (OUP: Oxford, 1980), p. 81. Henceforth cited as Dessain. Cf. also I.T. Ker, *John Henry Newman: A Biography* (Clarendon Press: Oxford, 1988), p 49. Henceforth cited as Ker, *John Henry Newman*.
3. Cf. I.T. Ker, *Newman on Being a Christian* (University of Notre Dame Press: Notre Dame, 1990), pp. 21-9.
4. Edward Hawkins was at that time Vicar of St Mary's, the University Church. He was later to become Provost of Oriel, and, as is well known, came to disagree sharply with Newman over the role of tutors in the college. Newman was, however, 'deeply influenced by a University Sermon which Hawkins had preached on tradition, to the effect that the Bible "was never intended to teach doctrine, but only to prove it, and that, if we would learn

doctrine, we must have recourse to the formularies of the Church".' Ker, *John Henry Newman,* p. 22.

5. *The Arians of the Fourth Century* (Pickering: London, 1883), p. 50. Henceforth cited as *Arians.*

6. *Ibidem*, pp. 36-7.

7. For a discussion of Newman's use of 'economy' and 'reserve' see R.C. Selby, *The Principle of Reserve in the Writings of John Henry Cardinal Newman* (OUP: Oxford, 1975). In Bremond's view, it is so important that he 'would advise somebody to read Newman from one end to the other, for the sole purpose of extracting from his works, a literary and religious manual of "economy"'. H. Bremond, *The Mystery of Newman* (Williams & Norgate: London, 1907), p. 6. For a discussion of *Arians* and Newman's methodological approach see R. Williams, 'Newman's *Arians* and the Question of Method in Doctrinal History' in I.T. Ker & A.G. Hill (eds), *Newman After a Hundred Years* (Clarendon Press: Oxford, 1990), pp. 263-88 (henceforth Ker & Hill); and for 'A note on Newman's historical method' see the brief treatment by J.D. Holmes in J. Coulson and A.M. Allchin (eds), *The Rediscovery of Newman: An Oxford Symposium* (Sheed & Ward: London, 1967), pp. 97-9.

8. This is discussed by C. Gunton, 'Newman's Dialectic: Dogma and Person in the Seventy-Third Tract for the Times' in Ker & Hill, pp. 309-322.

9. *Essays Critical and Historical,* 2 vols (Pickering: London, 1871) I, pp. 30-101. Henceforth cited as *Essays.*

10. *Arians*, p. 145.

11. *Ibidem*, p. 146.

12. See Newman's attack three years later upon the view of Dr Hampden that 'the Articles of the Nicene and Athanasian Creeds are merely human opinions, scholastic, allowing of change, unwarrantable when imposed, and, in fact, the produce of a mistaken philosophy; and that the Apostles' Creed is defensible only when considered as a record of historical facts'. *Elucidations of Dr Hampden's Theological Statements* (Baxter: Oxford, 1836) pp. 5-6; and see also 41, 46-7.

13. *Arians*, pp. 55-6.

14. *Ibidem*, p. 146.

15. *Ibidem*, p. 148.

16. *Ibidem*, pp. 149-50.

17. J.H. Newman, *Apologia Pro Vita Sua: Being a History of His Religious Opinions*: edited and with an Introduction by M.J. Svaglic (Clarendon Press: Oxford, 1990), p. 106. Henceforth cited as *Apologia.*

18. Benjamin Harrison was a don at Christ Church and a contributor to the *Tracts for the Times.*

19. The Abbé Jean-Nicholas Jager, was a French Catholic priest, whom Harrison had met in Paris, and who wanted to hold a debate about the

theology of the *Tracts* in the *Univers* newspaper. Newman took over the correspondence after Harrison had contributed two letters.

20. *Apologia*, pp. 102-3.

21. L. Allen, *John Henry Newman and the Abbé Jager: A Controversy on Scripture and Tradition (1834-1836)* (OUP: Oxford, 1975), p. 37.

22. *Ibidem.*

23. *Ibidem*, p. 15.

24. *Ibidem*, p. 33.

25. Both in the correspondence with the Abbé, and in the *Lectures on the Prophetical Office,* Newman can be seen searching for the categories of, and distinctions between, different truths, such as are to be found in neo-scholasticism.

26. Allen, *op. cit.*, p. 16.

27. *Ibidem*, pp. 16-17.

28. *Ibidem*, p. 17.

29. *Ibidem.*

30. *Ibidem*, p. 175.

31. *The Via Media of the Anglican Church,* 2 vols (Longmans, Green & Co: London, 1891), I, pp. 19-20. Henceforth cited as *VM*.

32. Allen, *op. cit.*, pp. 19-20.

33. *Ibidem*, p. 103.

34. *Apologia,* p. 103-5.

35. Allen, *op. cit.*, p. 20.

36. *Ibidem*, p. 12.

37. Along with Robert Williams, who was also a former pupil of Newman, Wood worked on an English translation of the Roman Breviary in 1837-8. Plans to publish it, however, came to nothing, when it encountered strong opposition from fellow-Tractarians. Ker, *John Henry Newman*, pp. 166-7.

38. As it is well known, Manning became Archdeacon of Chichester in 1841, before becoming a Catholic ten years later. In 1865, he succeeded Nicholas Wiseman as Archbishop of Westminster, in which capacity he exerted considerable influence at the First Vatican Council (1869-70). In 1875 Pius IX raised him to the cardinalate. For an account of Manning's life see E. S. Purcell's two-volume, *Life of Cardinal Manning, Archbishop of Westminster,* 2 vols. (Macmillan & Co: London, 1896). Purcell does, however, present a one-sided and inaccurate view of Manning at times. This, along with other works about Manning, is reviewed in D. Newsome's recently published, *The Convert Cardinals: John Henry Newman and Henry Edward Manning* (Murray: London, 1993), pp. 7-12.

39. J. Pereiro, 'S. F. Wood and an Early Theory of Development in the Oxford Movement' in *Recusant History,* Vol. 20, no. 4, October 1991, pp. 528-32.

40. *Ibidem*, p. 550.

41. Newman's former disciple, Mark Pattison, was also attracted to the concept of development. Cf. D. Nimmo, 'Towards and Away from Newman's Theory of Doctrinal Development: Pointers from Mark Pattison in 1838 and 1846' in the *Journal of Theological Studies*, vol. 29, 1978, pp. 160-2.

42. Letter to Francis, 22.10.1840. (Birmingham Oratory Archives). I am grateful to Mr Gerard Tracey, Archivist at the Birmingham Oratory, for bringing to my attention the archival material upon which I draw in this chapter, and which is identified in the notes with the initials BOA.

43. *Ibidem*.

44. *Ibidem*.

45. *Ibidem*.

46. *Ibidem*.

47. *Ibidem*.

48. Letter to Francis, 10.11.1840. (BOA).

49. *Ibidem*.

50. The first of Newman's examples is as follows: 'Supposing I were in some inferior command in a battle, and from the smoke and noise could not make out my commanding officer's signals, and could not act for the best, according to my best knowledge of what he was intending and what he was likely to intend, would this be to admit the principle that every one might fight, as he pleased, or by himself?'. *Ibidem*.

51. *Ibidem*.

52. *VM*, I, pp. 128-85.

53. Letter to Francis, 10.11.1840. (BOA).

54. *Ibidem*.

55. Richard Whately was a former Fellow of Oriel, who was, from 1825-31, Principal of Alban Hall, a position he relinquished upon his appointment to the Archbishopric of Dublin. When Newman first arrived in the Oriel Common Room in 1822, Whately was given the task of drawing the young Newman out of his shell. During this period Newman assisted Whately in research for his *Elements of Logic. John Henry Newman's Autobiographical Writings,* ed H. Tristram (Sheed & Ward: London, 1956), pp. 66-7.

56. Isaac Taylor, a convert to Anglicanism from non-conformity, is best known for his *Natural History of Enthusiasm* (1829). Cf P. Toon, *Evangelical Theology 1833-1856: A Response to Tractarianism* (Marshall, Morgan & Scott: London, 1979), p. 30.

57. Letter to Francis, 10.11.1840.

58. *An Essay on the Development of Christian Doctrine* (James Toovey: London, 1845), pp. 158-9. Henceforth cited as *Development* (1845). 'In this, Newman was also reversing his view on the seventeenth-century difference between the French Jesuit Petavius and the Anglican George Bull: Petavius had described, Bull had generally denied, a lack of doctrinal uniformity before

the Council of Nicaea'. S.W. Gilley, *Newman and His Age* (DLT: London, 1990), p. 230. Henceforth cited as Gilley.

59. J. H. Newman, 'Palmer's Treatise on the Church of Christ' in *The British Critic*, no. 24, October 1838, pp. 347-72. Re-printed in *Essays*, I, pp. 143-79.

60. Newman's firm belief in the importance of antecedent probability is also illustrated in a letter of 1853: 'Again, I stand by my (Oxford) University Discourses... and am almost a zealot for their substantial truth — and if I have brought out one truth in anything I have written, I consider it to be the *importance of antecedent probability* in conversion. It is how you convert factory girls as well as philosophers'. *The Letter and Diaries of John Henry Newman* Vols XI-XXXI eds C.S. Dessain, E.E. Kelly, T. Gornall (London 1961-72; Oxford 1973-7); Vols I-VI eds I.T. Ker, T. Gornall, G. Tracey (Oxford, 1978-84), XV p. 381. Henceforth cited *L & D*.

61. Letter to Francis, 22.10.1840. (BOA).

62. This method is summarised in a letter to W.E. Gladstone on 9 January 1868, in which Newman wrote: 'Next, passing from antecedent probabilities to history...'. L & D XXIV, p. 231-6.

63. An account of these can be found in Ker, *John Henry Newman*, pp.231-6.

64. Newman's own account of these years is to be found in the *Apologia*, pp. 90-213. See also Ker, *John Henry Newman*, pp. 158-315; esp. pp. 231-6.

65. The comparison was in an article in the *Dublin Review* VII (August 1839), entitled 'The Anglican Claim of Apostolic Succession'. In this, Wiseman 'employed Newman's favourite device of paralleling past and present by comparing the Anglican with the Donatist schismatics in Africa in the fourth century'. Gilley, p. 183.

66. *University Sermons: Fifteen Sermons Preached before the University of Oxford 1826-43*. Introductions by D.M. MacKinnon and J.D. Holmes (SPCK: London, 1970), p. 313. Henceforth cited as *US*.

67. *Ibidem*, p. 318.

68. *Ibidem*, pp. 331-2.

69. *Ibidem*, p. 320.

70. For a discussion of the relationship between the personal and the propositional in Newman's thought, see Ker, *Newman on Being a Christian*, pp. 21-7.

71. In his 'Introduction' to the *University Sermons*, D. M. MacKinnon notes 'Newman's own informality and untidiness, interrupted by passages of sharp and rigorous argument... One is aware of this as soon as one tries to identify Newman's views concerning the relations between faith and reason; nothing but the work as a whole is enough to show the reader what those views were'; pp. 10-11.

72. *US*, p. 316.

73. *Ibidem*, pp. 331 & 336.

74. *Ibidem*, p. 333.

75. *Ibidem*, pp. 251-77.

76. Ker, *John Henry Newman*, p. 49; and Williams, *op. cit.*, p. 263.

77. *Arians*, p. 179.

78. *US*, pp. 323.

79. *An Essay in Aid of a Grammar of Assent,* edited and with an Introduction by I. T. Ker (Clarendon Press: Oxford, 1985), pp. 82-3.

80. *US*, pp. 82-3.

81. *Development* (1845), p. 39.

82. Some of the entries are referred to briefly by O. Chadwick, *From Bossuet to Newman: The Idea of Doctrinal Development* (CUP: Cambridge, 1957), pp. 152 & 234.

83. Dated entry in appendix to personal diary, 17.03.1843. (BOA).

84. *Ibidem*, 07.04.1843.

85. *Apologia*, p.111.

86. Appendix, 07.10.1843. (BOA).

87. *Apologia*, p. 111.

88. Appendix, 25.01.1844. (BOA).

89. *Apologia*, p. 108.

90. *Ibidem*.

91. Appendix, 17.02.1844. (BOA).

92. *Ibidem*, 04.05.1844.

93. *Ibidem*, June, 1846.

94. *Ibidem*, July, 1846.

95. 'Ethos' is defined in *The Concise Oxford Dictionary of Current English* as: 'Characteristic spirit and beliefs of community, people, system, literary work, or person'. Such a definition would appear to cohere with Newman's use of the term.

96. *Apologia*, p. 111.

97. It might be added to this, that it is likely that there were many changes of mind and swings of mood during the period that led up to his reception into the Catholic Church and that trying to describe these (and the reasons for them) accurately must be nearly impossible. Bearing in mind Newman's maxim that 'the whole man moves', I have tried to avoid creating a sharp distinction between emotion and intellect, and the use of the word 'experiential' is intended to express the complex nature of the relationship between the two.

98. Although the 'Copybook on Development' has remained unpublished, Chadwick does make some use of it in *From Bossuet to Newman*, pp. 129, 139 & 232, including some very limited quotation. It is also referred to once by S. Thomas, *Newman and Heresy: The Anglican Years* (CUP: Cambridge, 1991), p. 231.

99. Copybook. (BOA).

100. *Ibidem*.

101. St Augustine regarded the Donatists, who had separated themselves from the Catholic Church on a point of discipline (they were doctrinally orthodox, but held strict views about sin and martyrdom) as schismatics. This was because they did not accept the teaching of the Universal Church, which is certain, hence Augustine's famous dictum which weighed so heavily with Newman, *securus judicat orbis terrarum*. Cf. J.N.D. Kelly, *Early Christian Doctrines* (A & C Black: London, 1985), pp. 409-17; W.H.C. Frend, *The Rise of Christianity* (DLT: London, 1986), pp. 488-92; 653-9; G.Barnes, *St Augustine of Hippo: Life and Controversies* (The Canterbury Press: Norwich, 1986), pp. 237-311.

102. Copybook. (BOA).

103. *Ibidem*.

104. *Ibidem*.

IV

NEWMAN AND EARLY
TRACTARIAN POLITICS

Peter B. Nockles

> There is now in France a High Church Party who are
> Republicans, and wish for universal suffrage, on the ground
> that in proportion as the franchise falls lower, the influence
> of the Church makes itself more felt.... Don't be surprised
> if one of these days ... [we turn] Radicals on similar
> grounds.[1]

Hurrell Froude's comment in May 1833 identifies the nascent Oxford
Movement with the movement associated with Lamennais in France,
in a repudiation of the civil as well as ecclesiastical *status quo*. Froude
believed that the Church in France as well as in England was op-
pressed by the State. Like Lamennais, Froude maintained that captivity
would cease if the Church's power basis was widened. The young
James Mozley in 1833 referred to the Oxford divines as 'the Democratical High Church school', and considered that Froude had imported
his notions of popular power from France.[2] In a letter to Matthew
Arnold in 1871, Newman confirmed the impact on Froude of Lamennais's notion that the Church must embrace democratic ideas. 'It was',
he commented, 'one of Hurrell Froude's main views that the Church
must alter her position in the political world — and, when he heard of
la Mennais, he took up his views with great eagerness'.
  Both Newman and Lamennais were inspiring and approximately
contemporaneous leaders of great religious movements. Both had
enthusiastic followers, Tractarians and Mennaisians respectively. The
parallel between Lamennais' call to the French clergy in 1829 to exert
'the liberty of your ministry' and Newman's message to the Anglican
clergy in *Tract 1* in 1833, 'Magnify your office', is clear enough.
Lamennais demanded a free Church in a free State, and the logic of
Tractarian anti-Erastianism pointed in the same direction. Christopher
Dawson and others have stressed Froude's knowledge of Lammenais's
writings and the kinship between the two.[4] Professor J.R. Griffin has

argued that having imbibed Lamennais' vision, Froude drew the early Tractarians into a position of political as well as ecclesiastical radicalism.[5] Professor Marvin O'Connell, however, cautions against pressing the links between the ideas of Froude and Lamennais too far.[6] I aim to build on O'Connell's reappraisal of Tractarian politics. I will argue that far from countenancing political radicalism, the Oxford Movement, at least in its early phase, entailed a positive enhancement of the Tory political inheritance of an older High Church tradition, although constitutional realities gradually forced the Tractarians to modify their stance.

According to James Mozley, Froude himself did not exactly know what he thought of 'these notions he has imported from France ... and he says, moreover, that there is no necessity for us in this country to form any judgment upon them'.[7] Moreover, apart from Froude, Lamennais had limited influence on Tractarian political thought. The authors of the *Tracts for the Times* remained more wedded to the spirit of the old political order than did the author of *L'Avenir*. Newman's diagnosis of the Church's thralldom to the State was similar to that of Lamennais, but his solution was not. Lamennais' ultimate error, in Newman's eyes, was his failure 'to recognize, nay to contemplate the idea, that rebellion is a sin'.[8] In fact, there was a close French parallel with Tractarian political attitudes, but it was between Newman and the Legitimist writers, de Maistre and Bonald, rather than between Newman and Lamennais.

The High Church religious connotations of 'Toryism' were recognised from an early date. 'High Church' and 'Tory' were almost synonymous terms during the reign of Queen Anne.[9] In his *Dictionary* (1755), Samuel Johnson defined a 'Tory' as 'one who adheres to the ancient constitution of the State, and the apostolic hierarchy of the Church of England'.[10] Jacobitism, which coloured early eighteenth-century Toryism, no longer represented a viable political grouping after the 1750s and 'Tory' ceases to be a precise descriptive label from between about 1760 and 1812.[11] Recent scholarship, however, points to the continuity of a set of 'Throne and Altar' values which survived the Stuart-Brunswick conflict. According to Jonathan Clark in his influential *English Society*, these values which he characterises as Anglican 'orthodox political theology', continued to underpin the English *ancien régime* throughout the eighteenth century to an extent hitherto unrecognised by secular historians.[12] Moreover, a non-Erastian Caroline ideal of Church and State that had been enunciated by Richard Hooker also characterised Hanoverian Anglicanism to a degree until recently underestimated.

Nevertheless, there was a shift in the mode and expression of the High Church Tory tradition in Anglicanism. In the three decades prior to the Oxford Movement, High Churchmen became the strongest opponents of Rome, linking theological objections to various Catholic beliefs and practices with an exaltation of the Royal Supremacy and attacks on divided allegiance.[13] From having been identified with closet Jacobitism as late as the 1750s, Anglican High Churchmanship by the 1820s had became identified with a robust defence of the Protestant Constitution and the House of Brunswick. Anti-Catholicism became the defining principle of what became known as Ultra-Toryism.[14]

Traditional Anglican political theology, misleadingly described by Griffin as 'Tory Erastianism',[15] survived the constitutional crisis of 1828-32 and was restated and only gradually modified by the early Tractarians in a new political context. Tractarian populism was subservient to Tractarian patristicism. It was not only with the ecclesiastical weapon of a call to apostolicity that the Tractarians challenged the Erastian threat to the Church of England in 1833; it was also with the political weapon of a call to monarchical authority, passive obedience and non-resistance. The two elements were not in tension. Tractarian anti-Erastianism entailed a repudiation not of the role of the State *per se* in matters ecclesiastical, but true to the Caroline model, repudiated only a secular or infidel and indifferent State enslaving the Church.

The early *Tracts for the Times* stressed 'apostolical descent' and exalted priestly and episcopal authority against the intrusion of the State. Yet the purely political origins of the rise of the Oxford Movement are too often overlooked.

Tractarianism represented a revolt of Oxford Toryism as well as an assertion of ecclesiastical independence against the reformist measures which the Grey ministry brought into Parliament in the early 1830s. Dean Stanley offended Anglo-Catholics when he made this point, but most historians taking their cue from Tractarian historiography regard the Movement as having been unconcerned with constitutional and political questions.[16] Pusey encouraged this misconception. When William Molesworth in 1864 asked Pusey for information on the political background to the Oxford Movement, he was dismayed that such a question should even be posed. Pusey shared the view expressed by his Tractarian friend, William Copeland, 'that the political element, the Reform Bill, had not any effect in producing the *Tracts for the Times*'.[17] Copeland maintained that Tractarianism had not been a response to the political crisis of the early 1830s. He could not 'imagine how the two subjects could be brought into any intelligible relation to each other'.[18] Later writers have seen a dichotomy between politics and theology in the Oxford Movement. Edward Norman has emphasised Newman's relative lack of concern for purely political questions. Holding that the sickness of human society was spiritual,

Newman was sceptical of political solutions that neglected a transcendent dimension.[19] But it is not true that the Tractarians in time retreated from the political sphere to the innermost sanctuary of religion'. John Rowlands has shown how Tractarian political thought was enshrined in the sermons and meditations of the Movement's leaders, and was thus more integral to Tractarian theology than is usually recognized.[20] For the early Tractarian Newman, the institutions of Church, State and University were real bulwarks of true religion against the forces of secularity; only gradually did he lose faith in them. Newman stressed the link between apostolicity and Toryism when he objected to the proposed introduction of modern history into Oxford's curriculum in the mid-1830s. As he told Charles Anderson in 1836, the difficulty as to modern history was 'the introduction of modern politics. The present school of philosophers are disgusted with our teaching religion on a positive basis — would they be better pleased if we taught Toryism as well? and it is quite certain that, if we taught the history of the last three centuries, we should interpret it in our own way'.[21]

At the root of Tractarian attitudes to politics, however, was what Rowlands calls an 'otherworldliness', which contrasted with the mentality of many contemporary Tory High Churchmen. Newman's religious individualism led him to foresee and brand as 'apostasy' our modern preoccupation with politics. Lamennais himself complained that the Tractarians treated political questions too theologically,[22] while Newman regarded Lamennais' vision as too political and naturalistic in texture. Certainly party politics was eschewed. Newman maintained: 'We have nothing to hope or fear from Whig or Conservative governments. We must trust upon our own ethos'.[23] Tractarian theological views increasingly cut across the political spectrum, with the liberal Conservative Roundell Palmer and even the Radical Whig politician Sir William Page Wood coming under the Movement's influence. The Toryism of the early Tractarians was primarily a moral Toryism that was distinct from the more political Ultra-Toryism espoused by Lord Eldon, the pillar of the pre-Reform Protestant constitution in Church and State. It also differed from what Copeland called 'the semi-infidel Conservatism of many of the maintainers of our so-called happy establishment'.[24]

It was a political episode, Oxford University's repudiation of Peel in 1829 for his *volte-face* in supporting Catholic Emancipation, that marks more accurately the true origin of the Oxford Movement than Keble's 1833 Assize Sermon condemning the suppression of the Irish bishoprics. For it was the campaign against Peel which first brought together the future Tractarian constellation on the basis of political discontent underpinned by moral principle. The campaign drew on the

'Church and King' traditions of the University, with Newman appealing to Romantic sensibility as well as religious principle in conjuring up potent images of historic Tory Oxford as a 'place set apart to witness to the nation'. Thus, Newman recalled that as he walked along 'the old road' from Oxford to visit his mother in the autumn of 1829, 'King Charles and his Bishop [Laud] seemed to rise before us'.[25] The anti-Peel lobby essentially represented the reassertion of an older anti-establishment tradition in Toryism that had been in abeyance since the accession of George III in 1760. For Newman, the defeat of Peel, 'proved the independence of the Church and of Oxford. So rarely is either of the two in opposition to Government, that not once in fifty years can independent principle be shown'.[26] Since the 1770s, Oxford had been a pillar of the establishment in the broadest sense. The defeat of the Home Secretary and Leader of the Commons represented a reversion to the University's eighteenth-century traditions of independence and opposition, in which a strong party within the University insisted upon Oxford's detachment from the political nation. Like Oxford Jacobitism in an earlier period, the Tractarian Movement for many years was to depend for its life-blood on the non-resident Tory country clergy and gentry represented in the University's Convocation. It was the Peel election which inaugurated the anti-liberal alliance on which early support for the Movement in the University rested. Newman invested the Peel election, in itself a merely political contest, with the character of an almost apocalyptic struggle against the forces of darkness. Oxford's orthodox Anglican consensus broke down. A moderate 'liberalism', which had been part of the earlier influence of Oriel *Noetics* such as Whately on Newman, was now branded as one of the satanic forces imperilling Church and University.[27]

Martin Svaglic has maintained that 'Newman's early political thought was a blend of the conservatism of Burke, which dominated Oxford, with the Nonjuring principle taught in the Anglican Homily on Wilful Disobedience (1569)'.[28] In the note on 'Liberalism' in the appendix to his *Apologia*, Newman included among the eighteen propositions that he had 'denounced and abjured', the tenets that 'the people were the legitimate source of power', and that 'it is lawful to rise in arms against legitimate princes. Therefore, e.g. the Puritans in the seventeenth century, and the French in the eighteenth, were justified in their Rebellion and Revolution respectively'.[29] In the face of the challenge of democratic ideas, Newman in 1833 was prepared to defend Church establishment as an instrument of the State. He even invoked a military analogy: the Church, Newman declared, was not only on the side of loyalty and civil order, but represented 'a standing army, insuring the obedience of the people to the Laws by weapons of persuasion'.[30]

The religious roots of Newman's politics were explicit. His Burkean scepticism about abstract political panaceas that overlooked original sin shaped his critique of Lamennais's ideas. Thus, he criticized Lamennais's belief in 'certain indefeasible rights of man, which certain forms of government encroach upon, and against which a rising is at any time justified', as flattering 'what we, in our English theology, should call the lawless and proud lusts of corrupt nature'. For Newman, Lamennais adopted the tempter's motto: 'ye shall be gods', so that he drew 'close to the democratical party of the day in that very point in which they most resemble antichrist'.[31] Newman's attitude here, like Froude's, was much closer to that of de Maistre and Bonald than to Lamennais.

Newman also assailed Benthamite Utilitarianism, with its Liberal theory of Education and glorification of natural and physical science as 'norms of truth'. The root of what Newman perceived as the false idols of Benthamism, which in his 'Letters on the Tamworth Room' he condemned Peel for taking up, lay in 'the cheerful, hopeful view of human nature, which prevails at all times (especially since the "Glorious" 1688!) Such was Paley's, Addison's, Blair's, and now Maltby's and the Liberals.[32] There was also continuity with the recent High Church past. In the 1790s, Bishop Horsley, Jones of Nayland and other Tory High Churchmen had indulged in prophetical interpretations of Scripture which branded Jacobinism as partaking of Antichrist. It was in similar vein in the 1830s, that Newman identified prevailing forces of rebellion, sedition and insubordination with that same spirit of Antichrist 'which scared the world some forty or fifty years ago'.[33] Newman wished for 'a rumpus', such as the Jacobin convulsion of the 1790s. This would 'shake people and make them talk sense.... Half the men one now meets would then turn Tories, e.g. just as your Tories at the beginning of the French Revolution'.[34] Froude agreed and also highlighted the link between the 1830s and 1790s. He gave his enthusiastic support in 1833 to a short-lived monthly, the *New Anti-Jacobin Review*, which advocated high Tory principles.[35] His private correspondence was full of diatribes against the evils of Whiggery as well as Protestant Latitudinarianism.[36]

With Keble, the link with the High Church political heritage was explicitly acknowledged. Keble's description of civil liberty as one of the promises of Satan was in the spirit and tone of Jones of Nayland's fulminations in the 1790s. Tory High Churchmen in earlier generations had equated Whig politics with Latitudinarian theology. Keble echoed this critique. As late as 1841, he devoted a review in the *British Critic* to castigating not only what he regarded as the lax theology but also the lax politics of the Whig school of the divine William Warburton in the preceding century. For Keble, Warburton's 'proud spirited' abstract notions of liberty were deemed to emanate from the same tainted source as his claims for religious enquiry and doctrinal latitude. It was a spirit which Keble detected and lamented even in some High Church and later Ultra-Tory eulogizers of the Protestant constitution and Revolution settlement. As Keble put it, 'in this overweening talk of human dignity and civil liberty, Warburton was but following the fashionable quasi-idolatry of that era, perhaps we might say, of our country, for a century and a half: a superstition not confined to any one school in theology'.[37] The Nonjurors had been different. They had invoked the true spirit of the primitive Christians first in passively obeying King James II and then at the Revolution of 1688 heroically refusing to compromise their principles and suffering for conscience's sake. For Keble as for Newman, an insistence on the duty of obedience and on the horror of rebellion as a form of blasphemy, stemmed from theological principle; it was but 'one inseparable branch of the universal doctrine of resignation and contentment'. Rebellion was akin to heresy; both were breaches of the natural moral order and forms of sacrilege.[38] As Pusey's biographer, Liddon, observed, it was Keble's 'moral temper' which 'led him to view reform and change with distrust: his faith in God's presence and guidance made all high-handed self-willed action on man's part appear more or less irreverent'.[39] Of course this message served political purposes. But Keble's political theology was not deterministically controlled by the dynamics of the *ancien régime*, but transcended the particular constitutional order under which it had been nurtured.

With Pusey, under the formative influence of Keble, an abandonment of a youthful political liberalism in favour of a 'moral Toryism', precisely coincided with his jettisoning of an early moderate Latitudinarianism and his emergence as one of the leaders of the Oxford Movement.[40] Given the popular historical assumption that Tractarianism was born out of its leaders having bade a farewell to Toryism, there was a paradox here, though one more apparent than real. A striking passage in a letter of Pusey to Edward Churton in 1865 has been cited to demonstrate Pusey's own 'farewell to Toryism'. Pusey told Churton, 'I could have been a Tory; but 1830 ended Toryism. I could not be a mere Conservative, i.e. I could not bind myself, or risk the future of the Church on the fidelity or wisdom of persons whose principle it is to keep what they think they can, and part with the rest'.[41] Yet the real implication of this passage was that Pusey actually regarded his theological *volte-face* into the vanguard of the Movement in the 1830s as a different expression of that deeper philosophical Toryism which the triumph of Reform appeared to have overthrown. Pusey rightly sensed that it was almost impossible in the wake of the events of 1828-33 again to translate such Tory principles into political reality. It was only when external political conditions had changed, and when the Tractarians regarded party politics as no longer a fitting forum for the pursuit of the High Church cause, that the tradition of orthodox political theology gained in Pusey a wholehearted convert.

The early Tractarians were also heirs of the orthodox political tradition in their espousal of a sacral or mystical theory of monarchy. Froude's reading in 1825 of Clarendon's influential *History of the Great Rebellion* (posthumously published in 1702) led him to 'adore King Charles and Bishop Laud'.[42] Keble shared such sentiments. His Toryism was infused by a romantic reverence for the House of Stuart and the potent symbol of Charles I as 'the Royal Martyr'. For Keble, the office of monarch represented the 'anointed of the Lord, a living type of the supreme dominion of Jesus Christ'.[43] Like pre-Tractarian High Churchmen, Keble's sacral royalism was reflected in a theological understanding of the Royal Supremacy. Against Whig ministerial interference in matters ecclesiastical in 1833-34, Keble sought part refuge in the ideal of the godly prince, as expressed in the text from Isaiah xlix, 23, 'And Kings shall be thy nursing fathers'. As the crown failed in the 1830s to protect the Church from secular encroachment, however, Keble's sense of the dangers of such reliance increased. Yet as with the Nonjurors with whom Keble identified, this did not diminish his faith in the old theory rightly interpreted. As he explained in 1839, for some the phrase 'nursing father', had 'acquired a trite and almost proverbial use ... in a very different sense: as though the Church were a helpless infant in the arms of some Defender of the Faith'. The true imagery of the text from Isaiah was of the Church as a mother with her children lodged in her arms; 'monarchs were essentially foster fathers and mothers'.[44]

Pusey acknowledged his conversion to Keble's brand of Toryism by his own changed attitude to the cult symbols of the royalist tradition in High Churchmanship. As he told Keble in November 1837,

> It was at Fairford, many years ago, when I was thoughtlessly or rather I must say confidently taking for granted that the Stuarts were rightly dethroned, that I heard for the first time a hint to the contrary from you; your seriousness was an intended reproof to my petulant expression about it, and so it stuck by me, although it was some time before it took root, and burst through all the clouds placed upon it'.[45]

Pusey's November 5th sermon in 1837, *Patience and Confidence the Strength of the Church*, symbolized by its dedication to Keble, was a fruit of the latter's influence.

The example of the Jacobite Nonjurors lurked as a potential reproach to the Tractarians. James Anthony Froude mockingly complained that his brother Hurrell and his Tractarian cohorts were guilty of a reconstruction of history which not only canonised and spoke of Charles I 'as the holy and blessed Martyr St Charles', but which led them 'to speak of James III instead of The Pretender'.[46] Pusey's repudiation of the 'Glorious Revolution' of 1688 led some to treat the sermon as an anachronistic piece of neo-Jacobite polemic, comparable to Sacheverell's notorious sermon in 1709, *In Peril among False Brethren*.[47] Just as Warburton and Samuel Parr had denounced the 'Jacobite' or 'Tory' politics of the sermons of Horne and Horsley in the 1760s and 1790s respectively, Thomas Arnold in January 1838 was complaining that Pusey had quoted texts 'which appear to advocate pure despotism'.[48] It was true that Pusey cited such authorities as Filmer, Overall's *Convocation Book*, Sanderson and Horsley in favour of the high doctrine of Non-Resistance,[49] but it was moral and religious lessons not party politics that concerned him. Those who accused Pusey of wishing to restore the Stuarts missed the point. As Pusey made clear, 'with regard to the special instance of the English Revolution of 1688, the question is now happily of practical importance only, as relates to men's feelings and principles, not to any political mode of acting'.[50] 'Non-resistance or passive obedience, in the sense to which they are generally limited' were 'but two sides of the same doctrine, — faith and humility in religion, obedience and submisssion in political allegiance'.[51] The contrast with Lamennais' approach, which Newman criticized as one of hurrying and thereby disrupting God's providential designs, could not have been greater. Far from contradicting the basic themes of the Oxford Movement as Griffin suggests,[52] the moral emphasis of Pusey's sermon was a genuine product of Tractarian spiritual teaching and *ethos*.

Keble's influence on Pusey was also exhibited by the latter's adherence to the notion of the monarch as 'nursing father' of the Church. In a sermon of 1838, Pusey stressed the rôle of the Crown in the Church's missionary endeavour, declaiming that the 'princes of this world shall reverence the Church, and shall find their glory and their joy in ministering to her necessities'.[53] Far from complaining of the monarch's interference, Pusey faulted the Crown's occasional failure to fulfil her duties of protection and succour. An instance of neglect was the failure in the previous century to introduce episcopacy to the North American colonies. The old theme of American Loyalists such as Jonathan Boucher that this failure had contributed to the revolt of the 1770s was reiterated by Pusey. But Pusey blamed ministerial advisers rather than the Crown itself.[54] Pusey criticized State interference in Church matters partly because it stifled the true rôle of the monarch as 'nursing father'. For Pusey, 'the blessed influence of George the Third' was a worthy model. But Pusey lamented, 'even he could not undo the evil which had been done by the ministers of the first two sovereigns of his line'.[55] Pusey complained that politicians had prostituted the episcopal office, but took comfort in the fact that 'their interference grew only with the weakness of the House of Hanover, and even Pitt could not carry his own Archbishop of Canterbury (Manners-Sutton)'.[56] Pusey maintained that 'this modern plan, wherein ministers are virtually the patrons, and the king a cypher, did not come in until the middle of the last century'. He hoped that 'with a struggle we might again recover the old system'.[57] Pusey's desire for a veto by the chapter and consecrating bishop in the case of bad episcopal appointments was not intended to restrict royal authority. He agreed with Keble that 'His Majesty's Prerogative would gain more than it would lose by taking from him the nominal appointment and giving the real one to that party who we know are always surest to stand by him'.[58]

Pusey remained committed to the ideal of sacral monarchy as a bulwark of the Church. In the Gorham crisis of 1850, it was an emphasis which divided him from other Tractarians and allied him with old High Churchmen with whom he had come to differ on sacramental teaching. In his *The Royal Supremacy not an Arbitrary Authority* (1850), Pusey appealed to that tradition of orthodox political theology which 'owned the ancient authority of the Crown' and which provided him with precedents of the role of early Christian Emperors in order to justify the principles which the Church had conceded'.[59]

Newman's royalist instincts were no less marked. He had a notorious horror of 'republicanism'[60] which was represented on the index of eighteen 'Liberal' propositions which he anathematised. Griffin is mistaken in his assertion that Newman ignored Anglican political liturgies as a Tractarian.[61] On the contrary, while he appears to have given up the November 5th service in 1834, Newman took up the traditional High Church cult of the Royal Martyr and like High Churchmen of an earlier generation scrupulously observed January 30th as the day of the Martyrdom.[62] Moreover, Newman shared the theoretical neo-Jacobitism of Froude and Keble. In contrast to the Ultra-Tory idolisers of the 1688 Constitution with whom he found himself in temporary alliance, by 1830 Newman had doubts as to 'whether we can consider our King as a proprietor of land in the old Tory theory'. Newman was convinced that 'the rightful heir was lost in the Revolution — then the nation took (usurped?) the property of the island (time has sanctioned their violence) and gave it to William and then to George on certain conditions, i.e that of being their chief magistrate. Has not the constitution since that time been essentially a republic?'.[63]

In spite of private misgivings over the legitimacy of the House of Brunswick, as with Keble and Pusey, Newman's royalist feelings found expression in a passionate appeal to the Crown to use her Supremacy to defend the Church against ministerial thraldom. When Bishop Phillpotts in a fighting speech in the House of Lords in June 1833 urged the Crown to veto Whig legislation by recourse to the Coronation Oath, thereby clashing with Lord Grey, Newman rallied to the former's side. After Newman's old mentor, Richard Whately, had defended Grey's interpretation of the Coronation Oath, Newman exploded, 'as to Whately and his evasions about the Coronation Oath, it is quite distressing to think about him'.[64] Newman still regarded the Royal Supremacy as a guarantor of the spiritual rights of the Church. Although William IV might not appear credible in the rôle of Christ's earthly Vicar, when Whig legislation threatened to infringe the Church's rights in 1833, it was natural for Newman to appeal to him as 'Defender of the Faith'. As Newman explained in a letter to the *British Magazine* in 1834

> If it be said that the Act of Settlement secures to the people certain liberties, I reply that the Coronation Oath has secured to the Church its liberties also to the utter annulment of all former precedents of tyranny — and that we stand by that oath as our law as well as our Sovereign's sanction and acknowledgment of it, and that any power in the State that innovates on the spirit of that oath tyrannises over us.[65]

When it became clear that William IV in 1833-34, unlike George III in 1801, was not prepared to stand by his oath in the way Tractarian leaders urged, Newman's disillusionment was patent. William IV's acquiescence in Peel's creation of the Ecclesiastical Commission in 1835 further deepened Newman's feeling that the Church was being betrayed by the Crown as well as by the Conservative party and that she would have to confide her trust elsewhere.[66] For Newman, William IV had proved as frail a reed for the Church to lean upon as the Bourbon monarch Charles X had proved in Lamennais' eyes.

Froude had never shared such illusions. His own devotion to the Royal Martyr had not been accompanied by any faith in a Royal Supremacy. His influence in lessening Newman's trust in the Supremacy was evident as early as the autumn of 1833, when Newman confided to his friend:

> It is most natural and right proper that the Monarchy and Aristocracy should be our secular instruments of influence — but if these powers

will not, lo! we turn to the people. The King has tied his own hands
— he has literally betrayed us ... Our first duty is the defence of the
Church. We have stood by Monarchy and Aristocracy till they have
refused to stand by themselves'.[67]

By 1837, Newman could sarcastically reflect that 'the gridiron of St
Laurence would be found a more effectual guarantee of Church
property than a Coronation Oath or an Act of Parliament'.[68] After all,
the fact that since 1707 the monarch presided as Head of a Presbyterian Kirk north of the Tweed represented a serious constitutional
anomaly and long-standing embarrassment for High Churchmen. By
1838 Manning was already alive to this anomaly. Manning denounced
the Ecclesiastical Commission as a surrender to Parliament of the
executive office of the episcopate. Parliament had become, in effect,
the Patriarch of the Church. But Manning conceded that the Act of
Union with Scotland had created an ominous precedent for the State
interference of the 1830s. For by consenting to make Presbyterianism
the State Religion in Scotland, Manning argued, the Church of England
had then allowed a new theory of Establishment to be substituted for
the principle of the Church.[69] In the wake of the Gorham Judgment in
1850, Manning, along with William Allies and William Dodsworth,
would conclude that the fatal act of subservience to the secular powers
had been made earlier still, being rooted in the Reformation Statutes
of the 1530s.

In the mid-1830s, Newman had to ask the question, which mattered
more, Monarchy or Church? As Jonathan Clark puts it, 'in 1688-9 the
political classes ultimately chose the second; in 1828-9 they reversed
that choice'.[70] Newman could not respect that reversal. Consequently,
he sought new 'secular instruments'. Yet, as he insisted to Froude,
'theoretically and historically, he remained a Tory'. It was only altered
external political circumstances that forced him to 'begin to be a
radical practically'.[71] Thus, he told Rose in 1836,

> Now suppose one had been born 30 years sooner, I think one should
> have kept quiet. But the times will not allow of this ... outward
> circumstances are changing ... we have a reason for being bolder ...
> men like Hooker, Andrewes, and Laud, acted in the system they
> found themselves. The single difference between their views and
> those I seem to follow is this — they had a divine right king — we,
> in matter of fact, have not.[72]

Robert Wilberforce was to make a similar point in 1854 in a work
marking his final abandonment of Tractarian Anglicanism for Roman
Catholicism. Wilberforce retained, even at this time, a certain nostalgia
for the Caroline ideal. He now believed that while the notion of the

monarch as Spiritual Governor was an innovation of the Reformation, yet in the seventeenth-century context it had retained a certain spiritual integrity. But Wilberforce insisted that in the nineteenth century when there was a parliamentary Sovereign with Parliament representing a divided nation, and with Presbyterianism established in Scotland, such a notion had lost all meaning. As Wilberforce put it, 'in the times of the Tudors and Stuarts, the Church seemed to come before the world as a living body, because the Royal Supremacy was alive and active; at present, the Church does nothing as a body, but leaves individuals to act as they will for themselves'.[73]

Froude helped undermine the basis of Newman's Toryism as a practical outlet for his ecclesiastical principles. But Newman's historical and emotional attachment to a Laudian monarchical and hierarchical ideal lingered on even into his later Tractarian years. This attachment was exemplified in 1840 by Newman's article on the 'Court of James I' in the *British Critic*. On reading the article, the Tractarian Charles Marriott confided to Newman, 'the very broad avowal of the Anglican notion of Royal Supremacy ... made me open my eyes an eighth of an inch wider than usual. But I think facts bear you out'.[74] Of course, there had been no stauncher Legitimist than Lamennais until his perception that the Church's interests had been sacrificed by the State led him to react against the politics of the *ancien régime*. Yet in spite of Newman's similar disillusionment with the Crown for failing to protect the Church from Whig encroachments, he refrained from following Lamennais into a repudiation of the 'Throne and Altar' principle. Although Newman felt the same outrage at the Church's subjection to State concerns, he actually criticised Lamennais for being too ready to forsake the House of Bourbon to whom the French clergy had returned in 1815. 'One might suppose', he complained, 'there were some old recollections of loyalty, or even vows of allegiance to attach them and to excuse their attachment to the sons of St Louis. Far from it; he [Lamennais] measures the unfortunate family only according to their power of advancing the interests of the Church; and considers they may be cast off without pity, if he does but succeed in proving that it is inexpedient to hold by them'.[75] In the spirit of traditional Tory Anglicanism, Newman regarded the challenge to the hereditary monarchical principle as an aspect of secularisation rather than as an assertion of ecclesiastical liberty. Newman's Tory and royalist sympathies acted as a brake in his drift towards Rome, even as his theological objections were overcome. In 1829, Catholic Emancipation had been gained partly by an appeal to abstract Whiggish principles of civil and political liberty which most of the Tory-minded future Tractarians had resolutely opposed. The apparent alliance of Roman Catholicism with the cause of Daniel O'Connell in Ireland and of the Whigs in England in the late 1830s disgusted Newman, as it also dismayed the Roman Catholic romantic and advocate of reunion, Ambrose Phillipps de Lisle. The antipathy was reciprocated.[76] As Sheridan Gilley has pointed out, the Ultramontane and O'Connellite editor of the *Tablet*, Frederick Lucas, who advocated that the Roman Catholic Church 'ally herself with the reforming and popular party in every nation', regarded the Tractarians as 'some of the most Hibernophobe High Tory members of the Anglican Church'.[77] On the other hand, if English Roman Catholics would break ranks with Whigs and Irish nationalists, Newman conceded that 'strong temptations will be placed in the way of individuals, already imbued with a tone of thought congenial to Rome, to join her communion'.[78] Certainly, Newman never found the political iconoclasm of some of the younger 'Romanising' adherents of the Movement such as W.G.Ward congenial. Wilfrid Ward later revealed the shock which his father caused when he declared at a dinner of Puseyites that Charles I had been rightly executed.[79] Newman's own comment about Ward on his joining the Movement in 1838 is a revealing mixture of spiritual empathy and political distaste: 'I cannot help liking him very much, in spite of his still professing himself a Radical in politics'.[80]

As Paul Misner, Sheridan Gilley and Rowlands have demonstrated, however, Newman's Toryism would be softened, and his passage towards Rome eased, by his rediscovery and reappropriation after 1840 of the 'Evangelical prophetical tradition, in which he had been educated'.[81] As 'the World' and its secular princes and powers began to assume the guise of Antichrist rather than Whiggery or Popery in Newman's always active eschatology, so his political Toryism was modified by an 'otherworldliness'.[82] This drew out of Newman that latent sense of the satanic significance of contemporary events which Sheridan Gilley has aptly described as the 'Protestant brimstone element' in his teaching about liberalism.[83] This element was not peculiar to Evangelical Protestantism but also characterized much Ultramontane Roman Catholicism in the wake of the French Revolution. Nonetheless, it represented in Newman one of several Evangelical traits that never left him. On the one hand, this trait had an anti-radical tendency, making it impossible for him to sympathize with a key theme in Lamennais's later teaching, the social regeneration of society as an end in itself. Yet, on the other hand, as Edward Norman argues, the same trait also had a radical tendency.[84] Newman's Anglican Toryism ultimately was undermined by his very detachment from worldly values and consequent view that all political ideas and institutions were unstable and transient.

The anti-establishment stance of the Tractarians increasingly qualified their authoritarian political attitudes. Froude's message was,

'Let us tell the truth and shame the devil; let us give up a national church, and have a real one'.[85] Establishment was an incubus and ought to be jettisoned; all 'secular' interference in the Church even by the Crown was an 'usurpation'. Froude's *Remarks on State Interference in Matters Spiritual* published in November 1833, in suggesting the possibility of the Church breaking its alliance with an Erastian State and appealing for popular support, echoed the radical line advocated in *L'Avenir*. Froude, however, sought to persuade rather than provoke Tory High Churchmen. In advocating that the Church face constitutional reality and adopt a new line of policy in relation to the State, Froude appealed to the very principles of Hooker's Church-State theory. It was only because Parliament was a lay synod of the Church, that Hooker justified himself in consenting to its interference in matters spiritual.[86] For Froude, the logic of the constitutional revolution of 1828-33 was that 'the *conditions* on which our predecessors consented to parliamentary interference in matters spiritual are *cancelled*'.[87] This enabled Froude to turn the tables on Tory High Churchmen with the retort, 'Open your eyes to the fearful change which has been so noiselessly effected; and acknowledge that *by standing still you become a party to revolution*'.[88]

Yet Froude's Church-State ideal was not the constitutionalism of Hooker nor the Laudian theocracy of the Caroline Divines or early Nonjurors. His vision was of ecclesiastical supremacy over the civil power in all capacities as symbolised by Becket and the twelfth-century Church dictating to monarchs.[89] Tory High Churchmen condemned the late-medieval Church's claim to spiritual dominion over the secular power as championed by Hildebrand.[90] In contrast, Froude faulted the Church for alienating too many of her ecclesiastical powers to the domain of temporal rulers in the fourteenth century. Froude argued that the 'usurpations' of Roman Pontiffs by the end of the fourteenth century, were 'usurpations' not on the rights of Kings and Governors, but on the rights of the Church itself, of the congregations of Christ's little ones, the poor, the halt, the lame and the blind'.[91] Froude lamented that fourteenth-century bishops had 'shrunk from asserting their station as successors of the Apostles, for fear of losing their station in society'.[92]

In the context of the High Church stand in the 1830s against Protestant Dissent, Froude's late-medieval frame of reference rendered him an unreliable ally. Froude's radical objection to the payment of tithes on the ground that it was enforced by the civil power and thus partook of 'desecration'[93] appeared to put him in league with Dissenters. To the dismay of Tory High Churchmen, Froude's brand of anti-Erastianism led him to identify with the anti-Church and State views of the early Puritans in their struggle with 'High Church' episcopal opponents such as Whitgift and Bancroft.[94]

Froude remained in one sense a Tory and 'romantic reactionary' in the continental rather than John Bull mould, but the radical implicat- ions of his anti-Establishment mentality seeped into the bloodstream of later Anglo-Catholicism and overshadowed the Tory and royalist character of the original Oxford Movement. By the late-1850s, the new spirit had inspired objections even to that Tory High Church red-letter day of the liturgical calendar, the Book of Common Prayer's January 30th Thanksgiving rite, on the ground that it was but a 'state service' imposed by the civil power.

Froude's influence in modifying Tractarian attitudes to establishment was potent. During the 1820s, Keble's constant refrain was of the 'danger to the Church Establishment'.[95] Even his 'National Apostasy' sermon was conservative in tone. In private correspondence by 1833, however, Keble began to sound more like Froude, eschewing compro- mise and even threatening dramatic gestures such as in August 1833 threatening to refuse the Oath of Supremacy 'in the sense which the legislature now puts upon it'.[96] But Keble did not put himself to the ultimate test, though again in 1850 he would contemplate the prospect of lay communion. Keble frequently acknowledged his personal debt to Froude in his later thinking on Church and State, for example, in his review of Gladstone's *The State in its Relations with the Church* (1838) which he regarded as exceptionally well-meant, but wanted 'a little reconciling with Froude's view'.[97] On the other hand, there were limits to Froude's influence on Keble. It was Nonjurors such as Leslie, rather than Becket or even Ambrose, who remained his ultimate guide on Church-State matters.[98]

Newman's initially conservative attitude to establishment was eroded by Froude's influence. The message which Newman sought to impress upon contemporary churchmen in articles such as 'The Church of the Fathers' in the *British Magazine*, was that following the example of the age of Ambrose and the Church of Milan, the Church of England might have to take a 'popular' course and 'flee to the mountains'. Yet this was not in itself an index of political radicalism. The Nonjurors and Scottish episcopalians had followed just such a path. Stephen Thomas suggests that Newman's conservative rhetoric such as his references to 'good King George' had only been designed to soothe his Tory country clerical readership which might otherwise baulk at the innovative and disturbing message he was delivering.[99] Whatever the truth of this, Froude encouraged Newman to re-read the whole history of Church-State relations in England with a new and more jaundiced eye, so that his tone changed. But in the Tractarian Newman there remained a tension between genuine nostalgia for the *ancien régime*, and the pull of a patristic ideal. He came to regard the Church of Henry VIII and William III as a 'law Church' as might be proved by the ready acquiesence in the establishment of Presbyterianism in Scotland in 1707. But even in 1837 he took consolation in the fact that Lamennais had represented the Church of Rome 'as much more of a law church in practice, than our own'. He even concluded that the main difference between the two churches was that 'we have hitherto been well-treated, and Romanists ill-treated, by the civil power'.[100] Newman was also still convinced at this time that the Church of England's position was not as subservient to the State as was the Greek Church wherein the Patriarch was in effect appointed by the Great Turk.

Newman's line, however, became increasingly subversive of the assumptions of Tory High Churchmanship. Whereas by the mid-1830s Tory High Churchmen rejoiced that the spectre of disestablishment was receding, Newman found little consolation in this development. Newman now concluded that the Liberals did not want disestablishment.

> They fear the Church too much to let her go; at present they are but weakening her, as they hope, while they retain her. It is the kind and considerate office you perform to birds when you clip their wings, that they may hop about on a lawn, and pick up worms and grubs. Liberals do but want a tame church'.[101]

By 1836, Newman had reached the view which underpinned his *Lectures on Anglican Difficulties* (1851), that 'Erastianism' was the Church of England's natural condition.[102]

Disillusionment with establishment modified the inherited Toryism of the early Tractarians. As C.K. Gloyn has argued, the Tractarians embraced a dynamic or progressive as well as a static concept of Church authority.[103] This entailed a reaction against the associations of wealth and privilege and the political entanglements of the older Tory High Churchmanship, symbolized by Froude's strictures on the 'gentleman heresy'.[104] This reaction, which reached an apogee with W.G. Ward's *Ideal of a Christian Church* (1845), mirrored, up to a point, that of the 'Liberal Catholic' or Ultramontane reaction in Roman Catholicism against the Gallican Church's compromises with the pre-revolutionary order of wealth and privilege. Although the links between Newman and Lamennais were tenuous, with both displaying physical insularity, the Oxford Movement itself was not an insular phenomenon.[105] On the contrary, at a political level it can be viewed as part of a pan-European disengagement from the idea of a confessional state towards religious pluralism that was evident not only in France but in Belgium and the Prussian Rhineland. Impressed by the 'popularity of High Churchism among the lower orders at the time of the Sacheverell trial',[107] Froude hoped that Anglo-Catholicism could become populist like contemporary Ultramontane Roman Catholic movements on the Continent. In Anglo-Catholic historiography the slum priest and Sisters of Mercy would become symbols of later Tractarian social concerns. But the ideal of the *Pauperes Christi* and a romantic view of the corporate collective character of medieval society destroyed by the Reformation and overthrow of monasticism, had already found expression in a series of articles by James Mozley and Frederick Oakeley in the *British Critic* in the early-1840s. Tractarian social teaching, with its assault on mammon worship, enshrined in those articles and in Newman's sermon on 'The Dangers of Riches', Manning's on Holy Poverty and Pusey's sermons on Almsgiving, deserves further study.[108]

The Tractarian reaction against the political *status quo* extended to a growing disenchantment with the world of royal favour and patronage.[109] This disenchantment was encouraged by Queen Victoria's early reliance on Whig Latitudinarian advisers and later support for the Presbyterian Kirk in Scotland. By the 1860s, the loyalty to the Queen exhibited in Presbyterian Scotland was being contrasted with the tendency among some English High Church clergy to dispense with prayers for the Sovereign. The change was well conveyed by Peter Maurice, the Evangelical Chaplain of Jesus College, Oxford, in a revealing comment to Dr MacBride, the Evangelical Principal of Magdalen Hall, in 1867:

> You could scarcely expect ... that in a place like Oxford, once so renowned for its loyalty and orthodoxy, that such a departure from the externals of both Church and State symbolism should have been permitted, and that so many of its churches should have neither the Royal Arms nor the Tables of the Commandments, as prescribed by law and ancient custom, for out of the eighteen there are only two in which the Royal Arms are visible.[110]

There was also a reaction against putting the trust of Church and University in the hands of even well-intentioned politicians such as Lord Eldon or the Duke of Wellington. This reaction was reflected in the private suspicion of the rôle of Wellington as Chancellor of Oxford University after 1834. Wellington was accused of sacrificing the Church and University's religious principles on the altar of academic order.[111] The experience of being at the receiving end of the University authorities in the early 1840s encouraged a more critical view of the 'powers that be' among even the most moderate supporters of the Movement. The process of disenchantment was such that one Tractarian writer in 1844, in his searching critique of what he regarded as the limitations of Lord Eldon's political mindset, was provoked into condemning Toryism as 'the ingenious device whereby politicians have endeavoured to enlist in their unholy warfare of partisanship those sentiments and feelings, whose rightful place is to be found in the blessed ranks, and among the sacred forces of our true Mother [the Church]'. Toryism was dismissed as 'the child of the world, the congenial offspring of a worthless parent'.[112]

Tractarian political disengagement was also aided by the continued identification of parliamentary Toryism with the fortunes of Protestantism. The Tractarians who had allied themselves with Ultra-Tory Protestantism in 1829 found themselves in dispute with it as the theological principles of the Movement developed in the direction of Rome. Not only were the Tractarians suspected of a theological leaning towards 'popery', but Tractarian strictures on the Revolution of 1688 put them in political conflict with the archaic brand of Whiggery hitherto espoused by the Ultra-Tory defenders of the Protestant constitution. The wonder is that the uneasy alliance between the neo-Jacobite Tractarians and neo-Orangeist or Eldonite Ulta-Tories survived so long. However, the Protestantism that partly underpinned the reconstruction and revival of the Conservative party in Parliament between 1838-41 was increasingly directed against the Tractarians.[113] Moreover, the rôle of the State as a partisan legal engine of Protestantism brought it into growing conflict with Tractarian claims. In various ritual cases from the 1850s onwards, Anglo-Catholics found themselves in direct constitutional opposition to the decisions of a Protestant State. Edward Norman's assertion that Newman's Toryism did not derive 'from the after-glow of the old world'[114] is open to question. Newman's Tractarian political ideology was infused by a romanticised historical identification with Caroline Anglicanism. Yet Newman's politics retained a pragmatic element. His espousal of modified divine-right monarchical theory well into the 1830s might seem anachronistic, but perhaps owed something to a subconscious doubt about Anglicanism which needed shouting down. For Newman in 1845, however, the transcendent order of God's way finally triumphed over the politics of national establishment. His conversion brought a sense of political as well as religious liberation. This feeling was manifest in a letter from Rome in 1847, wherein Newman likened the Jesuits there to the 'Conservatives of the political world' who had been dominant in the Oxford of sixteen or seventeen years previously. He was thinking of 'the Kebles, Perceval, etc. etc. and Froude before his eyes were opened to see through the hollowness of the then so-called Toryism'.[115] Newman finally had jettisoned the Anglican political lumber of 1829-32. The Roman Catholic Newman gratefully conceded that the rise of religious pluralism had destroyed 'the whole theory of Toryism' which

had underpinned confessional Anglicanism and historic Oxford. The
Tory theory, he exulted in 1851, 'came to pieces and went the way of
all flesh'.[116] In his letter to Matthew Arnold in 1871 following the republication of his essay on Lamennais, Newman even conceded,
'perhaps la Mennais will be a true prophet after all'.[117]

As Professor Ward has argued, such trends encouraged the rise of
an Anglican form of 'Liberal Catholicism' among the later Tractarians.[118] The advanced wing of the Movement associated with W.G.
Ward had always regarded the politics of Anglican confessionalism
with distaste and was closest in spirit to the movement of Lamennais
and Lacordaire in France. Ward's 'Ideal Church' was to assume as her
ordinary condition 'one of opposition to those high in worldly
station'.[119] A combination of High Churchmanship and Liberal
opinions in politics was much less unusual by the 1870s than it had
been in the 1830s.[120] Yet Anglican 'Liberal Catholicism', lacking that
source of ecclesial authority and unity which its Roman counterpart
found in the Papacy, remained a fragile plant, always vulnerable to the
secular political nostrums of the day. Conscious of the dangers of
ecclesiastical democracy, many Tractarians mistrusted Gladstone's
methods of reasserting the so-called liberties of the Church at the
expense of old Tory High Church ideals of Anglican confessionalism.
Some still regarded various outworks of the old constitutional order as
firmer guarantors of doctrinal orthodoxy than an unfettered ecclesiastical liberty. As Robert Wilberforce insisted, 'the Church was not a
mere democratic conferacy, having its principle of union in the consent
of mankind'.[121] Thus, in response to Gladstone's campaign to introduce
a lay element into synods of the Scottish Episcopal Church in 1852,
Robert Wilberforce was adamant that the Church would cease to be
Catholic if it accepted lay voting, while Keble 'thought it would be a
sin, but not a forfeiture'.[122] For Keble, the settling of financial points
by laymen was one thing, signing canons quite another.

Liberal Catholics, owing allegiance to a supra-national source of
ecclesiastical authority, could confidently appeal to the people and
claim freedom for all creeds from State control in the hope of
extending their own influence. Unlike traditional High Churchmen,
most Tractarians became impatient with the concept of the National
Church as a primary focus of allegiance. They lamented the insularity
of Anglicanism. Yet they became ever less sure about reliance on the
contemporary Anglican episcopate as representatives of doctrinal
authority even while they retained a faith in an historic undivided Early
Church. They clung on to the old political order of corporate Christendom and were reluctant to see the Church of England reduced to the
level of a sect as Gladstonian logic seemed to dictate. It was on the
assumption that the old order still existed, though modified, that

Newman and his followers in the 1830s and beyond endeavoured to restore the spirit of early ages into Catholic survivals in the Anglican framework by repairing and revivifying such institutions as the universities and cathedrals. The endeavour was not successful.

The anti-establishmentism of the Tractarians was essentially episodic in character. It only became pronounced at times of crisis in Church-State relations, as in 1833, 1847 and 1850. Moreover, the number of those such as Manning, Dodsworth and Robert Wilberforce whose anti-Erastianism led them ultimately to Rome was limited. Among the bulk who remained Anglican, as Gloyn argues, the dynamic concept of Church authority in Tractarianism actually fostered a concern to preserve a residual spiritual character to the State. Religion could not be compartmentalised and divorced from politics. The State's claim to sovereignty was a challenge to be overcome, rather than conceded by the Church's retreat to the margins of society.[123] Ironically, from the 1850s onwards it was Pusey who often upheld against the staunchly Anglican Gladstone the ideals of the old orthodox political theology, opposing the transition from what he called 'the Catholic to the infidel idea of the State'.[124] For Pusey, fears of the triumph of secularism outweighed any disadvantages of establishment. The Tractarians were not so much concerned with the Tory High Church rationale for establishment, that the Church should consecrate the nation, than with the idea that the Church should 'ensoul' society. The hope was that the Church could lead the State back into acknowledging her supremacy rather than alienating the State entirely by pressing for a premature divorce.

The uncompromising anti-Erastianism of the *Tracts for the Times* was not, as Griffin suggests, tantamount to political radicalism, any more than the anti-Erastianism of the Nonjurors had been. The early Tractarian appeal to the people, unlike in the case of Lamennais, had been largely rhetorical. For example, Keble was always threatening to turn his back on the State in private correspondence with Robert Wilberforce, but when a moment of truth came, and faced with the implications of a radical course, as in 1850-51, he drew back. Nor was Pusey the odd man out in his political conservatism. Those who were most strident in their anti-Erastianism such as Robert Wilberforce, Bishop Forbes and George Anthony Denison tended to be the staunchest Tories.[125] The Gladstonian 'Liberal Catholicism' espoused by the *Guardian* was also assailed as a betrayal of the Catholic cause by the extreme Anglo-Catholic and reunionist *Union Review* in the 1860s. The *Union Review* advocated 'uncompromising Toryism allied with untainted Catholicity', and asserted that the 'Catholic remembers the time when the State was in good sooth the protector of the Church, and eagerly looks for a return of those golden days'.[126] Of course, the

Anglo-Catholic had to be selective in his invocation of old-style Toryism. The political creed which was espoused, unlike in 1829, was 'not hampered with certain Protestant prejudices, thought by our ancestors to be inseparable from Toryism'.[127] A devotion to an historic Toryism which transcended and went behind the narrow Protestant constitutionalism of the 1820s remained a bond between old High Churchmen, such as Edward Churton, and Tractarians, such as Robert Wilberforce, even when the theological gulf between them was widening. Both chafed under the Whig ministerial régime of Lord John Russell. But as Churton commented to Wilberforce, in a conscious echo of an earlier era: 'under a Whig dynasty, "sufferance is the badge of all our tribe"'.[128]

Newman himself can be regarded as both a political conservative and a spiritual revolutionary. He was a prophet who, no less than radical Evangelicals with whom he retained residual points of affinity, believed that political events had to be interpreted theologically. While his spiritual journey inevitably reshaped the outward form and expression of his earlier political notions, there remained a degree of continuity in his political outlook. Even in 1875 in his *Letter to the Duke of Norfolk,* Newman was able to wax lyrical about 'Toryism, that is loyalty to persons', springing 'immortal in the human breast'.[129] Newman retained the conviction, expressed in his critique of Lamennais, that 'the spirit which could throw off civil authority might also deny the authority of religion itself'.[130] As applied to Lamennais, this proved to be a prophetic utterance.

1828-33 witnessed the shipwreck of the old constitution in Church and State. The Oxford Movement represented a response to the collapse of the *ancien régime* and heralded a new beginning. Toryism ceased to be the secular domicile of church feeling, loyalty and patriotism that it had hitherto been. Yet for many Tractarians, post-Reform politics presented an opportunity for new wine in old bottles. For as Thomas Mozley noted in 1839,

> ... though the objective part of the Tory system seemed thus to pass away, the sentiment could not, as it had deeper root than in the voices of a multitude, or the suffrages of a chamber of worldly statesmen. The feelings remained, though hopeless, orphaned and widowed. They could find no political centre.... Politically speaking, the greater part of the nation were become as sheep without a shepherd.[131]

The Oxford Movement initially harnessed and found a home for such Tory sentiments. It is in this context that Newman regarded Froude as having turned from being a Tory to an Apostolical,[132] and Frederic

Rogers judged Froude as being too High Church to be a Tory.[133] Clearly, Tractarianism transcended Toryism even while it subsumed it.

In retrospect, the Tractarians regretted that the Tory High Church-manship of preceding generations had become 'alloyed with faction'. But the fact that the battles of the Church had been fought, according to Mozley, 'in election committees and hustings; in pamphlets, popular addresses and newspapers', was blamed on circumstances rather than individuals. As Mozley argued, Tory churchmen of the pre-Reform era 'could not choose their own ground, or their own mode of warfare'. The Oxford Movement, however, in embracing the principles underlying the 'Church and King' tradition, acted, in Mozley's words, as 'the fan of the Winnower perpetually separating the chaff from the wheat, — purifying mixed motives, and testing the solidity and durability of principles'.[134] Religious truth had ceased to be bound up with dynastic legitimacy and other political questions, but the values which had underpinned adherence to such causes endured precisely because they transcended the causes themselves. Tractarianism signalled no 'Farewell to Toryism' as such, but represented the spiritual refashioning and reapplication of a sacred political creed.

NOTES

1. *Remains of Richard Hurrell Froude*, 4 vols, (London & Derby, 1838-9), vol. I (London, 1838), p. 312.

2. J.B. Mozley, *Essays Historical and Theological*, 2 vols, (London, 1878), vol. I, p. xix.

3. J. H. Newman to M. Arnold, 3 December 1871, C.S. Dessain & T. Gornall, eds, *Letters and Diaries of John Henry Newman*, vol. 25, (Oxford, 1973), p. 442.

4. C. Dawson, *The Spirit of the Oxford Movement* (London, 1933), pp. 59-65; W.G. Roe, *Lamennais and England: the Reception of Lamennaist Religious Ideas in England in the Nineteenth Century* (Oxford, 1966), p. 95; P. Brendon, *Hurrell Froude and the Oxford Movement* (London, 1974), p. 120. According to Bishop Knox, the real influence of Lamennais on Froude was in inculcating a hostile attitude to the Reformation, the impiety of which Lamennais had stressed in his *Essai sur L'Indifference en Religion*. E.A. Knox, *The Tractarian Movement, 1833-1845: a Study of the Oxford Movement as a Phase of the Religious Revival in Western Europe in the Second Quarter of the Nineteenth Century*, (London, 1933), pp. 49-51.

5. J.R. Griffin, 'The Radical Phase of the Oxford Movement', *Journal of Ecclesiastical History*, 27, (1976), pp. 47-56; J.R. Griffin, 'John Keble: Radical', *Anglican Theological Review*, 59, (1971), pp. 167-175.

6. M. O'Connell, 'Politics and Prophecy: Newman and Lamennais', in I. Ker & A.G. Hill, eds, *Newman After a Hundred Years* (Oxford, 1990), pp. 175-91.

7. Mozley, *Essays Historical and Theological*, vol. 1, p. xix.

8. J.H. Newman, 'Affairs of Rome', *British Critic*, 22, (1837), p. 274. The review article was reprinted as 'The Fall of de la Mennais', in J.H. Newman, *Essays, Critical and Historical*, 2 vols, (London, 1878), vol. I, pp. 102-36.

9. G. Every, *The High Church Party*, 1688-1718 (London, 1956), p. 1; G.V. Bennett, 'Conflict in the Church', in G. Holmes, ed, *After the Glorious Revolution, 1689-1714*, (London, 1969). p. 166.

10. See J. Sledd & G. Kalb, 'Johnson's Definitions of Whig and Tory', PMLA, 67, (September, 1952), p. 882.

11. J. Sack, *From Jacobite to Conservative. Reaction and Orthodoxy. c. 1760-1832* (Cambridge, 1993), chs. 3-4.

12. J.C.D. Clark, *English Society, 1688-1832: Ideology, Social Structure and Political Practice During the Ancien Régime* (Cambridge, 1985), especially ch. 4; R. Hole, *Pulpits, Politics and Public Order in England, 1760-1832* (Cambridge, 1989), pp. 12-21.

13. G. Best, 'The Protestant Constitution and its Supporters, 1800-29', *TRHS*, 5th Series, 8, (1958), pp. 105-27. For an example of the genre of Protestant High Churchmanship, see H. Phillpotts, *Letters to Charles Butler on the Theological Parts of his Book of the Roman Catholic Church*, (London, 1825).

14. Sack, *From Jacobite to Conservative*, ch. 9. See also D.G.S. Simes, 'The Ultra Tories in British Politics, 1824-1834'. D.Phil. thesis (Oxford, 1975). Sack (pp. 224-5) detects a more cordial attitude to Catholicism among Jacobite-orientated High Churchmen of the early and mid-eighteenth century.

15. J.R. Griffin, *The Oxford Movement: a Revision*, (Edinburgh, 1984), p.1.

16. See G. Best, ed, R. W. Church, *The Oxford Movement. Twelve Years, 1833-45,* (Chicago, 1970), pp. xxix-xxx. For Stanley's view, see *Edinburgh Review*, 43, 'The Oxford School,' (April, 1881), pp. 305-35. In contrast to later Tractarian historiography, Hurrell Froude's brother, James Anthony, described the Oxford Movement as 'toryism in ecclesiastical costume'. J.A. Froude, 'The Oxford Counter-Reformation', in *Short Studies on Great Subjects*, series IV (New edn, 1893), p. 249.

17. Pusey House, Pusey Papers (Liddon Bound Volumes), W.J. Copeland to E.B. Pusey, 30 October 1864.

18. PH, Pusey Papers, (LBV), W.J. Copeland to W.N. Molesworth, 2 November 1864.

19. E. Norman, 'Newman's Social and Political Thinking', in *Newman After a Hundred Years*, pp. 153-73. Newman certainly produced no systematic treatise of political thought. T. Kenny, *The Political Thought of John Henry Newman* (London, 1957), p. 144. On Newman's politics, see also A. Ryan,

'The Development of Newman's Political Thought', *Review of Politics,* 7, (1945), pp. 210-17.

20. J.H.L. Rowlands, *Church, State and Society: The Attitudes of John Keble, Richard Hurrell Froude and John Henry Newman* (Worthing, 1989), p. x. For an alternative, crudely reductionist view of Tractarian politics, see V. Pitt, 'The Oxford Movement: a case of cultural distortion?', in K. Leech & R. Williams, eds, *Essays Catholic and Radical* (London, 1983), pp. 205-224.

21. J.H. Newman to C. Anderson, 24 January 1836, G. Tracey, ed, *Letters and Diaries of John Henry Newman,* vol. 6, (Oxford, 1984), pp. 212-13. Hurrell Froude was an admirer of the Tory histories of Clarendon and the Nonjuror, Jeremy Collier. He wished for a continuation of Collier's two-volume *Ecclesiastical History of Great Britain* (1708-14). *Remains of Hurrell Froude,* vol. I, p. 339. See also n. 42.

22. Roe, *Lamennais and England,* p. 92.

23. J.H. Newman to Miss M.R. Giberne, 3 December 1837, Tracey, ed, *Letters and Diaries of John Henry Newman,* vol. 6, p. 174.

24. Pusey House, Pusey Papers, W.J. Copeland to Miss M. A. Copeland, 3 May 1836. For John Scott, Ist Earl of Eldon (1751-1838), see H. Twiss, *The Public and Private Life of Lord Chancellor Eldon With Selections from his Correspondence,* 3 vols, (2nd edn., London, 1844). For Tractarian strictures on Eldon's type of churchmanship, see *Christian Remembrancer,* 8, 'Life of Lord Eldon', (September, 1844), pp. 274-86. Eldon was notoriously neglectful of his churchly duties. See Twiss, *Life of Eldon,* vol. III, p. 488; W.E. Surtees, *Sketch of the Lives of Lords Stowell and Eldon* (London, 1846), p. 143.

25. J.H. Newman to J. W. Bowden, 17 January 1830, T. Gornall & I. Ker, eds., *Letters and Diaries of John Henry Newman,* vol. 2,. (Oxford, 1979), p. 189.

26. J.H. Newman to Mrs Newman, 1 March 1830, *ibidem* p. 125.

27. P.B. Nockles, 'An Academic Counter-Revolution: Newman and Tractarian Oxford's Idea of a University', *History of Universities,* 10, (1991)f pp. 148-50. 'Ultra-Tory' Evangelicals such as Sir Robert Harry Inglis (1786-1855), M.P. for Oxford University, in the 1830s allied themselves with the Tractarians against the Whig-Latitudinarian ministerial interest.

28. J.H. Newman, *Apologia Pro Vita Sua,* J. Svaglic, ed, (Oxford, 1967), p. 506.

29. *Ibidem,* pp. 260-2.

30. J. H. Newman, *The Via Media of the Anglican Church Illustrated in Lectures, Letters and Tracts written Between 1830 and 1841,* 2 vols, (London, 1877), vol. II, p. 84.

31. [Newman], 'Affairs of Rome', p. 274.

32. Gornall & Ker, eds, *Letters and Diaries of John Henry Newman,* vol. 2, p. 35.

33. J. H. Newman, *Discussions and Arguments on Various Subjects* (London, 1885), p. 68.

34. J.H. Newman to R.H. Froude, 10 September 1830, Gornall & Ker, *Letters and Diaries of John Henry Newman*, vol. 2, p. 289.

35. L.M. Guiney, *Hurrell Froude. Memoranda and Comments* (London, 1904), p. 127. The original *Anti-Jacobin Review*, a literary vehicle of Tory High Churchmanship had run from 1798 till 1821.

36. For example, see his comment in 1834: 'I have been much surprised to find that the first Latitudinarians were Tories: e.g. Hales, Chillingworth, and that set. How Whiggery has by degrees taken up all the filth that has been secreted in the fermentation of human thought! Puritanism, Latitudinarianism, Popery, Infidelity; they have it all now, and good luck to them'. *Remains of Hurrell Froude*, vol. I, p. 339.

37. [J. Keble], 'Unpublished Papers of Bishop Warburton', *British Critic*, 29, (April, 1841), p. 427.

38. J. Keble, 'The Danger of Sympathising with Rebellion', Sermon V, 'Preached before the University of Oxford on 30th January 1831, being the Day of King Charles' Martyrdom', in *Sermons Academical and Occasional* (Oxford, 1843), p. 124.

39. Liddon, *Life of Pusey*, vol. II, p. 29.

40. On Pusey's early political liberalism, see D. Forrester, *Young Doctor Pusey: a Study in Development* (London, 1989), pp. 14-18.

41. Quoted in Liddon, *Life of Pusey*, vol. IV, p. 199.

42. *Remains of Hurrell Froude*, vol. I, p. 177.

43. J. Keble, 'Kings to be Honoured for their Office Sake' [Accession Day Sermon, 1836], in *Plain Sermons by Contributors to the 'Tracts for the Times'*, vol. I, (London, 1839), p. 243; J. Keble, *'On the Death of a King'* [9 July, 1837], in *Plain Sermons*, vol. IV, (London, 1842), pp. 76-7.

44. [J. Keble], 'Gladstone — the State in its Relations with the Church', *British Critic*, 26, (October, 1839), pp. 374-5.

45. PH, (LBV), E. B. Pusey to J. Keble, 15 November 1837.

46. J.A. Froude, 'Oxford Counter-Reformation', p. 248.

47. Liddon, *Life of Pusey*, vol. II, p. 27. Even prior to the delivery of Pusey's sermon, the Evangelical *Christian Observer* accused Pusey of wishing 'to restore the doctrines and practices of Laud and Sacheverell'. Among these doctrines were included high notions of monarchical authority and non-resistance. *Christian Observer*, 37, 'Oxford Saintology', (September, 1837), p. 586; R. Fisher, *Tractarianism Opposed to the Truth* (London, 1843), pp. 15-16. Moderate High Churchmen also raised the spectre of Jacobitism. See J. Beaven, *Warnings from History, Political and Ecclesiastical. A Discourse Delivered before the University of Oxford on the 30th of January 1838. Being the Day of King Charles' Martyrdom* (Oxford, 1838).

The status of the 'Glorious Revolution' remained a source of contention among High Churchmen into the 1840s. Edward Churton cautioned his friend

William Gresley in 1845: 'those who submitted to the change of Government [in 1688], having no share in the guilt of the Revolution, acted on the old principles. I wish you therefore to speak with more moderation on this doubtful question'. Churton rejected the Tractarian tendency 'to attribute all the subsequent evils to this ancient date of the Revolution'. PH, Gresley Papers, Gres 3/7157, E. Churton to W. Gresley, 17 November 1845.

48. Quoted in A.P. Stanley, ed, *The Life and Correspondence of Thomas Arnold D.D.* (4th edn., London, 1845), vol. II, p. 93.

49. E.B. Pusey, *Patience and Confidence the Strength of the Church: a Sermon Preached on the Fifth of November, before the University of Oxford at St.Mary's,* (Oxford, 1837), p. xv.

50. *Ibidem,* p. vi. Liddon described the sermon as 'imbued with the old moral as well as political temper of Toryism'. Liddon, *Life of Pusey,* vol. II, p. 27.

51. Pusey, *Patience and Confidence,* p. v. The sermon was praised by a friendly reviewer for invoking the example of 'the saints and martyrs of our own Church, exhibited in all the beauty, dignity and loveliness of passive obedience and non-resistence'. [N. Goldsmid], 'Pusey's Sermon on the Fifth of November', *British Critic,* 23, (January, 1838), p. 144.

52. Griffin misinterprets the sermon as 'more a political treatise than a sermon'. Griffin, *Oxford Movement,* pp. 64-5. It is also interesting that a current historian of Jacobitism maintains 'that the last Oxford Jacobite sermon was preached by Dr Pusey on 5 November 1837'. P.K. Monod, *Jacobitism and the English People, 1688-1788* (Cambridge, 1989), p. 152.

53. E.B. Pusey, *The Church, the Converter of the Heathen. Two Sermons Preached in Conformity with the Queen's Letter in Behalf of the SPG* (Oxford, 1838), p. 23.

54. *Ibidem,* p. 56. For an earlier statement of this view, see J. Boucher, *View of the Causes and Consequences of the American Revolution in Thirteen Discourses* (London, 1797).

55. E.B. Pusey, *Remarks on the Prospective and Past Benefits of Cathedral Institutions, in the Promotion of Sound Religious Knowledge, and of Clerical Education* (London, 1833), p. 96.

56. Bodleian Library, Ms Wilberforce d. 17, fol. 336, E.B. Pusey to S. Wilberforce, 9 September 1836.

57. PH, (LBV), E.B. Pusey to W.E. Gladstone, March 1836.

58. Bodleian Library, Ms Wilberforce d. 17, fol. 338, J. Keble to S. Wilberforce, 19 September 1836.

59. E.B. Pusey, *The Royal Supremacy Not an Arbitrary Authority but Limited by the Laws of the Church, of which Kings are Members* (Oxford, 1850), p. 159.

60. On his Mediterranean journey in 1832-3, Newman refused even to look at the tricolour on a French vessel in the port of Algiers. Newman, *Apologia,* p. 97. For both Newman and Froude's defence of the Bourbon monarchy, see

n. 75. Sack (*From Jacobite to Conservative*, pp. 246-7) contrasts Newman's attitude with that of contemporary English Ultra-Tories whose inveterate anti-Catholicism inclined them, unlike their French counterparts, to take the liberal side in Continental politics. On the other hand, according to the unreliable Tom Mozley, 'all Oxford' was for the Bourbons and opposed to 'the Orleanist machinations'. T. Mozley, *Reminiscences Chiefly of Oriel College and the Oxford Movement*, 2 vols, (London, 1882), vol. I, p. 252.

61. J.R. Griffin, 'The Anglican Politics of Cardinal Newman', *Anglican Theological Review*, 55, (October, 1973), p. 435.

62. The entry in Newman's diary for 30 January 1836 reads: 'Saturday 30th January. The Martyrdom. I tried to find a church open in vain'. T. Gornall, ed, *Letters and Diaries of John Henry Newman*, vol. 5, (Oxford, 1981), pp. 220, 302. On the cult of the Royal Martyr in the High Anglican tradition, see H.W. Randall, 'The Rise and Fall of a Martyrology: Sermons on Charles I', *Huntington Library Quarterly*, 10, (1946/7), pp. 164-5; Sack, *From Jacobite to Conservative*, pp. 126-30.

63. J.H. Newman to R.H. Froude, 7 January 1830, Gornall & Ker, eds, *Letters and Diaries of John Henry Newman*, vol. 2, p. 186.

64. J.H. Newman to H.A. Woodgate, 7 July 1833, T. Gornall, ed, *Letters and Diaries of John Henry Newman*, vol. 4 (Oxford, 1981), pp. 26-7. Newman's attitude here mirrored that of conservative High Church supporters of the Oxford Movement such as Arthur Philip Perceval, later Chaplain to Queen Victoria. In 1833, Perceval accused the Whig Premier, Lord Grey, of undermining the monarchy. A.P. Perceval, *A Letter to the Rt. Hon. Earl Grey on the Obligation of the Coronation Oath* (London, 1833), pp. 6-7. On the religious symbolism of the coronation service, see E.C. Ratcliff, *The English Coronation Service* (London, 1937).

65. Gornall & Ker, eds, *Letters and Diaries of John Henry Newman*, vol. 4, p. 164.

66. J.H. Newman to J.W. Bowden, 5 February 1835, Gornall, ed, *Letters and Diaries of John Henry Newman*, vol. 5, p. 24.

67. J.H. Newman to R.H. Froude, 8 September 1833, Gornall & Ker, eds, *Letters and Diaries of John Henry Newman*, vol. 4, p. 33. The reluctant nature of the shift is clear from Newman's avowal: 'It is not we who desert the government, but the government that has left us; we are forced back upon those below us, because those above us will not honour us. There is no help for it, I say'. Newman, *The Church of the Fathers* (London, 1840), p. 3.

68. [Newman], 'Affairs of Rome', p. 270.

69. H.E. Manning, *The Principle of the Ecclesiastical Commission Examined, in a Letter to the Rt. Rev. the Lord Bishop of Chichester* (London, 1838), pp. 34-5.

70. Clark, *English Society*, p. 419.

71. J.H. Newman to R.H. Froude, 31 August 1833, A.Mozley, *Letters and Correspondence of John Henry Newman*, 2 vols, (London, 1891), vol. I, p. 450.

72. J.H. Newman to H.J. Rose, 23 May 1836, Gornall, ed, *Letters and Diaries of John Henry Newman*, vol. 5, p. 304.

73. R.I. Wilberforce, *An Inquiry into the Principles of Church Authority: or Reasons for Recalling My Subscription to the Royal Supremacy* (London, 1854); R.I. Wilberforce, *A Sketch of the History of Erastianism* (London, 1851), pp. 58-61. As Wilberforce explained: 'the Tudors had required all persons to agree with themselves; the Stuarts, with their Bishops; but William of Orange was indifferent what men believed, provided they differed from the Pope'. Wilberforce, *Church Authority*, p. 277.

74. PH, Ollard Papers, C. Marriott to J.H. Newman, 15 January 1840. See [J.H. Newman], 'The Court of James I', *British Critic*, 27 (January, 1840), pp. 34-5.

75. [Newman], 'Affairs of Rome', 276. Froude's pro-Bourbon attitude was also akin to that of the French Legitimist 'Ultras' and in contrast to the pro-Orleanism of the English 'Ultra-Tories'. Froude had been serious in 1830 when he expressed the hope that 'the march of mind in France may yet prove a bloody one'. *Remains of Hurrell Froude*, vol. I, p. 244.

76. 'I was driven, by my state of mind, to insist upon the political conduct, the controversial bearing, and the social methods and manifestations of Rome ... I had an unspeakable aversion to the policy and acts of Mr O'Connell, because, as I thought, he associated himself with men of all religions and no religion against the Anglican Church, and advanced Catholicism by violence and intrigue'. Newman, *Apologia*, (1st edn., London, 1864), p. 223.

The Tractarian romantic, Lord John Manners, likewise accused Catholics of 'shamelessly casting away your Stuart memories, your Jacobite predilections, your aristocratic sympathies, and your old English associations, to league yourselves with the legitimate descendants of those, who through long years of bitterness and reproach, ceased not to persecute your fathers'. [Lord John Manners], *What are the English Roman Catholics to do? The Question Considered in a Letter to Lord Edward Howard, by 'Anglo-Catholicus'* (London, 1841), p. 9.

On Phillipps de Lisle, a Tory Leicestershire squire who converted to Catholicism, see E.S. Purcell & E. de Lisle, *Life and Letters of Ambrose Phillipps de Lisle*, 2 vols, (London, 1900).

77. S.Gilley, 'Frederick Lucas, *The Tablet* and Ireland — A Victorian Forerunner of Liberation Theology', S. Mews, ed, *Modern Religious Rebels*. Presented to John Kent (London, 1993), p. 65.

78. Newman, *Apologia*, p. 237. Even when opposing Catholic Emancipation in 1829, Keble had looked to Catholics 'as possible allies instead of enemies in the struggles which seem to await us. It was so in the days of Charles I'. Bodleian Library, Ms Eng Lett d.124, fols.23-4, J. Keble to C.A. Ogilvie, 14 March 1829. But English Catholic nobles such as the Earl of Shrewsbury disappointed the Tractarians in their continued adherence to the Whig cause. See Earl of Shrewsbury, *A Second Letter to Ambrose Lisle Phillipps Esq. on the Present Position of Affairs*, (London, 1841). However, the *Catholic Magazine* shared the neo-Jacobite and Tory sympathies of the Tractarians. See

Catholic Magazine, I, New Series, 'The Last of the Stuarts', (March, 1843), p. 184.

79. W.Ward, *William George Ward and the Oxford Movement* (London, 1889), p. 214.

80. J.H. Newman to J.W. Bowden, May 1839, Mozley, ed, *Letters and Correspondence of Newman*, vol. II, p. 282.

81. See 'The Protestant Idea of Antichrist', in J.H. Newman, *Essays, Critical and Historical*, 2 vols, (London, 1871), Ess. II, pp. 112-85.

82. S.W. Gilley, 'Newman and Prophecy, Evangelical and Catholic', *The Journal of the United Reformed Church Society*, 3, (March, 1985), pp. 160-183; P. Misner, *Papacy and Development: Newman and the Primacy of the Pope* (London, 1976), pp. 50-77; Rowlands, *Church, State and Society*, pp. 181-96.

83. S.W. Gilley, *Newman and His Age* (London, 1990), p. 175.

84. E. Norman, 'Newman's Social and Poltical Thinking', pp. 165-6.

85. *Remains of Hurrell Froude*, vol. III, (Derby, 1838), p. 274.

86. *Ibidem*, pp. 199-200. Froude, however, used Hooker's views as an *argumentum ad hominem*. Privately, he conceded that he was 'out of conceit with old Hooker's notion of a lay synod: it is unecclesiastical and Whig. We must only be popular in the choice of Church officers'. *Remains of Hurrell Froude*, vol. I, p. 333. As early as 1836, one critic argued that the Oxford party had secretly discovered Hooker's doctrines [on Church and State] to be dangerous, though it is willing to shelter under his name still'. *State of Parties in Oxford* (Oxford, 1836), p. 16.

87. *Remains of Hurrell Froude*, vol. III, p. 207.

88. *Ibidem*, p. 196.

89. See Froude's article on Becket in the *British Magazine*, 2, (September, 1832), especially pp. 34-5. The article was reprinted as volume IV of the *Remains* (Derby, 1839). Even Newman thought that the 'Becket papers might frighten people considerably — on Church and State'. J.H. Newman to J. Keble, 13 September 1838, G. Tracey, ed, *Letters and Diaries of John Henry Newman*, vol. 6, p. 317. The most zealous lay participant in the early Movement, James William Bowden, was also sympathetic to Becket's standpoint. See J.W. Bowden, *The Life and Pontificate of Gregory the Seventh*, 2 vols, (London, 1840), vol. I, pp. 113-17.

90. For example, see W.F. Hook, *On the Church and Establishment. Two Plain Sermons* (London, 1834), p. 44; J.H. Pott, *The Rights of Sovereignty in Christian States Defended in Some Chief Particulars* (London, 1821). William Sewell later reminded his Tractarian friends that the Caroline Divines 'show no sympathy with Hildebrand ... still less would they hold up Becket to reverence, or allow him to be a martyr'. [W. Sewell], 'Divines of the Seventeenth Century', *Quarterly Review*, 69, (March, 1842), pp. 500-01.

91. *Remains of Hurrell Froude*, vol. IV, p. 273.

92. *Ibidem*, p. 227.

93. *Ibidem*, vol. I, pp. 414, 434.

94. *Ibidem*, vol. I, pp. 325-8. Frederic Rogers told Newman in 1837 that Froude had 'said to me ... that all our divines since the Reformation had been very dark about Church independence'. F. Rogers to J.H. Newman, 21 January 1839, G.E. Marindin, ed, *Letters of Frederic, Lord Blachford* (London, 1896), pp. 45-6.

95. PH, (LBV), J. Keble to A.P. Perceval, 29 June 1837.

96. J. Keble to J. H. Newman, 8 August 1833, Mozley, ed, *Letters and Correspondence of Newman*, vol. I, p. 441.

97. Keble College Archives, Keble Papers, J. Keble to J.H. Newman, 31 March 1839.

98. In his *Case of the Regale and of the Pontificale* (1700), the Nonjuror Charles Leslie had limited the Royal Supremacy to civil matters.

99. Thomas, *Newman and Heresy* (Cambridge, 1991) p. 52.

100. [Newman], 'Affairs of Rome', p. 261.

101. *Ibidem*, 278.

102. Newman asserted in 1851, 'that the established religion was set up in erastianism, that erastianism was its essence'. J.H. Newman, *Lectures on Certain Difficulties Felt by Anglicans in Catholic Teaching* (London, 1851), p. 223. But as early as 1836, Newman privately conceded to Pusey, 'that the English Church subsists in the State, and has no internal consistency ... to keep it together'. J.H. Newman to E.B. Pusey, 24 January 1836, Gornall, ed, *Letters and Diaries of John Henry Newman*, vol. 5, p. 214. Even by 1834-5, Newman had questioned the legitimacy of the Church's surrender of her juridical powers to the State in 1534. [J.H. Newman], 'The Convocation of the Province of Canterbury', *British Magazine*, 6, (October, 1834), pp. 517-24, 637-47; 7, (January-March, 1835), pp. 33-41, 145-54, 259-68.

103. C.K. Gloyn, *The Church in the Social Order: a Study of Anglican Social Theory from Coleridge to Maurice* (Forest Grove, Oregon), pp. 49-54.

104. By 1847, the High Churchman William Gresley was cautioning the more advanced Tractarians not to 'set down the old cry of "Church and King" as altogether Erastian. Good men used it as well as mere politicians'. W. Gresley, *A Second Statement on the Real Danger of the Church of England* (London, 1847), p. 14.

105. O'Connell, 'Newman and Lamennais', p. 177.

106. See Knox, *Tractarian Movement*, ch. 3.

107. *Remains of Hurrell Froude*, vol. I, p. 339. On popular Tory High Churchmanship in the era of the Whig trial of Doctor Henry Sacheverell (1709) for supposedly libelling the Revolution of 1688, see Monod, *Jacobitism and the English People*, ch. 6.

108. Important research on this topic is currently being carried out by Dr Simon Skinner of Mansfield College, Oxford.

109. See Thomas Mozley's comment in 1839: 'that times are changed in this respect is evinced by our being unable to estimate the feeling which made a Herbert, or a Laud, such zealous competitors for royal favour'. [T. Mozley], 'Church and King', *British Critic*, 25 (April, 1839), pp. 325-6.

110. P. Maurice, *The Ritualism of Oxford Popery. A Letter to Dr MacBride, Principal of Magdalen Hall, Oxford* (London, [1867]).

111.   See my forthcoming, 'Lost Causes and Impossible Loyalties: the University and the Oxford Movement, 1829-54', M. Brock & M.C. Curthoys, *History of the University of Oxford*, vol. 6.

112. *Christian Remembrancer*, 8, 'Life of Lord Eldon', pp. 285-6.

113. J. Wolffe, *The Protestant Crusade in Great Britain, 1829-1860* (Oxford, 1991), ch. 3.

114. Norman, 'Newman's Social and Political Thinking', p. 165.

115. C.S. Dessain, ed, *Letters and Diaries of John Henry Newman*, vol. 12, (London, 1962), pp. 103-4.

116. Newman, *Difficulties of Anglicans*, p. 267.

117. Newman to Arnold, 3 December 1871, Dessain & Gornall, eds, *Letters and Diaries of John Henry Newman*, vol. 25, p. 442.

118. W.R. Ward, 'Oxford and the Origins of Liberal Catholicism in the Church of England', *Studies in Church History*, 1, (1964), pp. 234-9.

119. W.G. Ward, *The Ideal of a Christian Church Considered in Comparison with Existing Practice* (London, 1844), p. 50.

120. J. Parry, *Democracy and Religion: Gladstone and the Liberal Party, 1867-1875* (Cambridge, 1986), p. 182.

121. R. Wilberforce, *Principles of Church Authority*, p. 65.

122. Liddon, *Life of Pusey*, vol. III, p. 351.

123. Gloyn, *Church in the Social Order*, pp. 66-9..

124. P.B. Nockles, 'Pusey and the Question of Church and State', in P. Butler, ed, *Pusey Rediscovered* (London, 1983), p. 291.

125. For Denison's political Toryism, see G.A. Denison, *Notes of My Life, 1805-1878* (Oxford, 1878), p. 64. Denison avowed, 'I am an old Tory. I never liked a Whig ... I am not fond of a Conservative either, as a Conservative'. G.A. Denison, *Mr Gladstone. With Appendix, Containing the Accumulated Evidence of Fifty-Five Years. A Retrospect and Prospect. With Summary* (London, 1885), p. 9.

126. *Union Review*, I (1863), 32.

127. *Ibidem*, 38.

128. PH, Churton Papers, Chur 2/4120, E. Churton to R.I. Wilberforce, 5 June 1849.

129. J.H. Newman, *A Letter to His Grace, the Duke of Norfolk on Occasion of Mr Gladstone's Recent Expostulation* (London, 1875), p. 72.

130. [Newman], 'Affairs of Rome', p. 283.

131. [Mozley], 'Church and King', p. 322.

132.   J.H. Newman to F. Rogers, 5 July 1837, Tracey, ed, *Letters and Diaries of John Henry Newman*, vol. 6. p. 89.

133. Birmingham Oratory, Newman Papers, B.12.1.220, F. Rogers to J.H. Newman, 14 August 1833. But for Thomas Mozley, Froude remained 'a Tory with that transcendental ideal of the English gentleman which forms the basis of Toryism'. Mozley, *Reminiscences,* vol. I, p. 228. It is significant that Froude never used 'Tory' in a pejorative sense as he did with the term 'Conservative'. See, *Remains of Hurrell Froude*, vol. I, p. 366.

134. [Mozley], 'Church and King', pp. 324-5.

V

EVANGELICAL PATTERNS OF CONVERSION IN NEWMAN'S AUTOBIOGRAPHICAL WRITINGS

Lothar Kuld

Newman research emphasises consistently his distancing from an Evangelical pattern of conversion.[1] This distancing can be clearly seen in Newman's own words in several of his autobiographical comments after 1826.[2] But even if we pursue this interpretation of Newman and do not see his conversion at the age of fifteen as an experience of an Evangelical nature, we are still confronted with the remarkable fact that he uses the pattern of accounts of Evangelical conversion in order to reconstruct his own conversion,[3] namely the religious autobiography of the Evangelical Thomas Scott, *The Force of Truth*, and the stages of the conversion *schema* which he worked out in a series of unpublished papers in 1821.

I will proceed chronologically and first of all provide a brief survey of Newman's understanding of the Evangelical concept of conversion in the papers of 1821 and then discuss Scott's religious autobiography *The Force of Truth* and the connection between Newman's *Apologia* and that book.

1. NEWMAN'S 'PAPERS ON CONVERSION' (1821) AND HIS LATER REFLECTIONS ON THE EVANGELICAL CONCEPT OF CONVERSION.

In June and July 1821 Newman wrote a series of six papers on conversion.[4] The method and content of the papers were Evangelical, in other words Newman derived the aspects of his concept of conversion strictly from those sections of writings which were known from literature on Puritanism, Methodism and Evangelicalism. The titles of the papers alone are clear evidence of this adherence: on the unconverted man, on law, on the scheme of salvation, on salvation by Jesus Christ, on conversion, on good works the necessary fruits of faith, on indwelling sin. After the collection of relevant writings on these headings Newman provided a summary in his own words. The paper, 'On Conversion', divides the conversion procedure into five phases:

— The recognition of sin. In this phase the changing of one's ways is still a step in the wrong direction. It is egocentric as it is self-seeking and self-centered and merely conducted out of fear of the judgement of God.

— This is followed by the will to mend one's ways.

— However, as soon as the will to change one's ways is present, the sinful human being breaks all his resolutions. He becomes more and more entangled in his sins. But now he is tormented by this state. He is desperate.

— This is the hour of God in which he rescues human beings from chaos. (Hence the image of the spirit of God above the waters which Newman uses here.) Human beings are seized by hope and fear before God.

— Finally Newman expresses the recognition: Man feels nothing in himself. Theologically speaking, the irredeemable and forlorn person is justified by God. At this point Newman's analytical style changes over to a very expressive one. He notes with great emotion: 'Happy, happy soul! ... he hath laid hold on the appointed mean of justification, he hath brought down from above the robe of righteousness.... Alleluja ... I was poor, and Thou hast made me rich; I was desolate, and Thou visited me; I wandered in a land of shadows, and Thou hast built my house upon a rock ...' Further exclamations and exclamation marks follow. They go beyond the confines of the sentence into a sphere of emphasis which can no longer be expressed in words. No human activity and no natural abilities can exert any influence here. Real conversion and justification are the result of God's initiative is what Newman wishes to express.

The Evangelical character of these papers is shown finally in the question of baptism, changing one's ways and regeneration.[5] Newman states in his paper, 'On the Unconverted Man', (June/July 1821) that man is also not converted through the waters of baptism — ' easy receipt, and of inestimable virtue! ... simple remedy for the radical disease of our nature! We have brought our children to the font — how rapturous will it be to observe, as reason begins to act, the daily unfolding and discovery of a regenerated nature, of an holy will and godly affections! Alas, experience teaches a different lesson, and we are constrained to admit that neither the hand of the baptizer, nor the voice of him that exhorteth, nor the example of pious friends, nor afflictions, nor mercies, nor anything human is [the] assured and certain method powerful to force the gift of God'.

L.H. Peterson assumed that Newman could have taken his description of the stages of the process of conversion directly from Dod-deridge's *Rise and Progress of Religion in the Soul* (1745).[6] In Peterson's view *Rise and Progress* was not an autobiographical work in itself yet it describes 'the stages in a Christian's journey from sin to salvation'. Doddridge's chapter-titles would outline 'the same progress of conversion that Newman describes: "The Careless Sinner Awakened", "The Awakened Sinner ... Cautioned against Delay", "The Sinner Arraigned and Convicted", "The Sinner Stripped of His Vain Pleas", "The Sinner Sentenced", "The Helpless State of the Sinner under Condemnation", "News of Salvation by Christ", "The Doubting Soul ... Assisted", "The Assistance of the Spirit of God", "The Christian Urged to ... an Express Act of Self-Dedication" etc'.

Five years after the completion of the script in 1826 Newman himself declared: 'I wrote *juxta praescriptum*'. (*AWr* 172. note from 26th July 1826). And it was a retraction when Newman went on to say: 'I am persuaded that very many of my most positive and dogmatical notions were taken *from books*. In the matter in question (conversion) my feelings were not violent, but a returning to, a renewing of, principles, under the power of the Holy Spirit, which I had *already* felt, and in a measure acted on, when young' (*AWr* 172). As early as June or July 1821 while he was working on these papers on conversion Newman also commented in his diary: 'I speak of (the process of) conversion with great diffidence, being obliged to adopt the language of books. For my own feelings, as far as I remember, were so different from any account I have ever read, that I dare not go by what *may* be an individual case'.[7]

At the beginning of 1825 he started to have doubts about the presentation of the regeneration of the converted person as being apart from baptism: 'I think,I am not certain, I must give up the doctrine of imputed righteousness, and that of regeneration as apart from baptism'.[8] (13 th. January 1825)

In 1874 Newman quoted these texts in his autobiographical *Memoir* and he added that he had been aware that he had always lacked those special Evangelical experiences. He wrote about himself: 'He was sensible that he had ever been wanting in those special Evangelical experiences, which, like the grip of the hand or other prescribed signs of a secret society, are the sure token of a member' (*AWr* 80). And after the publication of his *Apologia*, the account of his conversion, he received well-intentioned letters from strangers or anonymous writers in which they assured him that he still did not know what conversion meant and that he would have to undergo all the important changes were he to be saved (*AWr* 79). Newman confessed that these writers were right in their own way and that he had never really possessed a truly Evangelical understanding of conversion.

Stephan Dessain put forward the view that these words of Newman should be adhered to.[9] He arrived at the conclusion: 'Newman was never a real Evangelical, and had never been through the conventional experience of conviction of sin, terror, despair, followed by full assurance of salvation'.[10] He argued that Newman's conversion was of an intellectual and rational nature and differed fundamentally from the Evangelical understanding of conversion which was understood as an intense experience of sin, inner struggle and a final experience of mercy. In fact, on this point, Newman's postscript of 1826 on the scripts of 1821 draws a clear line. However, it has to be stated — contrary to Newman and the literature which then followed him — that his text of 1821 was not merely a copying of Evangelical authors. As has already been illustrated, the characteristic style of the paper is too emphatic and affirmative to be so.

2. 'CONVERSION' AS RECONSTRUCTION PATTERN OF STORIES OF FAITH IN THE WORKS OF THOMAS SCOTT AND JOHN HENRY NEWMAN

2.1. Newman — Scott

In the autobiographical *Memoir* of 1874 Newman mentioned the papers from 1821 as documents of his Evangelical phase. (*AWr* 80) He, in fact, spoke very positively of Evangelicalism. He wrote that Evangelicalism had sheltered and protected him in his most dangerous years and educated him in ways of piousness until the time came when he dedicated himself to the Christian ministry. (*AWr* 79) Newman mentions John Newton and Thomas Scott, Beveridge's *Private Thoughts upon Religion, and a Christian Life* (first published posthumously in 1709) and Dodderidge's *The Rise and Progress of Religion in the Soul* (1745) Of all these writers the Evangelical Thomas Scott (1747-1821) was 'the writer who made a deeper impression on my mind than any other'. He was the man 'to whom (humanly speaking) I almost owe my soul'. Newman wrote in the *Apologia* (1864) that Scott's religious autobiography *Force of Truth* (1779) had occupied his mind ever since his childhood.[11] Scott's story of conversion and the tradition of Evangelical autobiography was also known by Newman when he wrote the *Apologia* in 1864. Therefore it is no surprise to find traces of this tradition in Newman's autobiography.

2.2. Scott, 'The Force of Truth' (1779)[12]

The Force of Truth has three parts: Part 1: Life before Conversion; Part 2: Conversion; Part 3: Observations on the Report Presented.

The story of his conversion took up most space. Scott dealt quickly with what happened before. He started his story by saying that up to his sixteenth year he had never really had any firm religious beliefs: 'Till the sixteenth year of my age, I do not remember that I ever was under any serious conviction of being a sinner, in danger of wrath or in need of mercy.... But about my sixteenth year I began to see that I was a sinner'. He then resolved to improve his life but he was unsuccessful in this. So in order to placate himself he believed those people who relativised the sinfulness of mankind. He continued to explain that one could perceive the whole extent of his forlorn state in the motive which had led him to his ecclesiastical status: the desire for a comfortable life, for leisure and time for his literary interests. The first part of the story ends with this description of a religiously dead life rendered uneasy by the fear of the eternal penalty for his sins and therefore aimless.

Mercy came into his life through the influence of the Evangelical John Newton (1725-1807) who visited the sick in Scott's parish, a practice which for Scott was very unusual. Today one is more surprised by the behaviour of Scott than by the action of Newton. 'In tears' and 'without delay' he asked God for forgiveness for his transgression. This change may appear to have had no psychological preparation. It is conceivable in the light of faith in God's visible curative effect on each individual's life. For him an emotional shock is a sign of the experiencing of mercy.

The Evangelical change in his life, his conversion to so-called Methodism, was reconstructed by Scott in several stages: initially he wanted to force Newton into exchanging letters with him so that they could debate religious issues and he thus would attempt to refute Scott's views with rational arguments. Of course, Newton was not willing to do this. Newton was sure that one day Scott would recognise and adopt the same religious principles as his. Naturally, this offended Scott's self-assurance and self-admiration; With hindsight, however, Scott could see how this attitude of John Newton was evidence of his competence in spiritual matters: 'So clearly could he discern the dawnings of grace in my soul, admidst all the darkness of depraved nature, and my obstinate rebellion to the will of God!'

The next step was to embark on an intensive study of the Scripture. A criterion of truth is James 1, 5: the spirit promised to believers. 'I began to ask God to give me this promised wisdom'. Of course, the request alone was not sufficient. Scott wrote that, in addition, the behaviour of a child is necessary, a child who, as it were, sits at God's feet and only listens to him. He further stated that it was precisely this childish naivety which he had lacked when he had relied too heavily on his intellect. Step by step, however, parallel to this inner reorientation Scott began to follow Newton's example and to hold more 'Methodist' sermons, i.e. to extract all the arguments he used in his sermons from the bible and to develop them. In this way he moved instinctively nearer to the religious convictions of Newton and the Methodists. He moved closer to their 'scheme of doctrine' but at the same time he was unable to adopt it without a violent change in his own religious convictions. Scott wrote about his inhibitions, even his fear of being regarded as 'enthusiastic'. He claimed that this was merely evidence of his earlier lack of religious understanding[13] and that as a child 'of the world' he had not then understood that 'joy' was evidence of 'awakening' through Christ.

There followed an intensive dispute with the claims of theological positions from Anglican theologians. However, it was not through them but rather through Scripture that Scott discovered the doctrine of predestination and election which belong to the doctrine of Methodism. Here he found that Newton's interpretations were confirmed. He wrote that for this reason he then finally adopted the so-called Methodism of Newton, i.e. he adopted Newton's hermeneutics of an 'experienced knowledge' which encouraged the preacher to speak about himself and about God's story in his life. The fragments of the autobiographical confessions which arose in this way are for Scott the ideal way 'into the hearts and conscience of others'.[14]

Scott concluded his religious autobiography with a series of observations. This shows again very clearly the high degree of reflection in his account. It is analytical and educational.

1.   Scott regarded himself as an isolated example of conversion of a person under the guidance and teachings of the Holy Spirit. He wrote that he told his story first of all to strengthen those people who already knew and loved God and secondly to encourage others to take a serious look back at their religious perceptions and feelings.

2.   Scott said that in human terms everything worked against such a conversion. For years his religious convictions had stood in direct opposition to his present beliefs. He said that he had trusted in the strength of the human intellect and that his character was such that he was not very susceptible to undergoing a religious conversion. His situation had made an Evangelical conversion appear highly improbable. But: 'My leading resolve was to search for the truth diligently and to embrace it wherever I found it and whatever it might cost' (Scott, 95).[15] The title of the account of his conversion was derived from this attitude.

3.   According to Scott, the process of changing one's religious convictions happens very slowly and in stages. In his case, this process of conversion lasted around three years (between 1775 and 1777). 'I proceeded very gradually,and with extreme caution'(101). He wrote that his contact with other Evangelicals such as Newton during this period had not been vital for the process.In fact, he had rejected Newton for a long time. What had really brought about his conversion had been prepared by his study of the Scriptures, the search for truth and trust in the force of prayer. Yet it was not himself or other people

who had brought about his devotion to God but it was God himself
who had carried out his work on him.

2.3. Scott, Newman and the Evangelicals at the Beginning of the Nineteenth Century.

Scott's account of his conversion differs greatly from other classical
accounts of his religious tradition. It contains nothing of the torment
of Bunyan and nothing of the drama of the life story of Newton
(1725-1807) whom he took as an example. After an unsettled life at
sea during which he was for some time a slave dealer, Newton had
found his ecclesiastical vocation.[16] Scott recounted in great detail his
painstaking theological reading and the contradictions of Anglican
theologians of his century and the convergence of their ideas with
Evangelical 'Methodist' preachers and authors he had found. Apart
from the pastoral intention already mentioned, his book also possessed
a significant apologetic character. It defended Methodism against its
opponents in the Church of England. Scott wished to show these
opponents their rejection was based on prejudice and ignorance of the
fact that Anglican and Methodist doctrine had real similarities.

This positioning coincided with the ecclesiastical self-assessment of
the Evangelicals at the beginning of the nineteenth century.[17] On the
one hand, they recognized the necessity for a visible church and the
Church of England had such a function for them; on the other hand,
however, the real Church for the Evangelicals consisted of the invisible
church of the converted men. As one can imagine, this led to tension
concerning practical pastoral work when parishioners who regarded
themselves as converted men started to hold their own meetings and
itinerant preachers joined them and separated them from the rest of the
community (parish) of unconverted men. At the same time the
Evangelicals clearly accepted the fact that the visible Church had to
consist of a human formation of converted and unconverted men. The
dissenters from the visible Church were rejected by the Evangelicals
who at the same time distanced themselves from suspicions that they
were Calvinists and especially from the suspicion that they believed in
predestination.[18]

Scott also dealt with these borderlines very painstakingly in his
autobiography. He wrote repeatedly that so-called Methodism was
unifiable with the doctrine of the Church of England and Scott called
his Calvinism an intermediary phase from which he had moved
completely away. And again it was the example of an itinerant
Evangelical preacher, Newton, who had roused him in his parish from
religious lethargy and who must obviously have been competition for
him for a section of his parishoners.

The intellectual character of Scott's autobiography is finally evident in its critical annotation on the so-called enthusiasm of the Evangelicals. For his part Scott had to say: 'I never was taught anything by impulses, impressions, visions, dreams, or revelations'. Accordingly the emphasis of his autobiography is not placed on the process of the conversion as an emotional experience but rather on the conversion as a change of religious convictions in line with various Anglican authors. One can imagine how attractive Scott was within the Anglican Church and especially within Evangelically-minded circles. He legitimised its position within the State Church.

In the *Apologia* Newman made absolutely no attempt at legitimisation. Like Scott, however, he also fought for the recognition of the account of his religious convictions. In the *Apologia* he attempted to illustrate the inner harmony and intellectual integrity of the account of his faith. And the more he was able to relate his story within the Evangelical autobiographical tradition, the more he could rely on the acceptance of the Evangelicals and Anglicans. So Scott's autobiography provided Newman with a model, as Peterson quite rightly argues, as to how he could give an account within this Evangelical tradition without having to adopt the Evangelical concept of conversion in its strict sense.[19]

Peterson puts forward the theory that in the *Apologia* Newman was using the Evangelical conversion schema for the reconstruction of his own life story and this in the first three chapters. Then in the third chapter he took up the Augustinian or the Catholic tradition whose aim is to have the *confessio* in the sense of a profession of the doctrine of the Church not the *conversio* and the *explanatio* of this profession.[20]

The reading of the *Force of Truth* teaches us that this educational emphasis which Peterson accredits to the Augustinian tradition could already be perceived in Scott's writings, so that in this respect also Newman had a model from Scott which at the time of his completion of the *Apologia* must have undoubtedly been prominent in his mind and which he mentioned honestly in the *Apologia* as the only Evangelical book of any significance for the development of his religious opinions. The *Apologia* is the account of a change in religious convictions, the profession of faith and the apologetically sound presentation of those objects of faith which in the view of earlier co-religionists, in this case, the Anglicans, were seen as the difficulty and the reason for the rejection of that religious path which Newman was now treading. Just as Scott wished to clear up the Anglican misunderstanding of Methodist faith assumed by him, so did Newman for the Catholic doctrine. Just as Scott said that anyone who was to study the relevant theologians would finally end up in Methodism,

Newman claimed that anyone who was to study the Catholic position without prejudice would in the end espouse the Catholic truth in the same way. Another parallel with Scott was Newman's statement that only at the age of sixteen did he actually form a religious belief.[21] This same statement was, indeed, frequently expressed by young people from the Evangelical milieu in the eighteenth and nineteenth centuries.[22]

NOTES

1. S. Dessain, 'Newman's First Conversion', in *Internationale Cardinal-Newman-Studien*, *[NSt]* vol. III, pp. 37-53; Tristram (ed.), *J.H.Newman's Autobiographical Writings*, (London/New York 1956) *[AWr]*, p. 142; *Selbstbiographie nach seinen Tagebüchern*, (Stuttgart, 1959), *[SB]*, p. 181; P. Willi, *Sünde und Bekehrung*, (St.Ottilien 1992), p. 44, note 13; p. 53, note 48.

2. According to Tristram since 1822. (Tristram, *SB* p. 181).

3. Contrary to P. Willi, who wrote: *'Auch wenn sich die Bekehrung Newmans im 'Evangelikalen Milieu' vollzog, geschah sie doch nicht nach Evangelikalem Muster'*. (Willi, *Sünde u.Bekehrung*, p. 48, note 32)

4. Manuscript Nr.: A 9.1.c. The author thanks Gerard Tracey who brought this manuscript to his notice.

5. Newman wrote on the 29th. September 1820: 'I say then, that it is *absolutely necessary* for *every* one to undergo a total *change* in his heart and affections *before* he can enter into the kingdom of heaven.... The question *then* is, Do we, when children, receive this change in baptism? For myself I can answer that I did not; and that, when God afterwards in His mercy created me anew, no one can say it was only *reforming*. I know and am sure that before I was blind, but now I see' (*AWr* p. 165).

6. L.H.Peterson, 'Newman's *Apologia pro Vita Sua* and the Traditions of English Spiritual Autobiography', in: *Proceedings of the Modern Languages Association [PMLA]* 100, No.2 (1985) pp. 300-314, here: p. 313, note 6. Peterson refers to the paper *Memoir* of Newman (*AWr* p. 80).- Newman borrowed Dodderidge's *The Family Expositor*, (London, 1761), on the 27th July 1823 from Oriel College. About Newman's lendings of books at Trinity College we have no notes. (Letter from M. Steggle, Archive Assistant, Trinity College Oxford, 12 November 1993).

7. *AWr* p. 166

8. *AWr* p. 203; *SB* p. 262. The development of this change in Newman's religious opinions we may see in his diaries of that time: 'Had a conversation with Hawkins on real and nominal Christianity, in fact on conversion. He admitted there was a line, but he put it much lower than I should. The

majority, he said, of my congregation would not be touched by my preaching; for they would be conscious to themselves of not doing *enough*, not of doing *nothing*. May I get light, as I proceed'. (21 July 1824, *AWr* p. 201) — 'Lately I have been thinking much on the subject of grace, regeneration etc. and reading Sumner's *Apostolical Preaching*, which Hawkins has given me. Sumner's book threatens to drive me either into Calvinism, or baptismal regeneration, and I wish to steer clear of both ...' (24 August 1824, *AWr* p. 202) — 'I am lodged in the same house with Pusey, and we have had many conversations on the subject of religion, I arguing for imputed righteousness, he against it, I inclining to separate regeneration from baptism, he doubting its separation etc.' (16 December 1824, *AWr* p. 203).

9. *NSt* III, p. 53.

10. *NSt* III, p. 50.

11. The book he 'had been possessed of' since his boyhood; Newman, *Apologia pro Vita Sua*, ed. M.J.Svaglic, Oxford 1990, p. 18

12. All quotations are from Thomas Scott, *The Force of Truth*, Carlisle, Pennylvania 1984.

13. 'My understanding was not yet opened to understand such plain scriptures ...' (69) The same statement is known from many other Puritan and Evangelical authors. See for example Bunyan before his conversion: 'I heard, but I understood not'. (*Grace Abounding to the Chief of Sinners* (1666) § 37)

14. Newman's '*cor ad cor loquitur*' may be an echo of such an Evangelical experience.

15. See Newman, 24 August 1824: 'I think I really desire the truth, and would embrace it wherever I found it'. (*AWr* p. 202)

16. John Newton, *Out of the depths' being the Autobiography of the Rev. John Newton*, (London 1924 [first 1764]) — D.B. Hindmarsh, 'I am a sort of middle-man'. — *John Newton and the English Tradition between the Conversion of Wesley and Wilberforce*, D.Phil., Oxford 1993

17. For the following see G.F.A.Best, 'The Evangelicals and the Established Church in the Early Ninteenth Century', in: *The Journal of Theological Studies*, New Series (April 1959) Vol. 10, part 1, pp. 63-78

18. Best, pp. 70f; 75f.

19. Peterson, in: *PMLA* p. 302

20. *Ibidem.*

21. *Apologia*, p. 17. — Newman wrote in a letter to Keble: 'When I was a boy of fifteen, and living a life of sin, with a very dark conscience and a very profane spirit, He mercifully touched my heart; and with innumerable sins, yet I have not forsaken Him from that time, nor He me. He has upheld me to this hour, and I have called myself his servant'. *Correspondence of J.H.Newman with John Keble and Others 1839-1845*, ed. at the Birmingham Oratory, (London, 1917), p. 314.

22. William James quotes a statistical inquiry of Starbuck, who has shown

'how closely parallel in its manifestations the ordinary "conversion" which occurs in young people brought up in Evangelical circles is to that growth into a larger spiritual life which is a normal phase of adolescence in every class of human beings. The age is the same, falling usually between fourteen and seventeen. The symptoms are the same, — sense of incompleteness and imperfection; brooding, depression, morbid introspection, and sense of sin; anxiety about the hereafter; distress over doubts, and the like. And the result is the same — a happy relief and objectivity, as the confidence in self gets greater through the adjustment of the faculties to the wider outlook.... Conversion is in its essence a normal adolescent phenomenon, incidental to the passage from the child's small universe to the wider intellectual and spiritual life of maturity'. James, *The Varieties of Religious Experience*, [1901/1902], (New York, 1929), pp. 195f.

The author's thanks to Michael Payant

for his work of translation.

VI

NEWMAN'S CONVERSION OF 1845: A FRESH APPROACH

Vincent Ferrer Blehl

There are different ways in which one can consider the notion of conversion and therefore Newman's entrance into the Catholic Church on 9 October 1845. The method I propose to adopt in this article is to consider first what Newman had to say about conversion and then to apply this to his life up to and including the event of 1845. In so doing I will be showing that it was the result of a determined and continuous quest for both holiness and truth.

NEWMAN'S IDEA OF CONVERSION

Newman did not write any systematic treatise on conversion, but he spoke of it in various contexts and with relation to other views of conversion. One has, therefore, in attempting a synthesis, to be mindful of the occasional nature of his remarks. Newman remarked in one sermon that people commonly assign to certain times in their spiritual development the term 'conversion', for example when they begin to serve God more faithfully and seriously than before, or when they have made 'a sudden shoot forward', as it were. Others such as infidels, heathens or heretics assign the term to the time when their error fell off.[1] Such a religious mind is drawn from the error into truth 'not by losing what it had, but by gaining what it had not ... that portion of its original teaching which was to be cast off as absolutely false, would not be directly rejected, but indirectly rejected in the cognition of the truth which is its opposite. True conversion is of a positive, not a negative character'.[2]

Newman was suspicious of so-called 'sudden conversions' and he used St Paul to show that though his conversion seemed sudden, it was not so. He affirmed that there was a good deal in his character which remained unchanged after his conversion, but was 'merely directed to other and higher objects, and purified; it was his creed that changed, and his soul by regeneration'. He showed both before and after an energetic zeal for God, a scrupulous strictness of life and an implicit obedience to what he considered God's will.[3] In these various passages

Newman is referring to two distinct but interrelated developments: one spiritual or religious, the other theological or credal, and though the former especially is sometimes looked upon as the commencement of a serious endeavour to serve God, Newman denied that it was really a beginning. Moreover, in these experiences there is continuity amid change. The reason for this is that he defined conversion in opposition to the Evangelical understanding of conversion.

The Evangelicals asserted that conversion was a one-time affair, though it involved various stages such as 'conviction of sin, terror, despair, news of the free and full salvation, apprehension of Christ, sense of pardon, assurance of salvation, joy and peace, and so on to final perseverance'.[4]   Newman, on the other hand, asserted that conversion is 'the process, not the commencement of a religious course — gradual changing, not an initial change'. The only time that can be certainly designated as a beginning is Baptism, which Newman called 'God's first time'. In Baptism a Christian is given a new life, but this must grow and develop. This development, however, is irregular, because, despite the new nature, man contends with the remains of original sin within him: a principle of disobedience, of selfishness, of pride. Consequently, though generally speaking a baptized person is under a process of divine influence and sanctification, it is a process 'often interrupted, often given over, then resumed, irregularly carried on, heartily entered into, finally completed as the case may be'.[5]

Changes, though gradual, are not uniform, but proceed 'by fits and starts, being influenced by external events and other circumstances'. This Newman likens to the 'slow, gradual and continual growth of plants', but one day 'they grow more than another; they make a shoot, or at least we are attracted to their growth on that day by some accidental circumstance'.[6] Generally one is not conscious of the spiritual changes that are taking place in one's soul until suddenly one realizes that one is not the same as one had been but has changed. At this point it may perhaps be useful to keep in mind that Newman's concept of religious conversion is not the ordinary understanding of the term, though what he affirms is valid enough. Spiritual development is gradual and extends over a lifetime. One's beliefs or one's fuller understanding of those beliefs will, likewise, be expanded, developed and deepened. These developments will vary with the individual and are the results of grace accepted and acted upon.

'DIVINE CALLS'

Such growth and development is intimately connected with responses to calls from God. God calls us, Newman asserted, 'again and again in order to sanctify us. If we fall from our Baptism, He calls us to repent; if we are striving to fulfil our calling, He calls us on from grace to grace, and from holiness to holiness, while life is given us'.[7]

Newman explains that there is nothing miraculous in these calls. Christ works through our natural faculties of reason and conscience and in the concrete circumstances of life. Calls are often sudden and unexpected and 'indefinite and obscure in their consequences'. These are the various trials that come upon us, 'something which, if encountered well, will confirm a man in his present way ... and raise him into a higher state of knowledge and holiness'. Newman gives several examples based upon personal experience: it may be 'the loss of some dear friend or relative' or getting acquainted 'with some one whom God employs to bring before us a number of truths which were closed on us before; and we but half understand them, and but half approve them, and yet God seems to speak in them and Scripture to confirm them'. This is a case which not infrequently occurs, and it involves, says Newman, 'a call "to follow on to know the Lord."'[8]

The instances of divine calls in Scripture show that they require instant obedience, calling us to 'we know not what; they call us in darkness. Faith alone can obey them'.[9] Moreover these calls are part of the operation of God's providence, leading the individual soul, but are generally not recognized as such at the time. Newman gives as the reason God does not reveal where he is leading us that we might be frightened did we see the whole prospect at once. Trust in God, therefore, is an essential ingredient in the process of submitting ourselves to the guidance of the providence of God.[10]

NEXUS BETWEEN HOLINESS AND THE DISCOVERY OF TRUTH

There is a connection between growth in holiness and the quest for religious truth. The question is, where is such truth to be found? As an Anglican, Newman asserted that people embrace different religions but 'only one is the truth and the perfect truth ... God knows which it is; and towards that one and only Truth He is leading us forward', and by obedience to these calls 'we pass from one state of knowledge to another, we are introduced into a higher region from a lower'. Obedience to the light we possess is, therefore, the way to gain more light.[11]

The growing liberalism of the day concluded from the diversity of sects and religions that religion is only a matter of opinion and a man has a right to his own opinion so long as it is sincerely held. Newman opposed and criticized this position for leaving out of account the basic principle that truth must be sought through obedience to conscience. A person who follows conscience, even when that conscience is in error, will be led along the path to Truth, for his opinions will not be the result 'of mere chance reasoning or fancy, but of an improved heart'.

In several sermons, such as 'Truth Hidden When Not Sought After', 'Obedience to God the Way to Faith in Christ', and 'Obedience the Remedy for Religious Perplexity', Newman drove home this point.[12]

Let us now examine Newman's life and from the existing records show the major changes in his spiritual life and in his religious opinions. In so doing we can detect the going forward, the falling back, the return to spiritual ideals and the submission to God's will as manifested in calls. One can likewise perceive how his growth in holiness led him forward in his quest for Truth.

NEWMAN'S SO-CALLED FIRST CONVERSION

At Ealing School in 1816 with the help of Evangelical and Calvinistic authors Newman underwent a conversion experience which was really not a commencement but, as he said, 'a returning to, a renewing of, principles under the Holy Spirit which I had already felt, and in a measure acted on, when young'.[13] He changed from a life of sin and scepticism to live a strict religious life with daily reading and meditation on the Scriptures. This change also involved the reception of certain truths. He became certain of the existence of God 'as cutting at the root of doubt, providing a chain between the soul and God'.[14] He acknowledged too that he had 'received into his intellect impressions of dogma, which, through God's mercy, have never been effaced or obscured'.[15] He accepted, for example, the doctrine of the Trinity. He also accepted the Calvinist doctrine of election to glory and perseverence in grace, but these in time fell away. With the gift of Beveridge's *Private Thoughts*, given to him by Walter Mayers, his spiritual guide, he already began to reflect upon his beliefs and he continued to do so in the years to come.[16] And so Newman embarked on his quest for holiness and truth.

LIFE AT OXFORD

As an undergraduate at Oxford, Newman lived a religious life. He later revealed that he went through his residence 'without wounding my conscience by any gross or scandalous sin'.[17] After gaining a scholarship, however, his thoughts turned to a worldly career. 'I hoped great things for myself, not liking to go into the Church, but to the Law. I attended History Lectures (Professorial), hearing that the names were reported to the minister'.[18] In the solitude of the Long Vacation of 1820, while preparing for his examinations, he reflected on his life and, feeling he had become proud upon receiving the scholarship, he prayed not to take honours in his final exams if it would lead him into sin. He failed to take them but looked upon his failure as providential.[19] Returning to Oxford by reason of his scholarship he prepared to stand for the Oriel fellowship, which he gained in 1822.

The period between 1821-1824 was a time of marked change and development in Newman's spiritual life. His private journal reveals his constant and earnest endeavours to lead an interior life of prayer and to overcome what he considered his main sins and defects, especially pride, vanity, ambitiousness, anger and ill-temper (toward his brother Frank in particular) and contentiousness.[20] He spent hours in prayer and in reading the Scriptures. He took Holy Communion every fortnight and practised self-examination, especially before its reception. In 1823 he began to memorize large portions of the Bible, including whole books, and he contemplated becoming a missionary in foreign lands.[21] This period included an attempt to understand more fully his Evangelical beliefs. Starting in 1821 he spent the entire Easter term trying to systematize his beliefs under such headings as 'The Fall', 'The Gift of the Holy Spirit', 'On the Unconverted Man', 'Conversion', 'On Good Works, the Necessary Fruits of Faith', and 'Indwelling Sin'. He is surprised to find that his own conversion experience does not fit the pattern of Evangelical conversion, and hence he has to go by what is written in the books.[22] This period, which he later set down as one of the strictest in his life as an Anglican, ends with his decision to be ordained and to take the position of curate at St Clement's Oxford.[23]

As a curate he employed himself with enormous energy in visiting all his parishioners and preaching two lengthy sermons each Sunday. He also began to re-examine his Evangelical beliefs in light of Edward Hawkins's criticism of his first sermon for dividing the Christian world into two classes: the converted and the unconverted. His parochial experience convinced him that Calvinism is not 'a key to the phenomena of human nature, as they occur in the world' and that 'the religion he had received from John Newton and Thomas Scott would not work in a parish; that it was unreal'. Sumner's *Apostolic Preaching*, which Hawkins gave him, was influential in rooting out his Evangelical creed. Before the end of the two-year period he felt he had to accept some form of baptismal regeneration, normally denied by the Evangelicals.[24] Nevertheless he did not divest himself entirely of Evangelical views. In 1830 he still held to the Evangelical understanding of justification and sanctification. The in-dwelling of the Holy Spirit was only clearly and firmly asserted a few years later.[25]

Despite an earlier warning from his father, Newman felt certain he would never change his views. How did he explain the change? First, he realized that he had taken a good deal on faith from Scott and other Evangelical authors and upon examination did not find them confirmed in Scripture. Secondly, as he explained in the *Grammar of Assent*, a religion is a collection of various kinds of assent, some certain, others only opinion. Applying this to the change in his early beliefs, he affirmed that there were four doctrines which he held as if certain truths: those of the Holy Trinity, of the Incarnation, of Predestination, and of the Lutheran 'apprehension of Christ'. The first three, which are doctrines of the Catholic Church and, being such, are true, did not fade away, whereas the fourth, which is not true, though he thought it was, did in fact fade away.[26]

FALLING BACK AND MOVING FORWARD

In his farewell sermon at St Clement's in June 1826, Newman affirmed that in resigning his curacy and taking the position of tutor he believed he was following what God was calling him to do. He looked upon it as a pastoral charge and hence in harmony with his vocation as a minister of Christ. There was therefore continuity amid change. He devoted himself to his work with great enthusiasm and energy, but soon found himself caught up in the doings and politics of university life. According to his own account, he was drifting in the direction of the liberalism of the day and beginning to prefer intellectual to spiritual excellence. This was providentially cut off by ill-health and the death of his sister Mary.[27] As is clear from his poems about Mary and from some of his letters, he acquired a vivid realization of the invisible world behind the veil of the visible one into which Mary had departed and where she was now dwelling. He begins to feel that her presence is more real now than when she lived on earth. Secondly, he becomes more detached from the world.[28]

Later, in an account of conscience to Keble, he writes, 'He led me forward by a series of Providences from the age of nineteen (1820) till twenty-seven. "I was the work of His hands", for he repeatedly and variously chastised me and at last, to win me from the world, He took from me a dear sister — and just at the time He gave me kind friends to teach me His way more perfectly'.[29] These friends were Hurrell Froude and John Keble himself, whom Newman got to know more intimately; both of them greatly influenced his views spiritually and theologically. He began to pray against rising in the Church, thus completely conquering ambitious thoughts. Newman attempted to reform the tutorial system at Oriel in an effort to render it more pastoral and in so doing he came into conflict with the Provost, Edward Hawkins, who stopped his supply of pupils. He began to study the Fathers of the Church and to compose his first book, *The Arians of the Fourth Century*, on which he started work in June 1831. As a result he decided to remain at Oxford and to become a theologian.[30] In the same year he preached an ordination sermon, in which he viewed the ministerial office in a deeper and fuller light than when he was ordained.

Concerned about the state of the Church, its comfortable worldliness and the growth of liberalism, Newman argued that the Church from its earliest days had always opposed error and sought 'to promote Truth and Holiness'. It was therefore the special duty of a minister of Christ to have 'a systematic view of truth', and to hold theologically correct views, so as to guide others.[31]

After completing the *Arians* in 1832 and having travelled the Mediterranean with the Froudes, Newman returned alone to Sicily in April 1833 where he fell ill with a fever. The accompanying spiritual experience had a lasting effect upon him. He judged himself to have been guilty of pride and self-will, especially in his quarrel with the Provost and in returning to Sicily alone. Yet he kept saying to himself, 'I have not sinned against light'. He also felt he would not die because God had a work for him to do in England. He now resolved to search for God's will, not his own, and to conform his own will to God in loving surrender and with trust in his providence, as he expressed it in his famous hymn, *Lead Kindly Light*, and in the less well-known poem, *Providences*, beginning 'When I look back' ('*Semita Justorum*')[32] Like that of St Paul the change was not a radical change of principle, but his energies were channelled in a different direction and purified, or, as he said of himself, I was 'in all things the same, except that a new object was given me.'[33]

THE OXFORD MOVEMENT

Soon after Newman's return to England, Keble preached his assize sermon 'National Apostasy', 14 July 1833, from which time Newman dated the beginning of the Oxford or Tractarian Movement, of which he soon became the acknowledged leader. With enormous zeal and activity he promoted what he called Anglican principles: 1) the principle of dogma in opposition to doctrinal liberalism, i.e. that dogma is only opinion; 2) certain truths based upon dogma, e.g., a visible Church with sacraments and rites which are the channels of invisible grace; and 3) protest against Rome. The protest was directed against what were considered to be corruptions of the original doctrine by Rome and additions to it. He proposed therefore a *via media* between what he called 'ultra-Protestantism' or simply 'Protestantism', on the one hand and the corruptions of Rome on the other. He had supreme confidence in his position, based as it was on the Anglican divines.[34] In 1836 there is evidence of a clear development in Newman's spiritual life. The change is occasioned by the death of his close friend, Hurrell Froude, the death of his mother, and the marriages of his two sisters. On his birthday, 21 February, always a day of self-examination, he wrote: 'I think I am conscious to myself that, whatever are my faults, I wish to live and die to His glory — to surrender wholly to Him to be His instrument for whatever work and at whatever personal sacrifice — though I cannot duly realize my own words when I say so'.[35]

Froude's father asked Newman to accept some book from Hurrell's library as a memento. He chose Butler's *Analogy*, but it was already promised to someone else. Rogers suggested that Newman take Froude's Breviary. He did so and began to read it daily and to spend three to four hours in prayer. He published a tract (*Tract 75*)'On the Roman Breviary as embodying the substance of the devotional services of the Church Catholic'.[36] He suggested that it should be made the substance of daily devotion.[37] To his sister Harriett he mentioned the spiritual grace granted to him at this time, which was a renewal of what he felt when he lost his sister Mary. 'I am learning more than hitherto to live in the presence of the dead — this is a gain which strange faces cannot take away'.[38] At this time Newman also systematized his theological views in lectures on the 'Prophetical Office of the Church', offering them as 'helps towards the formation of a recognized Anglican theology'. He told Jemima that the lectures constituted 'no advance on any thing I have said — but a systematizing, consolidating, supplying premises etc.' He added, 'I say nothing, I believe, without the highest authority among our writers'.[39] The lectures show how the Anglican position differs from Romanism. He sees clearly the need of 'systematizing' the Anglican divines, and so he proceeded to do so in the '*Catena Patrum*' published as *Tracts* (Nos. *74* and *76*). Since, according to Anglican principles, what was held by the early Church constituted the norm of judging doctrine, he and Pusey started the *Library of the Fathers of the Church*. Once again it was the systematization of his views that constituted the object of his *Lectures on Justification* in 1837, published in the following year. The subject was in his thoughts for years, he wrote to Henry Wilberforce, 'yet I had nothing produceable scientifically'.[40] These lectures were another attempt to steer a course between Protestantism, on the one hand, and Romanism, on the other. No matter how many attacks were launched against the Tractarians and himself in particular, he retained confidence in the Cause.

FIRST DOUBTS ABOUT THE ANGLICAN CHURCH

In an article published in the August 1839 issue of the *Dublin Review*, 'The Anglican Claims of Apostolic Succession', Nicholas Wiseman examining the Donatist controversy argued that the Anglican Church was in schism. It was the occasion of Newman's first doubts about the Anglican Church.[41] On 21 September 1839 Newman noted in his private journal details of increased strictness in his customary private fasting, and concluded with the words: '*Gratias tibi Domine* — whither art thou leading me?' On 27 October he preached his sermon, 'Divine Calls', which concluded with the affirmation that nothing could be compared with this aim 'of not being disobedient to a heavenly vision', and the exhortation 'Let us beg and pray Him day by day to reveal Himself to our souls more fully ... so to work within us that we may sincerely say, "Thou shalt guide me with Thy counsel, and after that receive me into glory. Whom have I in heaven but Thee? and there is none upon earth that I desire in comparison of Thee; my flesh and my heart faileth; but God is the strength of my heart, and my portion for ever."'[42]

September 1839 to 1845 was a period of marked development both in Newman's spiritual life and in his religious opinions. These developments were mingled together, 'the strictest years of my life' as he later wrote to his sister Jemima. The period between his first doubts in 1839 and his entrance into the Catholic Church in October 1845 was one of intense prayer and fasting, of searching for God's will, of trying to discern where Truth lay, of inner probing of self and one's motives, of patient waiting for signs from God. Prudently he revealed his doubts only to two persons and later to a third. Believing it a duty to put aside objections to one's religious system, he composed an article in refutation of Wiseman's argument, 'Catholicity of the English Church'. Since the *via media* no longer provided a positive argument for the catholicity of the Anglican Church, his main argument for the Anglican claims now lay in the positive and special charges which he could bring against Rome, and so he lashed out against what he considered to be Rome's political and social line of action and her lack of morality and sanctity.[43]

In February 1841 Newman published *Tract 90* which presented a Catholic interpretation of the Thirty-Nine Articles. He did so, among other reasons, because it was objected that his position could not be reconciled with them since they were drawn up against Rome. In the uproar that followed he withdrew from the Movement but he continued to defend the Anglican position, though with other arguments. He did not answer the slanders that were spoken against him but retired to Littlemore in February 1842 to live a semi-monastic life of study and prayer.

What Newman called 'three blows' confirmed him in his doubts about the Anglican Church.[44] As a result of *Tract 90*, Dr Russell of Maynooth began to correspond with him and finally convinced him that what Newman called 'the secondary and traditionary system' of Rome had no existence in fact, nor did the ordinary books of devotion on Our Lady show any evidence that Rome 'suffered honours to be paid to the Blessed Virgin ... incompatible with the Supreme, Incommunicable Glory of the One Infinite and Eternal'.[45] 'Goaded', as he put it, by his conscience, Newman published in the *Conservative Journal* of February 1843 a retraction of his strong sayings against Rome, an act of great humility for one who had once been so confident in his position. The Lent of 1843 was the strictest for Newman as far as fasting was concerned. A meditation of an hour or an hour and a half was added every morning, and he and his companions made a retreat according to the Spiritual Exercises of St. Ignatius Loyola. On 7 September 1843, with the acquiescence of Keble, he resigned his position at St Mary's, as he no longer felt that he could in conscience be a teacher in the Anglican Church.[46]

The conviction that the Church of Rome was 'the one true fold of Christ' had grown stronger, but he could not calculate when it would affect his will and become practicable. In 1843 Newman was already convinced of the development of Christian doctrine, but by July 1844 he had progressed much further. 'I am far more certain (according to the Fathers) that we are in a state of culpable separation, than that developments do not exist under the Gospel, and that the Roman developments are not the true ones. I am far more certain that our (modern) doctrines are wrong than that the Roman (modern) doctrines are wrong'.[47] He therefore decided to put his views on development on paper and if, at the end, his convictions were not weaker, he would take steps to enter the Catholic Church. Before he finished the work he felt obliged in conscience to ask to be received.[48]

Why did Newman not do so sooner? First, he did not feel a clear call in conscience to do so. Secondly, if he were in error in entering the Catholic Church, he would lead others into error, or despairing of truth, into scepticism. Thirdly, he thought he might be suffering from 'judicial blindness', a punishment for some secret fault, and so he revealed his conscience to Keble. Fourthly, he had a dread of going by feelings and not by reason and conscience. As well as unsettling them in their beliefs, the pain he was giving to others was intense. He also recognized the price he would have to pay: for in joining a despised minority he would become ostracized from relatives and friends. In the Autumn of 1844 it made him ill and his doctor issued a stern warning, as a result of which he seems to have given up his fasting or at least to have mitigated it. In a poignant but painful correspondence with his sister Jemima he revealed his clear recognition of the sacrifices he was making in becoming a Catholic, but at the same time his complete trust in the providence of God.[49] A number of people, both then and subsequently, judged his action heroic.

CONCLUSION

If one accepts Newman's definition of religious conversion as a life-long process, then his conversion was not over in 1845. He continued to respond to calls from God, as I have sketched out elsewhere.[50] What about his theological or ecclesial conversion? In the *Apologia* Newman writes 'from the time that I became a Catholic, of course I have no further history of my religious opinions to narrate', but he goes on to say he does not mean that he had given up 'thinking on theological subjects'. Indeed the rest of Chapter Five shows that he had not. His adherence to the Catholic Church had brought peace and contentment and he persevered unto the end in it.[51]

'To live is to change, and to be perfect is to have changed often', Newman remarked in his *Essay on the Development of Christian Doctrine*.[52] In a sermon he once said, 'The perfect Christian state is that in which our duty and our pleasure is the same, when what is right and true is natural to us and in which God's service "is perfect freedom". And this is the state towards which all true Christians are tending ... an utter and absolute captivity of their will to His will, is their fulness and joy and everlasting life'.[53]

On the Sunday after his death, a fellow Oratorian preached on the applicability to him of the text, 'the just man made perfect'. Since then the Church has officially endorsed that judgment in declaring that Newman had indeed practised the virtues to an heroic degree.

NOTES

1. J. H. Newman, *Parochial and Plain Sermons* (London: Longmans, Green standard edition), VIII, sermon 15, pp. 226-27 [hereafter: *PPS*]. All references to Newman's works are to the Longmans standard edition, unless otherwise indicated.

2. J. H. Newman, *Discussions and Arguments*, p. 200.

3. John Henry Newman, *Autobiographical Writings*, ed. Henry Tristram (London: Sheed and Ward, 1956) p. 80 [hereafter: *AW*].

4. *PPS* VIII, 15, pp. 219-224, 227-28.

5. 'Remarks on the Covenant of Grace', 1828, Birmingham Oratory Archives, but the same view is given in his sermons, e.g. *PPS* VIII, sermon 15 and reaffirmed in letter of 2 June 1883 to George T. Edwards, *The Letters and Diaries of John Henry Newman*, eds. C.S. Dessain et al., 1961-, XXX, p. 224, [hereafter: *LD*].

6. *PPS* VIII, 15, pp. 225-26.

7. *PPS* VIII, 2, p. 23.

8. *PPS* VIII, 2, pp. 28-29.

9. *PPS* VIII, 2, p. 22.

10. *PPS* I, 26, pp. 348-49; *PPS* VI, 17. These concepts are more fully developed in Vincent Ferrer Blehl, S.J., *The White Stone: The Spiritual Theology of John Henry Newman* (Petersham, Mass.: St Bede's Publications, 1994) pp. 37-45.

11. *PPS* VIII, 2, pp. 27-28.

12. *PPS* VIII, 13 and 14; *PPS* I, 18.

13. *AW*, p. 172.

14. *AW*, p. 150.

15. J. H. Newman, *Apologia Pro Vita Sua* 4, [hereafter: Apo].

16. *LD* I, pp. 30-31.

17. *LD* II, p. 58.

18. *AW*, p. 45.

19. *AW*, pp. 159-60; *LD* I, 30, n. 1.

20. *AW*, pp. 174f, 188-89, 194, 196-98.

21. *AW*, pp. 165-66, 175, 194.

22. *AW*, pp. 166-67, 172.

23. *AW*, pp. 238, 198-99.

24. *AW*, pp. 76-77, 78f.

25. John Henry Newman, *Sermons 1824-1843*, vol. 2, ed. Vincent Ferrer Blehl, S.J. (Oxford: Clarendon Press, 1993) pp. xv-xvi, and Section II: *Sin and Justification*.

26. *AW*, pp. 80-82.

27. *Apo,* p. 14.

28. For a detailed account see Louis Bouyer, *Newman: His Life and Spirituality* (London: Burns & Oates, 1958) pp. 102-10.

29. *Correspondence of John Henry Newman with John Keble and Others ... 1839-1845* (London: Longmans, Green, 1917), pp. 315.

30. *LD* II, p. 367.

31. 'On the Ministerial order as an existing divine institution. Ordination Sermon' MS sermon No. 323, Birmingham Oratory Archives.

32. J. H. Newman, *Verses on Various Occasions* 187; *AW*, pp. 121f.

33. *PPS* VIII, 15, pp. 227-28; *Apo,* p. 36.

34. *Apo,* pp. 144-58.

35. *LD* V, p. 240.

36. *LD* V, p. 246 and n. 1.

37. *LD* VI, p. 66.

38. *LD* V, pp. 311-12.

39. *LD* VI, p. 6.

40. *LD* VI, p. 212.

41. 'It professed that the fact of isolation and opposition was always taken as a sufficient condemnation of bodies so circumstanced.... This was argued chiefly from the language of St Augustine, as elicited in the Donatist controversy, and the same sort of minute parallel was drawn between the state of the Donatists and our own, which I had felt on reading the history of the Monophysites'. Letter of J.H. Newman to Mrs William Froude, 9 April 1844, Birmingham Oratory Archives.

42. *PPS* VIII, 2, p. 32; *Apo,* p. 118.

43. *Apo,* p. 120.

44. In connection with his work on St Athanasius 'the ghost came a second time'. 'I saw clearly that in the history of the Arians, the pure Arians were the Protestants, the semi-Arians were the Anglicans and that Rome now was what it was then'. Secondly, the bishops one after another began to charge against *Tract 90.* 'I recognized it as a condemnation; it was the only one that was in their power'. The third blow came from the establishment by Parliament of the Jerusalem bishopric, allowing Protestants 'to put themselves under an Anglican bishop, without any renunciation of their errors or regard to their due reception of baptism and confirmation'. (*Apo,* pp. 139-46).

45. *Apo,* pp. 194-97, 148.

46. *AW,* pp. 221-28, *Apo,* p. 221.

47. *Apo,* p. 194f.

48. *Apo,* p. 234.

49. *Letters and Correspondence of John Henry Newman during his Life in the English Church* (London: Longmans, Green, 1891) II, pp. 439, 445, 450-51, 459-61, 464.

50. V. F. Blehl, 'Newman's Personal Endeavour as a Catholic to Follow the "Light" and the "Call"', in *Newman-Studien* 12 (1988) pp. 27-34.

51. *Apo,* p. 238.

52. *Essay on the Development of Christian Doctrine* (p. 40).

53. *PPS* IV, 1, p. 4.

VII

NEWMAN'S CONCEPT OF *'REALIZING'*

Bernhard Trocholepczy

It is proposed to show in this paper how Newman's concept of *realizing* is related to his principles of theology and what he calls the *'occasion'*. Thus we may bring into focus the relevance of Newman's understanding of the term *'mind'* and its importance both for the individual being and — in the context of an ecclesiological learning process — for the Church. I intend to present my considerations in three steps: First I will introduce *realizing* as a basic structure or a basic element in Newman's way of thought and living; then I will turn precisely to the question of how Newman acquired this structure of life and thought in his reception of Aristotelian philosophy — with reference to the *Nicomachean Ethics*; and thirdly I will reflect on some consequences of Newman's structure of thought for his understanding of the Church.

1. BASIC STRUCTURE OR ELEMENTS IN NEWMAN'S WAY OF THINKING AND LIVING: 'TO REALIZE'.

It is interesting that Manning provided an occasion for Newman to *realize*. Newman confessed in a letter to Henry Edward Manning that the latter helped him to 'realize my own views to myself; it makes me see their consistency; it assures me of my own deliberateness'.[1]

In 1843 when Newman reflected on leaving the Anglican Church he wrote, as he stated in his *Apologia*,

> to a friend, who had every claim upon me to be frank with him, Archdeacon Manning: — it will be seen that I disclose the real state of my mind in proportion as he presses me.[2]

By being pressed not to leave the Anglican Church Newman got a view of himself. He claimed that he had to leave the Anglican Church in order to be consistent with his own principles. The word 'view' is important for Newman because this word describes the contrary of mere theory and connects the truth with the person discovering it. Thus the understanding of Newman's use of the word 'view' is a first step to grasp what is meant by *realizing* which is rather more than a theoretical process.[3]

This biographical detail is mentioned because it shows at once that *realizing* is more than a principle of Newman's incarnational theology. It is very characteristic and typical of Newman — not only of him, but especially of him — that one cannot separate life and thinking.[4] It seems to be a good method to attain an understanding of the person and thought of Newman by considering his own principles and by observing how he himself *realized* them in different situations or — we may also say like Newman — *occasions* of his life.

First of all there are personal principles. For example: You have to do your duty.[5] As a young man he made a work plan for his studies. The schedule of his studies is preserved at the Birmingham Oratory and it indicates his reading for his final examination. It shows the accurate way Newman accounted to himself for the hours — sometimes eight or ten hours a day — he spent reading the authors of antiquity. Later on when Newman was 55 he wrote during his Dublin campaign to Mrs. J. W. Bowden : 'Years now are precious, because they are rare, like jewels'.[6]

Then there is another group of principles which are more directly religious: for example not to sin against the light. Newman could state during his illness in Sicily: 'I have not sinned against the light'.[7] Another principle of this sort he got from Thomas Scott — as we know from the *Apologia*: 'Holiness rather than peace'.[8]

Finally there are theological principles. They characterise his theological way of thinking: First of all there is the principle of incarnation — the central truth of Holy Scripture. Newman stated in his *Essay on the Development of Christian Doctrine*: 'I will consider the Incarnation the central truth of the gospel, and the source whence we are to draw out its principles'.[9] Another famous example of his theological principles is the principle of 'self' which not only means that one has to think independently with one's own head. The principle 'Myself and my creator'[10] is the starting point of Newman's theological inquiries. This principle Newman found during a period of isolation and illness when he was a boy of fifteen and attended a school in Ealing, near London. Later on he stated that the *Grammar* is an example of this *egotism* which he calls 'true modesty':

> I begin with expressing a sentiment, which is habitually in my thoughts, whenever they are turned to the subject of mental or moral science ... viz. that in these provinces of inquiry egotism is true modesty. In religious inquiry each of us can speak only for himself and for himself he has the right to speak. His own experiences are enough for himself, but he cannot speak for others: he cannot lay down the law ... if, as he believes and is sure, it is true, it will

> approve itself to others also, for there is but one truth. And doubtless
> he does find in fact, that, allowing for the difference of minds and
> of modes of speech, what convinces him, does convince others
> also.[11]

And further on Newman says:

> I am suspicious then of scientific demonstrations in a question of
> concrete fact, in a discussion between fallible men. However, let
> those demonstrate who have the gift ... For me, it is more congenial
> to my own judgment to attempt to prove Christianity in the same
> informal way in which I can prove for certain that I have been born
> into this world, and that I shall die out of it.[12]

What seems important is that we cannot separate the personal, religious
and theological principles, each of which we may use to introduce
someone to Newman's thinking and living. It is characteristic of him
that private, religious and theological principles are not in different
provinces or ranges: they should not relate to different parts of a
person's life. Newman stated in a University Sermon in Dublin in
1856: 'I want the intellectual layman to be religious, and the devout
ecclesiastic to be intellectual'.[13] One must always follow one's principles. And following them on the occasion of mastering different
situations one *realizes* what these principles are and thus who one is.
This may be one reason why Newman is called a somewhat unsystematic author. It is not only the logic of theology which is guiding
him in his enquiries but it is also his personal access to the truth.

What is meant by the term *personal access* and what is meant by the
word *realizing*? One of the key passages in which Newman explains
his view of *realizing* is found in a sermon he delivered in 1840. The
sermon is entitled *Subjection of the Reason and Feelings to the
Revealed Word*.[14] Here Newman gives an interpretation of 2 Cor.10:5

> Bringing into captivity every thought to the obedience of Christ
> [*et in captivitatem redigentes omnem intellectum in obsequium
> Christi*].[15]

This verse may even characterise all his considerations in the range of
the philosophy of religion. We learn from the title *Subjection of the
Reason* that reason (the notional range) is not standing by itself, but is
— as Newman explains in his letter to Flanagan — an instrument of a
faculty different from and more relevant than reason: that is the noetic
faculty, the mind, which controls its principles:[16]

> ... though religious men have gifts, and though they know it, yet
> they do not *realize* them.... [We] shall all confess that, at least, there
> is an abundance of matters which men do *not* realize, though they
> ought to do so. For instance, how loudly men talk of the shortness

of this life, of its vanity and unprofitableness, and of the claims which the world to come has upon us! This is what we hear said daily, yet few act upon the truths they utter; and why? because they do not *realize* what they are so ready to proclaim. They do not see Him who is invisible, and His eternal kingdom.[17]

Newman continues:

> Serious men may know indeed ... what their excellences are, whether religious, or moral, or any other, but they do not feel them in that vivid way which we call *realizing*, [my italics]. They do not open their hearts to the knowledge, so that it becomes fruitful. Barren knowledge is a wretched thing, when knowledge ought to bear fruit.[18]

To realize means that knowledge ought to bear fruit. This metaphor includes '*maturation*' and the dimension of time. It is directly related to Newman's early principle, 'Growth the only evidence of life',[19] which later finds its parallel in his theory of development. In his *Essay on the Development of Christian Doctrine* Newman stated: 'Here below to live is to change, and to be perfect is to have changed often'.[20]

Newman continues:

> When men realize a truth, it becomes an influential Principle within them, and leads to a number of consequences both in opinion and in conduct.[21]

He gives an example:

> The case is the same as regards realizing our own gifts. But men of superior minds know them without realizing. They may know that they have certain excellences, if they have them, they may know that they have good points of character, or abilities, or attainments; but it is the way of an unproductive knowledge, which leaves the mind just as it found it.... Another instance of this great gift of knowing without realizing, is afforded us in relation to subjects to which I will but allude. Men who indulge [in] their passions have a knowledge, different in kind from those who have abstained from such indulgence; and when they speak on subjects connected with it, realize them in a way in which others cannot realize them. The very ideas which are full of temptation to the former, the words which are painful to them to utter, all that causes them shame and confusion of face, can be said and thought of by the innocent without any distress at all.[22]

To explore more deeply Newman's understanding of *realizing* we must begin with what he called the *illative sense*, which is the organ of *realizing*.[23] To understand the *illative sense* is to understand *realizing*.

It was Johannes Artz who stated that the important terms of Newman like 'assent', 'certitude', 'implicit reasoning' are all functions of the so-called *illative sense*.[24] And Henri Bremond said, that the *Grammar* is a long definition of the *illative sense*.[25] The roots for an understanding of the term *illative sense* as well as of the term *realizing* lie in Newman's Aristotelian studies.

2. HOW NEWMAN ACQUIRED THIS STRUCTURE OF LIFE AND THOUGHT IN HIS RECEPTION OF ARISTOTELIAN PHILOSOPHY.

2.1. *Understanding of the illative sense and phronesis*

How does Newman define the *illative sense*? In chapter eight of the *Grammar* he quotes Book Six of the *Nicomachean Ethics* of Aristotle. He writes, there is

> a capacity sufficient for the occasion, deciding what ought to be done here and now, by this given person, under these given circumstances. It decides nothing hypothetical, it does not determine what a man should do ten years hence, or what another should do at this time.[26]

On the contrary Newman describes what gives the direction of the present act, 'not for the distant or the future'.[27] Newman calls this sense related to different situations the 'illative sense': 'A grand word for a common thing'[28] and he defines it as the *iudicium prudentis viri*.[29]

> It is the mind that reasons, and that controls its own reasonings, not any technical apparatus of words and propositions. This power of judging and concluding, when in its perfection, I call the Illative Sense.[30]

The *illative sense* is thus defined as a kind of personal voice of each individual, which guides the person in concrete situations. Neither science nor any system of thought is really able to help the individual confronted with a particular case.

On the other hand Newman underlines the possibilities of ethical systems:

> An ethical system may supply laws, general rules, guiding principles, a number of examples, suggestions, landmarks, limitations, cautions, distinctions, solutions of critical and anxious difficulties; but who is to apply them to a particular case?[31]

To recognize what has to be done here and now, the individual has to go back to himself: 'To learn his own duty in his own case, each individual must have recourse to his own rule'.[32]

Newman even defines the human being in contrast to the inferior animals around man by his ability to realize, that means using his *illative sense* step by step:

> What is the peculiarity of our nature, in contrast with the inferior animals around us? It is that, though man cannot change what he is born with, he is a being of progress with relation to his perfection and characteristic good. Other beings are complete from their first existence, in that line of excellence which is allotted to them; but man begins with nothing realized (to use the word), and he has to make capital for himself by the exercise of those faculties which are his natural inheritance. Thus he gradually advances to the fullness of his original destiny. Nor is this progress mechanical, nor is it of necessity; it is committed to the personal efforts of each individual of the species; each of us has the prerogative of completing his inchoate and rudimental nature, and of developing his own perfection out of the living elements with which his mind began to be. It is his gift to be the creator of his own sufficiency; and to be emphatically self-made.[33]

Thus it is the mind of the person which leads the human being in concrete situations. The mind of the individual 'is thus his own law, his own teacher, and his own judge in those special cases of duty which are personal to him'.[34]

2.2. *The Relation of Newman's Thought to Aristotle*

In the *Grammar* Newman takes up the subject of *phronesis*, of *prudentia*, in his introductory definition of the *illative sense*. He stresses that it is the *nous* which is responsible for the perfection of the *illative sense*. Newman develops this most characteristic and central sense of the human being by referring to Aristotle (*Nicomachean Ethics*, Chapter 6). The *Nicomachean Ethics* is a philosophical inquiry into practical truth: it answers the question what kind of truth accompanies the doings of a human being. Thus the subject matter of the *Nicomachean Ethics* is different from that of the *Metaphysics* of the Stagirite. The subjects of the *Metaphysics* are necessary, general and epistemical truth. It is very interesting that Newman, although he admired Aristotle and interpreted him all his life, never quoted this book of Aristotle.

The key question of the *Nicomachean Ethics* is: which kind of practical knowledge accompanies 'doing the truth'? The understanding of doing, of practice, is found at once — without reference to epistemical knowledge (*theoria*). Gadamer interprets Aristotle's understanding of '*Phronesis*' as follows: Practical knowledge differs from theoretical knowledge and is directed towards concrete situations. Practical knowledge has to understand circumstances in their infinite variety. The Aristotelian opposition between theoretical and practical truth means something other than only the opposition between the knowledge of general principles and the knowledge of the concrete, nor does it mean only the possibility to subsume the concrete under general concepts, which we call 'power of judgement'.

Moreover there is a positive, ethical measure. Apprehension and ethical mastering of concrete situations requires such subsuming of the facts into general terms, i.e. the end aimed at, that consequently follows what is correct. The subsuming of the concrete under general concepts presupposes the direction of the will, i.e. an ethical being.[35] The Aristotelian Phronesis is an 'intellectual virtue'. It is not a pure possibility (*dynamis*), but the destination of an ethical being. It can't be without all the ethical virtues. Conversely they can't exist without an intellectual virtue. Although this virtue, i.e. *Phronesis*, being exercised, has the result that one can distinguish what one should do from what one shouldn't do, it is not only good sense or general shrewdness. To distinguish what one should do from what one shouldn't presupposes an ethical habit.[36]

Thus Aristotle criticises the Platonic tradition.[37] By his limitation of Socratic-Platonic intellectualism in the range of the good, Aristotle becomes the founder of ethics as discipline, independent of the *Metaphysics*. By criticising the Platonic idea of the good as general and vague, Aristotle is interested in the human good which is the good for human practice [*cf. Nicomachean Ethics* A 4]. In the same way Aristotle contradicts the identification of virtue and knowledge, of *arete* and *logos*. This identification is the reason why the Platonic theory of ethics is criticized as an exaggeration. Aristotle reduced this exaggeration by demonstrating the *orexis* (which means everybody always strives for something) as the constituent element of man's ethical knowledge. The *orexis* tends to become a habit (*hexis*).[38]

2.3. *The Concept of the Illative Sense*

The Aristotelian concept of practical knowledge to which Newman refers[39] is the mind (*nous*), which cannot be separated from a growing being. Thus Newman shows that reasoning is a personal faculty. This seems to be the most important and significant element of Newman's adaptation of Aristotle: he wants reason understood in connection with the living, developing and growing person.

In this context it is interesting that Heidegger stated in his basic work *Being and Time* (twice at important places — at the beginning and at the end of the book): we have 'to make fast the guiding-line for all philosophical inquiry at the point where it *arises* and to which it *returns*'.[40] And this point is, in Newman's view, the mind of the living person and its first principles. *Phronesis* or *prudentia* which is the source of Newman's *illative sense* was Heidegger's basic phenomenon for a new analysis of existence [*Dasein*] in his basic work *Being and Time*. This is also shown in Heidegger's recently published volume 19, a lecture Heidegger gave in 1924/25 just before the publishing of '*Time and Being*' (in the beginning of 1927). There remains an important task which has so far not yet been undertaken to compare the two original drafts of Heidegger's and Newman's philosophy originating probably from the same phenomenological approach: one in the direction of anthropological analysis and one in the 'existential' analysis.

Heidegger in his interpretation of the *Nicomachean Ethics* doesn't hesitate to call *phronesis (iudicium prudentis viri)* the conscience: 'The phronesis is the movement of the conscience which makes the action transparent'[41] — in the same way Johannes Arzt calls Newman's *illative sense* the noetical parallel of the conscience.[42]

To return to Newman. He wanted to show an understanding of the reason which connects the reasoning faculty with the developing, growing, living ingredients of personal life. The competence of this faculty for judging, the *illative sense*, shows Aristotle's *phronesis* in a new perspective. The personal character of the *illative sense* is underlined by Newman's statement that it is 'not a constituent part of our nature, but a personal endowment'.[43] This endowment needs exercise and training: 'It comes of an acquired habit, though it has its first origin in nature itself, and it is formed and matured by practice and experience'.[44]

Newman cites Aristotle verbatim in order to underline the importance of practice, experience and habits. In the *Nicomachean Ethics* Aristotle deals with the *neoi*, young men without experience: [*Nicomachean Ethics* 1142 a1 1ff]:

> Young men come to be mathematicians and the like, but they cannot possess practical judgment; for this talent is employed upon individual facts, and these are learned only by experience; and a youth has not experience, for experience is only gained by a course of years.[45]

This means for Aristotle and Newman: practical knowledge is always combined with experience.

2.4. *Illative Sense and Reason*

The controversy in 1885 between Newman and Andrew Martin Fairbairn sheds light on the distinction between the *illative sense* and formal reasoning. In order to defend himself against the accusation of Fairbairn, Newman limited the range of reason — 'Reason is the power by which man deduces one proposition from another, or proceeds from premises to consequences; the rational faculty; discursive power'.[46] Newman made a distinction between *reasoning faculty* — the faculty and ability of abstracting — and the *constituent noetic faculty*.[47] The reasoning faculty is limited because it receives its antecedents — the point from which it starts — from other faculties.[48] Thus the *reasoning faculty* is an instrument: 'I have considered Reasoning as an instrument — that is, an instrument for the use of other faculties....'[49]

3. CONSEQUENCES OF NEWMAN'S STRUCTURE OF THOUGHT.

How does Newman explain the way in which the mind of the Church is *realizing*? One question we started with was: How does knowledge of truth become fruitful? There are at least two answers according to Newman: First of all, the principle, the antecedent — as Newman calls it — must be good and correct. And secondly: Newman mentions in his sermon *Subjection of Reason* that we have to open our hearts to the knowledge of the truth we acquire.

As regards the first answer we note what Newman stated in the controversy with Fairbairn:

> Still, what else can a man mean by speaking of a right use [of reason] but that there is wrong? — right [use of reason], because its antecedents are chosen rightly by divinely enlightened mind, being such as intuitions, dictates of the conscience, the inspired Word, the decision of the Church, and the like; whereas we call it false reason or sophistry when its antecedents are determined by pride, self-trust, unbelief, human affection, narrow self-interest, bad education, or other mental agencies, which are found in the world and in the individual'.[50]

Concerning the second answer to the question, it is consequently not reasoning which distinguishes the Church from the world, but the difference of principles from which either the Church or the World is starting. Newman included in his fifteenth University Sermon the verse of Luke 2:19: 'Mary kept all these things, and pondered them in her heart' as a short formula for his theory of *realizing*.[51] Mary in her meditative attitude is not only the ecclesial archetype of the development of doctrine. She is also a perfect exemplification of the realizing process in the Church. The decisive elements are:
a) to have a heart open to the reality of the divine message;
b) to be rooted in good principles.

It is from these elements, that the process of life, under the guidance of the Holy Spirit, becomes fruitful. While, on the contrary, a Church which only pursues principles and reduces life to formulae (one could almost say in a neology: a Church which reduces orthopraxis to orthodoxis) is correct but not fruitful. Newman would put it: 'Barren knowledge is a wretched thing, when it ought to bear fruit'.[52]

NOTES

1. Newman, John Henry: *Apologia pro Vita Sua,* London 1890, p. 222 [*Apo.*].

2. *Apo*, p. 219.

3. Cf. Lash, N.: *Newman on Development. The Search for an Explanation in History*, London 1975, pp. 35-36.

4. Cf. Merrigan, T.: *Clear Heads and Holy Hearts. The Religious and Theological Ideal of John Henry Newman*, Louvain 1991, pp. 1f.

5. Cf. Artz, J., in Newman, J.H.: *Über die Entwicklung der Glaubenslehre. Durchgesehene Neuausgabe der Übersetzung von T. Haecker. Besorgt, kommentiert und mit ergänzenden Dokumenten versehen von J. Artz*, Mainz 1969, p. 426: 'Newman wrote his *Grammar of Assent* in 1870 out of a feeling of duty ... just as he wrote his refutations of Pusey's *Eirenicon* and Gladstone's reproaches against the First Vatican Council.... If he wrote because of his responsibility for others before, now he felt compelled to write the *Development* out of a feeling of duty to himself. Action resulting from duty was a basic principle in Newman's life, especially in times of uncertainty, where there was a lack of clarity'. *[Trans: Br Anselm Brumwell, who has also translated notes 37, 38 and 42].*

6. *The Letters and Diaries of John Henry Newman.* Ed. C.S. Dessain et al., Vol. XVII, p. 378 [*LD*].

7. *LD* IV, p. 8.

8. *Apo*, p. 5.

9. Newman, J.H.: *An Essay on the Development of Christian Doctrine.* Foreword by I. Ker, Notre Dame (Indiana) 1989, p. 324 [*Dev.*].

10. *Apo*, p. 4.

11. Newman, J.H.: *An Essay in Aid of a Grammar of Assent*, ed. with introduction and notes by I.T. Ker, Oxford 1985, p. 248 [*GA*].

12. *GA* p. 264.

13. Newman, J.H.: *Sermons preached on Various Occasions*, London 1892, p. 13.

14. Newman wrote to his sister Jemina in 1841 (October 12th) that volume 6 of his Parochial and Plain Sermons in which he published this sermon is the most doctrinal set he published, and particularly on the subject of the Eucharist. Cf. *Letters and Correspondence of John Henry Newman during his Life in the English Church*, ed. Anne Mozley, vol. 2, London 1891, p. 352.

15. 18 December 1840; cf: Newman, J.H.: *Parochial and Plain Sermons*, Vol. VI, London 1881, p. 255, [*PPS* VI].

16. Cf: *The Theological Papers of John Henry Newman on Faith and Certainty*, ed. H.M. de Achaval and J.D. Holmes, Oxford 1976, p. 153 [*TP*].

17. *PPS* VI, p. 263.

18. *Ibidem.*

19. *Apo*, p. 5.

20. *Dev*, p. 40.

21. *PPS* VI, p. 263.

22. *PPS* VI, pp. 263f.

23. Cf: Artz, J.: 'Der *"Folgerungssinn"*' [illative sense] in Newman's *"Zustimmungslehre"* (*Grammar of Assent*), in: *Internationale Cardinal Newman Studien*. Ed. G. Biemer, H. Fries. Begründet von H. Fries, W Becker, Nürnberg/Sigmaringendorf 1948ff. Vol. II, p. 228: 'I.S. is a norm of certainty. It is also the organ of "realizing"'.[*NSt*]

24. *Ibidem*, p. 245.

25. Cf: *ibidem*, p. 219.

26. *GA*, p. 229.

27. *Ibidem.*

28. *LD* XXIV, p. 375.

29. *GA*, p. 205.

30. *GA*, p. 227f.

31. *GA*, p. 228.

32. *GA*, p. 229.

33. *GA*, p. 225.

34. *GA*, p. 228.

35. Cf. Gadamer: *Wahrheit und Methode. Grundzüge einer philosophischen Hermeneutik*, Tübingen 31972, pp. 18f. [*WuM*]

36. Cf: *ibidem*, p. 19.

37. Cf: Platons *Protagoras* 352 b1. Discussion between Plato and Aristotle cf.: Müller, A.W.: *Praktisches Folgern und Selbstgestaltung nach Aristoteles*, München 1982, pp. 15-25: 'In the *Protagoras*, to which Aristotle principally referred, Socrates had come to the least temporary conclusion, that bad behaviour is based on ignorance; in view of the more or less immediate consequences of this alternative form of behaviour, it is altogether better to

strive after ignorance. This conclusion implies important theses which Aristotle also presents as Socratic tradition: (1) actual knowledge occupies an undisputed ruling position in the human soul: it is not particularly subject to passion; (2) no-one willingly treats anything badly; (3) virtue is knowledge or insight; (4) virtue can be learnt. Aristotle examines all these theses in detail, after which they emerge in a more or less drastically modified form'.(16)

38. 'Owing to his restriction on Socratic-Platonic intellectualism in the search for Good, Aristotle becomes the well-known founder of ethics as an independent discipline, opposed to metaphysics. By criticizing the Platonic idea of Good as an empty generalization, he opposes the search for human Good, the Good in human behaviour [EN A 4]. In the trend of criticism the equating of virtue and knowledge, of *arete* and *logos*, on which the Socratic-Platonic teaching on virtue is based, proves to be an exaggeration. Aristotle brings it back to the correct measure, by showing the *orexis, Striving* and its shaping into a fixed attitude (*hexis*), as the basic element of a person's moral knowledge'. (*WuM* pp. 295f).

39. Cf. Newman's reception of Aristotle: William, C.F.: *Aristotelische Erkenntnislehre bei Whately und Newman*, Freiburg 1960; Sillem, E.J.: The Sources of Newman's Philosophy: Aristotle, in: *Ibidem; The Philosophical Notebook of John Henry Newman, Vol. I,* Leuven 1969, pp. 149-163; Verbeke, G.: Aristotelian roots of Newman's *illative sense*, in: *Newman and Gladstone. Centennial Essays* ed. J.D. Bastable, Dublin 1978, pp. 177-196.

40. Heidegger, M.: *Being and Time.* Translated by J. Macquarrie and E. Robinson, Oxford 1962, pp. 62, 487.

41. Heidegger, M.: *Platon: Sophistes, Vol. 19 (Gesamtausgabe),* Frankfurt am Main 1992, p. 56.

42. Cf. Artz, J.: Illative Sense und Gewissen, in: *NSt XI*, Heroldsberg 1980, 128: 'Also, one cannot simply identify the conscience with the illative sense, which merely functions as a conscience in a religious context. Rather, the "intellectual senses" which include the illative sense as well as the conscience, are not separated by immovable walls. They work together'.

43. *GA*, p. 205.

44. *GA*, pp. 228f.

45. *GA*, pp. 266f.

46. *TP* i, p. 141: Newman cites Dr. Johnson.

47. 'There is a faculty in the mind which acts as a complement to reasoning, and as well as having truth for its direct object thereby secures its use for rightful purposes. This faculty, viewed in relation to religion, is ... the moral sense; but it has a wider subject-matter than religion, and a more comprehensive office and scope, as being 'the apprehension of first principles', and Aristotle has taught me to call it *nous* or *noetic faculty*'. Note: '*Episteme*, Aristotle's second faculty, conversant with necessary truth, answers well

(analogically) to Reason, as I am considering it'. *TP* i, pp. 152f.

48. Cf. *TP* i, p. 141.

49. *TP* i, p. 153.

50. *TP* i, p. 154.

51. Newman, J.H.: *Fifteen Sermons preached before the University of Oxford between 1826 and 1843*, London, 1918, p. 312 (Sermon XV).

52. *PPS* VI, p. 263.

VIII

NEWMAN ON TRADITION
AS A SUBJECTIVE PROCESS

Günter Biemer

THE RELEVANCE OF NEWMAN'S THOUGHT FOR THE CHURCH TODAY

The Catechism of the Catholic Church[1] emphasizes that the ultimate reason for God's Revelation is his will that there be universal salvation (1 Tim 2,4): 'Christ must be proclaimed to all nations and individuals, so that this revelation may reach to the ends of the earth'.[2] God's salvific will is shown to be the origin of divine revelation not only culminating in the Christ-event but also in the apostolic succession, in Tradition and holy Scripture, in the institution of the teaching office of the Church, in the dogmas of faith and in the growth of understanding the faith. Quoting passages of *Dei Verbum* of the Second Vatican Council the *Catechism* says: 'The Church in her doctrine, life and worship, perpetuates and transmits to every generation all that she herself is, all that she believes'[3] and 'thanks to its supernatural sense of faith the People of God as a whole never ceases to welcome, to penetrate more deeply and to live more fully the gift of divine Revelation'.[4]

In comparison with the Council of Trent, where divine revelation is said to be contained '*in libris scriptis et sine scripto traditionibus*',[5] the most important difference of Vatican II which has reached catechetical relevance concerns the dynamic understanding of the process of tradition, the rôle of the laity in this process and the function of the teaching office of the infallible Church. These are certainly catchwords of John Henry Newman's ecclesiology. Thus far one can agree with David Newsome's statement that as Vatican I can be labelled Henry Edward Manning's Council, so Vatican II 'with some degree of truth' is Newman's.[6]

More than thirty years ago as a young man I tried to give a balanced report of what Newman scholars thought at that time to be only of minor importance in Newman's theological theories: his doctrine on Tradition as a source of Christian faith. Meantime other theologians took up the subject, writing on its details and aspects, like Jean Stern, Norbert Schiffers, Nicholas Lash and Aidan Nichols. Today looking back and trying to see more specifically what Newman's concern was, or had become in the course of his life, with regard to the subject of Tradition, I should like to sum up my observations in a hypothesis: Newman became more and more persuaded and finally convinced of the importance the subjective word of God (*Verbum Dei subiectivum*) has for handing on divine revelation in the history of humankind.

I shall try to illustrate this thesis in five steps.

1. FROM SCRIPTURE TO TRADITION (1816-1822/25)

Newman's 'inward conversion' of 1816 which made him 'rest in the thought of two, and two only, absolute and self-evident beings, myself and my creator',[7] had at least two important and lasting consequences for his life — existential and dogmatic. *Existentially* he became an actively religious person as a spiritual note shows (1816):

> 'In omnibus periculis 'Εγώ εἰμι nos liberabit si Illum in-vocaverimus'[8] [and] 'Nunc ego te, deus, oro quoniam mihi accidere potest ut in his venturis diebus invadar ab hoste, te oro, deus, ne me deseras'.[9]

In the beginning of 1817 Newman thanked Walter Mayers for sending him Beveridge's *Private Thoughts* and described in this letter very clearly the elements of the religious act:

> I sincerely trust that my conscience enlightened by the Bible through the influence of the Holy Spirit may prove a faithful and vigilant guardian of the principle of religion'.[10]

Newman understands Christian faith from the very beginning to be a practice which under the guidance of conscience involves the whole person, so that 'knowledge ... [would be] nothing compared with doing'.[11] At the roots of Newman's experience and understanding of religion faith is first of all a practice, a relationship, a communicative performance, and not only something to be known and contemplated. Religion is seated in the innermost personal faculty, in conscience. Conscience, he will say in his *Grammar of Assent* (1870), is the principle of religion as well as the principle of ethics.[12]

Importance of dogma.
Newman's 'inward conversion' of 1816 had not only existential consequences: he also 'fell under the influence of a definite Creed and received into ... [his] intellect impressions of dogma'.[13] In 1818 Newman listened to Edward Hawkins' sermon on 'unauthoritative tradition' without realizing yet its consequences for the dogmatic and

doctrinal understanding of Christianity. But between 1822 and 1825, reading Hawkins's text, he could see that Scripture 'was never intended to teach doctrine, but only to prove it' while conversely to teach or learn Christian doctrine we have to turn to Tradition, to have recourse to 'the formularies of the Church, for instance to the catechisms and to the creeds.... After learning from them the doctrine of Christianity, the inquirer must verify them by Scripture'.[14]

Writing about this new insight in his *Apologia*, Newman finishes up by saying: 'This view ... most fruitful in its consequences, opened upon me a large field of thought'.[15]

Newman had understood that the Bible was not the only source and record of the Christian faith; he points out that his continued membership in the Bible Society was from then on only a question of time.

2. LIVING TRADITION IN THE CHURCH OF ANTIQUITY

Newman's work on the *Arians of the Fourth Century* was simply part of his long-time study of the Fathers. He gained an extraordinary insight into the life of the early Church with specific knowledge about the modalities of how Christian faith was taught and practised, reflected upon and fought for. He received a clear understanding of Apostolic Tradition: a vision of how catechetical instruction was one of the main instruments of this Tradition of revelation. He found the roots and first traces of his later distinction between a static and dynamic Tradition, also reason for his lifelong emphasis on the witness of faith, in the rôle of individuals as well as on the level of the Christian laity.

The catechumenate in the Church of Alexandria was an 'introductory discipline' which effected the 'grounding in the faith', advancing 'from the most simple principle of Natural religion to the peculiar doctrines of the gospel' and 'from moral truth to the Christian mysteries'. The catechumens 'were taught the Lord's Prayer' and 'entrusted with the knowledge of the Creed'.[16]

The chief subjects of catechising in Jerusalem during the fourth century consisted of the doctrines of repentance and pardon; the necessity of good works; the nature and use of baptism and the immortality of the soul. By slow degrees and in due time the newly baptized could discover that Christianity consisted not only of doctrines and practices but was 'a profound philosophy'.[17]

In his search for the 'principle of formation' in 'that primitive age', Newman finds confirmation of Hawkins's theory that the Creed or Apostolical Tradition 'was practically the chief source of instruction':[18] 'Scripture being unsystematic, and the faith which it propounds being scattered through its documents and understood only when they are viewed as a whole, the Creeds aim at concentrating its general spirit, so as to give security to the Church, as far as may be, that its members take a definite view of that faith which alone is the true one'.[19] The text of Scripture is 'addressed principally to the affections and of a religious character' while the intellectual formulations of the Gospel truth in the text of the Creeds tranquillize the mind and are of 'a philosophical character'.[20]

According to Newman, there are two channels of handing down the Divine Revelation clearly marked out: a more systematic expression of the faith in the *symbola* or Creeds and the unsystematic expression of faith in Holy Scripture. Furthermore Newman discovers a twofold language in the stream of Tradition. Beside the 'decided and plain spoken' language of the Creeds[21] Newman seems to have a preference for 'natural and unpremeditated' statements in the works of the Fathers, comparable to the language of the inspired volume itself'.[22] It was the necessity of answering heresies which made theologians 'convert doxologies [of the Fathers] into Creeds'.[23] An outstanding principle of Tradition in the history of the Church that Newman discovered during his studies of the Arians is the personal representation of the revealed truth. At least there is a striking coincidence between the rôle which Athanasius has in Newman's history of the Arians and that in one of his *University Sermons* written in January 1832, half way between the summer of 1831 and the summer of 1832 when he wrote the book. It is in the chapter on the Council of Constantinople[24] where Newman calls Athanasius 'one who, after the apostles, has been a principal instrument by which the sacred truths of Christianity have been conveyed and secured to the world'.[25] And in his sermon *Personal Influence, the Means of Propagating the Truth*[26] Newman gives testimony of his conviction that 'a few highly-endowed men will rescue the world for centuries to come ... each receives and transmits the sacred flame ... to hand it on as bright as it has reached him....'[27] Though they are few 'they are enough to carry on God's noiseless work. The Apostles were such men; others might be named. ...'[28] And referring to Athanasius (in a footnote) Newman says: 'Before now even one man has impressed an image on the Church, which, through God's mercy, shall not be effaced while time lasts'.[29]

The value Newman attaches to oral tradition is testified in the often quoted summary of that sermon in which he says that the Apostolic Truth 'has been upheld in the world not as a system, not by books, not by argument, nor by temporal power, but by the personal influence of such men ... who are at once the teachers and the patterns of it'.[30] Systematically speaking in that sermon Newman calls Christ the great teacher of truth and his 'Blessed Spirit' a second teacher. The 'Primitive Church' in its collective holiness may be considered 'to make as near an approach to the pattern of Christ as fallen man ever will attain',[31] and those saintly witnesses who have made the Gospel the measure of their lives are his persons of reference. In this sense Newman prefers Tradition to Scripture: 'The Scriptures are thrown upon the world as if the common property of any who choose to appropriate them'. Their proper understanding depends on that spirit which is only handed on *cor ad cor*, or as Newman says in his sermon: 'The inspired Word being but a dead letter ... except as transmitted from one mind to another'.[32] In a later context of educational relevance, Newman will say that a principle can only be handed on by those in whom it lives already.[33] There remains tension between the need of qualified witnesses for handing down the faith and the high standard of qualification which is nothing less than holiness and confidence in God's providence, as Newman writes at the end of the *Arians*: 'That, should the hand of Satan press us sore, our Athanasius and Basil will be given us in their destined season, to break the bands of the oppressor, and let the captives go free'.[34]

Between April 1834 and February 1837 Newman displayed a new concept of Christian *paradosis* on four different levels of writing:

— in a 'controversial correspondence' with Jean Nicolas Jager,
— in an exchange of letters among friends with Hurrell Froude,
— in 'parochial lectures', held between May 16 and July 11 1836,
— in a book *On the Prophetical Office of the Church*.[35]

Newman's own state of mind at this time is mirrored in the *Via Media* where he opens his heart as to his experience with the Church: 'How much must be taken on trust, in order to be possessed; how little can be realized except by an effort of the will; how great a part of enjoyment lies in resignation. Without some portion of that Divine Philosophy which bids us consider "the kingdom of God" to be "within us", and which, by prayer and meditation, by acting on what is told us, and by anticipating sight, develops outwardly its own views and principles, and thus assimilates to itself all that is around us, not only the Church in this age and country, but the Church Catholic anywhere, or at any time, primitive, Roman, or reformed, is but a name....'[36] It was doubtless in the light of that Divine Philosophy that Newman designed his view of Christian Tradition in his correspondence and lectures. Basically there is what he learned in the Alexandrian School as the sacramental structure of the word of God as he wrote to Jager:

> Every word of divine revelation has a deep meaning. It is the outward form of a heavenly truth, and in this sense a mystery or a Sacrament. We may read it, confess it; but there is something in it which we cannot fathom, which we only, more or less as the case may be, enter into. Accordingly when a candidate for Baptism repeats the Articles of the Creed, he is confessing something incomprehensible in its depth, and indefinite in its extent. He cannot

know at the time what he is binding on himself, whither he is letting himself be carried'.[37]

In his personal history with the Word of God the Christian therefore 'receives with trust and unhesitatingly the interpretation which the Church gives of it'.[38] In order to avoid error as a consequence of applying private judgment in matters of doctrine, Newman drew up a series of rules about the interplay of the authority of Scripture, Tradition, Church, and private notions.[39]

Newman's vision of handing on the divine word in the Church through the centuries describes a threefold stream: Holy Scripture, and two different kinds of Tradition: one static and reliable, another dynamic and of changing reliability. Holy Scripture which according to the Thirty-Nine Articles 'containeth all things necessary to salvation'[40] has the preferable security of a written source of faith, 'fixed, tangible, accessible, readily applicable'.[41] It is 'the court of ultimate appeal which has the right of definitely settling all questions of faith'.[42] The relationship between Scripture and Tradition can be called a circular one. Newman 'considers that Tradition is as much necessary to explain Scripture as Scripture to verify and circumscribe Tradition; so that, where possible, neither should be used by itself'.[43] Although Newman is quite clear in stating that 'mere Tradition cannot be a 'sufficient voucher' for any part of the gospel',[44] the question of how Scripture's sufficiency can be guaranteed is answered in the form of a postulate: 'Scripture has one and but one sense ... it is the sense in which the Church Catholic has ever understood it'.[45]

The cross-reference of Scripture to Tradition and vice versa shows how important Tradition is for Newman in his Anglican ecclesiology. But is Tradition not a vague and unreliable source of faith? Newman's answer is 'Yes and No' because he finds two main streams of Tradition since the time of the Church of antiquity:

a) One is connected with the Apostles' Creed, and Newman would not call that unauthoritative as Hawkins did. 'The Apostles' Creed is a document as surely Apostolic, as far as the nature of evidence is concerned, as one of the epistles of St Paul,[46] it is of the nature of 'a written document' and has the same authenticity as the Scripture.[47] for 'this creed is received on what may be called apostolical Tradition'. It is 'a collection of definite articles passing from hand to hand, rehearsed and confessed at baptism, committed and received from bishop to bishop', and therefore Newman calls it 'episcopal Tradition' in his *Lectures on the Prophetical Office*.[48]

b) It is common terminology in Christian theology to distinguish between written Scripture and unwritten Tradition. If so there is reason to ask whether according to Newman there is not a third category of its own in between Scripture and Tradition, to be called 'written Tradition'?[49] It is 'that strict *Traditio* from one hand to another, from definite person to definite person, official and exact, which I may call apostolical or episcopal' — as he says in a letter to Hurrell Froude.[50]

c) Besides Scripture and written Tradition there is a *paradosis* full of life and change. Whoever reads Newman's own words cannot but feel how much he sympathizes with this stream of faith, so picturesque and yet not completely orthodox or reliable:

> God placed in his Church first Apostles, secondly prophets. Apostles rule, prophets expound. Prophets are the interpreters of the Divine Law, they unfold and define its mysteries, they illuminate its documents, they harmonize its contents, they apply its promises. Their teaching is a vast system not to be comprised in a few sentences, not to be embodied in one code or treatise, but consisting of a certain body of truths permeating the Church like an atmosphere, being irregular in its shape, from its very profusion and exuberance. That body of truth is part written and part unwritten, partly the interpretation, partly the supplement of Scripture; partly preserved in intellectual expressions, partly latent in the spirit and temper of Christians; poured to and fro in closets and upon housetops, in liturgies, in controversial works, in obscure fragments, in sermons. This I call prophetical Tradition, existing primarily in the bosom of the Church itself.. This is obviously a very different kind from the Apostolic Tradition, yet it is equally primitive and equally claims our zealous maintenance.[51]

Comparing both streams of Tradition Newman calls the latter 'like flesh covering a skeleton'.[52] While the 'apostolical Tradition is pure and worthy of faith ... prophetical Tradition may have been corrupted in details', and yet Newman insists that it deserves the 'greatest veneration' and is 'worthy of respect'.[53]

So far Newman's ecclesiology holds the classical *via media* position which he characterised himself in comparison with the Roman system in his second lecture on the *Prophetical Office*: 'Ours is antiquity, theirs the existing Church'.[54] Yet on the other hand it is quite obvious, as Allen observes, that in 'the notion of a prophetical office ... lay the seeds of development'.[55] Indeed Newman shows how articles of the faith have been transformed into new words and he is eager to show that they speak in both forms of 'but one and the same great and blessed doctrine, variously described and developed'. [56] It is in this sense 'that we must consider the Nicene and the Apostles' Creed as identical'.[57]

L.Allen and J.H. Walgrave discover early traces of the concept of development in Newman's *Arians* and *Prophetical Office* respectively,[58] Nicholas Lash on the other hand shows the connection between

Newman's option for the 'real' dimension of the *Grammar of Assent*
and his description of prophetical Tradition, while the notional
dimension seems related to the episcopal Tradition.

3. TRADITION AS DEVELOPMENT?

When Newman, looking back on his theory of development, wrote in
1846: 'I believe I was the first writer who made *life* the mark of a true
Church' [59] he presupposed the dialectical integration of the life element
of Tradition, i.e. prophetical, with the notionally identical Tradition,
i.e. episcopal. This dialectical interpretation is contained in the idea of
development.

On February 2nd 1843 Newman preached his last University Sermon
On the Theory of Developments in Religious Doctrine. In a letter to
Archdeacon Manning of the same year [60] he writes: 'The sermon on
development was a subject for years. And I think its view quite
necessary in justification of the Athanasian Creed'.[61] Nearly all the
elements of Newman's theory on Tradition which we have discovered
so far can be verified in that sermon. There is the sacramental
structure of the divine revelation in the text of the sermon: 'Mary kept
all these things and pondered them in her heart'.[62] There is the analogy
between the personal level of the individual Christian thinking about
the mystery of God in his revelation and the collective level of the
whole Church in her attempt to enter into and understand the gospel
message. There are movements of explication in other sciences where,
as Newman says, 'principles of philosophy, physics, ethics, politics,
taste admit both of implicit reception and explicit statement; — why
should not the ideas which are the secret life of the Christian be
recognized also as fixed and definite in themselves and as capable of
scientific analysis?'.[63] There is the movement of human reason dealing
with the words and facts of salvation so that

> one proposition necessarily leads to another, and a second to a third
> ... and the combination of these opposites occasions some fresh
> evolutions from the original idea, which indeed can never be said to
> be entirely exhausted. This process is its development and results in
> a series, or rather a body, of dogmatic statements, till what was at
> first an impression on the imagination has become a system or creed
> in the reason.[64]

To sum it up Newman says: 'One thing alone has to be impressed on
us by Scripture, the *Catholic Idea*, and in it they [i.e. developments]
all are included....' [italics mine].[65] Newman stresses the point of the
wholeness of the idea which is developed in the different branches of
the whole system. It would be the origin of heresy to 'go away with
this or that proposition of the creed, instead of embracing that one idea

which all of them together are meant to convey'.[66] Such an attitude would reveal that a [heretical] Christian does not realize that the message he is dealing with is a living truth and can only be understood if accepted in one's own life: 'Realizing is the very life of true developments; it is peculiar to the Church and the justification of her definitions'.[67] So it would be expressing the same to say that Mary kept all these happenings, *realizing* them in her heart.

What Newman called an *Essay on the Development of Christian Doctrine* was intended to be an answer to the antecedent probability of the Church of Rome being the one true Catholic Church of Christ in which the Church of antiquity had come to us through the centuries and was still existing with full apostolic authority. Archdeacon Manning had asked Newman after the latter's resignation of St Mary's:

> Has not God prospered you in the last ten years in a measure which makes it — may I venture to say — impatience something like Jonah's to ask or look for more?... Surely if one compares the English Church now with what it was ten years back it cannot be said truly that it is showing itself intrinsically alien from Catholic principles....'[68]

Newman answered him:

> My dear Manning ... I must tell you then frankly ... that it is from no disappointment, irritation or impatience, that I have, whether rightly or wrongly, resigned St. Mary's — but because I think the Church of Rome the Catholic Church, and ours not a part of the Catholic Church, because not in communion with Rome....'[69]

In his search of elements for a theory of Tradition the master-key to his essay is Newman's axiomatic statement:

> If development must be, then, whereas revelation is a heavenly gift, He who gave it virtually has not given it, unless he has also secured it from perversion and corruption, in all such development as comes upon it by the necessity of its nature....'[70]

Newman's seven notes of a true development suggest criteria of noetics and growth in concrete terms. Newman designs his theory as a phenomenological description of how ideas are moving. He reduces the history of Christianity to a movement of a central idea.

How much Newman was capable of what the phenomenology (of Edmund Husserl) calls *reductio ad essentiam* can be seen in his report about his first conversion, where religion is said to consist of the relation between 'two luminously self-evident beings, myself and my creator'.[71] Newman says the image of his creator realized in the process of months in 1816 'has never been effaced' in his life.

Similarly in order to enter into and live a Christian life,[72] Newman
says one thing only has to be impressed on our minds by Scripture,
'the Catholic idea'. In his justification of belief, which he called *An
Essay in Aid of a Grammar of Assent* Newman uses the term 'image
of Christ' being imprinted in the soul as a phenomenological reduction
of describing a Christian.[73]

Thus in his *Essay on the Development of Christian Doctrine*
Newman chooses the model of an idea for Christianity and con-
centrates on the central truth of the Incarnation; and from there three
main aspects take their rise: the 'sacramental, the hierarchical, and the
ascetical', because Christianity is at once 'dogmatic, devotional and
practical'.[74] The process of a strong or living idea is described by
Newman on the interpersonal and social level. In the process of time
'there will be a general agitation of thought, and an action of mind
upon mind....' The idea

> will in proportion to its native vigour and subtlety, introduce itself
> into the framework and details of social life, changing public
> opinion, and strengthening and undermining the foundations of
> established order. Thus, in time, it will have grown into an ethical
> code, or into a system of government, or into a theology, or into a
> ritual, according to its capabilities: and this body of thought, thus
> laboriously gained, will after all be little more then the proper
> representative of one idea, being in substance what that idea meant
> from the first, its complete image as seen in a combination of
> diversified aspects, with the successions and corrections of many
> minds, and the illustration of many experiences. This process,
> whether it be longer or shorter in point of time, by which the aspects
> of an idea are brought into consistency and form, I call its develop-
> ment, being the germination and maturation of some truth or
> apparent truth on a large mental field'.[75]

The criteria or rules of a true development can be understood as three
kinds of categories: — Testifying to *identity* of revealed truth, as for
example, 'preservation of its type', 'continuity of its principles';
'conservative action upon the past'. — Showing the process of
explicitation of what was so far implicit as, for example, in 'its logical
sequence', 'anticipation of its future' and — demonstrating the
progressive assimilating capacity in the struggle for survival: for
example, 'its power of assimilation'; 'its chronic vigour'.

It is Newman's merit that he established 'the fact of "development",
which he offered as a "theory", an "hypothesis", as an alternative to
"immutability" on the one hand and "corruption" on the other'.[76]

In order to discuss his theory with Roman authorities, Newman
wrote in 1847 his paper *De Catholici Dogmatis Evolutione* for
Giovanni Perrone which can be understood as a new presentation of

his dialectical design of Tradition drafted in the *Prophetical Office* and now combined with the notion of development. Newman distinguishes between an objective and subjective word of God in the course of handing on Revelation: '*Verbum Dei revelatum est illud donum veritatis evangelicae ... quod ... a Christo traditum apostolis, ab apostolis ecclesiae, transmittitur in saecula*'.[77] Newman does not mention the Hebrew Scriptures or the Old Covenant being included in this apostolical Tradition although Jesus as well as the Apostles were faithful Jews. Nor does Newman seem concerned with the difference of Scripture and Tradition; his interest is rather '*simplex illud et absolutum et immutabile (scil. mysterium)*' which can be most truly perceived in the revealed word when it is considered in its objective or dogmatic form. But is there an objective existence of the word of God at all since it exists always in the intellect of subjects? Newman's answer is 'Yes' if these subjects guarantee the sincerity, completeness, and splendour of the revelation. And this is only '*in intellectu Spiritus Sancti, in intellectu apostolorum*, and *in intellectu Ecclesiae Romanae*; in the latter as far as the revealed word has become or will become a dogma'.[78]

Summing up what Newman said about Tradition of the Revealed Word of God, one might say so far that it is nearly identical with 'that strict *traditio* ... from definite person to definite person, official and exact, which I may call apostolical or episcopal', as he wrote to Richard Hurrell Froude in July 1835.

The complementary concept is *Verbum Dei subiectivum* in so far as the apostolical faith dwells in the single minds of the faithful where it is looked at in its different aspects, because some people appeal more to one aspect and some to others.[79] And though all may have received the apostolical creed in a thorough catechetical course, yet there are '*propriae inquisitiones*'. This will be the very way in which God's word '*vi sua vitali*' in the course of time, is to reach its full explicitation [80]

On the collective level the divine word enters into the mind of the Catholic world, '*in mente orbis catholici*', and becomes a 'certain innermost sense', invisible but most powerful. 'It resides with the serving and with the teaching Church, is disposed of in parts, put in shape, propagated by proofs ... it will change its appearance, differ according to each age. As a phenomenon it is similar to philosophical ideas, 'it is a certain divine philosophy'.[81]

Obviously the working of the *Verbum Dei subiectivum* in the individual Christian as well as in the mind of the Church reminds one very strongly of the description Newman give to the process of Prophetical Tradition in the mid-thirties. But now, after his breakthrough to the idea of development, he can see how both forms of

Tradition, the episcopal and the prophetical, correlate and become a reliable texture which gives certainty to the faithful. He describes progress and growth in the Catholic mind as it takes place in due course. Thus the Church becomes fully conscious of what she knows about a certain content of her faith only in time: *'Sensus subiectivus ecclesiae transit in obiectiva dogmata'*.[82] One can say that the Church knows more now than in former centuries *'plus scire in theologia'*.[83] The means (*medium*) of this process passing contents of faith from subjective to objective relevance is the *'vox summi pontificis ex cathedra loquentis'* and the *'definitio oecumenici concilii'*.[84]

4. CONTRADICTORY MODELS OF TRADITION:
PERRONE — NEWMAN — MANNING

Perrone

Giovanni Perrone's understanding of Tradition is determined by his vision of a complete revelation in all details right from the beginning, received by the Apostles from Christ and handed on from the Apostles to their successors. The only possible change he can allow is not development but addition and explicitation: adding elements of revelation which scattered in different streams of Tradition since Apostolic times and the making ecclesiologically explicit what was implied in the original deposit of faith. The central teaching office of the Church is understood as a surveyor and custodian of the faith. Thus the Pope in Perrone's time could declare that faith in the immaculate beginning of Our Lady's life was contained in the universal faith of the people of God as testified by the bishops of the *orbis catholicus* and could therefore gain the quality of a dogma. Perrone's is a static and additive view of Tradition. Perrone's model of Tradition is anxiously tied to the objectivity of truth through the immutability or unchangeableness of the divine message.

Newman

Newman's insight into the movement and structures of Christian Tradition leads to a new approach based on salvation history and a balanced interplay between hierarchy, the *'schola theologorum'* and the laity as part of the People of God. It is a kind of summary or survey of his understanding of the dynamic process of doctrinal Tradition in the Church. Newman says in a letter to John Stanislas Flanagan[85] that the deposit of faith should not be understood as 'a number of for-mulae', nor as 'a list of articles that can be numbered' but rather as 'a divine philosophy', 'a system of thought'.[86] And since faith can be understood as 'a large philosophy, all parts of which are connected together' there is a logical and organic approach possible, 'so that he who really knows one part, may be said to know all, as *ex pede*

Herculem'. Newman is convinced that the Creed or Deposit of Faith 'was delivered to the Church with the gift of knowing its true and full meaning'.

But how does the mind of the Church work since it is not a person? Newman's answer involves the infallibility of the Church in Council or in the Pope: 'That when the Pope sits in St Peter's Chair, or when a Council of Fathers and the Doctors is collected round him, it (i.e. revealed truth) is capable of being presented to their minds with that fullness and exactness, under the operation of supernatural grace ... with which it habitually, not occasionally, resided in the minds of the Apostles'.[87] Newman's model of the Tradition of Christian Doctrine can be called 'synergistic' in so far as, in the stream of salvation history, the working process of the human mind represented in the mind of the Church comes together with divinely grounded intuition or instinct. Inspiration guarantees the divine origin of Holy Scripture, an illuminative power guarantees that the teaching office of the Church defines only as an article of faith what is contained in revelation.

Manning

There is certainly not enough space to give a fair account of Henry Edward Manning's idea about Tradition as a source of faith. Yet it is easy to find out that according to his theology the guarantee for the indefectibility of doctrine and infallibility of the Church resides in a very special way with the Pope. For Manning the Roman Pontiff does not seem to have infallibility only as a gift for scarce, exceptional and urgent moments in Church history in order to exercise his service as the bishop of St Peter's see for the unity of the Church. Rather the Pope is, so to speak, the fountain from which infallibility flows to the bishops and into the Church; he appears as the mediator of infallibility between Jesus Christ and, through his Holy Spirit, the Church. We read in Manning's Pastoral Letter '*The Centenary of St Peter and the General Council*':

> To the chief of his Apostles he [Jesus Christ] conveyed by the Holy Ghost all his communicable prerogatives, and thereby constituted him his vicar upon earth. Peter became the head and guide, the fountain of doctrine and jurisdiction, to the Apostles.... The organisation of the Church was unfolded from the plenitude of its head. The prerogatives of stability, perpetuity and indefectibility in the head became endowments of the body united to him. But they existed in Peter before they were communicated to the Church, before the Church was organised to which they were to be communicated.[88]

It is a logical sequence of the premise when Manning says that the gift of infallibility of the Church 'resides first in its head, next in the whole episcopate united with him.... It is manifest, that according to this doctrine, the fountain of infallible teaching is the Divine Head in Heaven, through the organ of the visible head of the Church on earth'.[89] James Pereiro focuses our attention on Manning's insistence that the Pope can act alone, apart from the Church: 'the declarations and condemnations of the head of the Church apart from the episcopate are infallible....'[90] To characterise Manning's idea of the Tradition of Christian Doctrine, I would call it a vertical, papal model in a pyramidal structure, the life of which depends very much on the office of the Pope. The legend about Pius IX is relevant: having been asked whether there are some obstacles in the Church's Tradition against the definition of papal infallibility he answered: 'I am the Tradition'. This legend becomes very understandable in the light of Manning's model of Tradition.

5. DIALOGIC TRADITION: NEWMAN'S PREFERENCE FOR A MODEL OF COINCIDENT OPPOSITES

Newman could indeed understand the models of his contemporaries in both Rome and London. He saw the point in Perrone's square static description of Tradition which guaranteed, as it seemed, the identity of revelation by means of a controllable list of articles of faith and by reducing any change to extrinsic causes without intrinsic growth. But this kind of theology in its neo-scholastic garb was bound to remain abstract in order to seem valid. It did not take into account faith in the hearts of the people, the charity which they practised in everyday life, the hope which they kept in the process of dying. Since life is more colourful than logic, Newman wanted his theology to contain the natural reasoning by which people lived and died, prayed and cursed, became holy or failed. His theory of Tradition should not only apply scientific or abstract processes but also take account of the movements of the people of God: 'In all times the laity has been the measure of the Catholic spirit', he said to his audience in Birmingham in 1851,[91] that is why 'I am accustomed to lay great stress on the *consensus fidelium* as an important channel of Tradition.[92]

Was it because concrete life escapes logic that Newman preferred the phenomenological approach in his way of thinking, in his style of describing and preaching? Phenomenological language allows, too, for the expression of the coincidence of opposites, of concrete and abstract, of theory and practice, of identity and change, of human and divine elements in biographies and human history. One of the striking examples describing Tradition in this style can be found in Newman's *Lectures on the Present Position of Catholics in England* where he says:

> It is impossible to learn what the Catholic spirit is if one does not

enter into the living contact with Catholics, with their Tradition. Somebody who wants to know who they are has to live with them.' Then only 'has he heard the words, seen the deeds, watched the manners, breathed the atmosphere, and so caught the true idea of the people; in other words he has mastered their Tradition. This is what Catholics mean by Tradition, and why they go so much by it. It does not prove our doctrines to the man in question, but it will tell him in a way no other informant can tell him, what our doctrines are.... It is we, our thinking, our speaking, acting self, our principles, our judgements, our proceedings.[93]

As regards Manning's vertical model of securing Tradition by means of an infallibility flowing down to the bishops and the Church from Christ via the Roman Pontiff, Newman could question its theological basis.[94] As has been shown, Newman's concept of Tradition takes full care of the hierarchical structure as one of the three main aspects of the Incarnation which is the central principle of Christianity. Yet he is also aware that it is the People of God whom God called to make them his *ek-klesia* and not only the hierarchy. 'The Church would look foolish without them' [that is the laity], Newman said once to his bishop.[95] Vatican II has not only taken up this comprehensive understanding of the Church as the People of God,[96] but also Newman's dialogic insight that 'there is something in the *pastorum et fidelium conspiratio* which is not in the pastors alone'.[97] And as a confirmation of Newman's line of thinking we read in the new Catechism that the activity of the laity in ecclesial communities ' is so necessary that for the most part, the apostolate of the pastors cannot be fully effective without it'.[98] To get finally to the core of the matter: is it not the simple consequence of the Church having an incarnational structure that the process of divinely assisted Tradition in the people of God shows all the human notions of a teaching and learning process? Indeed Newman in his beautiful little phenomenological essay 'What is a University?' compares learning and teaching with catechesis when he says:

> If we wish to become exact and fully furnished in any branch of knowledge ... we must consult the living man and listen to his living voice.... No book can get through the number of minute questions which it is possible to ask on any extended subject.... No book can convey the special spirit and delicate peculiarities of its subject with that rapidity and certainty which attend on the sympathy of mind with mind, through the eyes, the look, the accent, and the manner in casual expression thrown off at the moment and the unstudied turns of familiar conversation....[99] Religious teaching itself affords as an illustration [in so far as] its great instrument, or rather organ, has ever been that which nature prescribes in all education, the personal presence of a teacher or, in theological language, Oral Tradition. It

is the living voice, the breathing form, the expressive countenance, which preaches, which catechizes'.[100]

Newman's theology of Tradition is a theology that confides deeply in God's accompanying providence and thus in the power of truth — 'Veritas praevalebit' as he wrote in a letter to Manning.[101] Only by degrees and in due time will Christians come to realize that the Christian faith contains a 'profound philosophy'.[102] And 'without some portion of that Divine Philosophy which bids us consider "the kingdom of God" to be "within us" ... the Church ... is but a name'. [103] Yet with the discovery of that philosophy the Church becomes a divinely guided social process where people shape the course of their lives in the 'sympathy of mind with mind' ex umbris et imaginibus in veritatem.

ABBREVIATIONS OF THE WORKS QUOTED

Allen —   L. Allen, *J.H. Newman and the Abbé Jager*, London 1975.
Cons. —   J.H. Newman, *On Consulting the Faithful in Matters of Doctrine*, Ed: J. Coulson, London, 1961.
Cor. Keble —   *Correspondence of J.H. Newman with J. Keble and Others*, ed. at the Birmingham Oratory, London 1917.

Newman's Works in the Uniform Edition of 1868-81 (36 vols), Longmans, Green and Co.

Apol. —   *Apologia Pro Vita Sua*
Arians —   *The Arians from the Fourth Century*

Dev. —   *Essay on the Development of Christian Doctrine*, 2nd Ed.
HS —   *Historical Sketches*
LD —   *Letters and Diaries of Cardinal Newman*
OUS —   *Oxford University Sermons*
Pres.Pos. —   *Present Position of Catholics in England*
PS —   *Parochial and Plain Sermons*
VM —   *Via Media*

NOTES

1. *The Catechism of the Catholic Church*, (Geoffrey Chapman, 1994).
2. *Ibidem*, Article 2, 74.
3. *Ibidem*, 98.
4. *Ibidem*, 99.
5. 'In written books and in unwritten traditions': Council of Trent, IV sess. 8th Apr. 1546.
6. *Recusant History* vol. 21, No 2, 1992, p. 143.
7. *Apol.*, p. 4.
8. 'In all dangers "I am" will free us if we call upon him' (*LD* I, p. 29).
9. 'Now God I pray to you, since it can happen to me in days to come that I may be invaded by the enemy, I pray to you, God, not to leave me' (*ibidem*).
10. *LD*, I, p. 30.
11. *PS*, I, p. 27.
12 From the negative side Newman assesses his insight when he asserts to his brother Charles, 'rejection of Christianity [arises] from a fault of the heart, not of the intellect' [*LD* I, p. 219], the ethical obstacles being 'pride and sensuality'. [*Ibidem*. cf. *PS* I, p. 227; *Idea*, p. 111; *LD* I, p. 30].
13. *Apol.*, p. 4.
14. *Ibidem*, p. 9. Cf: Lk 1,4: The scriptural definition of the function of catechesis has the same structure: 'That thou mightest know the certainty of those things wherein thou hast been instructed'. [*LD* II, p.236; *PS* I, p. 27].
15. *Ibidem*, pp. 9f.
16. *Arians*, pp. 44f.
17. *Ibidem*, p. 43.
18. *Ibidem*, p. 135.
19. *Ibidem*, p. 147.
20. *Ibidem*, p. 146.
21. *Ibidem*, p. 147.
22. *Ibidem*, p. 179.
23. *Ibidem*, p. 180.
24. The First Council of Constantinople, 381 AD.
25. *Arians*, p. 375.
26. 2 January 1832.
27. *OUS*, p. 97.
28. *Ibidem*, p. 96.
29. 'Image of Christ'; cf: *GA*, p. 464. *OUS*, p. 97.
30. *OUS*, pp. 91f.
31. *Ibidem*, p. 82.
32. *Ibidem*, p. 94.
33. *HS*, III, pp. 8f.
34. *Arians*, p. 394.
35. cf: H. Tristram in *John Henry Newman, Centenary Essays,* London 1945, p. 202.
36. *VM* I, p. 331; cf. *LD* XI, p. 100.

37. Allen, p. 89; *VM*, I, p. 257.
38. Allen, p. 91.
39. *VM*, I, p. 134.
40. Article VI.
41. *VM* I, 291.
42. Allen I, pp, 117f.
43. *Ibidem*, p. 117.
44. *Ibidem*.
45. *Ibidem*, p. 121.
46. *Ibidem*, p. 119.
47. *Ibidem*, p. 94.
48. cf: Allen, p. 94 with *VM*, I, p. 249.
49. Allen, p. 176.
50. 20 July 1835.
51. Allen, pp. 94f.
52. *Ibidem*, p. 95.
53. *Ibidem*, pp. 95f.
54. *VM* I, p. 70 cf: footnote.
55. Allen, p. 14.
56. *VM* I, p. 226.
57. *Ibidem*, p. 227.
58. J.H. Walgrave, *Newman — Le développement du dogme*, Tournai, Paris, 1957, pp. 53-56.
59. *LD* XI, p. 101.
60. 25 October 1843.
61. *Cor. Keble*, p. 277.
62. Lk 2,19.
63. *OUS*, pp. 327f.
64. *Ibidem*, p. 329.
65. *Ibidem*, p. 336.
66. *Ibidem*, p. 337.
67. *Ibidem*, p. 337.
68. *Cor. Keble*, p. 274.
69. *Ibidem*, p. 276.
70. 2 *Dev*, p. 92.
71. *Apol.*, p. 4.
72. *OUS*, p. 336.
73. *GA*, p. 464.
74. *Dev*, pp. 36f; cf:pp. 323f.
75. *Ibidem*, pp. 37f.
76. N. Lash, in *Newman and Gladstone*, ed. J. Bastable, (Dublin, 1978), pp. 161f.
77. *De Cathaolici Dogmatis Evolutione*, Ch.I, p. 1.
78. *Ibidem*, Ch.I, p. 1.
79. *Ibidem*, Ch.I, p. 2.
80. *Ibidem*, Ch.II, p. 5.
81. *Ibidem*, Ch. III, p. 2.

82. *Ibidem*, Ch. III, p. 5.

83. *Ibidem*, Ch. IV, p. 4.

84. *Ibidem*, Ch. IV, p. 5.

85. 2 February, 1868.

86. H.de Achával, ed., 'An Unpublished Paper by Cardinal Newman on the Development of Doctrine', in: *Gregorianum*, 39, 1958, pp. 585-596.

87. *Ibidem*, p. 596.

88. 8 Nov, 1867.

89. H.E. Manning: *Petri Privilegium*, London 1871, pp. 22-24; *Arians*, p. 44f.

90. J. Pereiro, 'Truth before Peace — Manning and Infallibility'. In: *Recusant History* vol. 21, No 2, 1992, pp. 218-253; 246. It would of course be interesting to reflect on the question whether a Pope 'apart from the Church' is still a Christian and also whether there is a double mediatorship between God and humankind, first through Christ and then through the Pope.

91. *Pres.Pos.*, p. 390.

92. *Cons.*, p. 63.

93. *Pres.Pos.*, pp. 325f.

94. This was also George Talbot's view. He wrote to Manning: '*Sentire cum Petro* is always the safest side' [February 20th, 1866]. It is the same letter in which Talbot says: 'Dr. Newman is more English than the English. His spirit must be crushed'. (E.S. Purcell, *Life of Cardinal Manning*, 2 vols, London 1896, II, p. 323).

95. *Cons.* I, p. 9; Cf: *LD* XIX, p. 141, XX, p. 377.

96. *Lumen Gentium*, p. 12.

97. *Cons.*, p. 104.

98. *Catechism*, Article 9, 900.

99. *HS* III, pp. 8f.

100. *Ibidem*, p. 14.

101. 10 September 1836; cf: Purcell I, p. 223.

102. *Arians*, p. 43.

103. *VM*, I, p. 331.

IX

THE MYSTICAL BODY OF CHRIST: MANNING'S ECCLESIOLOGY IN HIS LATE ANGLICAN PERIOD

James Pereiro

In 1838, Henry Edward Manning preached his sermon *The Rule of Faith* on a text from the Epistle to the Galatians: 'But though we or an angel from heaven, preach any other Gospel unto you than that which we have preached unto you, let him be accursed. As we have said before, so say I now again, if any man preach any other Gospel unto you than that ye have received, let him be accursed' (Gal. 1, 8-9).[1] That was an everlasting injunction, and Manning felt the full force of it: 'We may no more swerve from the pure faith of Christ's Gospel, and be held guiltless, than the fickle Galatian, or the inflated Gnostic'.[2] Manning, from very early on in his ministry, was asking himself some very pressing questions: Was he teaching the truth of the day of Pentecost? How could he make sure that this was the case? The needs of souls, and a desire for peace of conscience urged theological study upon him in order to find that test of doctrine by which the revealed character of a particular truth or proposition might be ascertained.

In the course of his studies Manning soon adopted the High Anglican and Tractarian doctrines of Apostolic Succession and of the interpretation of Scripture by Antiquity as the Rule of Faith. This system he buttressed in 1842 with his book *The Unity of the Church*. The imposing edifice, though, was to be badly shaken by the crisis of the Oxford Movement in the early 1840s; Manning's old assumptions were then challenged and new questions opened before his mind. Years later, on the point of becoming a Catholic, Manning confessed to Robert Wilberforce that he had rested on his previous intellectual convictions until 1845, although with increasing difficulty. Newman's conversion and his parting shot as an Anglican, *The Development of Doctrine*, revealed to Manning the full force of the crisis. He read in Newman's book the demise of the Anglican Rule of Faith as a test of doctrine, and that led him to the realisation that 'to put Scripture and Tradition into the hands of the individual is as much private judgment as to put Scripture alone'.[3]

There followed many months of spiritual and intellectual crisis, which was probably at the root of the breakdown of his health in 1847. During those months of illness and convalescence he found the key that unlocked the answers to his many questions: the constant presence of the Holy Spirit in the Church as sanctifier and unerring teacher; the fact that the same divine teacher of the day of Pentecost is teaching infallibly nowadays in and through the Church.

The infallibility of the Church became Manning's main intellectual concern during the years that preceded his conversion; it found its way into his correspondence, and was finally brought to light in all its fullness in his fourth volume of Anglican *Sermons*. His intention in writing them was, as he confessed to Mary Wilberforce (2-XII-49), 'to publish as full a book on the subject of infallibility as I have a light to make. And by that book to take my path'.[4] At first sight, though, the fourth volume of *Sermons* reads more as a study on the nature of the Church, about the rôle of the Sacraments in its life and in the life of the individual Christian, than as a treatise on infallibility. This is understandable: Manning aimed at presenting the topic of infallibility within its proper setting; that is, the work of Redemption, and the nature and mission of the Church. He also dealt at length with the nature of the virtue of Faith, a topic intimately connected with infallibility.

Härdelin considered that no Tractarian — with the exception of Robert Wilberforce — had 'ever worked out a systematic and thorough ecclesiology, not to speak of an entire theological system'.[5] It could be argued, however, that Manning's fourth volume of *Sermons* is the expression, in a form that tends to disguise the systematic approach of his thought, of a rather complete conception of the Church as the Mystical Body of Christ. Manning's attachment to the literary form of the sermon as a means to convey ideas continued well into his Catholic period, although he had experience of its limitations. In 1865, in his Introduction to *The Temporal Mission of the Holy Ghost*, he mentioned how he had tried to publish a volume of Sermons on Reason and Revelation, but, he added, 'when I began to write I found it impossible to throw the matter into the form of sermons ... [and] I was therefore compelled to write this volume in the form of a short treatise'.[6]

The second edition of his fourth volume of *Sermons* came out within months of the first. Manning guided some of his friends like Gladstone, T.W. Allies and Robert Wilberforce to a full apprehension of his thought; it seems that many others failed to see the direction of Manning's ideas. That may partly explain the popularity of his last volume of Anglican *Sermons*.

I. THE MYSTICAL BODY OF CHRIST

Manning unfolds his conception of the Church as the Mystical Body of Christ within the general context of God's plan for man. The whole economy of creation and of grace are the manifestation of God's love for man, and the greatest sign of that love is his desire that men may be called and actually be sons of God. Original sin frustrated God's creative plan, and man's subsequent fallen condition made a work of restoration, amounting to a true new creation, necessary. In God's providence, Christ — the Creator of all things — is to be also the principle of their restoration, and the Incarnation the 'first act of the new creation'.[7]

Manning writes, the 'mystery of the incarnation is not a mere isolated fact, terminating in the personality of the Word made Flesh, but the beginning and productive cause of a new creation of mankind'.[8] The restoration of man's lost divine sonship, and, consequently, the restoration of the image of God in man follow on from it. Christ is the Son, the perfect image of God; and the Incarnation 'is the restoration of our manhood to God in the Person of Jesus Christ.... In the mystery of the Incarnation is contained ... the mystery of our renewal, in body, soul and spirit, to the image of God'.[9] Christ shares in our humanity in order to be the salvation of our nature and of each one of us through his sacrifice on the Cross, the foundation on which the new humanity is built: the 'mystery of the Incarnation is, indeed, a humanising of God, as it is also a deifying of man; for in Him the Godhead and the manhood are alike perfect and indivisible';[10] He shares in our humanity that we may share in his divinity.

Manning would describe the nature of this deifying procedure even further when he says: 'It does not mean that we are made partakers of the incommunicable Godhead, but that we are made partakers of the manhood of the incarnate Word. It is our nature made divine. We partake of Him: of His very flesh, of His mind, of His will, and of His spirit'.[11] Christ's human nature was divinised, without losing its human character, by his contact with the divine nature in the one Person; similarly we are divinised — according to Manning — by uniting ourselves to his human nature (substance). The 'Word, who is by eternal generation of one substance [nature] with the Father, by the mystery of the Incarnation became of one substance with us'.[12] Then, as the Son lives by the Father 'so we, distinct in person, but partaking of His substance, live by the Son'.[13]

Manning affirms that the union in Christ of the divine and human natures is not something merely accidental; rather, it is a substantial union; and he conceived our union with Christ to be of a similar character. His terminology at this point becomes somewhat obscure, particularly in the use he makes of the terms "substance" and "substantial": 'our union with the Word made flesh' — he would say — 'is not figurative or metaphorical, by affinity and relation of will, or love only, but in substance, spirit, and reality.... How can there be any living union which is not real? or a real union which is not substantial? ... Branches do not derive their life by a figurative engrafting, neither is the union of the trunk and the root a metaphor. The Incarnation is a real and substantial partaking of our manhood; and our union with Christ is a real, substantial partaking of His'.[14]

That sharing in Christ's manhood was not possible for man while he was still on earth. His presence was then local, and men's relation to it external. Manning would quote here Eph. 4,10: 'He who descended is He who also ascended far above all heavens, that He might fill all things'. The departure of Jesus was the necessary prelude to his return in a new mode of presence: 'by His departure His local presence was changed into an universal presence'.[15] Now the presence of His Mystical Body reaches the whole world and is able to embrace all men. The words of Heb. 10,5 (quoting Ps. 40, 6): 'You wanted no sacrifice or cereal offering but you gave me a body', are taken by Manning as referring not only to the physical body of Christ but also to the mystical one; a body, physical or mystical, in which and through which he carries out the work of Redemption.

The living principle of the Mystical Body was to be the Holy Spirit, and that made necessary Christ's departure from this earth. 'If He had tarried with us, He had abode alone; the Comforter had not come; His mystical body had not been knit together; His truth and spirit had not dwelt in us. While he was upon earth all was local, exterior and imperfect: now all is universal, inward, and divine'.[16] The coming of the Holy Spirit was conditional on Jesus's departure to the Father, from where he would send His Spirit. Then, the Holy Spirit, who had been the agent of the union of the divine and the human nature in Christ, would be the agent of our union with Christ. He partook of our nature (substance) 'by the operation of the Holy Ghost, and we of His by the power of the same Spirit. The miraculous Agent in the Incarnation and in the holy Sacraments is the same third Person'.[17] Man joins Christ, is incorporated into his Mystical Body, by Baptism, the Sacrament of man's regeneration in water and the Holy Spirit.

This new birth is a free gift from God; man can only be the recipient of it and in no way the agent: 'the dust of the ground [was not] more passive when the first man was made in God's likeness, than we, when, through baptism, we were born again as sons of God'.[18] Thus, Christ 'through His Holy Sacraments began a new line of spiritual generation'. We are new-born or regenerated in Baptism, but this — like our natural birth is only the beginning of life. 'The work of our renewal, indeed, is not perfected in regeneration [Baptism], but only begun'.[19] Man has been incorporated in Christ, whose Mystical Body 'is the whole fellowship of all who are united to Him by the Spirit'.[20]

The Mystical and the Physical Body of Christ are not independent, unconnected, realities in Manning's thought. 'The glorious Body of the Word made flesh is the centre of His mystical body, and, to it joins us one by one'.[21] Manning sees in the parable of the Vine an almost perfect image of the Mystical Body. 'In that parable we see the perfect outline of the Incarnation, or Christ mystical in all fullness: the root, the stem, the branches.... It describes by anticipation the life, growth, and fruitage of the Church, and reveals also the source and channels through which the quickening life passes into all its structure and farthest sprays',[22] the Sacraments being the 'channels through which the grace of it [Christ's sacrifice] flows to us one by one',[23]

> The natural body of our Lord Jesus Christ is, as it were, the root out of which, by the power of the Holy Ghost, His mystical body is produced'. [Men] 'were engrafted into the stock of the Word made flesh.... Then began the growth and expansion of the mystical vine.[24]

II. THE UNITY OF LIFE OF THE MYSTICAL BODY OF CHRIST

Christ and Christians become a unity of life; the many members become one body and share in one life. The Church is 'the production and overflow of His life and substance, — the fruit and fulfilment of His incarnation, — the complement and perfection of His mystical body. What is the Church but Christ's invisible presence openly manifested by a visible organisation? The Church is Christ's mystical body — the presence of Christ by the creative power of His incarnation, produced and prolonged on earth'.[25]

Manning would quote here Eph. 4, 22-23: Christ is the 'head over all things to the Church, which is His body; the fullness of Him that filleth all in all'. From that it followed that the prerogatives of the head became the prerogatives of the body: 'When he ascended up on high, the virtues of His glorified manhood were shed abroad upon His Church'.[26] 'Therefore the Church is one, because He is one; holy, because He is holy; catholic, because His presence is local no more; apostolic, because He still sends His own servants; indefectible, because He is the Life; unerring, because He is the Truth'.[27]

A community of life is, thus, established, between Christ and Christians, whereby the whole Mystical Body and the individual Christian share Christ's life, eternal life. 'As His Godhead and manhood are united in one divine person, so we and the Lord of the resurrection are united in one mystical body. A living head must needs have living members; and a Head that is risen must raise His members in due season.... He *is* our resurrection'.[28] Our Lord's words 'I am the Resurrection and the Life' did not only mean ' "I will quicken and raise mankind from the dead", but " I *am* the Resurrection, and all rise in me: I *am* 'the Life', and all live in Me"'.[29]

If the natural body of Jesus is the stock on which the Christian is engrafted, the sacramental body is the means by which his life is communicated to all the members of the Mystical Body and sustains them, his presence in them being their life: 'as the life and substance of the first creation are sustained and perpetuated until now, so in the second, which is the mystical Vine, He is root and trunk, branch and fruit; wholly in us, and we in Him'.[30] He will expand on the character of that presence by saying: 'the humanity of the second Adam is the immediate and substantial instrument of our regeneration and renewal. It has, therefore, a supernatural presence throughout the whole mystical body of Christ. As the substance of the first man is the productive cause of the whole human race, so the Manhood of the second, in its reality and presence, is extended throughout the Church. It is the presence of God which upholds all the creation of nature: it is the presence of the incarnate Word which upholds all the creation of grace'.[31] Manning does not seem to wish to develop further this theme which is dear to Tractarian thought, trusting perhaps his readers' familiarity with these ideas. Robert Wilberforce had described the concept in great detail in his recent book on the Incarnation (1848). It may be useful, however, for the sake of the modern reader, to describe it briefly as they are brought forward in Wilberforce's book. The first Adam, Robert Wilberforce had said, is not only the originating generative principle of human life but also the original on which all his descendants are generated. The unity of form is consequent to the law of descent from a single parent; that guarantees a perpetual succession of beings, in each one of whom the original type reappears. Analogically, Christ is the originating principle and the original of the new creation of the sons of God. 'The necessity then of Christ's Presence according to His humanity', wrote Wilberforce, 'rests upon His being that Pattern Man, in whom renewed manhood shone forth in its brightest colours, by reason of those supernatural endowments with which it was invested. So that it is essential that we should be as truly united to Him by grace, as we were to the first Adam by nature'.[32]

Manning pulls together the threads of his thought by saying: 'In one sense the Church is called the body of Christ, by metaphor and analogy to the members and unity of a natural body: in another sense mystically, because of its true and vital union with Him'.[33] The image of the vine has a similar representative value, for it expresses 'the intense inwardness and spirituality of the body of Christ, [it] expresses equally its visible unity and organisation. It is as visible, sensible, and local as was the natural body of Christ Himself. In all the world it is visibly manifest as the presence of its unseen Head. It speaks, witnesses, acts, binds and looses in His name, and as Himself'.[34] Thus, the unity of life of the Mystical Body implies also a unity of action, which manifests itself in its highest form in the sacrifice of Christ: 'This is the first foundation of the Church — its perfect unity of life and act with Christ its Head'. The priesthood of Christ, like his other prerogatives, descends 'from the Head to the body, whereby He offers the body in Himself, and the body, in and for itself, offers Him unto the Father'.[35]

That which holds together the Mystical Body of Christ is the law of love: 'The unity of love is a type of the unity of nature',[36] Manning says somewhat cryptically. The members of the Mystical Body cannot achieve the unity of the three Divine Persons in the oneness of God's nature, but they reflect it in the unity of love and its corollaries. The unity of love of God the Son and God the Father flows down from heaven unto the Church to make all one. Love 'is one of the names of Christ and of His Church. Its visible body is the earthly clothing, the mystical impersonation of the love of God, in which all, whether visible or invisible, are united to Him as the Father is in the Son'.[37] The 'unity and expansion of love is the cause and the law of unity and communion to the visible Church'.This unity 'had its beginning upon earth in Him who is Love incarnate; from Him it spread and embraced His disciples, binding them into one visible fellowship'.[38]

Manning will from now onwards affirm unequivocally that the unity of the visible Church is based on a communion of charity. This is a departure from his previous position, and he is conscious of it. In his book, *The Unity of the Church*, he had maintained 'that the unity of the Church is organic and moral — that the organic unity consists in succession, hierarchy, and valid sacraments, and the moral in the communion of charity among all the members of particular Churches, and all the Churches of the Catholic unity ... [and] that this moral unity might be permanently suspended, and even lost, while the organic unity remained intact, and that unity of communion belongs only to the perfection, not to the intrinsic essence of the Church'.[39]

In his third volume of Anglican *Sermons* he had still spoken of the theory of the Three Branches making up, though separate, the one Church. Now he had come to realise that the unity of charity and communion is an integral element of the unity of the Church; that visible unity, following from the law of charity, is an essential characteristic of the visible Church.

The Mystical Body is the revelation of the love which unites the divine persons; it is also the revelation of the love of God for man, just as Jesus Christ's physical presence among men had been: 'The

Love of the Father and of the Son was thenceforward manifest, not in a natural, but in a mystical body, which, from age to age, perfects itself by the inward working of its own principle of life. Its unity and growth are properties of its very being, descending from "the Head, even Christ: from whom the whole body, fitly joined together and compacted by that which every joint supplieth, according to the effectual working in the measure of every part, maketh increase of the body unto the edifying of itself in love" (Eph. IV. 15,16)'.[40]

The Church 'is, therefore, by its very nature and law one and indivisible, ever enlarging, all-embracing; gathering in all nations, fusing all races, harmonising all tongues, blending all thoughts, uniting all spirits: making the earth once more of "one lip", of one speech, of one heart, and of one will ... "There is one body and one spirit, even as ye are called in one hope of your calling: one Lord, one faith, one baptism" (Eph IV, 4,5), one altar, one holy sacrifice, one divine tradition of corporate identity and living consciousness, sustaining the illumination of truth, seen by love alone, and itself sustained by the Holy Ghost'.[41]

Schism is a most grievous sin, but it does not rend the unity of the Church: 'it is a sin against the indivisible love of God. To separate from the Church is to forfeit love; for love cannot be divided. Schisms do not rend it, but are rent from it. As the life retires into the living trunk when branches are cut away, so love still dwells undivided in the life of the Church when members fall from its communion'.[42]

Manning was conscious of this change in his way of thinking, and he would later offer an explicit retraction of the ideas he had previously expounded in *The Unity of the Church* (1842). In *The Temporal Mission of the Holy Ghost* (1865) he would point out the three errors into which he 'unconsciously fell' in his Anglican books and *Sermons*. Among them, he confessed that he 'had not understood from whence the principle of unity is derived. It had seemed to be a constitutional law, springing from external organisation, highly beneficial, but not a vital necessity to the Church. I seemed to trace the visible Church to its Founder and His apostles as a venerable and world-wide institution, the channel of grace, the witness of God, and the instrument of discipline and probation to men. I had not as yet perceived that the unity of the Church is the external expression of the intrinsic and necessary law of its existence; that it flows from the Unity of its Head, of its Life, of its mind, and of its will; or, in other words, from the unity of the Person of the Incarnate Son, who reigns in it, and of the Holy Ghost, who organises it by His inhabitation, sustains it by His presence, and speaks through it by His voice'.[43]

The unity of the Mystical Body corresponds to the unity of Christ's Body. There are not three bodies of Christ — physical, mystical and sacramental — but only one: 'one in nature, truth, and glory. But there are three manners, three miracles of divine omnipotence, by which that one body has been and is present; the first, as mortal and natural; the second, supernatural, real, and substantial; the third, mystical, by our incorporation. The presence is one, the manner threefold; the substance one in all three: all three one in Him'.[44]

III. THE INFALLIBILITY OF THE MYSTICAL BODY OF CHRIST

Christ, besides his life-giving and sanctifying work, also continues now his teaching action in and through the Church. After his Ascension the imperfect knowledge of the Apostles was to become full illumination in the Church by the working of the Holy Spirit. 'When He departed, the Spirit of Truth took up all that He had revealed, and unfolded it with great accessions of divine illumination. He then opened a ministry of interior and perfect faith, which has guided His Church in all ages and in all lands unto this day. His own teaching was partial and local: the guidance of the Holy Spirit is plenary and universal. And our Teacher departs not, but abides with us for ever: a guide ever present, though invisible; ever presiding, though in silence; unerring, though teaching through human reason and by human speech. The Spirit of Truth is Christ Himself by His Spirit guiding and teaching still ... the whole Church of God throughout the world; sustaining in its spiritual consciousness, in the successive and continuous line of its spiritual and intellectual life, the whole mystery of God, the unfading image of the heavenly Truth'.[45] Thus, there still is nowadays a living and divine voice speaking the truth of salvation in the world.

Manning had been looking, from his early days as a pastor in Lavington, for the faith of the day of Pentecost; now he had come to see that Pentecost was not an event of the past but a permanent reality in the Church. 'The day of Pentecost is an ever present miracle. It stands in its fullness even until now, and we are partakers of its presence and its power'.[46] The 'original inspiration has descended in a perpetual illumination';[47] 'the inspiration of the Apostles became illumination in the Church. The illumination of the Holy Ghost is as perpetual as His presence. His office is, as His presence, "for ever"; that is, unto the end of the world'.[48]

Thus, the infallibility of the Church is made up of two elements: 'perfect certainty in the object revealed, and spiritual illumination in the subject which perceives it, that is, the Church itself'. The infallibility of God who reveals is mirrored by the infallibility of the Church in receiving without distortion the content of the revelation. 'Shake this foundation', Manning would add, 'and faith becomes uncertainty'.[49]

Manning affirms that the 'perpetual preservation of truth is a part of the divine office of the Holy Ghost, ever present in the mystical body of Christ; and that the presence of an infallible Teacher is as necessary to the infirmities of human reason as the presence of an omnipotent Comforter is necessary to the infirmities of the human will; that both, the will and the reason, without such presence, omnipotent and infallible, would be in bondage to evil and to falsehood'.[50] The Truth revealed by God would soon have been deformed and corrupted had it been left to unaided human reason to understand, preserve and transmit it. 'Is it possible to believe', Manning asks, 'that the supernatural illumination of the Spirit was so given as to rest upon no higher base than reason, discovery, criticism, and analogies of nature?'[51]

He summarises his thought on the matter as follows: 'What has been said amounts to this: that the doctrines of faith, fully and clearly revealed by inspiration in the beginning, were fully and clearly apprehended by the Church'.[52]

IV. THE NATURE OF FAITH

Manning had definitively established two elements in the formula of the certainty of faith: the certainty of the original revelation, based on God's infallibility, and the certainty of the faith in its preservation and transmission, guaranteed by the presence of the Holy Spirit in the Church.

There was, however, another element in need of satisfactory explanation: how does the individual believer reach the certainty of faith? Any knowledge worthy of the name, as far as Manning was concerned, should be certain in the two senses of the word: the truth itself should be objectively certain, and the one who knows should be certain about it being true.

By what faculty is it that 'the truth [of revelation) is to be apprehended?', Manning asks. 'The whole word of God answers at once, By faith'.[53] Unfortunately, men seemed to have lost sight of its true nature. He considered that the controversies of recent centuries 'have committed two evils: they have dethroned the object of faith [which seems to refer to the Church, as formal object of the faith], and they have degraded faith itself [as a virtue]'.[54] Manning was not satisfied by the different definitions of the nature of faith being proposed: 'Some will have it to be a speculative assent to truths revealed; and some, to correct them, will have it to be a principle of moral action; and others, to set both sides right, join together these two definitions in one, and tell us that faith is a principle of moral action springing out of a speculative assent to truths revealed'.[55]

According to Manning, those were only partial answers; even more, they turned faith into 'an effect without a cause, or with a cause simply human, and within the natural endowments of the human intelligence'.[56] The latter was their more serious error: human reason can be neither the foundation of the knowledge of Faith nor the basis of certain knowledge about the supernatural, nor the origin of the act of believing. That is why he rejected the attempts of those who looked to the analogy of nature or to probabilities for the foundation and source of the act of faith. A human act cannot be the foundation of faith, in so far as human reason cannot reach the supernatural truths which are the object of Faith; neither can it produce certainty once those truths had been revealed to man by God. Nature is silent about the supernatural; to make the act of faith dependent on human reason would be to confine revealed religion to the level of natural religion and to destroy certainty.

Some would affirm, arguing from the analogy of nature that, 'as certainty is found nowhere in nature, it is not to be demanded in revelation; that a measure of uncertainty, that is, of probability, is involved in the idea of moral trial, and that the facts of nature show us on what laws revealed truth is to be sought and held; and that therefore the whole analogy of our condition is opposed to the supposition of an unerring witness preserving and propounding truth by Divine appointment in the Church'.[57]

Manning admits that the Analogy of Nature is an instrument at our disposal and at the service of God's revelation. 'It clears away supposed objections [preliminary objections to revelation and faith in general, or to particular doctrines of faith]; raises a probability that revelation is, like nature, the work of God; and that the analogy we trace in part, may extend beyond our range of observation. Thus far it invests nature with a divine character, and makes it the basis of faith'.[58]

Once revelation has been received, the analogy of nature becomes an instrument at our disposal for the better understanding of it. It would be a mistake, though, to use it antecedently to determine either the limit of the faith as to its content, or to prescribe the manner and kind of the divine procedure to be followed by God in revealing himself: it 'would be mere infidelity to take the analogy of nature as the measure or limit of revelation'.[59] 'We must receive it [revelation] in its own light and upon its own proper proofs.... What is, then, this proper evidence on which revelation, or, as we shall better say henceforth, the Church and the Faith, repose? Plainly, upon no presumption or probabilities deduced before the fact, that is, upon no *a priori* reasoning. We are not able to say before the fact whether any revelation shall he given or not; or, if given, to what extent, to what end, on what evidence, or how secured, and the like. In this, nature is silent as death. Analogies have no existence. All our proofs are after the event. The fact attests itself, and reveals its own outline, character, and conditions'.[60]

The proofs of revelation are not found in the analogy of nature, but 'in a series of supernatural facts, in original revelations, in spiritual consciousness, in the words of inspired Scripture, in apostolical traditions, in the testimony of the Church, in the definitions of Councils, in the collective discernment of men sanctified by the Spirit of God'.[61] Only these reveal the manner of God's dealings with man and the truths of faith. Those supernatural facts have no counterpart or analogy in nature. 'The supernatural inspiration of the Church is a perpetual illumination above the laws of nature. Its conditions, limits and modes of operation are all its own'.[62]

Manning considered as enemies of the faith those who apply wrongly the analogy of nature. 'They not only use the analogy of nature antecedently to the proper proof, so as to prescribe *a priori* the manner in which the Divine revelation has been put and left, but ultimately even against it. In fact, they are but the fine end of naturalism'.[63] When the analogy of nature is pressed beyond its proper range then the analogies existing between the counterparts 'soon run into a supposed identity, and the faith sinks into a mere natural religion'.[64]

Manning would insist repeatedly on the idea that what is natural cannot determine what and how the supernatural should be. If that were to be the case, it could be concluded that there are three Gods, because in nature each person is one man, and several persons, several human natures. The revelation is supernatural, and the supernatural has its own laws — different from and above those of nature — and it can be reached only by faith. Having settled that point, Manning adds rhetorically: 'because among men the father is before the son, cannot the ever-lasting Son be co-eternal with the Father?... Because human traditions grow corrupt, may not divine traditions be kept pure?.... Because natural truth is an uncertain light, may not the light of Christ be sustained by Himself infallible and clear?'[65]

So, what is faith and what are its sources? Action and consent spring from faith; 'but what is that cause or power' — asks Manning — 'which is before both the assent and action of faith?' And he answers: 'What but faith itself?'[66]

And faith has no human cause. Manning stresses the character of faith as an infused grace of God: 'Faith is a spiritual consciousness of the world unseen, infused into us, in our regeneration, by the supernatural gift of God'.[67] Faith means trust in divine authority: it is 'an infused grace of God, by which the soul casts its whole confidence upon the authority of God. The infallibility of God is the foundation of that trust'.[68] It generates a certainty founded on revelation. 'And what is the very first idea of revelation but a clear and infallible knowledge of the truth given direct from God?'.[69]

The Holy Spirit is the foundation of the certainty of revelation in itself and also of the certainty with which man accepts God's revelation: he inspires this certainty in man with the gift of faith. Probability, on the other hand, is the best 'that nature can give in most things, but the least truth in the kingdom of God is greater than it'.[70]

Having rejected the light of natural reason by way of the analogy of nature as guide to the knowledge of faith, Manning would also dismiss another approach to the understanding of the access to the truth of faith. The natural light of the individual mind, aided in some general way by grace, and taking into account the teaching authority of the Church without fully trusting it, would be the means for man to reach the truth of God.[71] The individual soul, according to this principle, would find truth by allowing itself to be guided by God, moral rectitude being the means which prepares the soul for God's light.

Manning answers this theory by saying that if this were to be the case, then the highest evidence achievable would be only a moral evidence. An evidence which 'is only probable; that is uncertain both in the subject and in the object. Is it possible to believe that this scheme of probabilities (that is, of uncertainty) in doctrine, and of imperfection (that is, of doubt) in evidence, is part of the probation of the regenerate within the revelation of the faith?'[72] Manning, as we will see, had a different idea about the nature of man's probation.

Faith, he would insist, is a gift, and it has the same structure in the Christians on the day of Pentecost as in the rest of believers down the centuries: 'this divine gift, as it was, at the first, not discovered but received, so it has been, not critically proved, from age to age, by intellect, not gathered by inductions or by the instruments of moral reasoning, but preserved and handed on by faith; that the office of reason [then and now] is, not to discover and attain, but to illustrate, demonstrate [!], and expound'.[73]

The knowledge of faith is a means, the most perfect one granted by God, for man to gain access to reality; it is 'that power of spiritual perception analogous to sense, that is, to sight, hearing, and feeling; and also to affection, that is, to love, fear, and desire. It is as wide as the whole soul of man, uniting it in one continuous act'.[74] Its object is a world of spiritual realities which cannot be apprehended except through it. Faith does not contradict or oppose the natural powers; its role is rather to complement and to perfect them. The senses give us

a perception of the visible world and the intellect adds its interpretation. 'Intellect corrects and exalts sense; faith corrects and exalts
both'.[75]

The gift of faith perfects the whole rational man: it 'has been
defined as the perfection of the will and of the intellect — of the will
as it sanctifies, of the intellect as it illuminates, of both at once as it
issues in its congenial fruits'.[76] Faith perfects both potencies, and helps
their proper acts; it is an active principle: 'Acting towards God, it
issues in trust, love, prayer, contemplation, worship; towards man, in
charity, gentleness, self-denial; upon ourselves, in abasement,
discipline, and penance'.[77]

Manning hastens to add that faith, like all other gifts from God, 'is
subject to the will of man. It is the matter of our highest probation. It
may be used or abused, matured or neglected, made perfect or
perverted'.[78] 'This supernatural gift was infused into us as a habit
[virtue] by the Spirit of God; but in its acting depends upon our will'.[79]
Faith 'is a moral habit, having its root in the will'.[80] Man's moral
nature has a determining influence in the act of faith; thus, the effort
to purify one's conscience, the habitual exercise of prayer and frequent
communion help faith to mature, while sin and worldliness deaden and
blur that spiritual perception, in the same way as human defects and
vices affect the exercise of the intellect and the will.

The home and resting place of the truth of faith is the Church of
Christ. Truth in the Church 'is one, perfect, absolute, and binding;
admitting no diminution or addition, election or choice. It is all
contained in the baptismal creed, as is all the law of sanctity in the ten
commandments, not expressly, but by deep implication; and the
authority on which we receive both is one, the Church teaching in the
name of Christ'.[81] The entirety of revealed truth, as proposed by the
Church, is binding on those who belong to it; the very nature of faith
excludes a partial reception of the truths proposed by the Church.

Manning considers the case of those who, because of not having the
truth proposed to them, do not come to know it, and of those who
because of some deeply ingrained prejudice cannot recognise the truth
of revelation when confronted with it. He affirms that 'no ignorance
of truth is a personal sin before God, except that ignorance which
springs from personal sin'.[82] If that is the case, why should men need
the teaching of a visible Church? Would it not be enough to leave man
to discover and follow truth with his own, unaided, reason?

To Manning's mind, the question ignores how great a treasure is the
possession of the truth of revelation; it brings life to those who possess
it, in the measure of their knowledge. At the same time, those who
asked that question did not understand the moral rôle of the Church as
a means for the probation of man. This is a theme that Manning had

dealt with at great length in *The Unity of the Church* (1842). Submission to the teaching Church is, in Manning's conception, an essential element of man's regeneration. It constitutes the probation of his intellectual nature. Man has a tendency 'to put subjective opinion in the place of objective truth'; that pride of the human intellect is countered in God's plans by the submission of men 'as learners to an order of men who are divinely commissioned to teach'.[83]

Man's rebellion, which destroyed the image of God in him, is corrected by his submission to the discipline of the Church. In giving this he conforms to the image of Christ, the obedient Son of the Father. 'By the illumination of the intellectual nature through the one objective doctrine, and by the purifying of the moral nature through the one objective discipline, the will is once more enthroned supreme, and its energies united with the will of God'.[84]

Thus, the probation of man does not consist in his discovering or not discovering the truth of faith by himself, aided by grace and his moral rectitude. Manning considers that this avenue leads to spiritual pride and rationalism. The Church's mission is not to call man 'to weigh the value of truth in the balance of the individual reason, but to call upon the individual will to surrender itself to the sweet yoke of Christ'.[85] 'Latitudinarian errors and proud indifference' were the very moral opposites of the humility required for the act of faith, and that they were not without moral responsibility.

Manning's fourth volume of *Sermons* builds upon contemporary Tractarian ideas on the Church, an ecclesiology to which he himself had made important contributions. The Tractarians' understanding of the nature of the Church developed gradually; 'the idea of the Church as an organism, as the mystical body of Christ, which forms so prominent a feature of the thought of the Fathers, was not developed by the Tractarians until a later stage'.[86] The principle of Apostolical Succession, the prerogatives of the Episcopate, the idea of the Church as a means of grace, the concept of the regeneration of Christians through their union with Christ and their life in him, were the steps that led the Tractarians to the vision of the Church as a living body: Christ's Mystical Body. It was a gradual, but it might be added, almost inexorable progress. To ask the question about the nature of the Church opened the door to a hundred others; thereafter, the logical development of their tenets and the reading of the Fathers could hardly fail to bring the doctrine of the Mystical Body of Christ to the forefront of Tractarian thinking about the Church.[87]

It would be no mean task to chart in detail the springs which feed Manning's thought. Rowell has pointed out that Manning's sermons bear in many, though not all respects, a notable likeness to Pusey's.[88] Manning, and also Robert Wilberforce, seem indebted to Pusey's *Tract*

67, Scriptural Views on Baptism, when they speak about the incorporation of the Christian into Christ and the Christian's life in him. It might be more difficult, and it would require detailed study, to ascertain the extent of Newman's influence — if any — on Manning's ecclesiology; echoes may have grown too faint here, and ideas too widely spread and generally accepted, to identify direct influences. It is, however, easier to detect the many obvious similarities between Manning's fourth volume of *Sermons* and Robert Wilberforce's book on the Incarnation; on the other hand, their regular intercourse and copious correspondence during the late 1840s and early 1850s would make it hard to determine the extent of their mutual influence, and what precisely they owed to each other. This is particularly the case where the theology of the Church and that of the Eucharist are concerned.

What is beyond doubt is that, from the basis of opinions commonly held among the Tractarians, Manning developed the concept of the Church as the Mystical Body of Christ, of its unity and infallibility, well beyond the ideas of Pusey or Wilberforce. The latter, in his book on the Incarnation, still spoke of the theory of the Three Branches and of the Church's loss of the gift of infallibility with their separation. Besides, Manning's doctrine about the nature of the virtue of Faith and its genesis can also be said to be a new development in Tractarian thinking.

There is one certain influence which Manning explicitly acknowledged: he had found in Melchior Cano's *De locis theologicis* the key that solved his perplexities about the 'Rule of Faith'; his ideas on unity and infallibility were developed from the reading of Holy Scripture and the Fathers — St Augustine in particular — in the light afforded him by Melchior Cano.

Manning's last volume of Anglican *Sermons* is a very important milestone in his theological development, and also of great significance for those who were still committed to the Anglican Revival which had its origin in the Oxford Movement. It is remarkable that, although scholars have been aware of Manning's influence on Pusey and Robert Wilberforce, there have been few studies of his theology. Härdelin, in the bibliography consulted for his great work about the Tractarian doctrines on the Eucharist, mentioned only one of Manning's published works: his 1842 *Charge*!

NOTES

1.   For an introduction to Manning's theological development and to his volumes of *Sermons* see G. Rowell, *'Remember Lot's Wife'* — *Manning's Anglican Sermons*, pp. 167-179; J. Pereiro, *'Truth Before Peace': Manning and Infallibility*, pp. 218-253; both in V.A. McClelland (ed), 'Henry Edward Manning (1808-1892)', *Recusant History*, (October 1992).

2.   H.E. Manning, *The Rule of Faith*, (London, 1838), p. 8.

3.   Correspondence and Papers of Henry Edward Manning and members of his family, at the Bodleian Library, Oxford, (*Manning Mss. Bod*), c. 656, Fol.107.

4.   *Manning Mss. Bod*, c.665, Fol.136.

5.   A. Härdelin, *The Tractarian Understanding of the Eucharist*, (Uppsala, 1965), p. 84.

6.   H.E. Manning, *The Temporal Mission of the Holy Ghost, or Reason and Revelation*, (London, 1909), pp. 1-2.

7.   H.E. Manning, *Sermons*, vol.IV, (2nd ed., London, 1850), p. 180.

8.   *Ibidem*, p. 92.

9.   *Ibidem*, p. 181.

10.   *Ibidem*, p. 52.

11.   *Ibidem*, p. 203.

12.   *Ibidem*, p. 184.

13.   *Ibidem*, p. 186.

14.   *Ibidem*, p. 187.

15.   *Ibidem*, p. 89.

16.   *Ibidem*, p. 103.

17.   *Ibidem*, p. 187.

18.   *Ibidem*, p. 27.

19.   *Ibidem*, p. 182.

20.   *Ibidem*, p. 201.

21.   *Ibidem*, p. 275.

22.   *Ibidem*, p. 190.

23.   *Ibidem*, p. 220.

24.   *Ibidem*, pp. 198-199.

25.   *Ibidem*, p. 93.

26.   *Ibidem*, pp. 181-182.

27.   *Ibidem*, p. 103.

28.   *Ibidem*, p. 345.

29.   *Ibidem*, p. 287.

30.   *Ibidem*, p. 198.

31.   *Ibidem*, pp. 92-93.

32.   R. Wilberforce, *The Doctrine of the Incarnation of our Lord Jesus Christ*, (London, 1848), p. 308.

33.   H.E. Manning, *Sermons*, vol.IV, p. 201.

34.   *Ibidem*.

35.   *Ibidem*, p. 224.

36.   *Ibidem*, p. 290.

37.   *Ibidem*.

38.   *Ibidem*, p. 296.

39.   H.E. Manning, *Temporal Mission*, p. 28.

40.   H.E. Manning, *Sermons*, vol.IV, pp. 296-297.

41.   *Ibidem*, p. 297.

42.   *Ibidem*, pp. 297-298

43.   H.E. Manning, *Temporal Mission*, p. 30.

44.   H.E. Manning, *Sermons*, vol.IV, p. 202.

45.   *Ibidem*, p. 97.

46.   *Ibidem*, p. 103.

47.   *Ibidem*, p. 172.

48.   *Ibidem*, p. 169.

49.   *Ibidem*, p. 171

50.   *Ibidem*, p. 172.

51.   *Ibidem*, p. 170.

52.   *Ibidem*, p. 172.

53.   *Ibidem*, p. 168.

54.   *Ibidem*, p. 376.

55.   *Ibidem*, pp. 376-377

56.   *Ibidem*, p. 377.

57.   *Ibidem*, p. 162.

58.   *Ibidem*, p. 157.

59.   *Ibidem*, p. 158. The visible world is seen as a type and sacrament of the unseen.

60.   *Ibidem*, p. 164.

61.   *Ibidem*, p. 168.

62.   *Ibidem*, p. 165.

63. *Ibidem*, p. 162.
64. *Ibidem*, p. 159.
65. *Ibidem*, p. 166.
66. *Ibidem*, p. 377.
67. *Ibidem*.
68. *Ibidem*, p. 171.
69. *Ibidem*.
70. *Ibidem*.
71. Cfr. *Ibidem*, p. 170.
72. *Ibidem*.
73. *Ibidem*, p. 172.
74. *Ibidem*, p. 378.
75. *Ibidem*, p. 379.
76. *Ibidem*, p. 380.
77. *Ibidem*.
78. *Ibidem*, p. 381.
79. *Ibidem*, p. 378.
80. *Ibidem*, p. 386.
81. *Ibidem*, p. 84.
82. *Ibidem*, p. 75.
83. H.E. Manning, *The Unity of the Church*, London, 1842, p. 268.
84. *Ibidem*, p. 251.
85. H.E. Manning, *Sermons,* vol.IV, p. 84.
86. Härdelin, op. cit., p. 72.
87. As an introduction to Tractarian ecclesiology see Y. Brilioth, *The Anglican Revival: Studies in the Oxford Movement*, (London, 1925), ch. XI and XIII; also Härdelin, op. cit., ch.2.
88. G. Rowell, op. cit., p. 170.

X

'A STRANGER AND DARK UNTO HIMSELF' MANNING'S SECOND 'CONVERSION' 1844-47

V. Alan McClelland

The first religious 'conversion' of Henry Edward Manning began its process while he was an undergraduate in Oxford and, in human terms, has usually been attributed to the strong influence of two people. The first of these was his brother-in-law, John Anderdon, that devotee of the unbending philosophy of character formation prescribed by the Baptist fundamentalist, John Forster[1] and the other, Favell Bevan, sister of an erstwhile school friend, a forceful and humourless woman governed by an evangelical 'high seriousness'in most of her undertakings. Recently, Christopher O'Gorman has questioned this interpretation of events,[2] maintaining that the considerable religious metamorphosis effected in Manning in the years between 1827 and 1834 was essentially the outcome of less clearly defined or overtly dramatic forces. In this analysis, the process of first 'conversion' consisted in subliminal understanding and, then, questioning of the old High Church principles of his family and upbringing, coupled with an increasing awareness of the nature of the Church and its Catholic heritage. It was certainly a gradual awakening, accompanied by a clearer definition of what was incumbent upon him in terms of personal commitment and religious practice. Pursuing this theory, then, the first 'conversion' does not appear to have been in the nature of a Damascus-experience but, more likely, the beginning of an evolving process that was to germinate and then burgeon in the midst of sacerdotal labour and pastoral commitment during the first ten years of Manning's charge at Lavington.

In old age, Manning reflected upon the nature of his theological standing as he commenced that initial decade of priestly work in the year when the first of the *Tracts for the Times* was published. 'The state of my religious belief in 1833,' he wrote 'was profound faith in the Holy Trinity and the Incarnation, in the Redemption by the Passion of our Lord, and in the work of the Holy Spirit and the conversion of the soul. I believed in baptismal regeneration and in a spiritual, but real, receiving of our Lord in Holy Communion. As to the Church, I had no definite conception'.[3] While we may make allowance for any deficiency in Manning's memory, it is with this last identified lacuna in his self-analysis that the period of second 'conversion' is essentially concerned.

In 1843, on a visit to Lavington, F D Maurice, admittedly evincing a certain trepidation, recorded his view of Manning as 'one of the completest men' he had ever encountered. The nature of the completeness was tempered, he considered 'with so much appreciation of everything good, such great refinement, tolerance, and kindliness, that I know not where one would look, rather, for a wise and true bishop in these times'.[4] Maurice's attempted panchromatic identification of the complete man was wide of the mark and, of course, never more so than in 1843 when Manning was undergoing a period of considerable spiritual stress and theological realignment. Furthermore, whatever *vocational* assurance Manning exuded within his pastoral obligations, the death of his wife Caroline, after less than four years of happy married life, had heightened in him an introspective recollection, a tortuous process of soul-searching that had become endemic in his daily living. That process of examination and analysis, apparent only to a limited circle of close friends, had led to a strengthening of his fundamental belief in the regenerative and directive action of the Holy Ghost, working within the Church and renewing her constantly, preserving her from error, guiding and fortifying her in her teaching and governing functions, as well as re-invigorating the spiritual life of her members.

Of the first seventeen *Tracts for the Times*, nine were written exclusively by Newman or in collaboration with him, and Manning showed considerable enthusiasm for their emphases upon dogmatic, historical and liturgical authenticity, for their reliance upon the teaching of the early Fathers of the Church and the early Oecumenical Councils. Similarly, he had admired Newman's *Parochial Sermons* when they appeared in 1834 for their felicity of language as well as spirituality — although it is significant that he told Samuel Wilberforce, by concentrating upon errors and abuses, they did not stress adequately the action of the Holy Spirit 'constantly present' as a Person, helping, teaching, fortifying and guiding. Indeed, it was the controversial polemic engendered by the aggressiveness of some of the Tractarians that Manning found distasteful, rather than anything in the *Tracts* themselves, the early ones of which were emolliently anodynous and gave valuable insights into the nature of Tradition, the visible evidence of the Holy Spirit brooding over God's creation and the dissemination of His truth. It was with committed alacrity that Manning agreed to join the team of authors to publish a *catena patrum* of the effusions of English divines from John Jewell in the sixteenth century to William van Mildert who died but a year before the publication of *Tract 78* in 1837. The aim of the collection was to illustrate how the true Creed of the Church was constituted. In the introduction to the *Tract*, Manning wrote: 'Catholic Tradition teaches revealed truth, Scripture proves it; Scripture is the document of the Faith, Tradition the witness of it; the true Creed is the Catholic interpretation of Scripture, or Scripturally-proved Tradition ... scripture and Tradition taken together are the joint Rule of Faith'.[5] The *Tract* was designed as a compendium to an edition of the work of Vincentius Lerinensis on heresy which Manning had issued the year before with Newman's encouragement.[6] In its 118 pages, the *Tract* vividly manifested the complementary rôles of Scripture and Tradition in the life of the *ecclesia docens* and lucidly endorsed the analysis of the constituents of the rule of faith foreshadowed by Wiseman's lectures on the Church given at St Mary Moorfields in 1835 and 1836. Wiseman had emphasized 'the threefold composition of the provision made by God for the acceptance of his holy religion: a divine revelation, having its essential basis in His written word; an unfailing authority to preserve, propose and explain it; and an inward aid to receive and embrace it'. And the emblem of these, 'as was done of old', Wiseman declared 'we carefully cherish in the tabernacle of God with men, which is His Church'.[7] For Newman, Wiseman's lectures proved beneficial mainly in the sense of awakening Anglicans to those Catholic principles too long dormant in the Church of England,[8] whereas to someone like David Lewis, Newman's curate, the lectures marked, even more so, the beginning of a serious revival of Catholicism in England.[9] Such views were to earn the stinging *riposte* of Hampden in his lecture on *Tradition* of March, 1839 : 'Let tradition be once established, whether doctrinal or interpretative, as a rule of faith and it will be sure in the event to supersede the written authority, or make it of none effect.'[10]

In Newman's reflective analysis, the *Tracts for the Times* had been founded upon 'a deadly antagonism to what in these last centuries has been called "Erastianism" or "Caesarism"',[11] the latter a term Manning was to employ himself throughout his long life to delineate the illegitimate secular interference of the State in matters ecclesiastical. Newman, in his letter to the Duke of Norfolk, written following Gladstone's polemical outburst against the first Vatican Council, maintained 'no ultramontane (so called) could go beyond those writers (of the *Tracts for the Times*) in the account which they gave of (the Church) from the Prophets', and he added 'that high notion is recorded beyond mistake in a thousand passages of their writings....'[12]

Impeccable Tractarian orthodoxy penetrated Manning's thinking by

1835 in response to his personal pilgrimage quest for the true basis of authoritative teaching in the Church : 'The first question that rose in my mind,' Purcell records of Manning 'was, what right have you to be teaching, admonishing, reforming, rebuking others? By what authority do you lift the latch of a poor man's door and enter and sit down and begin to instruct or correct him?' This train of thought he tells us in an autobiographical note 'forced me to see that no culture or knowledge of Greek or Latin would suffice for this. That if I was not a messenger sent from God, I was an intruder and impertinent'.[13] The sacerdotal witness of the clergy must ultimately rest upon proof of the apostolic succession of the episcopacy. 'How long so ever the line of transmission be drawn,' Manning was to preach in a sermon of 1835, 'the validity of all depends upon the soundness of the first, and the union between each successive link; so that if there be anywhere a break, the whole must fall, and what man dare on his own authority renew what the authority of Christ began?'[14] It was genuine personal necessity, indeed, that led Manning to seek the theological basis of his ministry and marked the beginning of an intensive period of private study of the Fathers.

Manning was critical of Melbourne's Act of 1836 setting up the Ecclesiastical Commission, not so much for what it would or would not do in practical measure but because it failed to recognize the immiscibility at the heart of claiming supremacy for the secular power over ecclesiastical matters intimately concerned with the teaching authority and essential polity of the Church. In a published letter to his bishop, William Otter, he made his belief clear that 'the Church by her Apostolical Commission is empowered to *govern*, as well as to *minister* in the name of Christ,' a power that was not only judicial but legislative through the ecclesiastical system of provincial and diocesan councils, 'the outward witness of her rights and the form of administering her legislative commission'.[15]

Manning was at pains to point out to his friends in 1836 that they misunderstood him if they associated him with any formal group or party within the Church of England, except insofar, as he told Andrew Hamilton, accidental agreement warranted putting him in the same category as others. He was his own man, he claimed, and his views were formed alone 'by the Word of God' and 'examination of the Christian Faith before Popery corrupted it, or Protestantism wrested it aside....'[16]

Manning's lucubration in relation to the establishment of the Ecclesiastical Commission on a permanent basis led to the re-editing, with his intense young friend Samuel Wood, of the treatise of the Jacobite non-juror Charles Leslie, *The Case of the Regale and of the Pontificat*. Originally published in 1700, Leslie argued in this study that the episcopate and episcopally-ordained clergy constituted a spiritual power, co-ordinate with that of the State. The re-issuing of Leslie's treatise constitutes an early indication of the road to Gorham and to Manning's ultimate realisation that, as a final resort, the Church of England had no stomach but to acquiesce in the over-riding judgement of the State, even in matters doctrinal.

For the succeeding few years Manning immersed himself in the study of Tradition, a period marked by the publication of his commitment to the theology of the Apostolic Succession in a sermon of 1838 on 'The Unity of the Church'. He had ingested Newman's lectures on the *Prophetical Office* published the year before, in which Newman had argued that it still remained to be tried 'whether what is called Anglo-Catholicism ... is capable of being professed, acted on, and maintained on a large sphere of action and through a sufficient period, or whether it be a mere modification or transition-state of either Romanism or of popular Protestantism, according as we view it'.[17] J.B. Mozley criticized this reflection later as evidence that Newman's approach 'fastens the one aspect of a book system upon [the Anglican Church]' and passes through her 'as if she were a phantom or exhalation, opposing no real resistance to the forcible theory that inwardly possesses him'.[18] In adopting such an approach, he maintained, Newman 'did not energize as a parish priest but as an author'.[19]

For his part, Manning was at one with Newman in identifying two essential ingredients in the search for assurance in the credentials of the Church of England: faithfulness to Apostolic precept and integrity of doctrinal belief with that of the early Church. Closely associated with such ingredients lie security in his own sacerdotal authenticity and advancement in his personal quest for conformity to the Divine Will.

In his important sermon on 'The Rule of Faith', preached before Bishop Otter in Chichester Cathedral in June 1838, the year in which the issue of Froude's *Remains* caused such *furore* in Anglican clerical ranks, Manning showed he had sympathy with the kind of yearning Froude evinced in his desire to follow Truth wherever he found it and whithersoever it might lead him. Manning's definition of the Church in that stressful year is that of an institution which was 'a living, responsible being; witnessing, defining old truths, condemning false novelties. Her charge is to sustain, from age to age, the whole body of revealed wisdom; to view each successive generations of her children with the conclusions of the faith, openly tendering, also, the proofs of Holy Scripture; and thus going before us from our childhood being ever herself of one ripe age, teaching us what things are necessary, probable or doubtful both what we must, and what we may believe; ever leading on those that will follow from conclusion to proofs, to inner ranges, and to higher paths of wisdom'.[20] It was an ecclesiology that unequivocally rejected private judgement in matters doctrinal and was one designed to challenge, if not to affront, evangelical conviction. The sure guidance of the Holy Ghost in her witness to the Truth, he declared, enables Christ's Church to protest 'against the claims, whether of churches or of individuals, to such an immediate guidance of that same Spirit by whom the Scriptures were dictated *as shall supersede this witness* in interpreting their sense'.[21] His attack upon 'the whirlwind of schism and heresy which burst, two centuries ago, upon our land, hurling down our sanctuaries and altars'[22] was an unequivocal testimony to his belief in the Catholicity of the Church and a rejection of the principles of the Reformers. The latter, indeed, he said, had 'deposited among their foundation stones noxious seeds, wafted from abroad, to mingle with the harvest of home-bred errors ... (and) left behind an abundant store, secretly to infest and overrun the courts of the Lord's house, when they were again builded as before'.[23] The peroration of the sermon was quite magnificent:

> But amid the windy storms and tempest of man's fleeting and turbulent opinions one thing is steadfast, 'Jesus Christ, the same yesterday, today, and for ever': the one faith unchangeable; the shadow of Himself. And in His awful presence we are set as witnesses. We may be cast out as obstinate and doating, as uncharitable and contentious, as hinderers of the vaunted common sense, as thwarting religious unity and popular co-operation and even, like the prophet of old, as troublers of Israel. Let us calmly answer, we have no power over ourselves. We testify to what we have received.[24]

By nailing his colours so firmly to the mast, Bishop Otter thought Manning had placed at risk his rôle within the diocese as a healer of division. Others accused him of investing the Church with the infallibility they saw as belonging only to Scripture. Again, he was accused of substituting Tradition for the word of God, of shifting Faith from Divine to human foundation. Far from being crushed by the swell of criticism, Manning answered it in an *Appendix* to his sermon of some 136 pages in length on which he advanced theological sources for the establishment of two major points:- that the Rule of Faith as he expounded it was the recognized principle of the reformed Church of England and, secondly, that it was also the universal rule of the early Church. His response was masterly and both the *Quarterly Review* and the *British Critic* lauded it with praise and enthusiasm.[25] Indeed, it was to be cited in the following year as a good defence of the Tractarian position *vis à vis* Wiseman's article in the *Dublin Review* indicating similarities between the Anglican dilemma and the position of the

Donatists of the fifth century, as condemned by St Augustine. Manning was under no illusion as to the power of Wiseman's argument which, for Newman, had 'pulverized' the theory of the *via media*.[26] Indeed, in his own words, Wiseman had left Newman with 'no positive Anglican theory'.[27] Manning's *Appendix* to the *Rule of Faith* was, thus, to gain wide circulation in 1839 when the Anglican shock troops found themselves in disarray. His view that 'the Roman Church, how much so ever it may appeal in words to antiquity, does in practice actually oppose it'[28] was an immediate, albeit, superficially polemical device upon which to rest for a time. Privately, Manning was as seriously disturbed as Newman by Wiseman's claim that the cornerstone of authenticity of faith and fidelity of teaching in the instruction of the Fathers was communion with the see of Peter.

Manning's book *The Unity of the Church*, which tried to address this issue, was published in 1842. It was in three parts, progressing from a presentation of the history and exposition of the doctrine of Catholic Unity, to an analysis of its moral design and, finally, to an examination of the concept of unity itself when applied to the actual state of contemporary Christendom. He argued boldly from the premise that unity is a duty and schism a sin, to showing that 'the polity of the Church, including the Apostolic succession as its primary condition, and what is vulgarly called Episcopacy as its aspect or countenance' is an organic part of the great phenomenon of objective unity 'through which the Holy Spirit works out, in the moral nature of man, the purpose of the Divine mind'.[29] Encapsulating much of Manning's thought is the sentence: 'The polity of the Church is subject to no control or judgement of man; and is absolutely immutable, except by the authority of God alone'.[30] The intellectual error is gross, he claimed, in those 'who change the polity of the body of Christ, and set up a system devised by the wit and moulded by the will of man, and call it a church'.[31] It is evident from contemplating such passages why Manning thought the arguments of *Tract 90*, published shortly before his own book in 1841, with their emphasis on the view that the Articles of the Church of England bear 'a highly Catholic meaning'[32] and, as Newman put it, 'that many doctrines, of which the Romanist are corruptions, may be held consistently with them' were not quite 'straight forward'.[33] Others of differing ecclesiastical positions agreed. Henry Wilson, for instance, summed up *Tract 90* as 'offering apologies for the doctrines (*sic*) of purgatory, pardons, image worship and invocation of saints',[34] all in the interests of halting the lemming-like drift to Rome. Manning's contribution to the ensuing debate was to attempt to raise the level by concentrating upon the nature and constitution of the Church and her teaching while emphasizing the need to strengthen individual piety and personal security in the faith. This is exemplified by his first volume of sermons, published in the same year as *The Unity of the Church*. Their pastoral themes could be embodied in the phrase : 'what a vast realm of spiritual life lies hid in each one of us'.[35] The seventeen sermons were designed to lay bare the fundamental yearnings of the Christian spirit.

The cataclysmic events of the decade 1840 to 1850 — the aftermath of *Tract 90*, the Jerusalem Bishopric affair, the conversion of Newman and many of his followers in the middle of the decade and subsequently, the appointment of Hampden to the see of Hereford in 1847 despite the unprecedented and voluble protests of fourteen bishops of the Church of England, to say nothing of the Gorham case itself — inevitably ensured Manning would have to play a more visible leadership rôle than hitherto. Already well-documented, this part of his career needs further investigation. The fundamental issue for him, underpinning most of the disputes, was the question of the increasingly aggressively interventionist rôle of the State in the polity of the church and, in the case of Hampden and Gorham in particular, it was an intervention presenting a challenge to orthodox doctrinal teaching.

By the beginning of the period of his second 'conversion', as it has been called, Manning had definitely abandoned any hope of compromise or middle way out of the ecclesiastical *impasse*. He could sympathise, he told Dodsworth, with those who believe the Roman Church to be right and the English Church wrong and yet remain as Anglicans 'in awe and fear lest they should tempt God by going over' but, he added, such men could not be Catholics worthy of imitation. 'Be sure of this,' he declared 'that the day I cease to be Anglican I shall be Roman'.

In 1841 Manning sensed that the white-heat of theological controversy and unrest was in danger of proving an obstacle to the untrammelled operation of the spirit within the Church of England. His sermons prepared for the university pulpit at St Mary the Virgin in 1841 were designed as careful, pious orations, ignoring by and large the Tractarian disputations. They concentrated upon the interior life of prayer and devotion, upon applying the word of God to human needs and situations. Similarly, when he preached the sermon on Trinity Sunday in 1841 in Chichester Cathedral at the first ordination service of Bishop Shuttleworth, he proclaimed 'it is only by holiness that we shall win the people to be holy' for 'even the lowliest and unlikeliest of Christ's servants gain by holiness an incredible dominion over the most stubborn and inveterate minds.... It is by gentleness, and a yielding temper, by conceding all indifferent points, by long endurance of undeserved contempts ... by asking reconciliation where others would exact apologies, that the sternest spirits of the world are absolutely broken into a willing and glad obedience to the lowliest servants of

Christ'.[36] It was a brave sermon on the dignity and heritage of the apostolic ministry, preached before a prelate who only three years earlier had himself written a powerful attack on Tractarian theology in *Not Tradition, But Revelation*, a treatise which scorned 'the superior wisdom of antiquity' and 'the blind adoption of primitive usages' as if the latter were 'only another name for Christian faith'.[37] In 1841, Manning resolved not to be drawn to a party spirit, or to adopt a destructive or refutative process. At this time he set down his views on his own relationship to the Church of England. In a document entitled *Religio Anglo-Catholici*, dated by Manning as 'written about 1841-42' and retained among his papers, he recorded: 'My allegiance to the Church in England' (and we note the significance of the word 'in') 'is on the hypothesis of its agreement and unity with the Church universal. Of that agreement I may play the judge if I will: but I shall be wiser if I forbear.... As by Baptism I was made a Christian so by partaking of the Church I was made a Catholic, that is, a member of the one, only, universal Church which comprehends all nations, extends into all lands, teaches all doctrines of truth, heals all the maladies of humanity .... For this reason I am not afraid to call myself an Anglo-Catholic, not imposing thereby a particular limitation on a universal term but intending to express a Catholic Christian born and dwelling in this Realm of England.' He continued: 'I have no sympathy for those that prison themselves within the small circle of national churches : nor with those that indulge in the empty theory of the church as a development or organisation of the national life : the one denies the Apostolic, the other the Catholic element of the Church; the one deals with its Polity as if it were a human, changeable, transitory thing : the other narrows the breath of Charity and tempts to a schismatical spirit. The duty of universal communion on the basis of truth is absolute'.[38]

This analytical reflection characterises the nature of Manning's interior struggle, the ingredients of his second gradual 'conversion' along a path that would relentlessly lead to Rome. As yet, he was bound to the Church of England because 'I dare not leave the Divine Presence working within her, I dare not sever myself from so much love which has been upon me and about me from my regeneration, from such tokens of grace, care, nearness, from such holy lives and deaths as are about me'.[39] Other reasons weighed heavily with him, not least the pastoral necessities of the faithful: 'all the trials of our Ecclesiastical and spiritual position are things to be endured: heavy, keen, searching, depressing as they are, they are to be borne and toiled under, and striven against for the sake of God's Elect in this land'.[40] His faith would be to endeavour to bring the Church of England and the Church of Rome closer together in an ecumenical drive that would restore Catholic teaching and practice in the Anglican Church, lessen divergence of view on specific points of difference and unite around the basis of Catholic truth.' He concluded: 'Next to the Church of England there is nothing between heaven and earth that commands from me so strong and fond a love than the Church of Rome'.[41] He set himself against individual defections to Rome, unless the working of the Holy Spirit was clearly manifest in them and his fifth of November sermon in 1843 at St Mary the Virgin has to be seen within that formal context.

On September 5, 1843, Manning was in Oxford and was informed by the bedel who arranged the programme of Select Preachers at St Mary's that Manning's next date to preach was November 5th. The time was intense. Newman was to resign the benefice of St Mary's on September 18th and the trickle of converts to Rome seemed to be gathering momentum. On October 14th, Newman told Manning that 'in proportion as I think the Anglican Church is showing herself intrinsically and radically alien from Catholic principles, so do I feel the difficulties in defending her claims to be a branch of the Catholic Church....'[42] Manning was, at first, overwhelmed at the level of despair Newman appeared to have imbibed: he seemed to be lost to the Church of England and it was but a matter of time before the final capitulation to Rome. Indeed, on October 25th, he informed Manning: 'I must tell you frankly, unless I combat arguments which to me, alas, are shadows, that it is from no disappointment, irritation, or impatience, that I have, whether rightly or wrongly, resigned St Mary's, but because I think the Church of Rome the Catholic Church, and ours not a part of the Catholic Church, because not in communion with Rome, and I felt I could not honestly be a teacher in it any longer'.[43] Remonstrance seemed pointless and Manning could only send him kind and affectionate greetings, together with the pious wish that 'by whatsoever path, may we be led home to the rest where there is no more going out'.[44]

Delivered ten days later, Manning's 5th of November sermon, entitled *Christ's Kingdom Not of This World*, remained within the pastoral framework he had devised for the series of sermons he gave at St Mary's but, in a time of exceptional crisis for the Church, it was intended to provide a solemn affirmation of confidence in the apostolicity of the Church of England, an attempt to pull men back from the brink of submission to Rome, an effort to posit a firm belief in the guidance of the Holy Spirit and a warning against the making of irrevocable choices or decisions as a consequence of human needs or personal loyalties.[45] He hoped to maintain the Anglican position without ambiguity and to pursue the work of rebuilding and regeneration within his immediate sphere of influence and, thus, to allow the interior life to grow in the Church, undisturbed by rancour or discord.

Although the old *via media* was no longer tenable, the Church of England still survived in her succession and her pastoral office. With the Greek Church and Rome, he felt, she shared a common faith, a unifying gospel under the guidance of the Holy Spirit. Following a short trip to Normandy with Henry Wilberforce in late September and early October, in 1844, Manning read W. G. Ward's *The Ideal of a Christian Church* which had been published in June. Apart from commenting upon its Luther-like protest, Manning remarked upon its subliminal effect and said to Gladstone 'how sorely true is his exposure of our miserable defects, discipline and practice,' for 'it is a perplexing dispensation when the Church cannot bear her diseases and will not have her remedies....'[46] The uncompromising call of *The Ideal* 'to sue humbly at the feet of Rome for pardon and restoration'[47] invited retribution. As for proceedings against Ward at Oxford, Manning could not subscribe to accusations of bad faith or to the proposed new statute on subscription and he considered the deprivation of degrees to be wildly disproportionate to the offence, if offence there was deemed to be. The political game he found frankly offensive and he told Pusey: 'I feel, day by day, that nothing but the hand of God can lead us out of our present stress and that feeling drives me to my altar and my flock where I thank God something higher and stronger than all evidence and reasoning assures me what our Church is and who is in it'.[48]

It was inevitable that the political and ecclesiastical events of the end of 1844 and the beginning of 1845 would rivet all minds firmly upon Newman and his fellows at Littlemore. Newman had informed Pusey in February 1845 that he was waiting before making a final decision on his future but he declared ominously 'it is only a matter of time'.[49] Having now despaired of Newman, Pusey was particularly anxious to stem the flow of converts, likely to follow in Newman's wake. He urged Manning to use the opportunity presented by his preparation of the archideaconal *Charge* he was to deliver in Chichester Cathedral in July to concentrate upon the theme of fidelity. Potential converts to Rome were seeking advice from Pusey and Manning himself had seven cases seeking direction in the same way.

It is a measure of his troubled spirits that Manning's *Charge* of 1845 was, in essence, the least inspiring of all his compositions as Archdeacon of Chichester. Less than a fifth of it was devoted to the subject uppermost in his mind, the rest being given over to immediate matters of worship, law, domestic discipline, parish and social life. He reaffirmed his belief in the power of the pastoral ministry to communicate the Divine Presence in the Church, a conviction he rested upon the marks of Divine mercy he saw evidenced in the Church and in his own daily life as well as in the trials the Church had endured and was called upon to endure. Response to these latter challenges had led to internal renewal and to an increase in sanctity. Internal ills would be reduced by humility not by dispute. The *Charge* was, in modern parlance, a 'low-key' affair, one calculated to reassure rather than to question.

On September 4th, 1845, Manning left for France for a short holiday in the company of William Dodsworth, his brother-in-law George Ryder and the latter's wife, Sophie, meeting them at Le Havre. The time was spent mainly in visiting churches and ecclesiastical establishments before the group split, the Ryder's going to Fontainbleau and the remainder to Rouen. The whole visit was swift and tiring and Manning had to be back at Lavington within ten days. He returned to further alarms, the news of Ward's confirmation by Wiseman, the determination of Ambrose St John and John B Dalgairns to be received into the Roman Catholic Church to be followed by others, and the resignation of Newman from his fellowship. On October 8th, the agonism of the remainder of the Littlemore group came to the inevitable conclusion. The news of Newman's conversion, expected as it was, was a considerable blow and Manning felt the immediate need for peaceful recollection. His sense of isolation is contained in a letter sent to Mary Wilberforce on October 19th, 1845: 'The other night', he told her, 'I was full of sad thoughts of things past and to come; and the past and the future jarred together and I could not talk of what I felt most'. He added: 'I trust you do love me, for I feel that I should grow worse if people left off loving me as I deserve they should....'[50]

To Gladstone Manning recorded his debt to Newman.... What do I not owe him?' he said. 'No living man has so powerfully affected me: and there is no mind I have so reverenced.... All I can do is still to love and pray for him, which I do very earnestly. I cannot but feel that it is a fact which must have its consequences, ethical and intellectual in our relation to Rome; and decidedly for good. They must learn to understand and appreciate us more truly: and, I trust, to love us more, which they have done but little as yet....'[51]

Manning's anxiety about the Church of England he confided to Robert Wilberforce was not concerned with any lack of being in the presence of Christ in the Church or her sacraments but with her fundamental theology. 'Our theology', he told him 'is a chaos, we have no principles, no form, no order, or structure, or science.' There must be 'a true and exact *intellectual* tradition of the Gospel'.[52] The Church of England had rejected Scholastic Theology but created a vacuum.

Newman's *Essay on the Development of Christian Doctrine* appeared on November 27th, 1845. In the case of T W Allies it was to direct his studies for the next five years, for 'it appeared to me then', he was to write later in his autobiography 'and has ever since, that the Papal Supremacy was the key to the whole controversy — the centre of the whole position'.[53] It led, indeed, to Allies's own important and much neglected study of the primacy which appeared in 1850.[54] The *Essay on the Development of Christian Doctrine* had a formative rôle upon Manning too. He read the book with extraordinary interest and told Gladstone: 'I remember no book that so held my attention from beginning to end. It seemed as if the doubts, difficulties and problems of the last ten years were suddenly brought to a focus external to my own mind, with the strength and light of another mind to whose powers I felt as nothing. It seemed to swallow me up with all the thoughts of years. But, in the end, I feel [I still am] where I was. There are some things which go before all reasoning, and survive all objections: of the former kind I feel is the invocation of God alone, and of the latter, the reality of the English Church...' Nevertheless, he felt the book would 'provoke some to scepticism and more to doubts ... not a few will it send, year by year, to Rome'. He was afraid 'it will open a running sore in our poor body.'[55]

Before the year was out Manning had to decide whether or not to succeed Samuel Wilberforce as sub-almoner to the Queen which post had a seeming entrée, not only to the Court but probably to a bishopric. He sought advice and prayed much before turning down the invitation. To Robert Wilberforce he confided: 'I feel safest for my own soul, both in regard to a clearer perception of the truth of our position and to a simpler line of practice, to keep myself as I am ... I know myself and am afraid of secularity. In my past life I have great causes of self-reproach: and, with God's help, I prepare to keep myself from all ways which are not within the compass of the Altar....'[56]

In May 1846, George and Sophie Ryder were received into the Roman Catholic Church, together with George's sister. Manning did not evince the bitterness that Samuel Wilberforce showed at the event, although he felt for his mother-in-law, Mrs John Sargent, and the pain she would experience at Ryder's public reception in Rome. The outcome was not a total surprise, however, and Manning was able to see in the event a deeper lesson: 'What does He mean us to learn by it? To be just, fair, and gentle towards the Church of Rome? I have often thought that it is in this way that He purposes to turn our hearts to each other. Certainly the converts have a truer intellectual apprehension of us'.[57]

Manning spent the months immediately following George Ryder's conversion in a searching self-analysis of his own theological position. He was now at ease with Marian devotion and found no theological difficulty in honouring angels and saints. By July he felt unable to say

Rome was in error.

In August, Manning, then 38 years old, began a serious stocktaking of the development of his theological position over the last decade. He diagnosed the ills which the Church of England was prepared to tolerate, noting her faults and setbacks. He tried to justify his own position in regard to the Church and the work he had undertaken towards her reform. He pondered on the difficulties of Roman doctrine and analysed his spiritual progress and personal weaknesses. Fundamental to the review was his belief in the infallibility of the true Church, by which he meant the infallibility of the Spirit sustaining the Church by His inspiration. With ruthless logic he then argued: 'The Church being infallible, the next question is to know what is that Church in which the gift of infallibility resides? Here comes in the question of Unity. For all agree there is but one Church'.[58] He recognised the primacy of Peter among the apostles, that the Church of Rome inherited among churches that primacy, that it had primatial and patriarchal functions, that the Eastern schism left Rome the inheritor and representative of the original unity, that the Church of Rome was the heir of infallibility and that the Eastern Churches 'give suffrage in almost all points to the definitions of Rome'.[59] He discovered he had no difficulty with the Creed of Constantinople or the definitions of the Council of Trent and he concluded that he believed the Pope to be primate.

In truly Ignatian manner, he then proceeded to record the deficiencies of the Church of England as he saw them. Primordially, there was the organic divorce from the see of Peter, then the acceptance of subjection to the Civil Power without final appeal, there was the abolition of penance, the extinction of the daily sacrifice, the loss of minor orders and, what he called, the mutilation of ritual. Functionally, he deplored the loss of the daily service, the lack of ecclesiastical discipline, the loss of unity in devotion and ritual, the lack of proper training for the priesthood , the unsacerdotal life of many bishops and priests, the effacing of the Church from 'the popular conscience', popular unbelief in the essential Christian mysteries and an insensibility of the invisible world.

Manning's catalogue of beliefs and doubts, taken together, constitute a true *bouleversement* of ideas, a second radical conversion. The way ahead now seemed less opaque. In 1847 he could not accept that, despite her organic and functional sickness, the English Church was other than an integral part of the Church catholic. He certainly retained belief in the validity of his own Orders and those transmitted within the Church of England and he believed in the efficacy of her sacramental life. He dared not envision that Divine Providence would be content to punish the English Church for so long by depriving her of the channels of sacramental grace. It was to be three more long years, in fact, involving prayer, reading, much controversy and ill health before a final 'conversion' lifted the veil that enabled Henry Edward Manning to consider he was then no longer 'a stranger and dark unto himself.'

NOTES

1. See 'The Essay on Decision of Character', published in John Forster's *Essays* (1805).

2. *Recusant History*, 21, 2, 1992, pp. 152-166.

3. E. S. Purcell, *Life of Cardinal Manning* (2 vols., 1896), I, p. 112.

4. F.Maurice, *Life of Frederick Dennison Maurice* (2 vols., 1885), I, p. 351.

5. *Tract 78* (1837), p. 2.

6. *Vincenti Lerinensis Commonitorum* (Baxter, Oxford, 1836)

7. N. Wiseman, *Lectures on the Principal Doctrines and Practices of the Catholic Church* (1867 ed.). Preface to the 1st ed., p. iii (1836), p. 62.

8. See Newman's article in the *British Critic*, December 1836.

9. W. Ward, *Life and Letters of Cardinal Wiseman* (2 vols., 1897), I, p. 233. Lewis served as Newman's curate at St. Mary the Virgin, Oxford, and was Fellow of Jesus College. He became a Roman Catholic in 1846.

10. R. H. Hampden, *A Lecture on Tradition read before the University in the Divinity School Oxford, on Thursday March 7, 1839* (Fellowes, London, 1839), 5 ed., p. 75.

11. J. H. Newman, *A Letter Addressed to His Grace the Duke of Norfolk on Occasion of Mr Gladstone's Recent Expostulation* (1875), p. 20.

12. *Ibidem*.

13. Purcell, *Op. cit.*, I, p. 112.

14. H. E. Manning, *The English Church: Its Succession and Witness for Christ. A Sermon Preached in the Cathedral Church, July 7, 1835, at the Visitation of the Ven, the Archdeacon* [Charles Weber], (Chichester, 1835) p. 9.

15. H. E. Manning, *The Principles of the Ecclesiastical Commission Examined in a Letter to the Right Rev, The Lord Bishop of Chichester* (Rivington, London, 1838), pp. 9ff.

16. Transcript of Letter in Manning papers, *(MP)* formerly at Bayswater, August 10,1836.

17. J. H. Newman, *Lectures on the Prophetical Office of the Church* (Pickering, London, ed. 1877) I, p. 17.

18. J. B. Mozley in *The Christian Remembrancer*, January 1846, p. 181.

19. *Ibidem*, p. 179.

20. H. E. Manning, *The Rule of Faith: A Sermon Preached in the Cathedral*

Church of Chichester, June 13, 1838, at the Small Visitation of the Rt. Rev. William Otter, Lord Bishop of Chichester (Rivington, London, 2nd ed., 1839), p.45.

21. *Ibidem*, p. 42.

22. *Ibidem*, p. 55

23. *Ibidem*.

24. *Ibidem*.

25. *Quarterly Review* 126, 1839, p. 530; *The British Critic*, 50, 1839, p. 470.

26. J. H. Newman, *Apologia Pro Vita Sua* (1864 ed., Longman, London) p. 212.

27. Ward, *op. cit.*, I, p. 333.

28. 'The Rule of Faith'. *Appendix*, p. 100.

29. H. E. Manning, *The Unity of the Church* (Murray, London, 1842), pp. 280-281.

30. *Ibidem*, p. 282.

31. *Ibidem*, p. 283.

32. *Letters of Rev J. B. Mozley, D.D., edited by his sister* (Rivington, London, 1885). Letter of Newman dated March 8, 1841.

33. *The Tablet*, 1892, I, p. 82.

34. Quoted in M A Crowther, *Church Embattled: Religious Controversy in Mid-Victorian England* (David & Charles, Newton Abbot, 1970), p. 111.

35 H. E. Manning, *Sermons* (Burns, London, 1842); 3rd. ed., 1844, p. 211.

36. *The Moral Design of the Apostolic Ministry. A Sermon Preached on Trinity Sunday 1841 at an Ordination held by the Right Rev Philip Nicholas Shuttleworth, Lord Bishop of Chichester, in the Cathedral Church by H. E. Manning, M A, Archdeacon of Chichester* (Murray, London, 1841), pp. 20ff.

37. P. N. Shuttleworth, *Not Tradition, But Revelation* (Rivington, London, 1838), pp. 149-150.

38. Manning Papers, *op. cit. Ms Religio Anglo-Catholici*, 1841-2.

39. *Ibidem*.

40. *Ibidem*.

41. *Ibidem*.

42. *Correspondence of John Henry Newman with John Keble and Others*, ed. at the Birmingham Oratory (Longmans, Green & Co., London, 1917). Letter of Newman to Manning, October 14, 1843, pp. 272-273.

43. *Ibidem*. Letter of Newman to Manning, 25 October, 1843, pp. 276-278.

44. *Ibidem*. Letter of Manning to Newman, October 27, 1843, pp. 278-279.

45. The sermon is printed as *Sermon IV* of H E Manning, *Sermons Preached Before the University of Oxford*, (Parker, Oxford, 1844).

46. *MP*, *op. cit.*, Manning to Gladstone, November 14, 1844.

47. Maisie Ward, *The Wilfrid Wards and the Transition* (Sheed & Ward, London, 1934), I, p. 6.

48. H. P. Liddon, *Life of Edward Bouverie Pusey*, (Longmans, Green & Co., London, 1893), II., p. 448. Letter to Pusey, February 25, 1845.

49. *Ibidem*.

50. Ushaw Papers. Letter of Manning to Mary Wilberforce, October 19, 1845.

51. *MP*, *op. cit.*, Manning to Gladstone, October 10, 1845.

52. Purcell, *op. cit.*, pp 504-505.

53. T. W. Allies, *A Life's Decision* (quotation taken from the new edition, Burns Oates, London, 1913, p 70).

54. *The See of Peter, the Rock of the Church, the Source of Jurisdiction and the Centre of Unity.*

55. *MP*, *op. cit.*, Manning to Gladstone, Feast of St Stephen, 1845.

56. *Ibidem*. Manning to Robert Wilberforce, December 20, 1845.

57. *Ibidem*. Journal entry, March 18, 1846.

58. *Ibidem*. July 12, 1846.

59. *Ibidem*.

XI

CROSSED VISIONS — THE ANGLICAN MANNING'S OPINION OF ROME AND THE CATHOLIC MANNING'S THOUGHTS ON CANTERBURY

James Pereiro[1]

A. MANNING'S ANGLICAN VISION OF ROME

1. *The Anglican Concept of the Rule of Faith and of Church Unity*

Until 1845, although with increasing doubts from 1842-1843 onwards, Manning remained rooted in High Church principles, and his approach to Rome in those years moved along lines clearly defined in the abundant Anglo-Roman polemical literature. Manning's first references to Rome, and to Roman doctrines, appeared in the books on the rule of faith and about the unity of the Church which he published in the late thirties and early forties. They were not polemical works but an affirmative expression of principle. However, his dominant interests in doctrinal issues coincided precisely with those points which defined the Anglican identity, as seen by the High Church tradition, the *Via Media* between Rome and Protestantism. He was bound to refer to Infallibility and Private Judgment, and to refute the absolute claims of the Roman Church.

In his sermon *The Rule of Faith* (1838), and in its *Appendix*, he criticised the Roman doctrine of the infallibility of the Church, and contrasted it with the Anglican rule of faith, which he described as follows: 'the Rule of Faith, as recognised and contended for by the reformed Church of England, is Scripture and antiquity, or Universal Tradition attesting both Scripture and the sense'.[2] The Roman Church, on the other hand, affirmed that 'the same Spirit which dictated the writing of the Scriptures, [is] directing the Church to understand them'.[3] The Church would, thus, be a living and infallible judge of interpretation. Manning saw an obvious danger in this principle: when doctrine is 'tied to follow the utterance of a *living* voice ... [it] must vary with its living expositor'.[4] That had actually been the case: doctrinal corruptions had found their way, as a consequence, into the

Roman Church; corruptions that Rome had tried to impose on other churches as points of necessary belief for salvation. Protestantism, on its part, because of its acceptance of the principle of private judgment, multiplied proportionally the danger of variations in doctrine. The Reformed Church of England, against both of them, held the rule of faith of the Primitive Church: Scripture and the sense of Scripture attested by universal Tradition. It was true that the Church of Rome also claimed to rest on Tradition, but she conceived it rather differently. She upheld that some points of belief 'were *not committed to writing in Holy Scripture* but rest on *oral* tradition *alone*'.[5] On this basis, Rome had defined, as points of necessary belief, *particular trȧditions* of which there were no traces in Scripture. The Church of England preserved the concept of Tradition of the Primitive Church, as expressed by Vincent of Lerins: antiquity, universality and consent. It followed, Manning concluded, that 'Christians cannot possibly admit that any doctrine, established by universal tradition, can be otherwise than *divinely, infallibly true*'.[6] This 'universal tradition of all ages', he added further on, 'is no less than the voice of God'.[7]

The nature of the Church, of Church unity and of what constituted it, was another bone of contention between Anglican and Roman controversialists. Manning had imbibed his ideas on the subject from the writings of Thorndike and Bramhall, whom he will quote frequently. From the traditional High Church perspective, he conceived the Church as being made up of local (or particular) Churches, under the jurisdiction of their respective bishops. The Universal Church was made up of local churches, without subordination or dependence from one on another: 'our bishop', he wrote in 1838, 'is to us the source of authority and the centre of unity in order, deliberation and discipline. ... We believe that no power, spiritual or ecclesiastical, excepted only the collective authority of the whole Episcopal order to which supreme jurisdiction all Bishops are severally subject, can reach us, unless it pass through his express permission'.[8] In 1850 he will repeat similar ideas, adding that the 'Church in every land is the Church throughout the world sojourning as in a place, and there teaching and ruling by the whole weight of the Divine Office committed to the Church Universal'.[9]

Manning, with Thorndike and Bramhall, admitted that the Church of Rome had a primacy of honour among the churches, based originally on the political preeminence of Rome, as capital of the Empire, and he would not object to 'a patriarchal power limited by the Canons of the Church and exercised in conformity with them'.[10] However, no local Church, not even a patriarchal see, could claim a supremacy of jurisdiction over other local churches. Their power descended upon each one of them directly from the divine Head of the

Church in Heaven. A local Church was competent to reform itself in those areas which were its own concern; when it came to doctrines of faith and discipline which affected the whole Church, the whole Church should be consulted, Rome first because of its primacy of honour. This, according to Manning, was the doctrine of Holy Scripture and the Fathers on the unity of the Church. What a local Church could not do was to impose its own practices or decisions on all other Churches, as if exercising a universal jurisdiction of divine origin.

2. *The Causes of the Church's Divisions*

Self exaltation, Manning thought, was the source of all strife, and had been the source of most of the evils of the Church. Rome's claim of a supremacy of jurisdiction over all other churches had been the main cause of the divisions within the Church. The blame for the division between the Eastern and the Western Church was to be laid at the doors of both of them, although the fault of the Greek Church was never so great as the usurpation of the Supreme Pontificate by the Bishop of Rome: 'if a more petulant temper be found among the Greeks, yet the formal and positive causes of division are to be laid to the charge of the Roman Church'.[11] The separation, having deprived them of 'the mutual check and mitigating influence of each on the other',[12] had given rise to corruptions in discipline and doctrine in both. Still, Manning concluded, 'on neither side is there either formal heresy or schism of such a kind as to cut either of them off from the one visible Church, and from communion with the one Head of the Church in heaven'.[13] Unity subsisted on the foundations of apostolic succession and in the preservation of the essentials of the faith. Unfortunately, the communion of charity between the churches which made up the Catholic Church had been broken, but that had not touched the essentials of unity.

The divisions within the Western Church, particularly that of the Church of England from Rome, had had the same cause: the Roman claim to universal jurisdiction. This time it was compounded by the Temporal Claims of the Popes, the deposing power among them, over sovereigns and princes.[14] Manning considered that the 'act of the sixteenth century was the last and the successful effort in a long series of ineffectual struggles against the secular encroachment of the Roman court.... And the principle on which they rested their act, and on which our relation to the Roman Church is still amply to be defended is this — that there is no one supreme prince or power in things temporal from whom the civil rulers of this realm derive their sovereign authority: neither by Divine right any one supreme spiritual head on earth from whom the pastors of this Church derive their apostolical commission: that both the Spirituality and Temporality of this Church and Realm severally possess full authority and jurisdiction derived to them by succession and devolution; and that both, under Christ alone, are within their respective spheres perfect and complete'.[15] There was no schism in rejecting the pretence of universal jurisdiction of divine right by a local Church; neither was there heresy. As a matter of fact, the aim of the Anglican reformers had been to restore the evangelical purity of doctrine, which had been compromised by Roman 'corruptions'. They had returned to the faith of the Primitive Church. In doing so, some Tractarians would add, they have had to remove also some true doctrines which had become contaminated and deformed with error.

Anglican High Church doctrine upheld the Branch Theory, acknowledging the Roman and the Eastern Churches as the other two branches which, with her, made up the Universal Church. Manning felt that this generous acknowledgement on the part of the Church of England of the Roman Church, 'in spite of the corrupt traditions and ensnaring doctrines with which it is darkened and disfigured',[16] was not reciprocated, and he considered this as a sign of schismatic temper. Wiseman, in his polemical writings, had introduced the famous reference to the Donatists; Manning did bring them in here, although under a different perspective. He thought that, in the disputes between the Roman Church and the Church of England, this latter one occupied the Catholic ground — acknowledging Rome as a sister Church, accepting the validity of her orders and sacraments, the possession of true faith in essentials, etc — while Rome, like the Donatists, denied the Church of England everything, including its reality as a Church. Manning resented that rejection, and also the fact that Rome used Catholic and Roman as convertible terms. According to the principles of the Branch Theory, Rome was promoting schism both in the East and England by setting 'altar against altar, and succession against succession. In the formation of sects in diocesan churches, in the exclusive assumption of the name Catholic, in the reordination of priests, and in restricting the One Church to their own communion, there has been no such example of division since the schism of Donatus'.[17]

The year 1843 saw a dramatic profession of Anglican principles by Manning. His 5th of November Oxford Sermon was prompted by a letter from Newman and by *The British Critic* antics of Ward and Oakeley. Newman, in his letter of 25th October, spoke of his resignation of St Mary's as being prompted not by disappointment, irritation or impatience, 'but because I think the Church of Rome the Catholic Church, and ours not part of the Catholic Church, because not in communion with Rome'.[18] Ward and Oakeley, on their part, were making Rome 'the Ideal Church', on whose pattern the Anglican Church should be reformed. In fact, they were subverting its very foundations.[19] Unrestrained praise of Roman doctrine and practices had a negative effect: it pushed people towards Protestantism and Rationalism, weakened the Catholic elements in the Anglican Church and strengthened the un-catholic elements in the Roman.[20] The Church of England, according to High Church principles, was the true representative of Primitive Christianity and the model on which the other Catholic Churches had to reform themselves, before reunion could be achieved.[21] In that vein, Manning ended his Sermon with a note of optimism: the Church of England, purified by her present trials, might still be 'a principle of reconciliation between east and west, and a law of unity and peace to mankind'.[22] The acts of the sixteenth century might have been the stern but necessary preparation for this mission. The special dispensation of divine providence which had since then protected the Church of England and the realm from falling under the secular dominion of Rome, while preserving in the Anglican Church the purity of ecclesiastical principles, had imposed on it the responsibility of being faithful to its trust, for the good of the Universal Church.

Pusey, and others, tried to restrain Manning's anti-Roman rhetoric. Their correspondence seem to have served little purpose except that of forcing Manning to declare his thoughts on Rome more explicitly. His letters to Dodsworth, after the Sermon at Oxford, clearly expressed his ideas on the matter. He felt 'fully persuaded that if the position of Thorndike and Bramhall is not tenable the Roman Church is right; I believe their position to be tenable, and I know that it is the only alternative to entering the Roman Church.... Be sure of this that the day I cease to be Anglican I shall be Roman. Nothing in the world could induce me to take up the fanciful, half and half, intermediate system [as propounded by men like Ward and Oakeley] which embodies the reality of neither, and forfeits the strength of both'.[23] To Pusey's remonstrances to show charity towards the Roman Church Manning would answer by defining the principles on which, as he saw it, their relationship with the Church of Rome should be based. Charity, indeed, was due to the whole Church, including the Roman, but that should not make them forget that they owed the largest and tenderest charity to their own Church. They should express that charity and act on it, aware of the fact that, for three hundred years, the Church of Rome had desired the extinction of the Anglican Church, and looked for ways to undermine and destroy it. He added: 'We owe it in charity to the whole Church and to the Roman inclusively to do all we can to deepen and perfect the spiritual life of the English Church ... I believe that the best hope of building up the spiritual life of the English Church, and so of bringing about a reconciliation of our Church with those from whom we are unhappily estranged is a clear, firm, unambiguous tone as regards the points at issue'.[24]

3. *Is Conversion Morally Defensible?*

The means of salvation — doctrine and discipline, apostolic succession and valid sacraments — were available in each of the branches of the Universal Church, and the way of salvation for the individual soul was to be found within the branch in which she had been baptized. From this perspective, conversion from one branch to another made little or no sense; even more, in most cases, it involved an act of schism. Manning's strategy to keep in the Anglican fold those who were 'on the verge of Popery' was outlined in some of his letters, when dealing with particular cases. First, from a doctrinal point of view, Manning would describe the 'Roman errors' — Infallibility of the Church, Transubstantiation, the Supremacy of the Pope, devotion to the Blessed Virgin Mary, etc. — making use of books like George Stanley Faber's *The Difficulties of Romanism (1826)* or William Palmer's *Treatise on the Church* (1838). These 'errors', however, did not touch the essentials of the faith. Consequently, the main thrust of Manning's argument to remain in the Anglican Church was moral. As he wrote to Pusey in 1839, leaving for Rome involved the sin of schism; it also implied 'the deliberate and formal incurring of all the abuses of Romanism'. Moreover, it meant ingratitude 'to God who has ordained our second birth through the English Church and given all things necessary for salvation'.[25] The safest path was to remain in the Church of England: 'A man sins heavily who leaves us, above all if he goes to Rome which is at variance with Catholic Tradition; is Schismatical in England, and idolatrous in its tendencies'.[26] Roman errors made him fear for the safety of those within the Roman Church.[27]

Manning's approach to the question of conversion changed slightly as years went by. In 1846, writing to Dodsworth, his main suggestion was to impress on the mind of the waverer that the bonds established by Baptism to a particular Church could not be undone lightly: 'No preference for the Roman or any other Church on the grounds of its order, definiteness, doctrinal system and the like cancel the filial duty springing from our regeneration'.[28] As he saw it, the 'question of forsaking or abiding in the Church of England simply stands thus: It is a sin to forsake it if it be not sin to abide in it. That it is a sin to abide in it involves the assumption that it is either no Church at all, or a Church in heresy, or in schism'.[29] In a letter to Pusey of 1845 he had pointed out that it was not for the individual to decide the above, that would be an unacceptable exercise of private judgment, a transit from faith to reason. It was a question between branches of the Church. 'I know', he wrote, 'only of two suppositions on which a person can be justified in leaving the Church of England while it continues on its present basis:

> 1. A judgment of the whole Church justly and truly taken condemning our present position, a thing next to impossible, and therefore confirming our case provisionally and ad interim, or
>
> 2. A belief of an individual mind that it cannot stay in it without mortal sin. Which latter case precludes all arguments or persuasion'.[30]

Manning's words encapsulated the dilemma of many who, like him, after having journeyed along the road towards more Catholic principles, felt attracted by Rome. Intellectually, and sometimes emotionally, they might incline towards the Catholic Church but they were pulled back from the brink by the fear of suffering from a delusion. In that state they remained, at times for many years, before taking the final step. Manning felt that intellectual convictions were not entirely trustworthy and, by themselves, were not enough to warrant a move: 'they are logical, and eminently liable to mislead from their very clearness: the error being in the subject matter: in the premises, not in the reasoning'.[31] Distrust for their conclusions, fear of private judgment, was usually accompanied by the painful awareness of their moral limitations: others, more learned and better, had abided unperturbed in the Anglican Church. All this told against haste in coming to a final decision. The issue had tremendous consequences for time and eternity! They looked for guidance and waited for the voice of God to make itself clearly heard, as in Samuel's case, by means of the three divine calls, a common practice among those on the brink of Rome.[32]

Manning's conduct in those years exemplifies the working of the rule that he had prescribed for others, i.e. that it would be a sin to leave the Church of England if it were no sin to remain in it. At the beginning of 1848, when writing to Robert Wilberforce of the consolidation of his conviction about the irreality of the Church of England and of his changed disposition towards the Church of Rome, he added: 'Still I can say I have never felt the fear of safety or pressure of conscience which alone justifies a change'.[33] And some time later, less than a year before his actual conversion, he could write: 'I have not yet heard Him in my conscience saying, "Flee for thy life". Till then, I will die rather than run the risk of crossing His will. I fear haste, and I fear to offend God, but I fear nothing else; and in that faith by His grace I will wait upon Him, humbling and chastening my own soul'.[34]

Manning, with Keble and Pusey, felt that the safest course was to remain in the Church of one's Baptism for as long as morally defensible. Their commonly held opinion was based on the fact that conversion, particularly to Rome, involved a rejection of the presence of the means of salvation in the Church *a quo*, and a judgment on the ecclesiastical character of that Communion. It was a morally dangerous step, involving an unjustifiable exercise of private judgment. Keble even maintained that English Roman Catholics should remain in their Church. He, however, did not rule out conversions entirely. It would be justified, in certain circumstances, to move from one branch of the Church to another, and, in the case of a move from Rome to Canterbury, the 'migration' involved a lesser moral danger, given that the rejection of that Church in becoming an Anglican would not be as absolute as if the move were the other way round.[35]

Manning, in *The Unity of the Church* (1842), had put forward his vision for Church reunion: visible and external unity was to be achieved by corporate reunion of the branches of the Church. The best way of achieving this would be by means of a truly ecumenical council, in which the Three Branches of the Church would be properly represented. While awaiting for the Council to resolve the differences between Orthodox, Anglican and Roman, we 'go on', Keble wrote, 'appealing to it, and in the meantime submitting our judgement to that portion of the apparent visible Church wherewith, by God's appointment, we are in communion'.[36] The imperatives of the individual conscience will soon make clear for Manning that personal convictions could not be sacrificed on the altar of corporate reunion.

4. *Perplexities and New Perspectives*

There were some areas in which the Church of England had to look to Rome, as having preserved primitive tradition. Newman, Pusey, Manning and others had soon discovered that, in applying the standard of Antiquity, many doctrines and practices of the Primitive Church had been lost in the Church of England, while still preserved in the Roman Church. This was particularly evident for Manning in respect to sacramental and ascetical practices. As early as 1838 he had expressed to Newman his perplexity about the limitations that the Anglican system imposed on the longings awakened in the faithful by the ideals of Christian life presented to them. Newman's response made clear their predicament: 'our blanket is too small for our bed ... I am conscious that we are raising longings and tastes which we are not allowed to supply — and till our bishops and others give scope to the development of Catholicism externally and wisely, we *do* tend to make impatient minds seek it where it has ever been, in Rome'.[37]

Manning felt the importance of confession and other ascetical practices, and lamented the lack of a proper spiritual theology in the Church of England. In his mind, he blamed her present deficiencies in this area on the reaction against the Roman corruptions which she had rejected in the Reformation. Some customs and devotions, though legitimate in themselves, had led to abuses, and the Reformers had been forced to discard them altogether. In 1840 he complained to Archdeacon Hare: 'The Romanist errors have bereft us of our inheritance of blessed contemplation'.[38] The English Church, he wrote later to Gladstone, was 'Catholic in dogma, and in polity, that is in all the objective being of a Church. But the subjective, the internal, ascetic, contemplative, devotional, moral, penitential elements were wasted down to a meagreness which is nigh unto death'.[39] These deficiencies, though, did not worry him unduly. The English Church had to develop those Catholic elements she had rejected at the Reformation, after having purified them from the deforming corruptions. That, she would do. She was 'a real substantial Catholic body capable of development and all perfection — able to lick up and absorb all that is true and beautiful in all Christendom into itself — and this is our problem'.[40]

In 1845 came the crisis caused by Newman's *Development of Doctrine*. Manning was not convinced by Newman's theory, but he saw in Newman's argument the crisis of the Anglican rule of faith: 'it opened my eyes to one fact, namely that I had laid down only half of the subject. I had found the *Rule*, but not the *Judge*. It was evident that to put Scripture and Antiquity into the hands of the individual is as much private judgment as to put Scripture alone'.[41] It was only in 1847, towards the end of a long and nearly fatal illness, that Manning discovered the principle which was to dispel the thick clouds which had covered his intellectual horizon for almost two years: the presence and action of the Holy Spirit within the Church. A discovery which brought with it a radical change in his concept of the Church and of the rule of faith. This new perspective he described, after some years consolidating the principle and deducing its corollaries, in his Fourth Volume of Anglican Sermons, published early in 1850. By then, Manning was fast slipping his moorings in the Church of England.

At the heart of his Fourth Volume of Anglican sermons is the idea that, when Christ ascended up on high, 'the virtues of His glorified manhood were shed abroad upon His Church'[42] by the Holy Spirit. 'Therefore the Church is one because He is one; holy, because He is holy; Catholic, because His presence is local no more; apostolic, because He still sends His own servants; indefectible, because He is life; unerring, because He is Truth'.[43] The Holy Spirit's union to the Church is an indissoluble one. Infallibility is, consequently, one of the essential properties of the Church. A Divine Teacher is still teaching in the world, through the Church, which is his body. When Christ departed, 'the Spirit of Truth took up all that He had revealed, and unfolded it with great accessions of divine illumination. He then opened a ministry of interior and perfect faith, which has guided His Church in all ages and in all lands unto this day. His own teaching was partial and local: the guidance of the Holy Spirit is plenary and universal. And our Teacher departs not, but abides with us for ever: a guide ever present, though invisible; ever presiding, though in silence; unerring, though teaching through human reason and by human speech'.[44]

Moreover, the presence of the Spirit of Love made the communion of charity a necessary part of the unity of the Church: she is a revelation of the love which inseparably unites the divine persons. The Church is one and indivisible, gathering in all nations, and making them 'of one speech, of one heart, and of one will'.[45] Schism is a most grievous sin, but it does not rend the unity of the Church: 'it is a sin against the indivisible love of God: To separate from the Church is to forfeit love, for love cannot be divided. Schisms do not rend it, but are rent from it. As the life retires into the living trunk when the branches are cut away, so love still dwells undivided in the life of the Church when members fall from its communion'.[46]

After a long crisis lasting several years, Manning would eventually conclude that the one true Church — undivided and indivisible — was the Church of Rome; within it, the Holy Spirit taught the faith of Pentecost, as he did nowhere else. The Anglican Church was no part of the Catholic Church, but a schismatic body. He was received into the Catholic Church on 6 April 1851.[47]

B. MANNING'S CATHOLIC VISION OF CANTERBURY

Manning was rather reluctant, after his conversion, to launch into an open attack against the Anglican Church; he did not want to be involved in controversy. He conceived the rôle of the Catholic Church in England as one of building up the whole edifice of revealed truth, completing the structure of partial truth preserved in the Anglican Church. It should not be a work of demolition. He was loath to contribute to the internal divisions already existing and multiplying within it. For him, it was a matter of personal feeling and also of charity: 'The Anglicanism of the Reformation is upon the rocks, like some tall ship stranded upon the shore, and going to pieces by its own weight and the steady action of the sea. We have no need of playing the wreckers. It would be inhumanity to do so. God knows that the desires and prayers of Catholics are ever ascending that all which remains of Christianity in England may be preserved, unfolded, and perfected into the whole circle of revealed truths and the unmutilated revelation of the faith'.[48] Still, the circumstances of the times, and the whole bent of his thought, forced him to speak frequently, sometimes even harshly, about the Anglican Church.

1. *The Anglican Reformation*

Manning's historical view of the Anglican Reformation was radically altered by the change in perspective consequent to his discovery of the active presence of the Holy Spirit in the Church and by the events, within Anglicanism, which preceded his conversion. After 1851 he would distinguish two clearly defined periods in the religious history of England between the mission of St Augustine and the separation from Rome under Henry VIII. The Saxon monarchy had been characterized, on the whole, by harmony in the relationship between Church and State; during that period, England became a land of saints and missionaries, where the crown was sometimes worn by holy men. The Norman rule, by contrast, was harsh and overbearing, ever attempting to interfere in ecclesiastical matters; and the martyrs and confessors of those centuries 'won their crowns in conflict with princes'.[49] The act of Henry VIII was only the last act in the drama: he gave 'final expression and effect to the secular and schismatical nationalism which the whole line of Norman kings had laid down in their legislation, and vindicated in their acts'.[50] The Anglican Church did not find its freedom, it became enslaved to the State.

The Anglican Reformation, moreover, had as its confessed aim to impugn certain doctrines, or corruptions, introduced into the purity of the primitive faith by the Church of Rome. In fact, Manning thought that it 'consists formally in the rejection of the Divine voice of the Church — in effacing from the minds of the English people the whole idea of a visible and divinely endowed Church, with supernatural offices',[51] 'teaching with a divine, and, therefore, infallible certainty'.[52] The vast majority of Anglicans, while disagreeing in almost every other aspect, found common ground in opposing the idea of an infallible teaching Church as 'a human superstition or a spiritual tyranny'.[53] His conclusion was that the 'master heresy of the English race is to deny the presence of any infallible authority upon earth'.[54]

'The reformers of the Church of England took for the basis of their religion, not the perpetual and infallible teaching of the Spirit of Jesus in His Church, but the Bible. A written book was erected in the place of the living Teacher, so as to exclude His supreme living voice. Anglican Christianity was to be based upon the Bible'.[55] That foundation, Manning contended, 'Anglicans have ruined under their own foot'.[56] The Scriptures, separated from the Church, which is their custodian and interpreter, became lost in a maze of contradictory interpretations. 'When right sense is lost, the Scripture is lost'.[57] The paradox of Anglicanism, and of Protestantism of every shade, was that those who had claimed to be most scriptural ended by being the most unscriptural; 'the system which founded itself upon the claim to be essentially and above all Scriptural, is ending in denying the inspiration and authenticity of Holy Scripture'.[58] Manning would quote the authors of *Essays and Reviews*, and Dr. Colenso's works, as samples of those who, encouraged by German criticism, were already moving in that direction.

It had taken many generations to unfold the consequences of the original error. The process had gone further and faster in Germany. Manning thought that only a divine intervention had prevented the Anglican Church from going that far: 'That which in Germany produced pure Rationalism, in England, but for the interposition of God, would have produced the same general disbelief of Christianity'.[59] The course of the Anglican Church, though, was a downward one; error grew larger all the time while truth disappeared. 'Every error which has sprung up in it adheres to it still. Its doctrines vanish, its heresies abide. All its morbid humours are absorbed into its blood. The Lutheranism of Edward the Sixth; the Hierarchical Calvinism of Elizabeth; the Ceremonial Arminianism of James; the Episcopalian Antiquarianism of the two Charleses; the Latitudinarianism of William the Third ... all coexist ... together, in open contradiction, and almost perpetual controversy'.[60] This was the inevitable consequence of the Anglican schism: 'because separation from the Holy See is separation from the Universal Church, and to be separated from the Church is to be deprived of its divine guidance and support',[61] i.e. the presence and assistance of the Holy Spirit. Truth, like a body deserted by the soul or like a branch separated from the vine, began its long process of decomposition within the Anglican Church. There was no provision in it to arrest that process.

The Church of England did not pronounce judgment among its factions, and there was not within it any infallible authority or test of certainty to be applied in order to discern truth from error. All the different and contradictory schools which made up the Church of England were in it by right. 'It would be untrue to represent any one of these schools of error as the legitimate voice or exponent of the Anglican Church. They are equally so, and equally not so. They each claim so to be, and deny the legitimacy of all the rest'.[62]

There had been, though, a reaction against that downward trend of faith within the Anglican Church, and that effort to recover the foundations of faith had begun with the rejection of the principle of private judgment. Manning would trace the origins of that theological school to the Elizabethan period. It had 'sprung up within the Established Church, basing itself upon Catholic tradition, and claiming to found its faith not upon private judgment, but upon the rule of Vincent of Lerins, namely, on that which was believed "at all times, everywhere, and by all men"'.[63] The representatives of this school had conducted a courageous campaign to recover the lost inheritance of Catholic truth, and to defend that under attack. A measure of their success was that they had created the illusion that the Anglican Church was still part of the great Catholic family. Unfortunately, they were only a school, and a small one at that, within the Anglican Church. Manning acknowledged, however, that they had performed a great service to Christianity in slowing down the decline towards rationalism within the Church of England.

There is, in Manning's thought and writings during the 1860s, a progressive recognition of the providential character of this movement towards Catholic faith and worship. It was the work of the Holy Spirit, 'drawing men, step by step, out of the illusions and falsehoods of the Anglican separation into the unity of the only Church'.[64] Newman and Manning consider that the internal logic of the Tractarian Movement, as intended by the Holy Spirit, led to Rome. However, it was a movement of men, not of the Anglican Church, 'an impulse of the Spirit of God preparing the hearts of men beforehand for the advance of His Church'.[65] It was providentially intended 'to restore the line of continuity between the intelligence of the English people and the intelligence of the universal Church',[66] by introducing Catholic doctrines and practices within the Anglican Church. These truths and practices, although not fully expressed and believed, were then preached and defended by a numerous body within the Church of England. Unfortunately, that return towards the truth was not general within Anglicanism, the hold of faith over the people of England had grown continually less: the 'masses', Manning wrote, 'are moving away, but individuals in great numbers are returning upwards to the light of faith'.[67] The heirs of the Oxford Movement were trying to cure the wounds that the Anglican Church itself was opening in its own body, but they were unable to identify and tackle the cause of the illness. They laboured under the same fundamental error as their opponents: they could not see that to enthrone man as judge of Scripture and Tradition was as much private judgment as making private judgment the interpreter of Holy Scripture. Manning considered them 'entangled in a circle which is never discovered until the divine fact of the presence and office of the Holy Ghost in the mystical body becomes intelligible to them'.[68] That was a Catholic truth which those who belonged to this school had still to recover. As he had written to Miss Stanley in 1851, 'The difference between the Church of England and the Church of Rome is not so much in *what* they respectively believe (though it is there also) but in *why* they believe it'.[69] That difference 'is not one of doctrine and details. It is a question of the Presence and Office of the Holy Ghost'.[70]

The process of dissolution was relentless, and the Anglo-Catholic party within the Church of England was powerless to arrest it; the general body was moving in a different direction and leaving those who held Catholic views more and more isolated. 'Whatsoever be the partial reaction of opinion in individuals or fragments of the Anglican body towards a more positive faith, I cannot note in the body as such, any tendency but one of further departure from unity, and of a lower descent in unbelief'.[71] Each period of its history brought with it a further erosion in the belief of Anglicans as a whole, and Manning saw each of these descending steps as the nemesis after a collision with the Church of God. This process of dissolution was aggravated by the national character of the Church of England. In a national church comprehensiveness takes the place of truth, and it necessarily has to do so if it is to preserve its character as a national church. Thus, 'the tendency of the Church of England to conform itself to the state of opinion among the English people, so as to reflect their subjective contradictions instead of witnessing to objective truths, has been elevated to a test of its perfection'.[72] Creeds were removed to make room for people. It had even been said that Christianity was not essential to a national church but only a blessed accident, a providential *bonus*.[73] As an Anglican, Manning had already noted with disquiet the theories being put forward in Germany claiming that the Christian Church in each country should be the spirit of the nation expressing itself through an organisation of its own. He felt that what in Germany was a philosophical doctrine had been long ago introduced in England on grounds of political expediency.

In the final analysis, the controversies of the last three hundred years had resolved themselves into a simple alternative: a choice between 'Rome and rationalism, between the divine certainty of faith, and the instability of human opinion: between the presence of a Divine Teacher and the solitude and darkness of the human soul'[74]; the human reason testing the doctrines of revelation or the human reason submitting as a disciple to the teaching of a Divine Person. It was no longer a matter of choice between 'Anglo-Catholicism and Roman Catholicism, but between Rationalism and Christianity; that is, Rationalism or Rome'[75]

Pusey was later to misquote those words, as he had misquoted Newman's reference to the Church of England. Newman had described it as a 'barrier against errors more fundamental than its own'; at the touch of Pusey's pen those words metamorphosed into 'a bulwark in God's hands against infidelity'. When it came to Manning, his alternative between Catholicism and rationalism became in Pusey's hands an alternative between Catholicism and atheism. Manning refuted that false accusation in his pamphlet *The Workings of the Holy Spirit in the Church of England*. 'I do not believe', he said, 'that the alternative before us is Catholicism or Atheism.... If a man, through an intellectual or moral aberration, should reject Christianity, that is Catholicism, the belief of God and of His perfections stands immutably upon the foundations of nature. Catholicism, or Deism, is the only ultimately logical and consistent alternative, though, happily, few men in rejecting Catholicism are logically consistent enough to reject Christianity. Atheism is an aberration which implies not only intellectual blindness, but a moral insensitivity'.[76]

Prejudice was a powerful force. The hatred of the Catholic Church — 'into which we English are born, as into the fall of Adam'[77] — was the fruit of centuries of anti-Catholic propaganda. And this deep-seated prejudice was married to the conviction that there is no divine voice now teaching on earth. This meant, that, as shown by the universal experience of those who had exercised the evangelical ministry in England, 'the last article of the Creed, which enters, and that slowly, and for a long time painfully, into the English intelligence, is the nature and office of the Church: or to speak theologically, the formal object of Faith, and the divinely ordained conditions of its manifestations to the world'.[78]

2. Schism and Heresy

Henry VIII had removed the English from their allegiance to Rome; a human authority had dismissed a divine one and enthroned itself in its place. That set in motion a process which, once initiated, could not be arrested. Because of its break with Rome, 'the mind and spirit of the Universal Church has no influx into the Anglican communion'.[79] England had rent itself from the source of certainty of faith. 'You know', Manning would say, 'how the rejection of this Divine authority [of the Church] has shattered the unity of faith in England'[80] 'With schism came contradiction; with contradiction uncertainty, debate, and doubt.... And private judgment, working out its result in individual minds, caused schism after schism'.[81]

He did not, however, utterly condemn his fellow Englishmen. 'The English people are indeed in heresy, but I do not call them heretics. God forbid!'.[82] The Anglican Reformation had been 'the sin of the Rulers, not of the people; of the Pastors, not of the flock. It was not until after long years of force, and fraud, and unrelenting cruelty, of persecution unto death, with frequent but fruitless armed risings in defence of their faith, that the poor of England fell under the power of their masters. They were robbed of their faith, and separated from the Church of God by conquest; and their children have been born into the ruin of their inheritance, and are in schism by no conscious, much less by any perverse election of their will'.[83] 'They have never known their rightful inheritance. They have grown up, believing what has been set before them by parents and teachers.... They have never made a perverse election against the truth'.[84] Those who had been born into schism were naturally less responsible than those who had caused it, and the moral guilt grew less at every step by which they were removed from the first authors of the schism or heresy.[85]

This condition of those outside the Church was a question which had exercised Manning's mind even before becoming a Catholic, and he had studied it as far as Dissenters and non-Christians were concerned. He had treated it in *The Unity of the Church* (1842), and in his *Fourth Volume of Anglican Sermons* (1850) he dedicated the sermon entitled 'Christ preached in any way a cause of joy' to this subject. Manning defined in it the approach, which he will maintain and develop after becoming a Catholic, to the difficulty presented by the multiplication of Christian sects and the moral status of those who belonged to them. He felt that any knowledge of God, even partial and perhaps contaminated with a certain degree of error, was better than no knowledge at all. The knowledge of God, he thought, brings about mighty changes in the soul; it is a living and life-giving truth. Through it, man becomes aware of God's love for him and of his sinfulness, and he is brought under the law of responsibility.

In 1890 he would describe how the Holy Spirit would be in action among those looking for truth with a sincere heart, although separated from the Church; particularly among those who had received the Sacrament of Baptism. True Catholic principles upheld that God wishes all men to be saved and that grace is given to all, even infidels; those who cooperate with it receive an increase of grace in their souls, while the virtue of penance restores grace to those who have lost it through sin and cannot receive the sacrament of penance; all those who seek truth belong, at least, to the soul of the Church. His personal experience confirmed the doctrine. He had 'intimately known souls living by faith, hope and charity ... in a word, living lives of visible sanctification, as undoubtedly the work of the Holy Ghost as I have ever seen.... Moreover, I have received into the Church I do not know how many souls in whom I could find no mortal sin'.[86]

Divisions were to be deplored, but Manning maintained that the right approach to those bodies was to rejoice in the good that they had and to work so as to build upon it. 'All that can be done to foster and ripen the elements of truth ... is the duty and work of charity'. He was

against an aggressive policy towards those communities: 'To overthrow, on the plea of re-construction, is to do the office of one whose
name is the Destroyer. God's temple is to be built up by a labour of
construction which preserves with jealous and loving tenderness all that
has life and truth.' He added that, by following this approach, in the
effort 'to add to and raise upward to perfection whatsoever of truth and
faith exists in the most imperfect, we should win many a soul. Men are
not won by contradictions, nor persuaded by refutations, but by the
expansion, enlargement, and perfect exhibition of the truths they hold
in germ. This is the only divine rule of controversy, the only evangelical principle of conversion ...'[87] After becoming a Catholic, he
would tell his co-religionists that they should be familiar with those
truths of faith solidly rooted in the minds of the people of England in
order to build upon them.

He acknowledged that some could object to the above concepts and
modus operandi: 'It may be said that this is equivalent to denying the
visibleness and the divine institution of the Church, the necessity and
grace of the holy Sacraments; that it substitutes personal sincerity for
the true faith, and goes all length with the latitudinarian theory, which
makes truth indifferent, or God all mercy'.[88] Manning answered by
saying that 'truth has life in it to those whose heart is right with
God'.[89] The measure of truth possessed or presented to individuals is
determined by circumstances over which they have little control. Truth
may have not been proposed to them or the education they have
received has created such a strong prejudice that it prevents them from
recognising truth when confronted with it. Invincible ignorance is no
personal sin, and 'no ignorance of truth is a personal sin before God,
except that ignorance which springs from personal sin'.[90] He would
add: 'If the heart be right with God, He will weigh the rest in a
balance of compassion'.[91] 'Truth is given for the probation of man;
the probation of man is not ordained for the sake of truth'.[92] Moreover, in the acceptance of the truth seen as such was also implicitly
contained many other truths, even the whole of revealed truth: 'No eye
but God can read the mysteries which are received by implicit
faith'.[93] These principles, he added, applied 'to every Christian sect
according to its measure, and to every individual born into it'.[94] In
a phrase, which seem to require some further clarification, Manning
would say: 'God has bound us to seek His grace through His Church;
but He has not bound Himself to give grace and salvation in no other
way'.[95]

This was not latitudinarianism. The 'duty of believing the whole and
perfect truth is still absolutely binding on pain of sin to all who know
it'.[96] That was a great responsibility. After his conversion, looking
back at those who had been with him for most of the journey,

Manning felt that among them were those who, having reached the threshold of truth, had recoiled from crossing into its fullness. God only could judge their reasons for doing so, but Manning thought that some were motivated by human considerations and he had serious misgivings as to their standing in God's eyes. In 1854 he wrote to Robert Wilberforce: 'I see men who once believed with even clearer light than I did, now professing not to believe this or that particular; and what is worst of all, I believe they say so truly; for what ought to be obeyed when believed, passes away.... If I trust the men who speak, I the more fear for them, for the truth has been lost'.[97] Their reaction before the perspective of conversion had been, in many cases, to throw themselves back 'in the direction of German criticism, as the only assignable reason for not submitting to the Catholic Church'.[98] It was an unavoidable declension. Some of them had since become prominent in the anti-Catholic movement.

Manning's main fears were for his friend Robert Wilberforce, afraid that he might be untrue to himself and to Truth. Robert, to Manning's mind, was looking 'for what God does not give': 'a conviction which precludes the exercise of faith. Except in figures and numbers there is no conviction which excludes the possibility of the contrary being true. It is not impossible even that Jesus Christ is not come in the flesh. I mean it does not involve a contradiction in its terms to suppose that the Christian History is a myth'. Private judgement stopped short of the final step, one which could only be taken by faith. 'A deist in becoming a Christian has no more than a conviction which excludes *reasonable* fear that Christianity may turn out not to be true. Reason can go no further, and until upon the motives of credibility supplied by reason he makes an act of faith, he can rise no higher'.[99] The proper use of private judgment was to examine the evidence as to whether God had instituted an infallible authority in the Church. 'We go by our own taper to the altar of light, and then put our taper out for ever'.[100]

During the Vatican Council, Manning would welcome the First Schema *De Ecclesia*, among other reasons, for its treatment, in Chapter VII, of the principle *extra ecclesiam nulla salus*. Manning felt that there was great ignorance on the subject, both among Catholics and non-Catholics. 'Catholics despaired of the salvation of non-Catholics and non-Catholics rejected the Catholic doctrine as incompatible with divine mercy and justice. This misunderstanding was a great obstacle to conversions, Manning complained, and his efforts to clarify the Church's position were met with the charge that he was mitigating the Church's doctrine without proper authority'.[101]

Englishmen were in a state of invincible ignorance, and their prejudices were so strongly rooted in their minds and hearts that, in good measure, they prevented them from being able to detect the light of the true faith. 'They were born into an atmosphere in which all lights are distorted and all colours change their hue. Truth and falsehood have shifted places, and the history of the English reformation is a traditionary fable'.[102] Manning was confident that the conjunction of the virtues of the English race and the grace of God might open their eyes to see the illusion and enable them to break the spell under which they had lived for so long. Ezekiel's vision of the 'Valley of the Dry Bones' was before his eyes, and he felt that Providence might again draw good from evil, and make the global empire of the British people a vehicle for the expansion of the Catholic Faith.[103]

3. *The Establishment: Nessus' Shirt?*

After the court decision on some of the authors of *Essays and Reviews* the old cry for disestablishment of the Anglican Church was raised anew: the ills of the Church of England, it was said, were consequent upon its condition as a Church by law established; remove the cause, and the Anglican Church would soon recover its former strength. Not many voices echoed that call.

The Parliamentary Statutes of the Tudors made it clear that the power to judge on appeal all causes of controverted doctrine belonged to the Crown, a judge which, like the Bishops, disclaimed infallibility. Even more, the Crown did not even claim to 'judge of the truth of the matter brought before it'[104]; it was 'invested with a power to admit or to exclude doctrines upon the exercise of its own *discernment*, all the while disclaiming the power to pronounce them to be *true*, and claiming only to pronounce them to be legal'.[105] The judgment of the Crown confined itself to declaring whether a particular doctrine was in open contradiction to the Anglican formularies. But, Manning would say, the cause of the evils which afflicted Anglicanism was the Anglican Church itself, not the Crown or its Privy Council. 'If the Church of England were the Church of God, the tribunals could do it no harm. It is Anglicanism which *generates* the errors. The tribunals only *legalise* them. The Anglican system is the source of all its own confusions, which the law contemptuously tolerates'.[106]

Those who looked on the Establishment as the cause of the Anglican Church's evils, and thought of disestablishment as the solution for its ills, were prey to a misconception. The Establishment was not Nessus' shirt for the Anglican Church; 'my belief', Manning wrote in 1864, 'is that when the Church of England lost its inherence in the universal Church, the principle of all spiritual and intellectual disease was developed in its blood, and ate into its bone. I do not believe that it is a poisoned vestment which is put upon it from without, but a morbid and manifold disease which is ever reproducing itself from within'.[107] Manning in the late 1860s, however, had a more positive vision of disestablishment. He acknowledged that some good had followed from the 'moral disestablishment' of the Church of England by the Test and Corporation Acts and by Catholic Emancipation. They had thrown the Church of England upon its inner spiritual and intellectual resources, and that had resulted in a revival, which further disestablishment would only accelerate. Manning considered this a highly desirable development which would increase the religious zeal and activity of the country as a whole. 'If this be so ... then the course of public legislation would assuredly not be less Christian. The public opinion of the country would be more so; and the legislation must ultimately be governed by public opinion'.[108] The preservation of Christianity, and the improvement of moral and social conditions in England was a task which required the cooperation of all the Christian denominations. Manning considered that Catholics were bound to cooperate with Anglicans and Dissenters 'in everything that is not contrary to faith or morals'[109]; and he was always ready to share a platform with Anglicans or Dissenters to defend a good cause — a practical ecumenism which did not imply a change in Manning's theological conception of the Church of England: Anglicanism was Protestantism.

Anglicans readily acknowledged that 'Protestantism is essentially rationalistic, but deny that Anglicanism is Protestant'.[110] Manning, on the other hand, maintained that they were intimately related, if not identical to each other: both appealed from the voice of the living Church; both alike rejected its divine infallible authority. It did not matter what they appealed to, the basis for that appeal was the same one: 'the refusal of the living voice of the Church as the rule of faith'.[111] If there was no infallible authority, the only criterion by which to interpret Holy Scripture — or Scripture and Tradition — was human reason, and the position was, therefore, essentially rationalistic: there is 'nothing intermediate', Manning would say, 'between divine faith and human opinion'.[112] In the Anglican system human reason was to determine which books had been inspired and their interpretation: the 'ultimate certainty upon which it rests, even the Scripture, its authenticity, interpretation, inspiration, is a human, and therefore a fallible, tradition'.[113] This was rationalism; this procedure could generate neither a human nor a divine certainty; it could not generate faith. A human authority 'can bind no man to believe in its decisions; for no man can be under obligation to make an act of faith in a teacher who may err'.[114] The individual was left to the devices of his private judgment; he was 'free to revise all judgments of a teacher who disclaims infallibility'.[115]

What Anglicans called 'faith' was a personal opinion based on reason or sentiment, or both. This erroneous concept of the act of faith made it very difficult for them to find the true faith, and it was a serious obstacle in their dialogue, or in controversy, with Catholics. The terms they used were equivocal. The Catholic position, Manning summed up, was that reason 'leads us to the feet of a Divine Teacher; but thenceforward His voice, and not our balancing of probabilities, will be the formal motive of our faith.... My faith terminates no longer in a cumulus of probabilities gathered from the past, but upon the veracity of a Divine Person guiding me with His presence'.[116]

Rationalism was not an external agent working on the Church of England from the outside. The door to it had not been opened by the Civil Courts. It was a habit of thought which had conceived Anglicanism and all the dissenting bodies which had separated from it. 'The Churchman differed from the Socinian, and the Socinian from the Deist as to the number of articles in his creed; but all alike consented to test their belief by the rational evidence for it'.[117]

4. *A Bulwark against Infidelity?*

The publication of *Essays and Reviews* (1860) had signalled the beginning of a new crisis in Anglicanism, and the subsequent court decisions on the contributions of Williams and Wilson added to the atmosphere of gloom among those of the Catholic party in the Church of England. The highest ecclesiastical tribunal, excepting only the Queen in Council, had pronounced in the cases of Williams and Wilson. Manning saw in the decision of the Court of Arches an official recognition of the legitimacy of rationalism within the Anglican Church. His analysis concluded that the decision, 'though in some degree adverse to the liberty claimed by the Rationalists, nevertheless gives to that school a substantive existence, and incorporates its principles by public law in the system and rights of the Church of England'.[118] In Manning's summary, the Court of Arches upheld the following principles: that the Church of England held as inspired and canonical the books of the Old and New Testaments, but it did not define what inspiration was; that the inspiration of parts of a particular book could be denied; that those parts which were considered inspired could be interpreted freely, provided the interpretation did not contradict the articles and formularies of the Church of England, which were vague and ambiguous enough 'to permit liberty and largeness of interpretation, of which everyone may avail himself as his conscience and critical faculty may require'.[119] This, for Manning, was pure rationalism: whatever was retained or rejected, was retained or rejected 'upon the principle of Rationalism, that is, of human testimony tried by the same criterion'.[120]

The judgment of the Court of Arches was raised in appeal to the Privy Council. The judgment was delivered on 8 February 1864. It went beyond the decision of the Court of Arches, 'it did open a large[r] area of biblical criticism and theological enquiry to free discussion among the clergy, and it rendered a large part of the conventional teaching of the Church unenforceable at law'.[121] The Anglo-Catholic party was not idle in the face of those events. Pusey's pamphlet on the legal force of the judgment of the Privy Council in Wilson's case (1864) was part of their response to the threat posed by *Essays and Reviews*. In his pamphlet Pusey made some remarks which were to stir Manning into action. He described the reaction of the English Catholics before the recent events as follows: 'A class of believers joined in the triumph. And while I know that a very earnest body of Roman Catholics rejoice in all the workings of God the Holy Spirit in the Church of England, (whatever they think of her,) and are saddened in what weakens *her* who is, in God's Hands the great bulwark against infidelity in this land, others seemed to be in ecstasy of triumph at this victory of Satan'.[122] It was generally believed that Manning was included among those who rejoiced at Satan's victory. He had recently been accused of having changed from being slow, cautious and moderate before his conversion to being violent and unreasonable; from being over-English before to being now Ultramontane. Pusey was to disclaim later on, in his *Eirenicon*, that he had included Manning and Wiseman in that group; by then, after Manning's broadside in his *The Workings of the Holy Spirit in the Church of England* (1864), they were already engaged in open polemic and more of the capital ships of both sides were about to join the action.

Manning felt that he could not leave unanswered Pusey's claim that the Church of England was a bulwark against infidelity. On the contrary, Manning thought that the Anglican Reformation and the Anglican Church were the 'true and original source of the present spiritual anarchy of England ... [The Church of England] so far from being a barrier against infidelity, must be recognised as the mother of all intellectual and spiritual aberrations which now cover the face of England'.[123] He tried to substantiate this charge by applying those principles that were so dear to him. The Church of England, he would admit, could be called a 'barrier against infidelity' by grace of the truth that she retained; but she was, at the same time, a source of unbelief in the measure in which she denied other truths, and, in particular, because she undermined the very foundations of the faith. The Church of England propagated unbelief 'by principle, and in the essence of its whole system. What is the ultimate guarantee of the divine revelation but the divine authority of the Church? Deny this, and we descend at once to human teachers. But this is what the Church of England formally and expressly denies. The perpetual and ever-present assistance of the Holy Spirit, whereby the Church in every age is not only preserved from error, but enabled at all times to declare the truth, that is the infallibility of the living Church at this hour — this it is that the Anglican Church in terms denies'.[124]

Manning did not regard the Church of England as a *teacher of truth*, 'for that would imply that it teaches the truth in all its circumference, and in all its divine certainty. Now this is precisely what the Church of England does not, and ... [it] has destroyed in itself the power of doing',[125] by rejecting the infallible authority of the Church. Manning was willing to call it 'a teacher of Christian truths', but not a teacher of Christian truth, 'because it rejects much of that truth, and also the Divine principle of its perpetuity in the world'[126]. It had to be admitted that the Anglican Church had preserved and taught more truths than the German Protestants, but it undermined the evidence of the truths it still retained in a double way, because:

> [a] 'It has detached them from other truths which by contact gave solidity to all by rendering them coherent and intelligible'.

> [b] 'It has detached them from the Divine voice of the Church, which guarantees to us the truth incorruptible and changeless'.[127] He concluded: 'How can this be regarded as "the great bulwark in God's hands against infidelity"?'[128]

These were hard words, and harder things were still to follow. Manning had borne witness 'to the presence and voice of a divine, and therefore infallible, teacher, guiding the Church with His perpetual assistance, and speaking through it as His organ'. He had also 'borne witness that the Church through which He teaches is that which St Augustine describes by the two incommunicable notes — that is "spread throughout the world" and "united to the Chair of Peter"'.[129] Manning was fully aware of the corollaries which follow from those premises: 'If the Catholic faith be the perfect revelation of Christianity, the Anglican Reformation is a cloud of heresies; if the Catholic Church be the organ of the Holy Ghost, the Anglican Church is not only no part of the Church, but no church of divine foundation. It is a human institution, sustained, as it was founded, by a human authority, without priesthood, without sacraments, without absolution, without the Real Presence of Jesus upon its altars'.[130]

The fact that Manning recognised the workings of the Holy Spirit in the Church of England could not be of great consolation for men like Pusey. The Holy Spirit, Manning had added, was active in the whole world and among every nation even before the Church came into existence. He continued now his operations in individuals outside the Church, and his presence and action would necessarily be more abundant among those who have been regenerated by Baptism. Manning qualified this statement by saying: 'What I have said does not recognise the grace *of* the Church of England as such'. Grace 'works not *by* it, nor *through* it, but *in* it and among those who, without faults of their own, are detained by it from the true Church of their baptism'.[131]

He added that he did not rejoice, but lament, any further loss of truth in the Anglican Church. In the introduction to *England and Christendom* (1867) he would quote an old sermon 'Christ preached every way a cause for joy'(1850). There he had affirmed that any light is better than darkness, and that in the least measure of truth there is cause for rejoicing. His belief was that anything which undermined the truths still taught by the Church of England drove the people further and further away from the Catholic Church. He did not look forward to the Anglican Church being swept away by a flood of infidelity. He desired to see the Church of England passing away 'under the action of a higher and more perfect truth' that would make the lingering embers in it rise into a burning flame. Then, all the Christianity 'which survives in Anglicanism would be perfected by the restoration of the truths which have been lost, and the whole would be fixed and perpetuated by the evidence of a Divine certainty and the voice of a Divine Teacher'.[132] The mission of the Church in the world is not to destroy but 'to fill up the truth'.[133]

5. An 'Eirenicon' and the A.P.U.C.

Manning's judgment of the Church of England could not but draw a response from Pusey; he had denied to the Anglican Church everything the latter felt it stood for. Pusey wrote to Newman expressing how hurt he was by Manning's letter: he has 'denied us everything, except what in a greater degree Dissenters had too...'[134] He seemed to have forgotten, though, that Newman had said as much in his *Difficulties of Anglicans* (1850): 'If I let you plead the sensible effects of supernatural grace, as exemplified in yourselves, in proof that your religion is true, I must allow the plea to others [i.e.: Wesleyans] to whom by your theory you are bound to deny it ... [H]ave they not more remarkable phenomena in their history, symptomatic of the presence of grace among them, than you can show in yours?'[135]

Manning's charges against the Anglican Church, Pusey thought, could be grouped together under two counts: a) the errors of the Anglican Church; b) the rejection of the infallibility of the Church. He would counterattack by saying that the Catholic Church itself was not free from error — devotion to our Lady being a conspicuous example;

indeed, the Anglican Reformation had been a protest against such abuses. Manning's fundamental charge, though, was that the Church of England had rejected the doctrine of the Infallibility of the Church. Pusey did address it in detail, and made use of Ward's articles in the *Dublin Review* to rebut the charge and turn it against Manning.

'The last charge which Dr. Manning brings against the Church of England', Pusey wrote, 'is that "it formally denies" the "perpetual Divine voice" of the Church'.[136] He rightly pointed out that the main stress in Manning's words was laid on the term 'perpetual'. Pusey claimed that the Anglican Church did not deny the infallibility of the Church, in the past or at the present time. Manning's mistake, according to him, originated in a false assumption: 'that, in denying the infallibility of the Roman Church by itself, we are "denying the infallibility of the living Church at this hour"; because, on his hypothesis, the Roman Church is, alone, the living Church, to the exclusion of the Eastern Church and of ourselves'.[137]

The Church of England, Pusey claimed, was in possession of infallible truth resting on an infallible authority, that of the Primitive Church, and, he added, 'we do not need the present agency of an infallible Church to assure us of the truth of what has been ruled infallibly'.[138] Besides, the Church of England not only accepted that the Church had taught infallible truth in the past, but also that it could also do so now if she were to be united and act in unison. The Holy Spirit still speaks in the Church when its three branches 'teach the same faith which was from the beginning ... and, if need required, they could at this day declare concurrently any truth, if it should appear that it had not, as yet, been sufficiently defined, against some fresh heresy which should emerge'.[139] The 'whole' Catholic Church had not collectively sanctioned error, and what it had or might collectively sanction in the future would be certain truth: a truly 'Oecumenical Council, if such were now held and received by the whole Church, would, by that reception, have the seal of infal-libility',[140] as had those of the Primitive Church. Moreover, 'if the same doctrines were enunciated at once by the whole Church, the East, West, and our own, separately but concordantly ... the doctrine, so simultaneously enunciated, would be infallibly certain'.[141] This, Pusey felt, was the theory of the Gallican divines, which sets the test of infallibility in the reception of a particular doctrine by the whole Church. To Pusey's mind, the main difference between him and Manning was that the latter identified the Church with the 'Roman Church', while Pusey saw it in the union or concurrent action of its three constitutive branches: the Anglican, the Roman and the Orthodox.

Pusey seemed to acknowledge the infallibility of the present-day

Church almost as much as Manning did.[142] The all-important difference consisted in their divergent notions of what the Church is and,
therefore, of what constitutes its unity. Manning's concept of the
Church, as we have seen, rested on the perpetual and inseparable union
of the Holy Spirit to it, and the consequent perpetual endowments of
unity (intrinsic and visible at the same time), of holiness and of
infallibility. Pusey's idea of the *Ecclesia Anglicana* rested on the
acceptance of an externally divided Church which, at the same time,
had preserved its essential unity. The Universal Church was still
infallible, although its infallibility was suspended in so far as the
Church was prevented from acting in unison by the divisions which
had broken its unity of communion. Ironically, Pusey, in his *Eirenicon*, had repeated, almost verbatim, the ideas about unity which
Manning had published in *The Unity of the Church* (1842), and which
he would formally retract in *The Temporal Mission of the Holy Ghost*
(1865).

Manning — who, in the meantime, had been made Archbishop of
Westminster — did not answer Pusey's *Eirenicon* directly. He thought
that it had been written at Keble's instance, and in order to prevent
people from entering the Catholic Church. To Manning's mind, Pusey
had confirmed the contention put forward in *The Workings of the Holy
Spirit in the Church of England*. There Manning had claimed 'that the
Anglican Church appeals from the living voice of the Church at this
hour, thereby denying its Divine authority'; he felt that Dr. Pusey in
the *Eirenicon* had done precisely that, 'thereby confirming the
argument of my Letter'.[143] Still, the points raised by Pusey would be
taken into consideration in his subsequent works. *The Temporal
Mission of the Holy Ghost* addressed some of the issues, others were
to be tackled in his Pastoral on the A.P.U.C.

Manning dwelt on the concept of unity in his Pastoral *The Reunion
of Christendom* (6 January 1866), and in doing so addressed together
the issues raised by Pusey and the A.P.U.C. He saw them sharing the
same basic error on a fundamental point of faith, and he felt the need
to act on the matter promptly and clearly; principles vital for the
Church were at stake. As he had written in 1852: 'The unity and the
infallibility of the Church of Jesus Christ, these are our principles, and
these shall be our safety'.[144] These principles were now openly
attacked by Pusey, and, at the same time, they seemed to be obscured
in the minds of many of those Catholics who had given their names to
the A.P.U.C.

The *Association for Promotion of the Unity of Christendom*, heir to
previous initiatives for corporate reunion, had grown out of the
enthusiasm and sanguine hopes of Ambrose Lisle Phillipps. In his
letters to Propaganda he gave the impression that the number of

Anglicans committed to the scheme of reunion was much larger — and their determination to seek reunion with Rome stronger — than they actually were. Those who had set up the Association declared that they looked forward to a corporate reunion of those three great bodies which claim for themselves the inheritance of the priesthood and the name of Catholic. They claimed that they did not want, at that stage, to compromise any principles that those separate bodies might uphold; their only aim was to pray for unity.

The Catholic Hierarchy, from very early on, looked with suspicion on the initiative. In 1857, within a year of the setting up of the Association, Cardinal Wiseman wrote a strong Memorandum to Propaganda about the A.P.U.C. However, no action was taken about discouraging Catholics from joining the Association, and, one year after its formation, it counted a thousand Catholics among its membership of seven thousand. The majority of members of the Association, though, belonged to the Anglo-Catholic party, and they became the dominant influence within it. Wiseman had promised Propaganda to keep an attentive eye over its doings, and to act if action were to be required. The need for action presented itself to the bishops after the foundation of the *Union Review* by Lee, as a successor to the *Union Newspaper*. The latter, till then the organ of the Association, had, by its advocacy of 'Romish' practices, alienated many moderate High Churchmen. The newly born *Union Review*, as a reaction, 'was anxious to adopt a measured and cautious tone, but in developing this approach to assuage Anglican susceptibilities it succeeded in offending Roman Catholics by a sustained antagonism to individual conversions and bitter attacks upon well-known converts'.[145] The *Review*, willingly or unwillingly, was 'encouraging disharmony among the body of Roman Catholics, setting "old Catholic" against convert'. What galvanized the bishops into action, though, was its decided advocacy of the 'Branch Theory': 'ample evidence could be culled from it [the *Review*] of the views of leading members of the Association to give weight to the papal rescript when it declared that the Association "has resulted from a view put forward by it in express terms, that the three Christian Communions, the Roman Catholic, the schismatic Greek and the Anglican, though separated and divided one from another, yet with an equal right claim the title Catholic"'.[146] Not all the members of the Association held those views, but most of them did, and there was a danger of scandal, as it could be presumed that the Catholic members partook of those ideas. In his address to the Academia in 1863 Manning had made a reference to some Catholics who thought that 'the duty of Anglicans is to remain where they are with a view to spreading their opinions in the Established Church: in other words that individuals may postpone, or even refuse, to submit to the Church in the hope of bringing about what I may call a corporate union of the Churches'. He considered that this opinion involved a fundamental misunderstanding; it could only 'rest upon the erroneous assumption that the Anglican Establishment is as truly a Church as the schismatical Greek Church'.[147] That was not the case, given that the Church of England lacked the essential elements which made up a particular Church: apostolic succession, valid orders, valid sacraments and orthodox doctrine.

The Catholic bishops commissioned Bishop Ullathorne to write to Propaganda to denounce the Association and its principles, which he duly did on 26 April 1864. He also sent some issues of the *Union Review*, to illustrate the case. The Holy Office's answer — dated 16 September 1864 — came as a cold shower to the members of the Association. It condemned the Branch Theory, implicit in the declaration of the A.P.U.C., as 'a heresy overthrowing the nature of unity, and the Divine Constitution of the Church'[148]; consequently, it added, it would be unlawful for a Catholic to join the Association, 'in as much as it is an implicit adhesion to heresy, and to an intention stained with heresy'.[149]

The disappointment of members of the Association was great, and they felt themselves gravely misunderstood. An *Address*, signed by 198 Anglican clergymen, was sent in the summer of 1865 to Cardinal Patrizi trying to clarify those points which they considered the Holy Office had misinterpreted. The essential point they made concerned the question of the three branches, or communions. They clarified that when they had previously said that Anglicans, Orthodox and Roman Catholics had an equal claim to call themselves 'Catholic' treated of the question of *fact*, not of *right*.

The new Archbishop-elect was asked by Rome for his comments on the address, and he was not slow in sending them. The Association had been '*in no sense misunderstood*'. Their answer clearly manifested their mind: 'They say that they do not believe that there are three Churches *de jure*, but only *de facto*. But this denies (1) the exclusive unity of the Catholic and Roman Church, and (2) its exclusive infallibility, and (3) the universal duty and necessity of submission to it. These three points they do not hold. They hold that the three are all alike *de facto* Churches.... Under the disguise of this theory lies hid the old assumption of the *divisibility* [breach of the visible unity] of the Church, and its consequent loss of *perfection* only. And this assumes also the suspension of infallibility, and, therefore, of the perpetual Divine assistance of the Holy Spirit'.[150]

Manning's letter, and consequent visit to Rome, had considerable influence in shaping the answer of the Congregation of the Holy Office to the letter of the 198 Anglican clergyman. He felt the urgent need for an authoritative declaration. The 'unionists', he wrote to Ullathorne, claimed the support of the bishops, and many Catholics were being deceived. He considered that the way to clarify those misunderstandings would be for each bishop to publish individually the forthcoming document from Rome, and to show their personal sentiments. 'For my part', he added, 'I am ready to come out more strongly than ever'.[151]

The letter of the Congregation, dated 8 December 1865, was handed first to the representatives of the Anglican clergymen who had written to Card. Patrizi. Talbot sent a copy to Manning as soon as he possibly could. In the accompanying letter he told Manning: 'I think you will admire it. It contains all your ideas on the subject, as they made your instructions their rule'.[152] Manning, however, was not entirely satisfied with the Congregation's reply. He felt that the letter was 'very solid and dignified, as far as it goes'. Still, he had hoped for more, 'but it will do'.[153] To make it really do Manning published the letters from Rome with a long commentary, where he developed at great length the points made in them. He prefaced his remarks with a summary of the events which had led to the exchange of letters, and then summarized the answer of the Holy Office for the benefit of his flock:

> 1. That the unity of the Church is absolute and indivisible, and that the Church had never lost its unity, not for so much as a moment of time ever can.... There is, therefore, both *de jure* and *de facto*, only one Church, one by a numerical and exclusive unity.

> 2. That the Church of Christ is indefectible, not only in duration, but in doctrine, or in other words, that it is infallible, which is a Divine endowment bestowed upon it by its Head; and that the infallibility of the Church is a dogma of faith....

> 3. That the Primacy of the Visible Head is of Divine institution, and was ordained to generate and to preserve the unity both of faith and of communion, that is, both internal and external, of which the See of Peter is the centre and the bond.
> ...

> 4. That therefore the Catholic and Roman Church alone has received the name of Catholic....

> 5. That no one can give to any other body the name of Catholic without incurring manifest heresy....

> 6. That whosoever is separated from the one and only Catholic Church, howsoever well he may believe himself to live, by the

one sin of separation from the unity of Christ, is in the state of wrath.

7. That every several soul, under pain of losing eternal life, is bound to enter the only Church of Christ, out of which is neither absolution nor entrance into the kingdom of heaven'.[154]

The fundamental difference involved in the exchange of letters between the Association and Propaganda or the Holy Office, as with the controversy between Pusey and Manning, was about the concept of unity of the Church. Manning's Pastoral on the A.P.U.C. was considered generally as aimed against Pusey's *Eirenicon*. It is safe to say that Manning's main concern, and also Propaganda's, was not what Pusey and the Anglican members of A.P.U.C. might think about the unity of the Church, but how far the existing ambiguity could go to confuse the issue in Catholic minds.

For Manning, unity could only take place in truth. 'We are ready', he wrote in his Pastoral, 'to purchase the reunion of our separated brethren at any cost less than the sacrifice of a jot or a tittle of the supernatural order of unity and faith'.[155] Agreement in truth should always precede unity, and the signatories of the letter to Card. Patrizi could probably have underwritten that statement. 'Truth alone generates unity. It was the dogma of faith which united the intellects of men as one intelligence.... From this unity of intellects has sprung the unity of wills'.[156] But truth could not be found 'till we have submitted ourselves to a teacher who cannot err'. The only infallible teacher is God Himself, and unity was to be achieved 'by surrendering reason and will to His divine voice, teaching through His only Church. We must be taught of God before we can be at peace one with another'.[157] The unity of the Church is created 'by the submission of all wills to one Divine Teacher through the pastors of the Church, specially the one who is supreme on earth'.[158] Thus, there could be no unity which did not accept this fundamental truth of faith: 'We can offer unity only on the condition on which we hold it — unconditional submission to the living and perpetual voice of the Church of God. If this be refused, it is not we who hinder unity. For it is not we who impose this condition, but the Spirit of Truth who abides in the Church for ever'.[159] The visible unity of the Church was the 'landmark which God has set up to bound the Fold of Salvation.... They who teach that the Anglican separation and the Greek schism are parts of the Catholic Church violate a dogma of faith'.[160] This was a truth that Christians were as bound to believe as that of Baptismal Regeneration.

Manning admitted that some Anglicans were ready to accept the decrees of the Council of Trent, but that was not enough for reunion, as they would accept the decrees according to their own interpretation. 'To profess a readiness to accept the Council of Trent, if it be interpreted according to our opinion, is not to subject ourselves to the authority of the Council, but to subject it to our own judgment'.[161] That was equivalent to receive the Council upon the principle of private judgment. This procedure 'would make no man a Catholic. To receive the Council of Trent only because we critically believe its decrees to be true, and not only because its decrees are infallible, is private judgment'. And, Manning added, in that case we 'should not be submitting to them, but approving them. The formal motive of our approval would be not the divine authority of the Council, but the judgment of our private spirit'.[162] The A.P.U.C. and Pusey occupied the same ground. 'If a man were to hold the whole Catholic Theology and the decrees of the eighteen General Councils on the principle of the *Eirenicon*, he would not be a Catholic. He would be as true a Protestant as Luther or Calvin. It is not the believing of isolated doctrines, but the act of Divine Faith, terminating in its formal motive, the veracity of God through the living voice of the Church, that makes us Catholic Christians'.[163] 'The Anglican system, — including its most advanced developments of Anglo-Catholicism, Unionism, Ritualism, — rests upon one and the same basis; and the period which commenced with 1830 and the *Tracts for the Times*, diverse as its phenomena may be, is nevertheless in principle, in procedure, and in result, as purely and simply rationalistic as the period from 1688 down to that date'.[164] Ritualism, to single one out, was just 'private judgment in gorgeous raiment'.[165] Pusey, Manning claimed, had not answered his argument, he had merely confirmed it, and he added: 'every *Eirenicon* against the Catholic Church is a fresh reinforcement to the Rationalism of England'.[166]

Reunion was not just a question of believing a bit more or a bit less of dogma. It was based on a fundamental choice between a divine faith and rationalism. 'Unionism is outwardly a reaction against Latitudinarianism; inwardly it promotes it. There can be but two principles and two tendencies: the one, divine faith ... the other, of human criticism, disguise it as you may in texts of Scripture, or in patristic learning, or in sceptical history, or rationalistic interpretation, the tendency of which is always to wider formulas and diminished truth, to comprehension of communion, and loss of faith'.[167]

There was no point in talking about the 'essentials' of the faith. What are essentials? Who has the power to determine what is essential and what is not? By whose judgment are we to ascertain it? 'I had thought', Manning would say, 'that the word "essentials" had long ago departed with "fundamentals", into the Limbus of infantine theology'.[168] 'The Church', Manning said, 'knows only one essential truth, and that is, the whole revelation of God'.[169] For those who accepted the principle of infallibility there was no question of a little more or a little less of dogma; implicit in their faith on the infallibility of the Church was the belief in everything that the Church had defined as revealed or might define in the future as belonging to the deposit of revelation. In his speech to the General Congregation of the Vatican Council on 25 May 1870 Manning would affirm that belief in the infallibility of the Church is the only adequate motive of conversion to the Catholic Church.[170] For those who did not accept the principle of infallibility, there was no question of more or less. They did not have faith, only an opinion based on private judgment. In any case, Manning would add, the 'circle of essentials [in the Anglican Church] has so short a radius, that it is difficult to enclose in it any perfect Christian truth'.[171] Manning put it very simply in a letter to Ullathorne: 'I am very glad you have written about Dr. Pusey's Book. What you say is most true. It shows a simple unbelief in the two articles of the Creed, — the Holy Ghost and the Church. I am surprised and sorry that men should fail to appreciate this.... I see Dr. Pusey is again writing in answer to me about "*explanations*" [i.e.: of terms and concepts used]. What can explanations do for a man who does not believe the Voice of the Explainer to be divine? He may agree with the explanations, but that is not faith. Can Dr. Pusey be really so blind?'[172] Pusey wrote two more *Eirenicons;* they went unanswered. The argument, as far as Manning was concerned, had already been exhausted.

The rule of faith and the nature of the Church's unity were, for Manning, the two points on which all ecumenical dialogue resolved itself. He thought that the convocation of Vatican Council I offered a new ecumenical opportunity. The Archbishop of Westminster, when announcing it to his flock, clearly defined the terms of communion: 'The General Council ... will be convened by the Pope; and will be composed of those who believe, as an article of Divine faith, the visible unity and infallibility of the Catholic and Roman Church'.[173]

ABBREVIATIONS

Appendix   H.E. Manning, *The Rule of Faith. Appendix to a Sermon* (London, 1838).

APUC   H.E. Manning, *The Reunion of Christendom. A Pastoral Letter* [dated Epiphany 1866] (London, 1866).

ASer   H.E. Manning, *Sermons*, Vol. IV (2nd ed., London, 1850).

CSer   H.E. Manning, *Sermons on Ecclesiastical Subjects,*

| | Vol. I (Dublin, 1869) |
| | Vol. II (London, 1872). |

E&C   H.E. Manning, *England and Christendom* (London, 1867).

I. Preface

II. The Crown in Council, on the Essays and Reviews. A letter to an Anglican Friend (dated 8 March, 1864)

III. The Convocation and the Crown in Council (dated 25 July, 1864)

Four Evils   H.E. Manning, *The Four Great Evils of the Day* (8th Edition, London, n.d.) (First 1871).

Grounds   H.E. Manning, *The Grounds of Faith* (new ed., London, 1856) (First 1852).

LD   *The Letters and Diaries of John Henry Newman*

Vols. I-VI, eds. I. Ker, T. Gornall, G. Tracey (Oxford, 1978-84)

Vols. XI-XXXI, eds. C.S. Dessain, E.E. Kelly, T. Gornall (London, 1961-72; Oxford, 1973).

Manning Mss.

Bod.   Manning Papers at the Bodleian Library, Oxford.

Pitts. Manning Papers at Pitts Theological Library, Emory University, Atlanta (U.S.A.).

West.   Manning Papers at Westminster Diocesan Archive, London.

P   E.S. Purcell, *Life of Cardinal Manning*, 2 vols. (London, 1896).

Privilegium   H.E. Manning, *Petri Privilegium: Three Pastoral Letters to the Clergy of the Diocese* (London, 1871).

I. The Centenary of Saint Peter and the General Council (November 8, 1867)

II. The Oecumenical Council and the Infallibility of the Roman Pontiff (Rosary Sunday, 1869)

III. The Vatican Council and its Definitions (Feast of St Edward the Confessor, 1870)

TM   H.E. Manning, *The Temporal Mission of the Holy Ghost, or Reason and Revelation* (6th ed., London, 1909) (First 1865).

Unity   H.E. Manning, *The Unity of the Church* (London, 1842)

Workings   H.E. Manning, *The Workings of the Holy Spirit in the Church of England. A letter to the Rev. E.B. Pusey, DD* (London, 1864).

NOTES

1. I am grateful to Dr. Peter Erb for his comments and suggestions while discussing the topic of this present paper; I am also grateful to Dr. J.C.D. Clark for his helpful comments on an earlier version of the present text.

2. *Appendix*, p. 33.

3. *Ibidem*, p. 82.

4. *Ibidem*, p. 85.

5. *Ibidem*, p. 82.

6. *Ibidem*, p. 112.

7. *Ibidem*, p. 133.

8. H.E. Manning, *The Principle of the Ecclesiastical Commission Examined, in a Letter to the Right Rev. Lord Bishop of Chichester* (London, 1838), pp. 5-6.

9. H.E. Manning, *The Appellate Jurisdiction of the Crown in Matters Spiritual. A Letter to the Right Reverend Ashurst-Turner, Bishop of Chichester* (London, 1850), p. 22.

10. *Unity*, p. 363. In this book Manning dedicated some long notes to discuss the nature of the precedence of the Church of Rome (i.e. notes in pp. 98-99 and 152-154).

11. *Ibidem*, p. 359.

12. *Ibidem*, p. 360.

13. *Ibidem*, p. 359.

14. Cfr. *Ibidem*, pp. 360-366.

15. H.E. Manning, 'Christ's Kingdom not of this world', in *Sermons preached before the University of Oxford* (Oxford, 1844), pp. 91-92. A year later, in a letter to Oakeley (21-XII-44), Manning will paint a somewhat different picture of the Reformation in general, also embracing the English one. He believed that 'its moral and theological character to be in great measure evil', but he believed with equal conviction that 'the position in which it has placed us to be tenable; and that we have cause to be thankful to God for great, and extraordinary mercies in the over-ruling and result' of it (*Manning Mss.Bod.*, c. 654, Fol. 68)

16. *Unity*, pp. 365-366.

17. *Ibidem*, p. 364. The Jerusalem Bishopric was seen by Manning as an act which undermined the first principles of the Church of England. It was an unwarranted act of intrusion: the Anglican Church could not 'by any fiction treat as void, and under our jurisdiction, sees which if they belong to any certainly do not belong to us'; this act would only 'add another to the number of contending claims' (*Manning Mss.Bod.*, c. 653, Fol. 177; letter dated 28-X-41).

18. *Manning Mss.Bod.*, c. 654, Fol. 52.

19. Manning felt that they could not be agents in the growth of Catholic principles and practice within the Church of England. As Manning wrote to Oakeley (22-XII-44): 'To those who believe that Catholic and Roman are not convertible terms, the unprotestantizing of the English Church does not signify the Romanizing of it' (*Manning Mss.Bod*, c. 654, Fol. 71).

20. Cfr. *Pusey Mss.*, Pusey House, Manning to Pusey, Let. 22, dated 8-VIII-45.

21. Cfr. P. Nockles, *The Oxford Movement in Context* (Cambridge, 1994), pp. 162ff.

22. H.E. Manning, *Sermons preached before the University of Oxford*, p. 95.

23. *Manning Mss.Bod*, c. 658, Fols. 26-27; letter dated 13-I-1844.

24. *Pusey Mss.*, Pusey House, Manning to Pusey, Let. 22, dated 8-VIII-45. Pusey felt that he could not take any offensive ground against Rome. He even hoped at the time 'that it may prove that the Council of Trent may become the basis of union, that those assembled there were kept providentially from error', and that it 'might, by subsequent reception, become a General Council' (*Pusey Mss.*, Pusey House, Pusey to Manning, Let. 47, dated 20/22-VII-45).

25. *Pusey Mss.*, Pusey House, Manning to Pusey, Let. 2, dated 7-XII-39 (Copy).

26. *Ibidem.*

27. In 1842 he did not want 'to go into the question of the comparative openness of the way to life in the two Churches, of the means of knowledge and grace, and the fostering and disposing causes which tend towards salvation' (*Unity*, p. 365). However, in 1844, writing to Oakeley, he would express his misgiving and fears for the reality, life and safety of the Roman Church (cfr. *Manning Mss.Bod.*, c. 654, Fol. 70; letter dated 21-XII-44).

28. *Manning Mss.Bod.*, c. 658, Fol. 60; letter dated 29-VIII-46.

29. *Ibidem*, Fol. 59.

30. *Pusey Mss.*, Pusey House, Manning to Pusey; letter dated 25-VII-45.

31. *Manning Mss.Bod.*, c. 655, Fol. 137; letter to Mary Wilberforce, dated 2-XII-49.

32. Cfr. D. Newsome, *The Parting of Friends* (London, 1966), pp. 329 and 366.

33. *Manning Mss.Bod.*, c. 655, Fol. 62.

34. *P*, I, p. 474; letter to unknown correspondent, dated 6-V-50.

35. Cfr. J. Keble, *Sermons Academical and Occasional* (Oxford, 1847), see pages XXXI and LXIX, particularly note *m* in the last page mentioned.

36. *Ibidem*, p. XLII.

37. *Manning Mss.Bod*, c. 654, Fol. 36. Manning felt that, although the Anglican Church had to learn some things from Rome, there were 'some of God's great mercies, which they may learn from us' (*Pusey Mss.*, Pusey

House, Manning to Pusey, Let. 22, dated 8-VIII-45)

38. *Ibidem*, c. 653, Fol. 50; letter dated 20-XI-40.

39. *Manning Mss.Pitts*, 411111mg, Chapeau, p. 93; letter dated 11-XI-41.

40. *Ibidem*, 410417 mg; letter dated 17-IV-41.

41. *Manning Mss.Bod.*, c. 656, Fol. 107; letter to R. Wilberforce, dated 22-I-51.

42. *ASer, IV*, pp. 181-182.

43. *Ibidem*, p. 103.

44. *Ibidem*, p. 97.

45. *Ibidem*, p. 297.

46. *Ibidem*, pp. 297-298. The article *The Mystical Body of Christ* on Manning's Anglican ecclesiology in this same volume (pp. 168-86) studies in detail the themes developed in Manning's Fourth Volume of Anglican Sermons. It may be useful to refer to it now — if the reader has not already done so — before reading the next section of the present article.

47. The steps leading to this conclusion exceed the scope of the present paper. I hope to deal with this point in a further study.

48. *TM*, pp. 225-226; see also *Grounds*, p. 13.

49. *CSer*, I, p. 218.

50. *Ibidem*, p. 30.

51. *Ibidem*, p. 34.

52. *Ibidem*, p. 58.

53. *Ibidem*, p. 41.

54. *Ibidem*, p. 56.

55. *CSer*, II, pp. 191-192.

56. *Ibidem*, p. 192.

57. *TM*, p. 205.

58. *Ibidem*, p. 207.

59. *Grounds*, p. 88.

60. *CSer*, I, p. 57.

61. *Ibidem*, pp. 25-26.

62. *Ibidem*, p. 57.

63. *Grounds*, pp. 41-42.

64. 'Inaugural Address to the Academia' (Session 1866-7), in *Miscellanies*, I, p. 178. See also pp. 182 and 183.

65. *Ibidem*, p. 187.

66. 'On the Subjects proper to the Academia' (Session 1863-4), in *Miscellanies*, I, p. 83.

67. 'Inaugural Address' (Session 1866-7), in *Miscellanies*, I, p. 178. Manning considered that the two schools which were tearing Anglicanism apart, the Anglo-Catholic and the Critical, were moving so fast away from each other 'that nothing can restrain them from reaching their natural points of rest', Rome or Rationalism ['Inaugural Address' (Session 1868-9), in op.cit., p. 262].

68. *TM*, p. 78.

69. *Manning Mss.Bod.*, c. 660, Fol. 59; letter dated 4-VII-51.

70. *Ibidem*, Fol. 184; letter dated 29-XII-53. See above p. 16.

71. *CSer*, I, p. 67.

72. *E&C*, I, p. LXXXVII. Similar expressions can be found in Newman's *Difficulties of Anglicans* (London, 1897), vol. I, pp. 13-22.

73. Cfr. *Ibidem*, p. XCI.

74. *Ibidem*, p. 60.

75. *E&C*, p. 79.

76. *Workings*, pp. 24-25.

77. *Privilegium*, I, p. 102.

78. *CSer*, I, p. 58.

79. *Grounds*, p. 77.

80. *Four Evils*, p. 22.

81. *Grounds*, pp. 2-3.

82. *Four Evils*, p. 23.

83. *CSer*, I, p. 72.

84. *Four Evils*, p. 23.

85. Cfr. *Unity*, p. 315.

86. 'Autobiographical Note'; *P*, II, pp. 780-781. The same Note described how different was the general perception of Catholics at the time.

87. *ASer*, IV, pp. 73-74. In 1890 he contrasted the two methods: 'There are two ways of proving a problem. The one to show that every other conception is impossible; this is polemical and destructive. The other to show that the true conception is evident. This is positive and expository'('Autobiographical Note'; *P*, II, p.789).

88. *Ibidem*, p. 74.

89. *Ibidem*.

90. *Ibidem*, p, 75.

91. *Ibidem*, p. 79.

92. *Ibidem*, p. 78.

93. *Ibidem*, p. 80.

94. *Ibidem*, p. 77. In 1842 he had said how a body which had broken away from the Church had forfeited the character of a Church, but that it would be false to conclude that its members had forfeited their hope of salvation (cfr. *Unity*, p. 349).

95. *Ibidem*, p. 82.

96. *Ibidem*, p. 80.

97. *P*, II, p. 36; letter dated 20-I-54.

98. *CSer*, I, p. 61.

99. *P*, II, p. 36; letter to Robert Wilberforce, dated 20-I-54.

100. *Manning Mss.Bod.*, c. 656, Fol. 200; letter to Robert Wilberforce, dated 16-VI-51.

101. F.J. Cwiekowski, *The English Bishops and the First Vatican Council* (Louvain, 1971), p. 220. Manning considered that English Catholics — because of 'an antagonistic attitude of mind, bitter and hardly charitable' towards Anglicans — 'held with all rigour the axiom *extra ecclesiam nulla salus*' — ('Autobiographical Note'; P, II, p.778). An attitude born of centuries of persecution and discrimination.

102. *CSer*, I, pp. 192-193; see also *Workings*, p. 15.

103. Cfr. *CSer*, I, pp. 112-114 and 378ff; see also *CSer*, II, pp. 351ff.

104. *E&C*, III, p. 56.

105. *Ibidem*, p. 44.

106. *E&C*, II, pp. 28-29.

107. *Ibidem*, p. 24.

108. 'Inaugural Address' (Session 1868-9), in *Miscellanies*, I, p. 291. J. von Arx has studied some of these points in his article 'Manning's Ultramontanism and the Catholic Church in British Politics', in *Recusant History* (May 1989), vol. 19, n. 3, pp. 332-347.

109. 'Autobiographical Note' (1890); *P*, II, p. 782.

110. *E&C*, III, p. 50.

111. *Ibidem*, p. 51.

112. *Ibidem*, p. 53.

113. *Ibidem*, p. 57.

114. *Ibidem*, p. 59.

115. *Ibidem*.

116. *Ibidem*, pp. 75-6.

117. *E&C*, I, p. XXIII.

118. *CSer*, I, p. 52.

119. *Ibidem*, p. 53.

120. *Ibidem*, p. 54.

121. J.L. Altholz, *Anatomy of a Controversy: the Debate over Essays and Reviews, 1860-1864* (Aldershot, 1994), p. 109.

122. E.B. Pusey, *Case as to the legal force of the Judgment of the Privy Council in re Fendall v Wilson* (London, 1864), pp. 3-4.

123. *Workings*, pp. 29-30.

124. *Ibidem*, p. 34.

125. *Ibidem*, p. 21.

126. *Ibidem*, p. 22.

127. *Ibidem*, p. 30.

128. *Ibidem*, p. 35.

129. *Ibidem*, pp. 41-42.

130. *Ibidem*.

131. *Ibidem*, p. 20.

132. *Ibidem*, pp. 28-29.

133. *Ibidem*, p. 24.

134. *LD*, XXII, p. 99.

135. J.H. Newman, *op. cit.*, vol. I, p. 88.

136. E.B. Pusey, *An Eirenicon, In a Letter to the Author of 'The Christian Year'* (London, 1865), p. 82. Pusey's argument against papal infallibility and Manning's response are secondary to the main argument about the infallibility of the Church and it is not dealt with here.

137. *Ibidem*, pp. 83-84.

138. *Ibidem*, p. 96.

139. *Ibidem*, p. 84.

140. *Ibidem*, p. 97. The appeal to a future Council was for Manning a 'plea for insubordination' and it implied uncertainty as to the faith for centuries, until the Council were to meet (cfr. *Grounds*, pp. 70-71).

141. *Ibidem*. There is a certain ambiguity in Pusey's expressions when referring to infallibility. He seems to hesitate between two different positions: acknowledging the infallibility of the Church or accepting the existence of infallible truth handed on by a non-infallible Church.

142. In 1863 Manning had remarked how the developments in Anglican thinking which had taken place in the last thirty years had led some Anglican clergymen to believe in the infallibility of the Church [see 'Inaugural Address' (Session 1863-64), in *Miscellanies*, I, p. 81].

143. *E&C*, I, p. XIV.

144. *CSer*, I, p. 194.

145. V.A. McClelland, 'Corporate Reunion: A Nineteenth-Century Dilemma', in *Theological Studies*, March 1982, p. 25.

146. *Ibidem*, p. 27.

147. *Miscellanies*, I, p. 82.

148. Translation in *APUC*, p. 6.

149. *Ibidem*.

150. Letter to Talbot (18-VII-65); *P*, II, p. 281.

151. *Manning Mss. West.*, Manning-Ullathorne Cor., *U* 34; letter dated 25-VIII-65.

152. Talbot to Manning (1-XII-65); *P*, II, p. 284.

153. Manning to Talbot (11-XII-65); *P*, II, p. 284.

154. *APUC*, pp. 8-10. The last two points need to be read in the light of Manning's ideas, described already in this paper, on the position of those who are outside the Church

155. *Ibidem*, pp. 16-17.

156. *Ibidem*, pp. 23-24.

157. *CSer*, II, pp. 238-239.

158. *APUC*, p. 24.

159. *Ibidem*, p. 17.

160. *Ibidem*, p. 26.

161. *Ibidem*, p. 39.

162. *Ibidem,* p. 41.
163. *E&C*, I, pp. LXXXII-LXXXIII.
164. *Ibidem*, pp. LI-LII.
165. *Ibidem,* p. LXXXIII.
166. *Ibidem*, p. LIII.
167. *APUC*, pp. 66-67.
168. *E&C*, I, p. LXIV.
169. *Grounds*, p. 25.
170. Cfr. *M*, 52, col. 258A.
171. *E&C*, I, p. LXV.
172. *Manning Mss.West.*, Manning-Ullathorne Cor., *U* 40; letter dated 15-III-66.
173. *Privilegium*, I, p. 88.

XII

MANNING: THE CATHOLIC WRITINGS

Sheridan Gilley

The mere listing of the writings of Henry Edward Manning occupies twelve columns of the *British Museum Catalogue of Printed Books*, and by far the greater number of these titles belong to his career as a Roman Catholic. On closer examination, this hefty heap of volumes is less impressive than it seems. In an era in which print was the only medium of mass communication, every public utterance by a distinguished man tended to end up in printed form, and a large part of Manning's output consists of addresses, occasional sermons, pastoral letters to his archdiocese and introductions and prefaces generously given to do a little good and to puff the work of other people.

True, the evidences of the author's unflagging industry are remarkable. Manning's pastoral letter of 1867 on the eighteenth centenary of St Peter's martyrdom and the summoning of the Vatican Council runs to 105 pages, exclusive of Latin appendices[1] while the three collected pieces in *England and Christendom* are casually assigned an 109 page introduction.[2] Such prolixity was not uncommon in the nineteenth century, and some of it is the product of a special interest, like the Cardinal's temperance speeches, published after his death by an admirer, C. Kegan Paul.[3] Other parts are polemic called forth by circumstance, like the large body of sermons and lectures in defence of the Pope's Temporal Power against the *Risorgimento*, some of the most notable of which were brought together in a major work published in 1861, *The Temporal Power of the Vicar of Jesus Christ*;[4] supplemented later by essays like the attack on Garibaldi's visit in a public letter to Edward Cardwell in 1864.[5] *Caesarism and Ultramontanism* was written in response to the *Kulturkampf* in Prussia,[6] while Manning's subsequent answer[7] to Gladstone's attack on papal infallibility was eclipsed by a more famous reply by Newman. Again, the echoes of past controversies sound through Manning's writings on education, around the time of Forster's Education Act, and on the long shadow cast on British politics by Ireland.

Yet the sheer bulk of the *omnia opera* is a little deceptive, as some of the volumes, like the collected thirty-eight sermons in the three volumes of collected Catholic sermons[8] and the three volumes of miscellanies,[9] and the smaller works of extracts assembled for instruction or devotion, are re-publications of already printed material. Moreover certain themes, phrases and ideas recur from one work to another. Yet there are no wasted words in any particular work. Manning's Catholic writings are clear and concise, a point which I want to expand. But they are for the most part pastoral or practical or political in intent, called forth by a special need or occasion, as the outpourings of a great ecclesiastical statesman and busy shepherd of souls, written for the moment, and, like the moment, quickly gone.

Given their immediate character, most of these writings are not calculated to win Manning a readership today; and as far as I can discover, the only one of his books to remain in print well into the twentieth century, in a period when his type of Ultramontanism was still regnant in the Church, was his classic *The Eternal Priesthood*.[10] Nor is the style of his works very attractive. Manning lacked Newman's magic gift of creating a literary masterpiece from a passing controversy. Manning's tone is too often that of a dogmatic debater, which probably goes back to his days as a young man at the Oxford Union in the late 1820s; that is, his writings read as the work of someone accustomed to public speaking and debate, who had 'learnt very early', as Manning put it himself, 'to think on my hind legs'.[11] His mode of mental composition was through numbered points, and can be seen at its barest in his surviving sermon notes and memoranda, as in the example which was published as of interest to the curious in his own life time in the first volume of the *Strand Magazine*, soon to be made famous by the adventures of Sherlock Holmes.[12] It has been noted that G. K. Chesterton's style is a fat man's; it grows by the accumulation of illustration and paradox. Manning's, by contrast, is usually lean to the point of emaciation, the mode of self-expression of the ascetic who never ate or drank at the London banquets placed before him. It is as if the work was laid down as a sequence of points and quotations, and then threaded together with a brisk economy of words.

Indeed Manning's Catholic writings are sometimes hardly more than a slight expansion on a pattern of bare headings, amounting to bald assertions, with contrary arguments as briefly stated in order to be thrust aside. The result is that some of his most important books like *The Temporal Mission of the Holy Ghost*[13] can be quite effectively read through the summaries in the introductory table of Contents, and in the text the bones still show beneath the flesh. The humour, when it comes, as it seldom does, is of the briefest and driest: my favourite is

the remark in *The True Story of the Vatican Council* about the great
storm which accompanied the final vote in St Peter's on the infallibility
decree. 'Other critics', wrote Manning, quoting *The Times*'s correspondent, Newman's brother-in-law Tom Mozley, 'saw in this
thunderstorm an articulate voice of divine indignation against the
definition. They forgot Sinai and the Ten Commandments'.[14]

Even Manning's *bon mots* had the virtue of brevity, and his habit of
concise logical statement and counter-statement may well have been
influenced by the dogmatic catechisms and scholastic manuals of his
day, which also come to firm conclusions. Such manuals do, however,
put the counter-case and Manning's way of writing, in origin a
debating skill, is more than catechetical; it has the one-sidedness of
debating in English public life. It is not the debater's job to grant an
inch to an adversary. The youthful Manning may have been considered
a possible Prime Minister, but neither the British parliamentary
tradition nor the Law Courts, which so often lead to it, waste time in
putting an opponent's case. That is his job, and he will be just as one-
sided as his adversary. Manning would have been a superb barrister or
parliamentary orator. Give him his brief or despatch box, and he
showed no mercy.

There is, then, in Manning, an element of the intellectual bully: he
will never give one reason when five will do. Take his defence of the
rights of property: they are 'founded on the law of nature, sanctioned
in revelation, declared in the Christian law, taught by the Catholic
Church, and incorporated in the civilisations of all nations'. Mercy,
cries the reader. Will not one of these suffice? The merits and defects
of Manning's approach appear in his *Religio Viatoris*, written, as he
put it, while for many days on a journey without work or books, and
containing a brief and rapid sketch of his whole body of beliefs. The
outline of the four chapters into which the work is divided is charac-
teristically skeletal:

> The four following truths are the four corners of my faith:
> I.   A necessity of my reason constrains me to believe the
> existence of God.
> II.   My moral sense, or moral reason, or conscience,
> constrains me to believe that God has revealed Himself to me.
> III.   My reason and moral sense constrain me to believe
> that this revelation is Christianity.
>
> IV.   My reason is convinced that historical Christianity is
> the Catholic Faith.[15]

From God to Roman Catholicism in four simple steps: all this is
capable of certain and irrefragable proof. The weakness of such proofs

so brilliantly stated in debate is that, when translated to the printed page, they lack the very quality in which Newman excelled, of disarming the hostile reader by explaining his own case so plausibly that he hardly feels the pain of its refutation. Manning, however, has no time for such frivolities. His job is not to spare, but to strike.

This ruthless, bullying quality might be illustrated from the four main points in the *Religio Viatoris*. His first is that reason requires him to believe in God because he cannot believe he is uncaused, or self-caused, and these notions he demonstrates to his own satisfaction to be 'strictly incredible, inasmuch as they are intrinsically absurd and self-contradictory'.[16] The notion of being 'self-caused' puzzlingly includes descent from an ape or an animal origin, which Manning sweeps aside with five differences between men and animals: powers of language, of abstract thought, of creative mind, of moral reason and of moral self-government. The denial of such differences between man and the animal creation involves 'mental suicide'. Now whatever one thinks of Manning's arguments — and they seem to me good arguments — they hardly settle the issue of mankind's origins in the half dozen pages which he has devoted to discussing them. Yet he offers his refutation as though it were as self-evidently certain as the multiplication table, where Newman would have presented it as a probability, subtly predisposing the mind to a certainty for which it has been carefully prepared.

This is not to say that Newman would have rejected Manning's arguments; indeed Manning adopted the very starting-point of the individual self from which Newman also began. But Newman did not offer his proofs as knock-down Euclidian theorems which only a fool could refuse. Again, Manning's proof of God from conscience in the second chapter of *Religio Viatoris* is not unlike Newman's, and indeed seems to me to be morally superior to Newman's, for where Newman's proof of God's existence from conscience is couched primarily in terms of obedience in guilt to a righteous judge, Manning's proof stresses the 'interior peace and joy' and happiness which the conformity of conscience to the divine judge brings. Yet the reader sympathises more readily with Newman's guilt than with Manning's peace and happiness, and the reason is that the one presents a hard external scientific proof; the other gently urges the force of his own experience, and appeals to a like experience in his hearer.

There is the same contrast in Manning's defence of his third and fourth propositions, that true religion is Christianity and that the one divine form of Christianity is the Roman Catholic. Again, he does not differ fundamentally from Newman as to the need for a universal ecclesial body united in the Holy Spirit. Where he differs is his insistence on the certain deductive argument for ecclesial authority. As he wrote elsewhere, 'Authority is, therefore, not an imperious act substituting command for reason ... but it is reason and evidence speaking by a legitimate voice.... It is not authority that generates truth, but truth that generates authority....'[17] Just as mankind receives its science and medicine on good authority, supported by evidence and reason, so reason and evidence inexorably point to the authority of an infallible Church.

The difference from Newman is that Manning's Church was defended with proofs calculated to appeal only to someone looking for a logically water-tight ecclesiology, one of those closed thought systems made so unpopular by Karl Popper and by Fascism and Communism in this century. Newman's defence of the same Roman Catholic position seems the more subtle in that it was moderated by a vivid consciousness of the objections attending it, and the accompanying reassurance that the reader could raise these objections without feeling like a knave or a fool.

In saying this I do not mean to damn Manning. There is a place for both types of teaching the faith, the manner authoritative and the manner persuasive. But Manning and Newman set out their wares in a very different fashion. Newman was autobiographical. He exposed the processes by which he came to his conclusions. Manning gave his conclusions, without personal preliminaries. Newman had an incurably *literary* mind. This was partly why he was so distrusted, for an insidious and plausible rhetoric which, as Kingsley said, planted a whole line of thought by a mere hint or suggestion. Manning was by no means ignorant of the arts of rhetoric. There are especially moving passages in the sermons and pastorals, and I do not want to set a fashion of contrasting the Cardinal rhetorician and the Cardinal logician. But for Newman, truth too often defied propositional form, and was to be approached through an implicit logic not always conscious of its own assumptions and conclusions. For Manning, truth was always propositional, and the only logic possible was an explicit one.

But Manning's mind was made for action, and his powers of public argument were sharpened and honed by a ceaseless round of preaching and public performance as a Catholic priest, first as right-hand man to Cardinal Wiseman and then for twenty-seven years as Archbishop of Westminster. Newman wrote to seduce. His was a personal influence finely tuned to the prejudices of his Protestant fellow-countrymen. But Manning came among them with the full weight of the authority of Rome in her most Ultramontane mood. When he spoke, it was *ex cathedra Westmonasteriensis*, as one whose office from 1865 was archiepiscopal and primatial, and whose rôle was to expound Rome's case without frills and contradictions. This was part of his style, of the air he carried with him, for all his humility, as the great high priest of the Great High Priest. It was one with the mystical sense which pervaded his conception of priesthood in *The Eternal Priesthood*, 'Thou art a priest forever after the order of Melchisedech', and his favourite phrases from the Book of Revelation like 'the great white throne'.[18] No ecclesiastic so answered to the hymn '*Ecce sacerdos magnus*'. He taught, like his Master, as one with authority, with a singleminded clarity and force that all could understand if not receive.

These two different habits of mind, Manning's and Newman's, the authoritative and the persuasive, are in a sense complementary and though much has been made of the damage to the Roman Catholic cause from their conflict, it could equally be argued that it benefited that cause to have enjoyed the support of two leaders of such supreme abilities in quite different ways as Manning and Newman. The superiority of the power persuasive, however, is that it passes insensibly into the citadel that it is trying to subvert; the power authoritative is more like the bombardment of the outside wall. Again, one should not exaggerate the difference between them. Manning and Newman shared a horror of the rising tide of unbelief, and indeed both derived it in individuals from a failure of the moral or spiritual sense. But both also recognised an intellectual challenge, and while Newman's sheer originality of mind furnished arguments to meet that challenge, it was Manning who was prepared to brave intellectual irreligion in its most sophisticated form in the Metaphysical Society, a celebrated chat club for eminent Victorian intellectuals, founded by his fellow-Ultramontane William George Ward, where Newman remained aloof.

'In the Session before last', Manning patiently began his own first address to the Society, 'we came out of the discussion of the question, "Has a frog a soul?" with one point conceded, that is to say, that men differ from frogs, in that they have a will and a moral consciousness'. From this, Manning derived the existence of a personal self, possessing both intelligence and will, but endowed with the intuitive prior sense of its own existence as a 'self' or 'I'. It is on the certainty that 'I' exist, he argued, that all subsequent certainties of intellection or willing depend; but as I exist, before such intellection or willing, so does my immortal soul.[19] Manning was quite prepared to argue for his certainties to his fellow though doubting Metaphysicals and to state his case before an educated public through the semi-learned periodical press, the *Dublin Review* to Catholics of course, but also to informed middle class opinion through the *Nineteenth Century* and the *Contemporary* and *Fortnightly Review*.

Talking politely to agnostics like Huxley in the rarefied intellectual atmosphere of the Metaphysical Society was, however, one thing; it was quite another when it came to practical life. Manning's normal response to infidelity was straight denunciation, nowhere more severely than of its implications for the education of the poor. 'These last generations', he wrote, 'have become fruitful of impiety and of immorality of a stupendous kind; and among other of their impious and immoral offspring is a pestilent infidel school, who, with an audacity never before known in the Christian world, are at this time assailing the foundations of human society and of Divine Law ... this morality without God for school-children, is bottomless impiety if it be not the stupidity of unbelief'.[20]

To Manning, it was the great merit of the definition of papal infallibility that it answered the unbelief of the nineteenth century, but there is a great deal more to Manning than hard-hearted denunciation and external argument. The foundation of his conviction about the Pope was his doctrine of the Church, itself the product of his discovery of the doctrine of the Spirit's presence in the Church, as recently most ably elucidated by Father James Pereiro, in the finest essay ever written on Manning's theology, in Professor McClelland's recent edition of *Recusant History*.[21] In his major Anglican treatise, *The Unity of the Church*, Manning defined an objective ecclesial unity with Christ and the Apostles and a subjective ecclesial unity with one's local pastor and other churches. Manning's reading of the *De Locis Theologicis* of the sixteenth-century divine Melchior Cano suggested, however, a deeper supernatural unity in the Church which was the work within her of 'the Personal coming, abiding and office of the Holy Ghost', endowing her with infallibility in her teaching.[22] In fact, what Manning found in the doctrine of the Spirit's presence in the Church was a living ecclesiology, the principle of the Church as Christ's Mystical Body, and Manning's major Catholic treatise on the Holy Spirit, *The Temporal Mission of the Holy Ghost*, is the enunciation of a dynamic ecclesiology which is far more impressive than its rather grim mode of self-expression.

But his doctrine of the Spirit was also universal: as he wrote in his letter on *The Workings of the Holy Spirit in the Church of England* to Pusey, 'the operations of the Holy Spirit of God have been from the beginning of the world co-extensive with the whole human race'. In that, the very heathen are moved by the Spirit of God. Yet Anglicans possessed a privilege denied to the heathen. Manning insisted that 'in denying the Church of England to be the Catholic Church, or any part of it, or in any divine and true sense a Church at all, and in denying the validity of its absolutions and its orders, no Catholic ever denies the workings of the Spirit of God or the operations of grace in it', or the validity of an Anglican baptism when properly performed. If validly baptised, — and Manning denied that Anglican baptisers had always followed the necessary form — the Anglican might well have received that perhaps ultimately salvific initial supernatural grace from which Manning himself derived his own conversion. These 'many belong to the Church who are out of its visible unity'.[23] Children, the poor, women and the uneducated could not be blamed for being shut off from Catholicism by an invincible ignorance imposed on them by others, and indeed Dissenters, further from the Catholic Church than Anglicans, often had a deeper personal devotion to Our Lord.

There were limits to this charity. Manning regarded the Church of England, already reeling under the publication of the Liberal *Essays and Reviews*, less as a bulwark against infidelity than as a carrier of the infidel infection, and he condemned the Association for Promoting the Unity of Christendom, a society of Anglicans and Catholics to pray for reunion; but the universal office of the Holy Ghost meant that God's grace was at work in the Church of England as well.

It is, however, the doctrine of the universal office of the Spirit which inspired Manning to recognise its presence wherever it was to be found, whether among the Nonconformist Joseph Arch's agricultural labourers or the philanthropy and preaching of the Salvation Army. The paradox was that the very exclusiveness of his Spirit ecclesiology was part and parcel of his own practical universalism. In defending Russian Jews against pogroms, in consorting with trade unionists who were championing the poor, he was acting with those who did the Spirit's work even if they knew it not themselves.

Moreover as Father von Arx has shown, in his study of *Caesarism and Ultramontanism*,[24] Manning defended Ultramontanism as necessary to the protection of the freedom of the Church from the idea of the newly emergent omnipotent and omnicompetent nation state, so that the Church was thereby the protector of other freedoms as well. The rights and dignity of labourers or of poor abused children were one with the Church's freedoms. Moreover as Manning asserted in his subsequent controversy with James Stephen, every Church, and not merely the Catholic, must claim this freedom from the State for its very existence, as it declared an otherworldly origin and authority separate from the State in a Revelation from God and a foundation in Christ. All Churches assert their authority, as all claim to be organs of the Paraclete, and so all require freedom to exercise that claim. Thus Manning's political crusades did not appeal to the sanction of the Roman Catholic Church's distinctive claim to infallibility. Rather, they arose from that demand for the freedom to preach the moral law, to require justice and mercy, and to witness to the Spirit, which was rightly put forward by all good Christians, and even by pagans of good will.

Of course, Manning also thought that the Catholic Church had a distinctive voice in demanding political justice, as the one true Church, which was also the shrine and organ of the Paraclete and the guardian of the universal moral law. Again, he saw a distinctive role for his own Church as the trusted leader of the working class, hoping to give it the role of leadership in England which it already enjoyed in Ireland. There is, moreover, a connection between the exalted conception of the priestly office set forth in *The Eternal Priesthood*, of the priest who lives a life of Holy Poverty and all but heroic sanctity and self-denial, and Manning's own claim to speak with authority on social and political issues, as a high priest forever, after the order of Melchisedech. It might be said that the practical justification of such claims as Manning's to sacerdotal power is the manner in which it is exercised. The view of Manning as a power-hungry ecclesiastic was passed into popular currency by his biographer E. S. Purcell, and it was the late Michael Ramsey, Archbishop of Canterbury, who remarked to me in criticism of Purcell's biography that it took no account of Manning's greatness as a spiritual writer. Alas, I never followed through this hint to enquire of Ramsey in what he thought this greatness to consist; my own suggestion is that it was the application of the spiritual authority of the Catholic priesthood to believers of an assurance of forgiveness, salvation and love. Manning's certainties were ultimately pastoral: the sinner could only know that his sin was forgiven if the Church spoke with an infallible assurance in the power of the keys and that she had this God-given power to forgive.

There is a great deal of nonsense now talked of the Catholic sense of guilt. It would be truer to speak of the Catholic power of pardon. In fact, both Victorian Protestantism and Catholicism possessed a strong sense of sin, and both sought to overcome it in the power of the Cross. It has been frequently remarked that there was a close temperamental affinity between Victorian Roman Catholicism and Evangelicalism, as in the remark attributed to Cardinal Wiseman that the Methodists preached from the pulpit the sacrifice which he offered at the altar. Nowhere was this more marked than in the shared language of salvation by the Precious Blood, though in popular Protestant revivalism such Passion devotion had become separated from the Eucharistic devotion with which it was fused in popular Catholicism. In Protestantism, the tendency of such Passion devotion was anti-Calvinist, as it was anti-rigorist and anti-Jansenist in Roman Catholicism; both preached man's sinfulness but both stressed the universal action of God's forgiveness.

Ralph Gibson has noted this current in nineteenth-century French Catholicism, softening the terrors of an older emphasis on the fewness of the elect and everlasting punishment,[25] and in England, the tendency has been described by Geoffrey Rowell as a widening of the bounds of Purgatory.[26] The great apostle of the trend in England was Manning's fellow convert from Anglicanism, the ex-Evangelical Father Frederick William Faber, in whom one can see the genial spirit of the faith under clear blue Mediterranean skies, as in a cheerful procession behind a Madonna in petticoats. As Faber wrote:

> For the love of God is broader
>   Than the measures of man's mind;
> And the heart of the Eternal
>   Is most wonderfully kind.
>
> But we make his love too narrow
>   By false limits of our own;
> And we magnify his strictness
>   With a zeal he will not own.
>
> There is plentiful redemption
>   In the Blood that has been shed,
> There is joy for all the members
>   In the sorrows of the Head.[27]

This is not quite Manning, for whom the contrast between English and Mediterranean religion was one between awe and homeliness. One of his loveliest letters, written in 1849, describes the sun rising from the Mediterranean between Nice and Genoa like the Monstrance lifted at Benediction, and even while in Rome he thought of his Anglican parish of Lavington at Christmas, 'the dressings of Holly, and the Altar, the Charity and Xtmas communion, alms and kindliness, bright hearths and loving faces, and the homely plain open Xtmas joy of the Church of England'. Then he thought of 'the severe majesty and awful near reality of the Roman Church, with its claims and its denials'.[28] By contrast, other ex-Evangelicals like Faber found Rome domestic and relaxed where English religion was conventional, stiff and hidebound, and even Newman took a Roman holiday in his *Difficulties Felt by Anglicans*, in which he describes how the religion of Catholic countries could coexist with a kind of fairground immorality and disobedience to the Church. For Newman and Faber, conversion to Rome meant a return to Evangelical freedom, but I am not sure that the same was true for Manning, and indeed the reality of his Evangelical conversion at the hands of Miss Favell Lee Bevan has been recently questioned by Christopher O'Gorman.[29]

Yet Manning's spiritual writings seem to me to be pervaded by an Evangelical temper. It was just such a sentiment as Faber's from St Alphonsus Liguori, 'O, poor blood of Jesus Christ', in reprimand of rigorism, with which Manning opens his *The Love of Jesus to Penitents*, a defence of the sacrament of penance as 'the special Sacrament of the Compassion of Jesus', as the manifestation of 'the special tenderness of the love of Jesus', drawing the penitent to itself 'by the efffusion of special gifts of grace'. 'In the Holy Eucharist', writes Manning, 'Jesus manifests Himself in His royalty, power, and glory. In the Sacrament of Penance, in His tenderness as a Physician, and His compassion as the Good Shepherd. In the former He attracts and transforms us chiefly by His divine attributes; in the latter by His human experience, sympathy, and pity'.[30] The only sin, Manning stresses, which cannot be forgiven is the sin against the Holy Ghost; and that sin is impenitence, not seeking forgiveness. In the chapters which follow, on self-knowledge, contrition, reparation and per-severance, Manning is quite severe enough on the conditions for such forgiveness, but he has led the shrinking reader in by putting the divine pity first. In brief, what Manning offered penitents in the confessional was this assurance of the divine compassion by the power of the priestly office to offer it. In this, Manning's high claims for himself were but a means of mercy, the quieting of the anxious conscience which could hardly believe that its sins could be forgiven.

There is a contrast here with Newman, whose moral severity as an Anglican was Jansenistical: 'we need the Law's stern fires'. Indeed as David Newsome has pointed out in his work *The Convert Cardinals*, Manning's Anglican sermons contain a great deal more about joy, love and mercy than Newman's. Even as a Roman Catholic, Newman published one terrifying hell-fire sermon, 'Neglect of Divine Calls and Warnings',[31] the more frightening because everlasting loss appears as the result of a very ordinary careless worldly state of mind, in which the humanity of the victim pleads in vain in mitigation of divine judgement. Manning never wrote anything as terrible, though of course he preached the eternity of Hell, as in his Lenten discourses, *Sin: and its Consequences*, which draws the doctrine out of the terrifying gulf between human sinfulness and the transcendant glory and holiness of God. Manning's stress, however, in this work lay on eternal punish-ment as the consequence of conscious choice, for which a remedy lies to hand in the tears and contrition of the penitent. In fact, the general gloom of the first seven addresses, on sin, mortal sin, venial sin, sins of omission, penance, temptation and dereliction, is dissipated in the sunlight of the conclusion, on 'The Joys of the Resurrection', of faith, vision and the direct sight of God, in which the sufferings of the Sacred Humanity in sympathy with human suffering grant the gift of life everlasting.

This was a major theme in Manning's spiritual writings: Christ's identification through his suffering with suffering mankind. It was, however, the very intensity of Manning's own identification with human suffering, which had been dignified and ennobled by Christ's suffering, and his own pastoral experience of how terrible such suffering was, that lay behind his involvement with political reform. The vision of heaven was rest and relief from the anguish of earth. Addressing a well-to-do congregation, he said

> rest from toil, rest from labour, rest from eating your bread in the sweat of your face — that which the multitudes and the millions of Christendom, in all lands and all languages, have for their earthly lot — the poor labourer, the tiller of the ground - those who wring hard sustenance out of the hard earth, who live lives of cold, and pain, and disease, and privation, in homes that are bare, with hungry children, with those that are dearest to them languishing, and fading for want of the food which their toil cannot supply — this is an earthly burden of which you who hear me perhaps know little. But in heaven 'they shall hunger no more, they shall thirst no more, neither shall the sun light upon them nor any heat; but the Lamb which is in the midst of the Throne shall rule over them, and shall lead them by the fountains of the waters of life, and God shall wipe away all tears from their eyes'.[32]

This compassion on the multitude, the compassion in which Manning sought to follow Christ, undergirded his political involvements, and bound together his two-fold crusade, for the Pope and the poor. In his own eyes, the two were one. In the late 1850s, Manning became the unwearied propagandist in England for the Pope's Temporal Power; but his defence of Rome was essentially religious, indeed Evangelical in character, that this was a part of the age-old battle between the Church as an otherworldly power, the Kingdom of God on earth, and its enemies the flesh and the devil in the kingdom of this world. Thus his view of the matter was apocalyptic, a mirror image of the Evangelical view which saw in the fall of the Roman Whore of Babylon a sign that the Second Coming was near at hand. In the first age of the Church, Manning argued, she was persecuted until rescued by Constantine; then she enjoyed a millennium of peaceful activity; but since the Reformation she had been returning to the condition from which she came, and in these no doubt the prelude to the last days, of 'the final dethronement of Christendom and of the restoration of society without God in the world',[33] her end would be as her beginning. When Manning appealed for Peter's Pence, he spoke of the Pope's sufferings from the *Risorgimento* as 'a renewal of the humiliations of the Son of God'.[34] The Pope's cause was the cause of Christendom, of the inferiority of the temporal to the eternal; it was the cause of the poor against the rich, for it was the rich who sought the plunder of the Church. And in the end, that power in the Pope was one which had the sanction of the popular will.

At the end of his life, Manning himself decided that papal authority was no longer best served by the Temporal Power in its form before 1870, yet the principle of his defence remained clear: that the freedom of the Church is the foundation of all freedom, and truth and justice. It was this fearless apocalyptic otherworldliness, in defiance of the Protestant and Liberal public opinion in his own time, which bred in him the Mosaic Radical ready to denounce the exploitation of the English village labourer and the white slave trade of the modern Babylon of which he was Archbishop, and the cruelty of the English savage to his children. And it was Manning's apocalyptic vision of the double crisis of his age, a crisis of unbelief requiring an infallible Church, a crisis of poverty requiring a compassionate Church, which gave depth and consistency to his conviction that the compassionate Church must have the authority of the infallible Church for its compassion to serve a materialistic and apostatising world.

This then, seems to me the strength of Manning's message. There is nothing wrong with political activism; but it requires religious dogma for its ultimate sanction. There is no point in linking political radicalism with theological Modernism: such Modernism has no dogmatic authority, and its radicalism has no authority either. The Church which has power to teach the truth has the power to forgive; but if there is no such power to teach the truth, then there is no forgiveness. It is no use the Church espousing social and political causes however worthy, unless she is sure of her own religious authority first. But it is no use preaching a religion which has no practical and political implications in justice for the poor. Manning is a sign that the Church has everything to gain from her militant ecclesiastical politicians; but they must be militant Christians strong in the Holy Spirit first.

NOTES

1.   *The Centenary of Saint Peter and the General Council* (London, 1867).

2.   *England and Christendom* (London, 1867); see also note 23.

3.   *The Temperance Speeches of Cardinal Manning* (London, 1894).

4.   See E. R. Norman, 'Cardinal Manning and the Temporal Power', in Derek Beales and Geoffrey Best (eds), *History, Society and the Churches: Essays in Honour of Owen Chadwick* (Cambridge, 1985) p. 239.

5. *The Visit of Garibaldi to England: A Letter to the Right Hon. Edward Cardwell, M.P.* (London, 1864); reprinted in *Miscellanies* Vol. I (London, 1877).

6. *Caesarism and Ultramontanism* (second edition, London, 1874).

7. *The Vatican Decrees in their Bearing on Civil Allegiance* (London, 1875).

8. *Sermons on Ecclesiastical Subjects*, 3 vols (London, 1863-73).

9. *Miscellanies*, 3 vols (London, 1877-88).

10. *The Eternal Priesthood* (London, 1883). I have a cheap English edition of 1931.

11. Maisie Ward, *The Wilfrid Wards and the Transition I. The Nineteenth Century* (London, 1934), p. 220.

12. *Selections from the Strand Magazine* Vol. I 1891 (London, 1966) pp. 32-4.

13. *The Temporal Mission of the Holy Ghost; or, Reason and Revelation* (London, 1865).

14. *The True Story of the Vatican Council* (London, 1877), p. 147.

15. *Religio Viatoris* (4th edition, no date, end of preliminary discourse).

16. *Ibidem*, p. 8.

17. Henry Edward Manning, 'That Legitimate Authority is an Evidence of Truth' (read 14 May 1872), p. 7 [*Papers read before the Metaphysical Society, 1871-79*] (London, 1871-79), British Library, Cup.400. c.2 (7).

18. See, for example, Maisie Ward, *The Wilfrid Wards*, p. 222.

19. Henry Edward Manning 'What is the Relation of the Will to Thought?', (1871) p. 1. [*Papers read before the Metaphysical Society, 1871-79*] London, 1871, British Library, Cup. 400.c.2 (1).

20. *Sin: and its Consequences* (London, 1874), pp. 9, 11.

21. James Pereiro, '"Truth Before Peace": Manning and Infallibility', *Recusant History*, Vol. 21. No. 2 (October, 1992), pp. 218-53.

22. *The Unity of the Church* (London, 1842).

23. *The Workings of the Holy Spirit in the Church of England*, (originally published London, 1864: reprinted in *England and Christendom*, 1867), pp. 88-9.

24. Jeffrey P. von Arx, S.J., 'Archbishop Manning and the *Kulturkampf*', *Recusant History*, Vol. 21, No. 2 (October, 1992), pp. 254-66.

25. Ralph Gibson, *A Social History of French Catholicism, 1789-1914* (London, 1989).

26. Geoffrey Rowell, 'The Bounds of Purgatory', *Hell and the Victorians* (Oxford, 1974), pp. 153-79.

27. 'There's a wideness in God's mercy', *The English Hymnal* (London, 1906), pp. 396-7.

28. David Newsome, *The Parting of Friends: The Wilberforces and Henry Manning* (London, 1966) p. 326.

29. Christopher O'Gorman, 'A History of Henry Manning's Religious Opinions, 1808-1832', *Recusant History*, Vol. 21, No 2 (October, 1992), pp. 152-66.

30. *The Love of Jesus to Penitents* (Dublin, 1866), pp. 12, 9, 11.

31. John Henry Newman, *Discourses Addressed to Mixed Congregations* (London, 1850), pp. 23-44.

32. *Sin: and its Consequences*, p. 246.

33. *The Present Crisis of the Holy See Tested by Prophecy* (London, 1861) p. xii, and pp. 87-8. See also E. R. Norman, *op. cit.* pp. 239-41.

34. *St. Peter's Pence: An Address to the Congregation of S. Mary of the Angels, Bayswater* (London, 1861),p. 20.

XIII

CHRIST AND THE CHURCH IN ROBERT ISAAC WILBERFORCE'S *DOCTRINE OF THE INCARNATION*

Geoffrey Rowell

Robert Isaac Wilberforce (1802-1857) was the second son of William Wilberforce (1779-1833). He, and his younger brother, Henry, eventually found their home in the Roman Catholic Church. Samuel, three years younger than Robert and two years older then Henry, remained in the Church of England as an outstanding Bishop of Oxford. It was Robert who was the most significant as a theologian. His theology was expressed in three major theological works, *The Doctrine of the Incarnation* (1848), *The Doctrine of Holy Baptism* (1849), and *The Doctrine of the Holy Eucharist* (1853). This paper will be particularly concerned with the first of these works, which has as its full title *The Doctrine of the Incarnation of our Lord Jesus Christ, in its relation to Mankind and to the Church.*

The book falls roughly into two halves. The first is Christological, tracing the doctrine of the Person of Christ through the debates of the early centuries. The second section builds on this and develops the consequences of the doctrine of the Incarnation for understanding the Church and salvation.

In the introduction Wilberforce indicates one of his major concerns. The dispensation of the Gospel is personal, objective and revealed. 'It rests not, like the theories of Rationalistic philosophy, on the self-relying advent of an external Saviour'.[1] Wilberforce is conscious, from his own Evangelical family roots, of the power of the subjective aspects of religious faith. Yet, if religion is a divine reality, it 'implies the existence of certain outward facts, external to ourselves, which have a being independent of our thoughts, and are the objects of our consideration'. If our inward feelings are not to be 'only a delusive dream', the Incarnation and the Atonement must have 'an actual place in the world of realities'. Subjective feelings require an objective correlative if they are to have substance and the power to endure. More is needed than the conviction of a Harriet Martineau that 'the value is in the act of faith, more than in its object'.[2]

Throughout *The Doctrine of the Incarnation* Wilberforce contrasts Rationalist philosophy (by which he often, though not always, means Romantic subjective idealism) with a religion of revelation:

> Rationalism makes the individual the starting point for improvement whereas the Church's starting point is Christ. The first is for dealing with nature as it finds it; it takes man such as he is, with the powers and faculties which he possesses, and supposes that their cultivation may enable him to shake off the evils and infirmities which all deplore. The man himself, therefore, is the commencement of all renewal; he may use God's grace — indeed he may invoke the name of Christ — but in himself is the ultimate principle of renovation.[3]

His conversion, or transformation, precedes any relation to Christ. By contrast, for the Church it is Christ who is the origin, channel and centre of regeneration. 'In Him and not in them is the original principle of movement':

> The restoration of the ancient pattern of man is not attained through the natural perfection of individuals, but because in Christ, Our Lord, was the personal presence of that Divine Word, which was above nature.

Through the sacramental system we are bound to Christ, 'and the restoration of every man is due to that great gift which was bestowed upon our common nature through the Incarnation of Christ'.[4]

In education the Church bases its teaching on 'the improvement of that renewed nature which, in Christ, our Lord, has been bestowed upon His brethren' — a reminder of the importance of the doctrine of baptismal regeneration to the Tractarians, a doctrine which John Keble affirmed as the very basis of pastoral, parochial and educational practice. By contrast 'Rationalist' philosophy appeals to 'natural gifts' and 'intellectual endowments', making these 'a sufficient ground for reform'. Again there is a reminder of Newman's strong emphasis, both in the Tamworth Reading Room Letters and in the later *Idea of a University*, on the necessity for more than knowledge if moral improvement is to be effected.

The Incarnation is the foundation of the Church system: 'Rationalism has its real foundation in that theory of Pantheism, which ends in deifying the natural powers of man', for

> put the Incarnation out of view, and Pantheism is the natural resource of reflective minds.

It implies 'that in man's life is a divine principle, akin to that all-embracing power which pervades the universe'. The truth, Wilberforce asserts, 'is not that man is naturally God, but that God has mercifully become man'.[5] Christ is the Pattern Man, by Office, by Nature, and by Sympathy.

In the succeeding six chapters Wilberforce builds on a patristic base to expound the doctrine of Christ as Very God and Very Man. He cites Hooker and Beveridge, and among German scholars builds particularly on the work of Dorner. Wilberforce is also familiar with Möhler's *Symbolik* and Baur's critique.[6] He insists that 'the Divine Nature which is at once the highest object of contemplation and the primary source of being' is necessarily the measure of our human conceptions: 'Our notions ... of things human, and the conceptions of mankind, are rather to be measured by this standard, than to measure it'. Like F. D. Maurice in his controversy with Mansel, he appeals to the Johannine text: 'This is life eternal, to know Thee the only true God, and Jesus Christ whom Thou hast sent' (John xvii.3):

> When men attempt therefore, as was done by Plato of old, and has been done with less excuse by the thinkers of modern Germany, to invent an intellectual Theogony out of their own conceptions, the attempt is so far useful, as it is looked upon as an illustration only and shadow of those great realities, which exist around and above us, and by Revelation have been made known to our minds.[7]

The intellectual schemes of German philosophical theologians from Kant to Hegel are, says Wilberforce, 'not without interest'. Simply because man was created in the image of God, 'there will be some appetency to admit those truths, which have their original in Him'. All speculative discourse about God is, however, fallacious, as it rests 'only on human conceptions and on the requirements of man's mind'.

> Unless the reality and original of all things be fixed in the actual Being of the self-existent Godhead, there can be no basis on which to ground our thoughts. The real existence of the Ever-Blessed Trinity must be received as before all creation, and as underlying all knowledge.[8]

Wilberforce cites Augustine's *De Trinitate* to underline this point: '*In illa Trinitate summa origo est rerum omnium, et perfectissima pulchritudo et beatissima delectatio*'.[9]

In chapter seven Wilberforce turns to consider 'the effect which has been produced upon the condition of mankind by our Lord's Incarnation' — the doctrine of Mediation.[10] He sets out this argument in seven chapters leading to some ten pages of conclusion. The chapter divisions are as follows: (1) The teaching, example and sacrifice of

Christ; (2) Christ as Advocate — his heavenly intercession; (3) The Spiritual Presence of Christ as Mediator; (4) The Presence of Christ in his Church, his mystical Body; (5) The theology of corporate worship in relation to the Church; (6) Sacraments as means of union with the manhood of Christ; (7) Christ as Mediator — the source of holiness and knowledge to mankind.

The mediation of Christ flows from his two-fold nature: 'To man He was manifested as a teacher and an example, while He offered to God the perfect sacrifice of our redemption'.[11] Through the life of Christ we are instructed in the precepts of the Gospel, 'reason has its employment and love its pattern'.[12] But it is not only an example of moral living that Christ gives us, it is more importantly an example of obedience to God. Wilberforce cites Bishop Butler — 'Submission to the will of God may be said to be the whole of religion' — and this Christ both exemplified and acquired 'through the perfect road of experience'.[13] And that obedience is 'an obedience unto death', the total offering of himself as the true sacrifice which in one sense fulfilled the law, and in another showed the true ground of the law: 'The offerings of the Law were built upon the offering of Christ: they were the type of a future reality, which cast its shadow beforehand on the Jewish nation'.[14] Christ is the centre in which all the ancient varieties of sacrifice meet. Christ, the God-man, was 'fitted by the wisdom of God for the service of mercy which he discharged': 'From Christ's Divinity there flowed such consecrating virtue, as made Him a fitting *Priest*, and such atoning efficacy as made Him a sufficient *Victim*'.[15] A priest, Wilberforce continues, 'is a Mediator in action', and Christ's priesthood is rooted in his constitution. 'It is the result of that personal union which binds man to God'. Citing John Damascene, Wilberforce argues that Christ's priestly consecration 'was that uniting of His Divine to His human nature whereby He was anointed the Son of God'.[16]

Turning to the Atonement, Wilberforce notes Anselm's position stated in *Cur Deus Homo* i.12, that 'it is not fitting that God should forgive sins without punishment'.[17] Such a view is, he suggests, speculative, and has neither direct Scriptural grounding, nor support in the Fathers, and he appeals to both Athanasius and Bishop Butler in support. There is a wise reserve in refusing to speculate on what abstract justice might make necessary.[18] What Christ achieved, through his sacrificial death, is a new life which needs to be communicated to mankind in as substantive a way as the death consequent upon the sin of Adam. That bond exists in sacramental grace and Church union, 'but the gift itself was purchased for humanity at large, when its Head suffered in our common nature'.[19] The treatise of Richard Field, *Of the Church*, (Book V, 1610) is quoted in conclusion. Our 'restoration could not be wrought but by Him that should be the root, fountain, and beginning of supernatural and spiritual being, in whom the whole nature of mankind should be found in a more eminent sort than it was in Adam'.[20]

The Epistle to the Hebrews above all the New Testament writings emphasises the High Priesthood of Christ and his heavenly intercession. Having expounded its teaching Wilberforce comments that both Arian and Sabellian tendencies were current in contemporary theology and that in the end, though starting from different directions, they amounted to much the same thing. According to the Sabellian theory, he writes, 'there is no pleading of man's nature with God: the Son is merely a title substituted for His Father's name during the mediatorial government of the Church — the reality of His acts is evaporated — and a practical unbelief in His operations is justified by His real nonexistence in the world of external realities'.[21] The heavenly worship described in the Book of Revelation supplements the teaching of the Epistle to the Hebrews, and Wilberforce notes how Irenaeus, Clement and Origen link their understanding of the Church's worship closely to their belief in the reality of Christ's heavenly intercession and the worship of the heavenly places. The mediation of Christ is not something over and done with, an event in the past, but it is a present work. 'To this all prayer is relevant — on this all worship depends. The Church's service goes on from year to year, as His intercession is perpetually made and perpetually accepted.... Every prayer which we conclude in His name, is as much an appeal to His man's nature, as though in Psalm or Litany we were to number all His limbs and recount all the circumstances of His Passion'.[22]

To speak of Christ's *Presence* is, Wilberforce suggests, to sum up his actions as Mediator towards man: 'The efficacy of Christian prayers is because He is in the midst ... and the peculiar blessing conferred by the gift of the Holy Ghost, is explained to be his own return: "I will not leave you comfortless, I will come to you"'.[23] But how is this presence to be understood? Wilberforce is concerned to distinguish it from any idea of the immanent presence of God within the world. That, although true, remains at the level of natural religion. The Presence of Christ which is spoken of in Scripture is 'through that human nature which He has taken as the means of union between heaven and earth'.[24] Hooker, he notes, in the fifth book of *The Laws of Ecclesiastical Polity*, acknowledges that 'God hath in many ways, above the reach of our capacities, exalted that body, which it hath pleased Him to make His own'.[25] Hooker in turn is building on St Augustine: 'It behoveth us to take great heed, lest while we go about to maintain the glorious Deity of Him, which is man, we leave Him not the true bodily substance of a man'.[26] There can be little doubt that

Wilberforce would have been as doughty an opponent of many contemporary theologians who seem to have little serious place for the glorified humanity of Christ, as he was with the Sabellians of his own day. He was well aware of the problem of theological language, arguing strongly that it is a mistake to assume that because language is founded upon terms which derive from the world of sense, it therefore follows that what such language is used to denote is merely figurative: 'The necessary deficiencies of language do not derogate from the certainty of those existences to which our consciousness witnesses, and which lead us up by the shortest track to the very throne of God'. 'Presence' may be a figurative term, but it is no less a reality. It is through the Spirit that the 'sanctified humanity of the Son of God exerts its renewing influence upon the defiled humanity of His brethren'.[27]

The end and purpose of the Spirit's work in enabling Christ's presence within us, is *theosis* or 'deification' — a theme which was very important to the Tractarians, as also to the Greek Fathers, and to many of the seventeenth-century Anglican divines. It is no accident that Wilberforce quotes Lancelot Andrewes, who in his fourth sermon on the Nativity (1609) speaks of our adoption as sons of God: 'We made the sons of God, as He the Son of man; we made partakers of His divine, as He of our human nature'.[28] The union of mankind with Christ is not, affirms Wilberforce, 'a mere imitation — the following of a good model, the fixing of thoughts upon One who has shown in the clearest manner, how God may be served and man benefitted — it is an actual and real union, whereby all renewed men are joined to the second, as they were by nature to the first Adam'.[29] Christians are engrafted into Christ's glorified human nature. St Cyril had reproved those who taught that 'only the Deity of Christ is the vine'. 'Christ ... both as God and man', Hooker writes, 'that true vine, whereof we both spiritually and corporally are branches':[30]

> The assertion then of Our Lord's Presence according to His human nature, and of our real union with the manhood of Christ, is no technical or unnecessary dogma, but that pregnant fact on which is built our present regeneration and our future hope.[31]

Wilberforce's concern is to defend Catholic orthodoxy against both Arian and Sabellian error:

> To what would the Arian supposition lead men, save to trust in the Mediation of a created being, and thus to reverence the creature rather than the Creator. And this was the very stain of Pagan worship. And what is the tendency of Sabellian error, save to lose sight of any mode of Mediation, and in the pride of intellect to

betake itself to the abstract contemplation of God? And the result in
this case would be the bare Theism of the philosophic or the dreamy
Pantheism of the poetic mind.[32]

The reality and presence of Christ is objective. Our participation in his
manhood, is brought about in our union with the Church. And the
description of the Church as Christ's mystical body is fundamental.
And the unity of the Church flows out of its nature as Christ's body:

> If the unity of the Church were nothing but that those who bear the
> same name may be classed together, as we bestow the name of
> Platonists on those who followed the disciple of Socrates, its
> assertion as a doctrine would be altogether unmeaning.[33]

The Adam-Christ parallel is fundamental. Christ, the Second Adam,
who is 'a life-giving Spirit', is the means whereby the life of glory is
communicated to us. The Laudian divine, Thomas Jackson, wrote that
although 'the Divine Nature ... is the prime fountain of life to all', and
though it is 'inexhaustible in itself', yet it is 'a fountain whereof we
cannot drink, save as it is derived unto us through the human nature
of Christ'.[34] It is this spiritual reality which is at the heart of the
Church's unity. And the unity of the Church, Wilberforce affirms, is
the earthly counterpart of the communion of the Trinity.

The Trinitarian basis of the Church's unity is mediated through the
manhood of the Incarnate Word. It is this peculiarity which stands
opposed to the theory of Rationalism:

> The principle of Rationalism is, that man's improvement may be
> effected through those gifts which God bestowed upon him by
> creation, inasmuch as sufficient means of intercourse with the
> Supreme Spirit were provided by the law of his nature. Whereas the
> Church deals with man as a fallen race, whose original means of
> intercourse with God have been obstructed, and which needs a new
> and supernatural channel for the entrance of heavenly gifts. And this
> channel has been provided throught the Man Jesus Christ.[35]

The ordinances of the Church — sacraments, holy things, places and
persons, 'are a series of instruments whereby the sanctified manhood
of the Mediator diffuses itself as a life-giving seed through the mass of
humanity'.[36] To reject those sacraments and ordinances is tantamount
to rejecting the mediation of Christ.

If contemporary philosophical and unsacramental religion was a
prime target for Wilberforce, he sees the Quakers as exemplifying
similar characteristics in an earlier generation. The Quaker disuse of
sacraments and appeal to the inner light meant that, although Quakerism 'might retain the phraseology of the Gospel', it tended to substitute

natural religion for revealed. Wilberforce cites the Non-Juror, Charles Leslie (1660-1722), the author of several substantial anti-Quaker treatises, notably *The Snake in the Grass* (1690). A strong defender of orthodox Christianity against contemporary Deism, Leslie also saw the illuminism of Quakers and other 'inner-light' groups as ultimately inimical to Christianity. Whereas Jeremy Taylor had followed the Fathers in speaking of the Blessed Sacrament as the extension of the Incarnation, the Quakers by their rejection of sacraments, and their substitution of 'a dreamy notion of the abstract intercourse between the minds of faithful men and the governing Mind of the Universe', opened the door to Rationalism. And 'Rationalism', Wilberforce comments, 'is but the entrance to that deeper abyss of Pantheism, towards which the rejection of the sacramental system has a tendency to conduct'.[37] A religion of inner feelings, and a religion of abstractions, bypasses the sacramental system, the appointed means of grace. Wilberforce notes that Hooker had seen a resemblance to the Gnostic repudiation of the sacraments in those who 'fixing their minds wholly on the known necessity of faith', imagined 'that nothing but faith' was 'necessary for the attainment of all grace'.[38] Hooker is supported by Thomas Jackson who stresses that God's forgiveness and reconciliation is only mediated to us through his Son, 'that is, through His humanity, as the organ or conduit, or as the only bond by which we are united and reconciled unto the Divine nature'.[39] Quakerism, anticipating Rationalism, is a kind of Sabellianism, which implies (like Joachim of Fiore in an earlier age) that the work of the Spirit supersedes the work of Christ, as the institutional church of Peter with its order and sacraments will be replaced by the spiritual church of John. The Quakers, says Wilberforce, citing Leslie, 'deny any proper Incarnation of Christ ... yet they allow Jesus to be called Christ, from the dwelling of Christ in Him; but for the same reason they take the name of Christ to themselves and say that it belongs to them as well as to Jesus'.[40]

Turning from the Quakerism of the past to contemporary theologians, Wilberforce cites Schleiermacher and Archbishop Whately as instances of a connection between inadequate views of Christ's nature and 'a low estimate of the gifts of grace'. Schleiermacher, he notes, had contrasted Catholicism and Protestantism in the following manner:

> Catholicism is that system which represents the relation of the individual to Christ to be dependent on his relation to the Church; Protestantism that which represents the relation of the individual to the Church to be dependent on his relation to Christ.[41]

To make such a statement involves, Wilberforce claims, 'a virtual denial of the spiritual nature of the Church', and makes of the Church no more than 'a human system devised for the more convenient working of religion among men'.[42] Following Dorner's critique of Schleiermacher, Wilberforce points out that it is Schleiermacher's denial of the Son of God taking man's nature into the unity of his Person, and so making the personality of Christ dependent on the Personality of the Second Person of the Trinity, that undermines any real grounding for a high doctrine of the Church. Whately is likewise defective, having a low view of the sacraments and yet a high view of Church authority, with the consequence that 'harshness and technicality' are infused into the Gospel system:

> The Kingdom of Christ seems as though it was designed to limit the gifts of grace rather than to extend them. The Church assumes the austerity of a Sabine mother rather than the affectionate loving-kindness of the daughter of Zion.[43]

The doctrine of our union with the manhood of Christ in his mystical body, and Christ's true Presence and Mediation are the true security against the substitution of the Church as a formal system. The life of the Church depends 'not on gifts of government but on the gifts of grace'. Forgetfulness of the inward spiritual principle of the Church's life leads to external party bickering and conflict. The holiness which springs from union with Christ is essential to the true unity of the Church:

> Church-obedience depends on the authority to bless, not on the power to govern. Its rule is not coercive, but parental; it stands on the communication of gifts, not the enactment of penalties.... Thus in the world of grace, as in that of nature, is affection the root of duty; and men's relation to the Church of their Baptism is built on that fundamental law, which is the basis of social life.[44]

> The Church of Christ is His Body; His Presence its life; its blessing the gift of spiritual union with His man's nature. Where this is given there is opened for men the gift of life, and state of salvation. Our duty towards that portion of it, in which our lot is cast, arises from love to itself, not from hatred to others; the lines of our heritage are marked out by affection and not by antipathy. For in it lies our actual participation in the Mediation of Christ.... For such has been the appointment of His sovereign wisdom, that so in the person of a Mediator the true ladder might be fixed, whereby God might descend to His creatures, and His creatures might ascend to God.[45]

Common worship gives expression to the 'quickening energy' of Christ which is at the heart of the life of the Church. It fulfils all to which the worship and ritual of Judaism had pointed. Christ's mediation, moreover, is at the heart of Christian worship, and, rightly understood, means that there can be no merely individual relation to Christ, independent of a corporate participation in the worship of the Church: 'A system of worship upon earth is the necessary correlative to a work of intercession in heaven. The one implies the other'.[46] Earthly worship is the correlative of the heavenly intercession of Christ and therefore 'those things which were done on earth in the Church's united acts' were 'made part of that grand sacrifice which has its consummation in heaven'.[47] All Christian worship is therefore sacrificial, but the Eucharist, the heart of Christian worship, which is the centre of union with Christ, is 'most emphatically the Christian sacrifice'.[48] Wilberforce interestingly cites the millenarian Joseph Mede (1586-1638), who believed the Pope to be Antichrist, and yet defended strongly a sacrificial understanding of the Eucharist, to the effect that 'when the Lamb of God lies slain upon the holy table', then was the moment when the 'sacrifice of Praise and Prayer through Jesus Christ' was 'mystically represented in the creatures of bread and wine'.[49] But the only ground on which the Eucharist can have that character of a sacrifice is 'through its participation in the central work of Mediation, the offering, *i.e.* of the body of Jesus Christ once for all':[50]

> Through this bread and this cup, that which is offered as a true sacrifice in heaven, is present as a real though immaterial agent in the Church's ministrations. So that what is done by Christ's ministers below, is a constituent part of that general work which the one great High Priest performs in heaven: through the intervention of His heavenly Head, the earthly sacrificer truly exhibits to the Father that body of Christ, which is the one only sacrifice for sins; each visible act has its efficacy through those invisible acts of which it is the earthly expression; and things done on earth are one with those done in heaven.[51]

If Christian worship, and especially the Eucharist, is something done, Wilberforce writes, 'merely within man himself, in the region of his own feelings and intellect', then the language of sacrifice would be inappropriate. But if it is something belonging to the whole Church, and linked to Christ the Mediator, then such language is indeed appropriate. Is Christ's Incarnation a truth, or a fictitious representation (the doctrine Wilberforce labels as Sabellian)?

For Wilberforce the truth of the Incarnation and its concomitant the truth of Christ's heavenly intercession and continuing mediation, supplies both the grounds for a sacrificial understanding of Christian worship (and particularly the Eucharist), and for the justification of ministerial priesthood:

> If Christ is still maintaining a real intercession — if He still pleads that sacrifice, in the merit whereof we must partake if we would be truly joined to His man's nature — then is there ample scope for that sacerdotal system, by which some actual *thing* is still to be effected, and in which some agents must be still employed.[52]

If Sabellianism is true, then Christ's office is at an end and there is no longer any need for ministers; but if his office continues, then 'for its participation' certain acts and agents are needed and 'we have an exact precedent in the Jewish system for bestowing the name of sacrifice and priesthood upon the media which are thus employed'.[53] Public worship and public ministry, liturgy and ministerial priesthood, go together. The set forms of worship with their prescribed responses give a place for the service of the whole community. Where such a responsive pattern of worship is lost, the minister comes to be seen mainly as a teacher 'whose office is not to address God but themselves'. The Protestant churches of Europe have sadly succumbed, Wilberforce suggests, to the exaltation of the preacher. To the loss of the collective or corporate character of worship, Wilberforce believes, is to be attributed the growth of unbelief in many parts of the Continent.

In Chapter XIII Wilberforce turns more particularly to a consideration of the sacraments. 'They are channels to the faithful of those supernatural gifts whereby God renews the soul'.[54] Sacraments lead to union with Christ, they are not merely acted prayer nor a teaching by example. They are both, in the words of the Prayer Book Catechism, an 'outward and visible sign' and 'an inward and spiritual grace'. Wilberforce is a strong believer in baptismal regeneration, but notes that such a high doctrine of baptism means only that it is regarded as 'the appointed means for that union with Christ, whereby men may obtain strength to serve Him'. 'Baptism neither exempts devout men from the necessity of a watchful life, nor careless men from the necessity of conversion. It is a reason why the watchfulness of the one should be more unvaried, and the conversion of the other more complete.... To receive gifts of grace is in itself not security against losing them'.[55] The first gift of life is derived from that union with Christ which he originally bestows. Grace is prevenient. 'Unless the beginnings of the spiritual life are laid in this antecedent gift of union with Christ, we pass over of necessity to the Rationalistic principle which would attribute them to that natural relation of the soul to God which it had by creation'.[56] The Eucharist was declared by Hooker to be recognised by all as 'a true and a real participation of Christ, who thereby imparteth Himself, even His whole entire Person, *as a mystical head* unto every soul that receiveth Him'. But since the beginning of the eighteenth century the latitudinarian denigration and disparagement of the sacraments by those who, like Bishop Hoadly, regarded them as

no more than enacted sermons, a lower view had prevailed. This led
to the practical Sabellianism of Wilberforce's day. 'The real objection
against the sacramental system', he notes, 'does not arise from any
deficiency in its Scriptural authority ... but from the abstract improbab-
ility that external ordinances can be the means of obtaining internal
gifts'.[57]

In his final chapter Wilberforce endeavours to draw out on a larger
canvas the meaning of Christ's Mediation. In its effects on mankind at
large, he declares, 'it may be affirmed to be the producing principle
of holiness and of knowledge'.[58] Human expectations and longings are
fulfilled in the coming of Christ. The dream of a millenium or a
golden age speaks of a society which will bestow blessings on every
individual. In a surprising and interesting reference, Wilberforce cites
D. F. Strauss's *Leben Jesu* as a witness to such a longing: 'the key of
the whole Christian system; and ... the subject of all its assertions we
must take not [to be] an individual, *i.e.* Christ, but an idea — a
realized and actual idea ... this idea is humanity viewed collectively:
humanity is the union of two natures, it is God incarnate'.[59] For
Wilberforce this is just a strong assertion of the error of supposing that
the regeneration of mankind will flow from social attempts. It denies
any reality of or necessity for grace. Through Christ God bestows on
us both holiness and knowledge, as 'an imputed and an infused or
'engrafted' gift' — 'bestowed from without upon the faithful, as an
object of contemplation; and communicated likewise to the body of the
Church, as an internal principle of teaching and guidance'.[60] The
Church receives an imparted treasure of truth — the Scriptures — and
an engrafted principle enabling those Scriptures to be comprehended.
We have been given the gift of reason, but reason alone will not
suffice. Both Locke's empiricism and Kant's categories are too
narrowly limiting: 'Our individual reason is not large enough to satisfy
the cravings of our hearts'. It is faith to which we are called. Yet that
faith requires interpretation and guidance, and this cannot be left
simply to the individual, the appeals to the inner light of Quakers in
England or Semler in Germany. Both the claim to an autonomous
superior reason and the claim to individual illumination are in the end
denials of Christ's mediation (once again Wilberforce's *bête noire* of
Sabellianism appears). Church authority is, for Wilberforce, the place
where faith is rightly judged and guided, and to maintain such
authority is 'to assert the empire of grace as opposed to that of
nature'.[61] Although, as with the nature of moral rules, there is an
inevitable uncertainty, there is a broad consensus of faith that is clear
enough, summed up in the creeds of the undivided Church. Just as the
corporate faith of the Church supersedes private judgement, so the
collective testimony of the Christian community must outweigh the

private judgement of any single portion of the Christian body. Always it must be remembered that in the perfect condition of the Church, 'unity is as plain a characteristic as holiness':[62]

> Knowledge and holiness, coming to us through Christ our Lord, are attributes of His Body Mystical by grace, as to His Sacred Person they pertain by nature. Now division in this Body is sin; and sin being the privation of the one of these is fatal to the other. And their blending and commingling nature is evidenced by their perfect union in Him, in whom alone either dwells completely. For knowledge is not perfect, save in Him whose nature is love. And if in man it is to be completely manifest, it can only be through the acquisition of that state, of which man's first dwelling-place was an anticipation, when the Tree of Knowledge stands by the Tree of Life in the midst of the Paradise of God.[63]

NOTES

1. R. I. Wilberforce, *The Doctrine of the Incarnation of our Lord Jesus Christ, in its Relation to Mankind and to the Church* (London, 1849), [*DIJC*], pp. 1-2

2. *DIJC* pp. 4-5, 6

3. *Ibidem*, p. 12

4. *Ibidem*, pp. 12-13

5. *Ibidem*, pp. 13-14

6. *Ibidem*, pp. 72-3, 123 & n.

7. *Ibidem*, p. 178

8. *Ibidem*, pp. 178-9

9. Augustine, *De Trinitate*, vi. 12, cited, *DIJC* p. 179n.

10. *DIJC* p. 211

11. *Ibidem*, p. 219

12. *Ibidem*, pp. 220-1

13. *Ibidem*, pp. 222-3

14. *Ibidem*, p. 225

15. *Ibidem*, pp. 228-9

16. *Ibidem*, p. 230

17. *Ibidem*, p. 235

18. *Ibidem*, pp. 237-8

19. *Ibidem*, p. 239

20. *Ibidem*, p. 242. Field, *On the Church*, V.11.

21. *DIJC* p. 255

22. *Ibidem*, p. 263

23. *Ibidem*, pp. 264-5

24. *Ibidem*, p. 273

25. *Ibidem*, p. 276. R. Hooker, *Laws of Ecclesiastical Polity*, V.54.9.
26. *DIJC* p. 278
27. *Ibidem*, p. 286
28. *Ibidem*, p. 292. Lancelot Andrewes, *Sermons*, I, L.A.C.T., p. 59
29. *DIJC* pp. 292-3
30. *Ibidem*, p. 298; Hooker, *Eccl. Polity*, V.59.9.
31. *DIJC* p. 298
32. *Ibidem*, p. 308
33. *Ibidem*, p. 316
34. T. Jackson, *Commentary on the Creed*, xi.3.10, *DIJC* pp. 318-9n.
35. *DIJC* pp. 321-2
36. *Ibidem*, p. 322
37. *Ibidem*, pp. 329-30
38. *Ibidem*, p. 333
39. *Ibidem*, p. 334, Jackson, *Commentary on the Creed*, xi.3.12.
40. C. Leslie, *The Snake in the Grass*, Works, II, p. 67
41. *Die christliche Glaube*
42. *DIJC* p. 342
43. *Ibidem*, pp. 345-6
44. *Ibidem*, p. 350
45. *Ibidem*, p. 351
46. *Ibidem*, p. 366
47. *Ibidem*.
48. *Ibidem*.
49. J. Mede, *Works*, ii.2., p. 357, 'That the Christian Service is an Oblation provided by the Father'. *DIJC* p. 368
50. *DIJC* p. 369
51. *Ibidem*, pp. 371-2
52. *Ibidem*, p. 381
53. *Ibidem*, p. 352
54. *Ibidem*, p. 406
55. *Ibidem*, p. 439
56. *Ibidem*, p. 442
57. *Ibidem*, p. 454
58. *Ibidem*, p. 457
59. *Ibidem*, p. 460. D.F. Strauss, *Leben Iesu*, Sec. 149, Vol. ii, p. 767
60. *DIJC* p. 474
61. *Ibidem*, p. 523
62. *Ibidem*, p. 529
63. *Ibidem*, pp. 529-30

XIV

'THE MOST TURBULENT PRIEST OF THE OXFORD DIOCESE': THOMAS WILLIAM ALLIES AND THE QUEST FOR AUTHORITY 1837-1850

V. Alan McClelland

Judgements of the personality and significance of Thomas William Allies (1813-1903) have been richly diverse. To David Newsome in *The Parting of Friends,* Allies was 'the most turbulent priest of the Oxford diocese',[1] a man variously characterized as 'prickly and stubborn',[2] driven by 'Puseyite excesses',[3] 'a very tiresome man', both 'peevish and querulous'.[4] Although such acidities are diluted in Newsome's more recent study, *The Convert Cardinals,*[5] he sees the main importance of Allies as encapsulated within the context of an influential relationship with Manning, not dissimilar from that acknowledged between W G Ward and Newman in the 1840s. As Ward's articles in *The British Critic* and his publication in 1844 of *The Ideal of the Christian Church* precipitated Newman towards the irrevocable step of submission to Rome at the time when, he declared, he wished to remain in peace and stillness,[6] so Allies, with an equally urgent logic, by the publication four years later of his *Journal in France*, is seen to impel Manning to confront more rapidly the final crisis generated by his theological position.

Other scholars have viewed Allies in a less constricted way. Professor A.C.F. Beales considered that after the conversion of Allies to Rome in 1850, he became 'the greatest of the Catholic lay leaders in the entire century',[7] a view endorsed by the biographer of Mary Frances Lescher, 1825-1904,[8] who regards his work for education in general and teacher-education in particular, between 1853 and 1890, to have been crucial for the growth and development of the Roman Catholic community in England. This analysis of his Catholic life has been confirmed by Mary Griset Holland in her doctoral study on *The British Catholic Press and the Educational Controversy, 1847-1865.*[9] In a different context, Dwight Culler and Sheridan Gilley have shown how concerned Newman was to secure the services of Allies to teach the philosophy of history at the Catholic University in Dublin,[10] that curious subject the parameters of which were defined by Newman as the 'science of which historical facts are the basis, or the laws on which it pleases Almighty Providence to conduct the political and social world'.[11] Although Allies was disconcerted at the comprehensiveness of the brief, his selection by Newman was a tribute to his intellectual and scholarly reputation, to which he responded with verve and imagination. Newman was impressed by the skill of Allies as a writer and he once commented favourably upon the eloquence of his prose.[12] Other scholarly testimonies have been offered: Owen Chadwick to Allies's great work for elementary education,[13] Edward Norman to his administrative wisdom. [14] Anne Pollen was perhaps his greatest admirer. Writing the life of her father, she described Allies as 'a mental athlete', possessed of 'disinterested courage',[15] a thinker and writer of considerable ability, zeal and honesty. These qualities are exemplified in considering the contribution of Allies to the main theological debates of the years 1837 to 1850, a period embracing the dates of his ordination to the diaconate in the Anglican Church and his ultimate conversion to Rome. His autobiography, *A Life's Decision*,[16] when published in 1880, was described by Newman as a 'document' not to be measured by 'a market price'.[17] The book was a singularly honest, if somewhat patchy analysis that was to form the basis of the short biography written by his daughter in 1907.[18]

In 1833, the year when *The Arians of the Fourth Century* was published, containing what Wilfrid Ward described as Newman's 'remarkable generalisations on the genesis and rationale of creeds and dogmatic formulae',[19] Thomas William Allies entered upon the eight-year tenure of his fellowship at Wadham College. It was the momentous year when the first of the *Tracts for the Times* appeared. It was the year in which Henry Edward Manning quitted his fellowship at Merton to begin a curacy with John Sargent, the rector of Lavington. He was shortly to embark there on a three-year study of Tradition that would led to the publication of his views on the nature of the Apostolic Succession in a sermon of 1835 on 'The Unity of the Church', followed by an edition and subsequent translation of St Vincent of Lerins on 'The Antiquity and Universality of the Catholic Faith against the Profane Novelties of our Heretics'[20] and then, the *Catena Patrum*, which formed Tract 78 of the *Tracts for the Times* before it was encapsulated by Keble into the new edition of his sermon on *Primitive Tradition*.[21]

In 1833, Allies was twenty years old; the oil painting executed by Mrs Carpenter when he was seventeen[22] endorses Anne Pollen's comment of a 'handsome' and 'dapper' young man[23] exuding a measure of self-assurance and sartorial elegance that sometimes accompanies smallness of stature. A subsequent description of him as that 'little bantam cock' was not entirely misplaced if applied to both his appearance and personality.[24] The son of the rector of Wormington, near Cheltenham, Allies was the surviving child of his father's first marriage, his mother having died, aged twenty-one, one week after the birth. Following a sojourn at Bristol Grammar School, Thomas Allies was educated at Eton before entering Wadham College, Oxford, in 1830, then one of the centres of Evangelical tradition in the University.[25] As a Fellow he served under the wardenship of Benjamin Symons, a ponderous, humourless Evangelical destined to become one of the strongest opponents of Tractarianism among the college heads.[26] Even within the defences of Wadham, however, the Tractarian amoebae began to extend their pseudopodia in one direction or another. Allies found Richard Church at Wadham since 1832, for instance, before he took a fellowship at Oriel five years later.

The main formative influence upon Allies in early life was undoubtedly Edward Coleridge in whose house at Eton he had resided. Coleridge was the son-in-law of John Keate, headmaster of Eton from 1809 to 1834. When Edward Hawtrey succeeded Keate in 1834, Coleridge was allowed a good deal of reforming latitude. A committed high churchman, Coleridge brought a new sense of care and professionalism to his tutorial duties that won an instant response from the young studious Allies. The two were to remain constant and cherished friends. Allies was the first winner at Eton of the Newcastle Scholarship in the year it was established and he was to gratify Coleridge by returning to Eton in 1838 to help him prepare a clutch of other promising youths for the examination. Richard Ollard has observed that 'Coleridge's high church convictions perhaps played their part in disposing so many of his ablest pupils to follow Newman into the Church of Rome'.[27] Be that as it may, he certainly introduced a new philosophy into Eton life that changed the relationship of teacher to pupil for the better. It was Coleridge who recommended Allies to attend, when in London, the Margaret Street Chapel in Cavendish Square where the Cambridge Tractarian, William Dodsworth, who was to become a close confidante of Manning in 1835, conducted dignified liturgical celebrations and preached Tractarian theology from the pulpit.[28] There, Allies maintained, he imbibed higher views as to the nature of the Church, the episcopate and the sacraments. 'From the first', he subsequently reflected, 'I determined never to leave the church when there was a communion, and this was every Sunday at Dodsworth's. I always had a great reverence for that sacrament, and remember the thrill with which I first assisted as a deacon in that church'.[29]

Allies was made deacon in 1838 and began to take pupils in London. It was a lonely and isolated year, his father having died unexpectedly at a time when he felt unformed in his religious views. He outlines his sense of bewilderment and his lack of system and order: 'my mind was ever longing for a connected and consecutive system *in rebus divinis*. I sought it hither and thither, in a desultory manner, and in heterogeneous authors, without knowing what I was in search of'.[30] In seeking such a *lebensraum* he considered it, in later life, to have been unpredictable which choice of theological opinion he would adopt. But through all his beliefs, he could discern the need for the Church to be visibly one and for the sacraments to be seen as the treasured conduits of grace. In 1838 he dined with W G Ward who told him much about Tractarian beliefs and, subsequently, Coleridge reinforced Ward's arguments, pointing out that any reasonable man must agree with the Oxford School.

Allies began to read some of Newman's sermons. 'The sense of physical isolation and solitude which had affected his spirits grievously was resolved by marriage in 1840 to Eliza Hall Newman, the fulgent eighteen-year old half-sister of the Revd Thomas Herding Newman of Magdalen with whom he had become friendly in Oxford. In May of the same year he became chaplain to the Bishop of London. Charles James Blomfield has been reported as being by nature 'high-handed, sarcastic, meddlesome, hasty, overbearing', his critics maintaining 'even when he smiled, he smiled episcopally', that 'he was always conscious of dignity'.[31] Although an efficient administrator and, indeed, an eloquent preacher, Blomfield lacked the common appeal and he bore criticism and opposition ill. In theological issues he was a moderate high churchman but one reluctant to be associated with coterie or party. With a reputation among Tractarians of being something of a trimmer, he was to favour the Jerusalem Bishopric scheme in 1841 and oppose Hampden's appointment to the see of Hereford six years later. In the year of the nomination of Allies to be his chaplain, Blomfield subscribed £50 to the cost of the memorial to Cranmer, Latimer and Ridley in Oxford. For Allies to be chaplain to such an unpredictable prelate was fraught with difficulty from the outset and, not being accustomed to remaining quiescent when matters of principle were at stake, he soon fell into disfavour.

Two years into his priesthood, the commitment of Allies to Tractarianism was still in its infancy. He was eager to learn. At a single stroke, he tells us, he purchased a hundred-pounds worth of the Fathers (Augustine, Chrysostom, Basil, Athanasius and others) and began regular study.[32] Prior to this, what he knew of the Fathers was derived from Newman's works and the *Tracts for the Times*. In later years, he was to analyse this period of theological development, referring to two sermons he preached on the unity of the Church. He dwelt 'on the *sacramentum* of unity as all-important' and his belief 'in such a doctrine of unity, as again in the doctrine of the Real Presence, of baptismal regeneration, and the apostolical succession' was stronger even at that time than his belief in the Anglican Church.[33] Throughout the period of his chaplaincy his sympathies were with the Tractarian position and, under the spiritual direction of Dodsworth, he began to pray earnestly and to fast, especially on Fridays. Two questions he set himself to answer: is the Anglican Church faithful to the Apostolic precept and is it identical with the teaching of the Fathers?

Allies had seen the publication of the first part of Froude's *Remains* in 1838 as part of the desire to elevate and purify the Church of England rather than an attempt to Romanize it. The publication of the *Remains* has been described as 'the greatest tactical mistake in the history of the movement'; it polarized viewpoints, 'alienated the sympathy of moderate high churchmen and aroused the suspicion and hostility of its opponents'.[34] Yet, Allies would have found sympathy with the view that Froude had the most right to the title 'Anglo-Catholic' because he went beyond the apologetic task of proving the Church of England to be truly Catholic to the one of following Catholic principles to a legitimate conclusion. Froude's open exposure of himself to the Spirit of Truth, wherever he encountered it, found a warm reception in the thought of Allies, as articulated in *A Life's Decision*.[35] If he had been asked in 1842, before he left the service of Bishop Blomfield, as to the basis of his belief in a particular doctrine, he would have answered 'Because the Catholic Church believed it'. He would then have looked for evidence to the Church of the fourth and fifth centuries.

With the brashness of a young man of twenty-eight holding decided views, Allies fell foul of Blomfleld by enunciating the Puseyite viewpoint in informal discussions. Blomfield was driven to informing Allies that all *he* approved of was 'moderate Oxford' and he plainly thought the views of Allies to be extreme.[36] The final *dénouement* arrived when Allies supported, in argument, the views held by Tractarians that Blomfleld had countenanced a Protestant, the King of Prussia, acting as one of the godfathers at the baptism of the Prince of Wales. Allies tells us that Blomfield's action 'deeply offended my Church principles', adding that 'with more sincerity than prudence I stated my scruple to the Bishop, who was not a little nettled at this remark of his chaplain'.[37] Within a few days, Blomfleld proposed Allies take the living of Launton, near Bicester, in Oxfordshire. There was little doubt this was a serious blow to the prospects of a young and recently married clergyman at the beginning of his career. More seriously, it removed him from the spiritual support of Dodsworth and the consolation of the Margaret Street liturgical revivalism. The living was pleasant enough at £60 a year with a secluded rectory and a large garden. The location was rural and isolated and, when he was inducted on his twenty-ninth birthday, Allies saw his life as one essentially of banishment from a future of intellectual and spiritual stimulation to that of a bucolic lifestyle, the rôle of a country parson in a State establishment. 'My heart sank within me', he wrote 'at the prospect of going there; sank within me during the interval between accepting the living and going to reside on it; sank within me on the evening of arriving there; and my wife shared in these feelings'.[38] Furthermore, he discovered his new parishioners were engrossed in rural pursuits and there was no intellectual challenge awaiting him. Immorality and irreligion were everywhere evident. He found it a depressing and daunting assignment.

The contrast with Manning's arrival at Lavington some nine years earlier is startling. A.E. Knox has referred to the 'dark hanging woods of Lavington, to the clump of beech and juniper giving it character, to the picturesque valley of the Rother and the circumjacent heathery commons, evergreen woods, brown copses, and cultivated fields'.[39] The beauty of the place was compelling and Manning was later to record how it soon captured his heart: 'I loved the little church under the green hillside, where the Morning and Evening Prayer and the music of the English Bible for seventeen years, became a part of my soul'.[40] Within seven years Manning had introduced two services each feast day as well as weekly communion, and in 1840 he began the practice of hearing confessions, having won the hearts and minds of his people. He instructed the poor in their homes as well as in the church, he concentrated upon eminently practical teaching on work, common and family life, poverty and death, as exemplified in the four published volumes of his Anglican sermons, a pastoral programme directed to the every-day needs of his shepherds and country farmers.[41]

The task of Allies was more difficult! He wished for a missionary rôle, similar to that of Dodsworth, by which he could bring the benefits of Tractarian scholarship and teaching to an appreciative people. He did not feel any bent to the pastoral office *per se*, but, he wrote, he had considerable love of preaching and 'very great feeling and love of theology as an organic structure of Divine doctrines'.[42] He attributed peevishness to Blomfield in selecting a vicarage that would be calculated to dampen down his Tractarian proclivities. Later, however, he was to see the banishment as a blessing in disguise. He soon realised he had time on his hands and he could now continue the study of the Fathers in earnest, a desire inflamed by his first meeting with John Henry Newman at a visitation in Oxford in June 1842. This meeting led to a correspondence between them in which Newman gave advice on reading the Fathers in a systematic way, ensuring that the process proceeded together with a study of divinity and/or ecclesiastical history.[43] As he saw the mighty folios ranged around his room, Allies felt he was not alone or isolated in his faith — 'I had a ground for what I believed (and) I stood on a higher footing than the system in which I lived, and was acquainted with those who enabled me to *judge* that system'.[44] The contact and correspondence with Newman was to continue and the latter was to become his confessor in 1844 and his spiritual adviser.

The first two years of the incumbency of Allies at Launton were given over to study, spiritual reflection and an attempt (without noticeable success) to reform and revitalize the spiritual commitment of his parish. It was a dispiriting time in which his parishioners did not respond to his warnings or consolations and did not seem to value his ministrations. With such a response he found that his reading and his pastoral duties, 'theory and practice, thought and works, seemed to fit into each other, and together produce dissatisfaction with the Anglican Church'.[45]

Following a short trip to Ramsgate and a visit from W.G. Ward in February 1843 (who spoke glowingly of the daily celebration of Mass by French priests), Allies decided to spend two weeks in France in 1843. Nothing interested the Tractarians more than to discover all they could about the religious habits, observances and inner life of the inhabitants of towns visited when journeying abroad. Their diaries indicate that although they were far from devoid of the normal interests of the tourist and that they could be enraptured by a splendid *vista,* an architectural gem or a public spectacle, it was essentially the ecclesiastical polity and quality of religious observance that really captivated their interest. Allies was not an exception to this generalization and he was accompanied to France by his wife, his sister-in-law and her husband. The visit embraced Rouen, Amiens, Beauvais, Nantes, Chartres and Evreux. Along with many Anglican clergy visiting the continent at this time, he realised how insignificant and unimportant was the Church of England as he put his foot down upon French soil. Reflecting on the visit he wrote 'for the first time it seems to have been brought home to me that our Blessed Lady had a share in the Incarnation! For the first time I made an effort to arrive at the *rationale* of the regard which Catholics pay to her and to the saints'.[46] Similarly, he was struck by the fact that 'abroad the Church, however lamentably it has been assailed by revolutionary impiety, or decorated in false or meretricious taste, is still recognized by all as the *house of prayer*, intended primarily for *worship*, not for *instruction*, still less for the *display* of the priest's oratory' and he asked himself the question 'what would be thought here (in England) of a person kneeling down to pray when he entered the church? Would he be set down as a hypocrite or as an enthusiast?'[47] He found the Mass solemn and beautiful, was critical of the lack of concelebration, but praised the opportunity provided for taking Communion on a daily basis. He convinced himself that the Roman Catholic did not confuse the reverence due to the Mother of God with the worship owing to her Son, writing 'it rather seems as if, in his mind, *she* were the connecting link between us and Him — so that the Virgin is inextricably mixed up in his feelings with the Incarnation....'[48] Furthermore, he wrote, 'without churches open all day, and the habit of praying in them, I do not see how it is possible for the great mass of Christians to realise the Communion of Saints; and that the good and serious do realise it abroad to an extent we have no conception of here, I feel convinced. What would I give to be able to keep the doors of my church open from morning to night, and to see my parishioners come there not only to join in public, but to offer private devotions, and confess to their priest, as I witnessed on Monday, August 14, at the village of Poix! Such a thing in England seems beyond the reach of the wildest imagination'.[49]

Despite these criticisms and notes of admiration, Allies did not return with overtly germinating seeds of conversion in his heart! The Church of England 'was simply a church with divine powers to be restored' and the Tractarians had been raised up for the purpose 'if the Bishops would only let them'.[50] In June, 1843 he had written to Blomfield to seek another parish but, on being ignored, took it as a sign he should remain at Launton. On his return from France, he published a volume of sermons in 1844, inspired by Tractarian themes and his intensive work on the Fathers. The volume was dedicated to Newman, by then living in retirement at Littlemore.

Unlike Newman, Allies welcomed the publication of W.G. Ward's *Ideal of a Christian Church* which appeared in 1844. Ward argued that the Roman Catholic Church alone could be considered the 'ideal' Church and that the formularies of the Church of England were sufficiently all-embracing that he could hold and teach all the doctrines of Rome while still remaining, in good faith, a member of the Church of England.[51] Newman did not approve of the final sentiment, of course, but the Church of England had been broad-based enough to contain unitarianism, why not Wardism? To Allies, Ward's book had a greater function: it supplied him with the *reasons* for the difficulties he was experiencing. Hitherto, he had viewed the Anglican Church as 'simply a *machine out of order* but one *restorable* by the Tractarians'; now it was presented to him as 'a monster with two heads and no feet'.[52]

Allies began to worry lest his 'secret and yet undefined dread' that the Church of England was a schismatical church was true. 'All that I see around me', he wrote, 'seems so little like the Church, as either revealed in the Bible, or realised in early ages. Confusion of face meets us on every side. In this respect, Ward's book gave but an articulate voice to the conclusion to which I had been for some time more and more inclining. This is a fearful vision hanging over the future. "In all things may I know God's will, and at all times be ready to fulfil it"'[53]

The need to address this question constituted the next phase of Allies' search and led to the publication in 1846 of *The Church of England Cleared from the Charge of Schism*, an attempt to show that the Anglican Church preserved intact the fullness of the faith professed by the Fathers. It was welcomed by many high churchmen reeling from the shock of Newman's conversion to Rome in 1845 and the publication of his *Essay on the Development of Christian Doctrine*. Allies had warning of the impending cataclysm. With Dodsworth he had visited Newman at Littlemore on May 19, 1845 when the latter had told them of his determination to leave the Church of England. Reflecting on the event, Allies wrote: 'His mind had been for many years educating mine: his books were the instruments by which I was drawn out of my foreign radicalism, and loose, incoherent Protestantism. His influence was my real *point d'appui* in the Anglican Church. This same month, having completed a course of thirteen sermons on Abraham, I was led to give up this part of pastoral work. By the prospect of Newman's leaving us, as well as from its own internal progress, my mind was put wholly in a controversial state...'[54]

Following the conversion of Newman, Allies began to draw nearer to Manning, mainly because of the close relationship that existed between the Archdeacon and Dodsworth. Manning's sojourn abroad which began in July 1847 was destined to occupy almost a year of his life before he returned to Lavington. He was determined to attend as many Roman Catholic ceremonies as possible to observe their effect upon worshippers, while seeking out an Anglican establishment for his regular Sunday obligation. During his absence, Dodsworth had accepted an invitation to settle his wife and family in the vicarage at Lavington for the summer where they could benefit from country air and long walks. He promised to join Manning subsequently as the latter decided to progress gradually through Belgium and Germany before wintering in Rome. Laprimaudaye, Manning's curate, would handle the spiritual care of Lavington and Dodsworth would visit the vicarage, as would Allies.

Shaken by Newman's conversion, Allies had consulted Manning about his own proposal to devote three years to a study of the nature of the Church. Whatever might be his convictions, he resolved to do nothing during that time of study by way of changing his personal position. Manning's advice was to reinforce that determination, suggesting to Allies that 'God's voice is to be waited for *thrice*, as in Samuel's case.'[55]

In June, 1847 Allies met with John Hungerford Pollen and John Wynne in Oxford. Wynne was six years junior to Allies and Pollen was seven years younger. They were both disturbed by Newman's conversion. Pollen, Fellow of Merton, had been ordained deacon by Richard Bagot at Oxford and was finding his work in the parish of St-Peter-le-Baily as frustrating as Allies was finding work at Launton. Wynne, Fellow of All Souls, had been at Eton with Pollen. He was eventually to become a Roman Catholic in 1850 in Jerusalem and subsequently became a Jesuit. The 'three British lions', as they dubbed themselves, embarked upon a fact-finding trip to France, especially to discover how the French clergy dealt with the poor in their congregations.

Allies kept a detailed journal of this visit, the second Continental visit in two years. In 1846 he had spent two weeks with Coleridge and other companions in Belgium and on the Rhine. The Paris expedition with Pollen and Wynne lasted for seven weeks. Writing in his journal, Allies saw the keynote of all the Roman services as 'The Word was made Flesh, and dwelt among us'. 'The Real Presence', he wrote, 'broods like a spirit overall: gives meaning to every genuflection: life to every hymn: harmony to that wonderful "cloud of witnesses", with the Virgin Mother at their head, who intercede with the Most Holy Trinity, and join their praises with the angelic hosts, and voices of feeble men suffering the conflict of the flesh.... The Real Presence is the secret support of the religious orders, as of the priests' self-denying mission; by it the most lonely feels that he is not alone.... And a concomitant of the true doctrine of the priesthood is that system of confession which is the nerve and sinew of religion in Catholic countries....'[56]

To this realisation, Allies related the causes of his own ineptitude at Launton: 'The efficacy of a pastor must depend entirely on the knowledge of his people's state ... on his power to guide them in their penitence ... and in Catholic countries, we see the priest — however much he may earn the dislike of the worldly — respected, cherished, and obeyed by his people....'[57] The *Journal* then points the contrast with the Church of England: 'Are our universities at present a fit school for preparing men for a life of patience, self-denial, and humiliation? What sort of labourers, how grounded, disciplined, and tried, have *we* been sending forth to the Church's forlorn hope in her assaults on the stronghold of heathenism?... Are *we* never to reform?

Not by introducing novelties, but by recurring to ancient practices ...
for the Prayer Book of the Church of England has the deepest
accordance with the Catholic system....'[58] By removing misconceptions
and ignorance, the *Journal* would make a positive contribution to the
mutual understanding of Christendom and the ultimate reconciliation
of the churches. From France 'the three lions' journeyed to Italy,
leaving Allies at Padua to find his way home.

In 1848, the second edition of Allies's *Defence of the Church of
England from the Charge of Schism* appeared, enlarged and extended.
He began also to consider the possible publication of his *Journal* of the
tour to France and, to that end, to provide a more complete picture,
decided to go to France again for a short second visit in 1848,
accompanied for part of the time by James Laird Patterson, curate of
St Thomas's, in Oxford. Immediately on his return, Allies went to see
Manning about the possible publication of the *Journal*. His visit to
Lavington on August 18th was to seek Manning's impressions of
continental Catholicism and compare them with his own. Edward
Coleridge, also on a visit to Lavington, urged Allies not to go ahead
with publication until he sought the judgement of Manning. This he
was happy to promise, informing Manning that the days he had spent
at Lavington 'were to me the most valuable ones in all my vacation'.[59]

Manning delayed his judgement until October. The *Journal* interested
him greatly but from the beginning he saw its effect upon others would
be decidedly Romewards. Writing on 10th October from Eaton Place,
where he was with Henry Wilberforce, Manning declared Allies's
manuscript had deeply affected him and renewed in him thoughts such
as Rome used to awaken day by day when he was there. When he
came to consider its publication, however, he saw:

I.   (i) that its *whole effect* is persuasive of going to Rome;

(ii) that its *whole effect* is dissuasive of rest in the Church of
England; this I think is the tone of the whole.

II.   Next the details are favourable in the same direction, eg:

(i) the exhibition of celibacy as the practical centre of all works of
direction and charity;

(ii) the *spiritual* necessity of confession;

(iii) the Patronage and Office of the Blessed Virgin;

(iv) the miracles.

III.   Then the direct contrasts and comparisons of the Churches of
            England and Rome — eg: note at the end of the *Journal* of 1845.
            And the tone of unrest and mistrust in which you write.

IV.   Equally your manifest delight and preference of the Roman Ritual
            and Offices.

            Now all these things make me believe the effect of publishing it
            would be rather to send people to Rome than to raise the Church of
            England and, also, as I said in my last letter, to make your life a
            burden. I mean that the self-devotion of a Cedrus would be nothing
            to it. Before it comes out it will be well to lean on a javelin and
            devote yourself to the gods infernal. But I am speaking of it as a
            whole. I think it contains most valuable and useful matters, as

            1. A statement without inferences or contrasts of the work and
            conditions of the Church in France, especially its Religious Ideas.
            2. A quiet exhibition of the practical effect of celibacy on the service
            of the Church.
            3. And of Confession upon Education, and therefore on our whole
            life.
            4. All your conversations which show the charity and earnestness of
            our brethren abroad.

            Now I cannot deny the truth of what you have written in the main.
            But I feel that it is so far in advance of all except for individual
            minds, that the effect would be to provoke hasty and therefore
            adverse resolutions, and heap perpetual annoyance on yourself....'[60]

Allies, who could not get to London to see Manning, decided to accept
his advice. Two days later Manning asked leave to show the *MS* to
Henry Wilberforce. The outcome of this reflection was that it was
suggested that the *MS* might be published, after some revision. Allies,
however, found it difficult to divine how the book could be revised
without comparisons being made with the practice of the Anglican
Church, to the latter's detriment. Manning gave the general guidelines
of how he thought this could be done in a letter of October 13th. Allies
would need, however, to undertake the revision himself.[61] It was clear
that a desire for reconciliation between the Churches should be
admitted, that there should be a recognition of all that is divine, good
and legitimate in the Roman Church, that anything human, ques-
tionable or apparently bad should be exposed in truth and loyalty in
both systems and that obstacles to unity should be removed and
remedies proposed.
    Allies took the *MS* to S.W. Heathcote of New College, Oxford, a
friend of Hungerford Pollen, 'impartial' and, we are told, 'imbued
with Mr Keble's mind'. Heathcote, too, suggested certain corrections
but was so much in favour of publication that he offered to be editor

if Allies did not wish to print it under his own name. Eventually, the emendations were completed and Allies showed the *MS* to Manning on December 14th. Manning's view, while favourable, still feared the reaction for Allies.

On his return to Lavington, Manning received a letter from Pusey, dated December 19th, 1848, which indicated he had wind of the proposed publication, very likely from Charles Marriott. 'I hear you have undertaken the responsibility of sanctioning the printing of Allies's *Journal*', he wrote. 'I do most earnestly hope that you will undertake the additional responsibility of revising for the press'. He considered Allies's mind to be 'so sharp, hard, angular, controversial, acrid' that he would expect everything 'to be written as distressingly as it can be for a member of the Church of England, raising questions but affording no clue through them'. Manning was reminded 'it was a principle of dear J.H.N., when he was with us, never to shatter people without need....'[62]

Manning had already warned Allies of the difficulties and felt he could do little more now, except urge him to ask Heathcote to read over the proofs and refer any doubts to Pusey. Allies wished to dedicate the book to Manning, but the latter suggested a suitable form of words dedicating it to the Church of England which might help to protect Allies from any possible future attacks and show his loyalty to the Church. This suggestion Allies also accepted.

The first copies of the *Journal* arrived from the printer on February 19, 1849. A storm of protest was let loose in high church circles, although Allies did receive congratulatory letters from Newman, Palmer, Wynne, Pollen, Edward Coleridge, Dodsworth, Henry Wilberforce and James Patterson. Samuel Wilberforce had already had a clash with Allies in 1847 when the latter had reported to him the vicar of Bicester for alleged unorthodoxy on the matter of baptismal regeneration. Wilberforce had refused to take public action, although he had admonished the vicar privately. Samuel now turned the tables on Allies by impugning the *Journal in France* as denying the dogmatic formularies of the Church of England. He demanded retraction. Allies, for his part, before the altar, felt he had now 'discharged a sacred debt to the Roman Church'.[63] Nevertheless, he was undergoing a more severe spiritual cross than anything his bishop could lay upon him:

> The thought that one is *out* of the Catholic Church, that one's Baptism, Eucharist, Orders, are all unreal, is hardly supportable. It is a chain from which by day and night one is never free — the last thought in the evening, the first in the morning, intruding at the most awful moments, shaking one's confidence when it is most needed, harassing one in the very labours of charity. May it work in me a

more entire resignation, patience, and faith. It is indeed *waiting* for
the Lord.[64]

Newman considered the *Journal in France* must subserve the cause of
Catholic Unity, adding 'of which you must know I think there is but
one way'.[65] Manning commented 'the amount of valuable, instructing,
shaming, stirring matter is great, and this is what I wished to see,
without any reflections. I fear that some heads will remember only the
reflections and forget the facts. Parts of the book are very beautiful
and true'.[66]

Samuel Wilberforce attacked the book for its teaching on the Mass
and the Eucharist and for statements that he found irreconcilable with
the Thirty-Nine Articles. Allies defended himself briskly and masterly,
answering the Bishop's adverse comments *seriatim* and alleging
Wilberforce had misapprehended the drift of the book in relation to
such topics. The Bishop was imperious:

> You cannot, I conceive acknowledge the authority of my office,
> without allowing that you are bound, on my requiring it, as I again
> do, to explain, justify, or retract distinct passages in your published
> work against which I except as directly contradicting the letter and
> spirit of our Articles and Formularies.[67]

In a lengthy response, Allies defended his doctrinal position thoroughly
and vigorously, citing a long *catena* of Anglican authorities, and,
gallingly, challenging the right of Wilberforce to ask questions in the
form in which he did. The Bishop asked Allies to submit his book
either (1) to the Archbishop of the province or the judgement of his
peers *or* (2) to the Regius Professors of Divinity, Pastoral Theology
and Ecclesiastical History in the University of Oxford, to determine the
question whether or not the statements Wilberforce complained of were
contradictory, or not contradictory, to the Thirty-Nine Articles or any
of them. Allies declined the trap! 'To decide whether my statements
are or are not agreeable', he responded, 'to the letter and meaning of
the Articles, would be, in fact, to decide what the sense of the Articles
is on certain disputed points. This is a matter which for three centuries
has been left open by the Church of England, and I feel that it would
not be right to accept a particular sense put upon those Articles from
any individuals (however fitted by station or qualification to give a
judgement) nor from any authority short of the Church of England
herself, either assembled in Synod or represented in her courts of law
especially as a decision either way must produce an extensive and
lasting effect on the Church herself'.[68]

Samuel Wilberforce was on the point of prosecuting Allies in a legal
tribunal when Manning intervened with his brother-in-law. Manning
committed himself to state categorically that in his view the book

contained no Roman doctrine properly so called, that it contained no proposition or word contrary to the Catholic faith and that it contained no doctrinal statement at variance with the Thirty-Nine Articles.[69] A legal action would have wide implications and would lead to defections to Rome which might implicate members of Wilberforce's own family. Samuel had to accept from Allies a promise that there would not be a further edition of the book and a regret for publishing 'what seemed to his Bishop an infraction of the Articles'.[70]

When the quarrel was over, Allies, leaving his wife and family at Lowestoft, left for Rome and Naples with Wynne. Allies was determined to present a copy of his book to the Pope, Pius IX, who was then taking refuge in Gaeta. Wynne gave an interesting account of the audience to Mrs Allies:

> Allies will have told you how fortune or the good angel favoured us in the undertaking, how gracious a reception we met with from the Holy Father, how complimentary he was to your husband, and how parental in his parting benediction. He made special reference to recent events in England, and you must never let them fret you any more. If England is unkind, Italy opens her arms to those who love the faith of Christ....'[71]

The Gorham Judgement of 1850 was the final straw, not simply because 'the judgement of the Privy Council in favour of Gorham ... involves us (ie the Church of England), if, unreversed, in heresy' but because the case 'had brought out incidentally the nature and extent of the Royal Prerogative' which he felt 'at once to preclude my remaining in the Anglican Establishment, independently of the decision itself on the question of Baptismal Regeneration'.[72] His final position was that the Royal Supremacy effectively *annihilates* the Church of England as a Church. Mrs T.W. Allies was received, ahead of her husband, into the Roman Catholic Church on 9 February, 1850 by an octogenarian priest (recommended by Newman) in London. Her husband was received by Newman at Cotton some four months later. His new book, *The See of St Peter*, was a justification and vindication of his long journey in the quest for authority.

What did the future hold at that certain — and yet in the material sense fundamentally uncertain — moment? A future of poverty and temporal failure presented itself. Perhaps the last word can be left with Thomas William Allies as he contemplated that future:

> *To have this world, and the next too, is more*
> *than Christ had, and more than he promised*
> *to His followers.*[73]

ABBREVIATIONS

L.D.   T.W. Allies, *A Life's Decision* (1880).

M.H.A.   Mary H. Allies, *Thomas William Allies*, (1907).

NOTES

1. David Newsome, *The Parting of Friends*, (1966), p.298.

2. *Ibidem*, p. 333.

3. *Ibidem*.

4. *Ibidem*, p. 342.

5. David Newsome, *The Convert Cardinals: John Henry Newman and Henry Edward Manning*, (1993).

6. *Ibidem*, p. 161.

7. A.C.F. Beales in G.A. Beck (ed.), *The English Catholics, 1850-1950*. (1950), p.372.

8. Anon, *Sister Mary of St Philip (Frances Mary Lescher), 1825-1904*. (1920), pp. 48 *seq.*

9. Mary Griset Holland, *The British Catholic Press and the Educational Controversy, 1847-1865*, (1987), p. 240.

10. A. Dwight Culler, *The Imperial Intellect*, (1955), pp. 133, 195, 219, 269; Sheridan Gilley, *Newman and His Age*. (1990), p. 267.

11. Charles Stephen Dessain (ed.), *The Letters and Diaries of John Henry Newman* 16, (1964); Letter of Newman to Allies, September 3, 1854.

12. Charles Stephen Dessain and Thomas Gornall (eds.), *The Letters and Diaries of John Henry Newman* 30, (1976); Letter of Newman to Allies, May 21, 1882.

13. Owen Chadwick, *The Victorian Church — Part Two*, (1970), p. 416.

14. Edward Norman, *The English Catholic Church in the Nineteenth Century*, (1984), p. 169.

15. Anne Pollen, *John Hungerford Pollen, 1820-1907*. (1912), pp. 62, 63, 369.

16. *L.D.*, (1880).

17. Dessain and Gornall, *op.cit*, Newman to Allies, November 26, 1881.

18. *M.H.A.*, (1907).

19. Wilfrid Ward, *Ten Personal Studies*, (1908), pp. 280-281.

20. *Vincenti Lirinensis Commonitorium*, (1836); *Vincentius of Lerins's Commonitory*, (1837).

21. *vide*, pp. 93, *seq.*, John Keble, *Primitive Tradition Recognised in Holy Scripture: A Sermon Preached in the Cathedral Church of Winchester at the Visitation of the Worshipful and Reverend William Dealtry, D.D., Chancellor of the Diocese, September 27. 1836*, (2nd ed; 1837).

22. Reproduced as the front piece of *M.H.A.*

23. Anne Pollen, *op.cit.*, p. 62.

24. *L.D.*, p. 8.

25. J.S. Reynolds, *The Evangelicals at Oxford 1757-1871*, (1953), p. 95.

26. C.E. Mallet, *A History of the University of Oxford*, (1927), 3, pp. 413-415.

27. Richard Ollard, *An English Education: A Perspective of Eton*, (1982), pp. 58-59.

28. *vide*, his connection with Faber. Raleigh Addington (ed.), *Faber, Poet and Priest*, (1974), pp. 163, 193, 224, 226, 229.

29. *L.D.*, p. 5.

30. *Ibidem.*

31. Chadwick, *op.cit.*, p. 133.

32. *L.D.*, p. 14.

33. *Ibidem*, p. 8.

34. C. Dawson, *The Spirit of the Oxford Movement*, (1933), p. 118.

35. *L.D.*, p. 9.

36. *M.H.A.*, p. 42.

37. *L.D.*, p. 10.

38. *Ibidem*, p. 10.

39. M.A. Lowther, *A Compendious History of Sussex, Topographical, Archaeological and Anecdotal*, (1870), 2, pp. 271-272.

40. Manning papers formerly at Bayswater, *Autobiographical Notes*, Book 4.

41. H.E. Manning, *Sermons*, 4 vols., (1842-1850).

42. *L.D.*, p. 11.

43. *Ibidem*, The letter of Newman dated September 30, 1842 is given *in extenso.*

44. *Ibidem*, p. 17.

45. *Ibidem*, p. 18.

46. *Ibidem*, p. 20.

47. *Ibidem*, p. 26.

48. *Ibidem*, p. 29.

49. *Ibidem*, p. 29-33.

50. *Ibidem*, p. 36.

51. Ian Ker, *John Henry Newman: A Biography* (1988), pp. 294-295.

52. *L.D.*, p. 51.

53. *Ibidem*, p. 52.

54. *Ibidem*, p. 57.

55. *Ibidem*, p. 113.

56. T.W. Allies, *Journal in France*, (1849), pp. 2-9.

57. *Ibidem*,

58. *Ibidem*,

59. Manning Papers, *op. cit.*, Allies to Manning, August 6, 1848.

60. *Ibidem*, Manning to Allies, October 10, 1848.

61. *Ibidem*, Manning to Allies, October 13, 1848.

62. *Ibidem*, Pusey to Manning, December 19, 1848. Manning did not reply to this letter until January 26th and it therefore becomes clear that Allies's account in *A Life's Decision*, (pp. 141-143) is inaccurate. Pusey's letter did not reach Manning until after he had written to Allies with the views of Henry Wilberforce and himself.

63. *L.D.*, p. 122.

64. *Ibidem*, p. 133.

65. *Ibidem*, p. 153. Letter of Newman to Allies, February 20, 1849.

66. *Ibidem*, pp. 146-147. Letter of Manning to Allies, March 23, 1849.

67. *Ibidem*, p. 166. Letter of Samuel Wilberforce to Allies, March 24, 1849.

68. *Ibidem*, p. 181. Letter of Allies to Samuel Wilberforce, St Mark's Day, 1849.

69. *Ibidem*, p. 186. Letter of Manning to Samuel Wilberforce, May 16, 1849.

70. Pollen, *op. cit.*, p. 129.

71. *M.H.A.*, pp. 57 *seq.* Letter of John H. Wynne to Mrs Allies, August 25, 1849.

72. *L.D.*, pp. 241-242.

73. *Ibidem*, p. 285.